Hollywood Stunt Performers

Hollywood Stunt Performers

A Dictionary and Filmography of Over 600 Men and Women, 1922–1996

by

GENE SCOTT FREESE

McFarland & Company, Inc., Publishers
Jefferson, North Carolina and London

British Library Cataloguing-in-Publication data are available

Library of Congress Cataloguing-in-Publication Data

Freese, Gene Scott, 1969–
    Hollywood stunt performers : a dictionary and filmography of over
600 men and women, 1922–1996 / by Gene Scott Freese.
      p.   cm.
    Includes bibliographical references and index.
    ISBN 0-7864-0511-2 (illustrated casebound : 50# alkaline paper) ∞
    1. Stunt performers—United States—Biography—Dictionaries.
I. Title.
PN1995.9.S7F67   1998
791.43'028'092273—dc21
[b]   98-2733
                                                        CIP

Manufactured in the United States of America

*McFarland & Company, Inc., Publishers
  Box 611, Jefferson, North Carolina 28640*

Table of Contents

Introduction

The life of a stuntman is an interesting one. These men (and women, though for the most part this book uses "stuntman" for both) routinely risk life and limb for the sake of the movies, sometimes receiving very little compensation and, more often than not, even less glory. Yet members of this rare breed of society are undeniably skilled at what they do, and the increased demand for large-scale action films over the past decade suggests that audiences appreciate their talents. But does anyone remember their names?

The career of a professional stuntman has few guarantees and little financial stability. A performer can earn several hundred thousand dollars one year and less than ten thousand the next, depending upon a number of variables. An injury could not only take a chunk out of one's livelihood, but put a permanent stop to an entire career. Advancing age can do the same. It only makes sense that the body will not be able to do at the age of 45 what it could at 25. Professional athletes will attest to this, and a professional athlete is essentially what a stunt performer is—a person skilled in a variety of physical pursuits.

While the general public may consider them to be nothing more than crazy daredevils, the ones who have had lengthy careers have done so through intelligence and precautionary measures, not foolhardy recklessness. Many veteran stunt performers become stunt coordinators or second unit directors when they sense their own physical skills decreasing, using their knowledge and experience in a different capacity. A stunt coordinator hires the stunt personnel for a film, arranges each bit of action described by the script, and determines whether the feat required is safe and possible to perform. A second unit director often controls the entire crew during action scenes.

While there may be as many as 400 to 500 qualified stunt performers in the industry at any one time, generally speaking only about a fifth of these individuals will get the work that's available. It's a tough business to get into, especially considering that several stunt dynasties have developed. Names such as Epper, Orsatti, Baxley, Burton, Wilder, Orrison, Gilbert, and Rondell tend to dominate the stunt field and have done so for a number of years. What's more, the profession itself has changed drastically from the old days, when specialists handled vehicular stunts, fight scenes, and horse falls independently. Over the years high-fall, aerial, and fire specialists emerged, but today one must be skilled in all of the above to truly make a living in the industry. A specialist with only one skill will find it hard to survive. In addition to the types of stunts just mentioned, most of today's stunt performers are also skilled in gymnastics, the martial arts, and all types of water sports.

Stunt schools have emerged to train prospective stunt people, though many already in the industry scoff at their existence, feeling that they are a waste of money. Many stunt performers have entered the business simply by chance, by being in the right place at the right time and meeting the right individual. But to get into the fraternal stunt organizations—the upper echelon of the industry—one must already be a member of the Screen Actors Guild, be invited to join by existing members, and show proof of earnings of more than $50,000 paid exclusively for stuntwork in any given year. It's not an easy requirement to meet, and many stunt performers remain independent throughout their careers.

Up until the late 1970s stunt performers weren't even given onscreen credit for their work. Thus it is virtually impossible to compile a complete set of credits for many of these individuals. Many stunt performers are never visible on screen, even when they're working steadily. A few stunt performers, however, have become recognizable faces in their own right, chiefly through bit parts on TV and film. Producers would understandably prefer to hire a stunt performer who can handle a couple of lines of dialogue, rather than hire both an actor and a stuntman for the same part. Men such as Bob Minor, Nick Dimitri, Chuck Hicks, Dick Durock, Gene LeBell, Fred Lerner, Henry Kingi, and Al Leong fall into this category.

Some stuntmen have gained fame in the movie business for a single scene or stunt: Ernie Orsatti for his backward fall into glass in *The Poseidon Adventure,* Bud Ekins for Steve McQueen's motorcycle jump in *The Great Escape*, Loren Janes for his cactus jump in *How the West Was Won*, Bob Herron for crashing a car through a barn in *Convoy*, Carey Loftin for coordinating the car chase in *Bullit*, Nick Dimitri for his fistfight with Charles Bronson in *Hard Times*. The list goes on and on.

Others have gained recognition in the science fiction and horror field for a single role: Dick Durock as the comic book character *Swamp Thing* or George P. Wilbur, Dick Warlock, and Kane Hodder as Jason and Michael in the *Friday the 13th* and *Halloween* film series. One of the most deserving cult reputations in the fantasy field goes to Patricia Tallman for her gutsy lead performance in the remake of *Night of the Living Dead*. Tom Savini, that film's director and a noted makeup and effects expert, has often done stuntwork as well.

A few stuntmen have become genuine legends through their longstanding associations with the stars that they doubled. Chuck Roberson was John Wayne's stuntman for 30 years and even wrote a book about his life (*The Fall Guy*). Joe Canutt is associated with Charlton Heston, and Hal Needham with Burt Reynolds.

On rare occasions a stuntman will graduate into character parts or leads, Richard Farnsworth being a shining example. Jock Mahoney even went on to become *Tarzan*. The multi-talented Branscombe Richmond landed the second lead on the popular television series *Renegade* and has garnered a loyal following. Sonny Landham portrayed a memorable villain in *48HRS*. Steve James became a supporting player and action lead in films of the late eighties before dying unexpectedly of pancreatic cancer. Even the late Oscar winner Ben Johnson began as a stuntman and horse wrangler in the 1940s before director John Ford gave him the lead in *Wagon Master*.

Five of the best screen villains of the 1970s all began in the industry as stuntmen. William Smith (*Rich Man, Poor Man*) was an Air Force weight-lifting champ and arm wrestling champion of the world. Don Stroud (*The Buddy Holly Story*) was a champion surfer who was hired off the beach to double Troy Donahue on television's *Hawaiian Eye*. Robert Tessier (*The Longest Yard*) was a real biker who was hired to stage the action in the motorcycle film *Born Losers*. Roy Jenson (*Chinatown*) was a former professional football player in the Canadian Football League. Lance LeGault (*Coma*) was Elvis Presley's double throughout the sixties.

Additionally, *Grizzly Adams* star Dan Haggerty was an animal trainer and stuntman; Robert Fuller of the television westerns *Laramie* and *Wagon Train* broke into films as a stuntman; sixties leading man Gary Lockwood once doubled for Anthony Perkins; and even Burt Reynolds got his start because he was willing to dive through a window. A few stuntmen have become directors, Chuck Bail and *Smokey and the Bandit*'s Hal Needham being the best known.

Unfortunately, the business is not without its risks. A number of stuntmen have lost their lives in the line of duty, most notably Dar Robinson, who held several world records for high falls and was a celebrity with the general public thanks to his many appearances on the television show *That's Incredible*. The deaths of A.J. Bakunas, Reid Rondell, and Sonia Davis also made headlines, while Heidi Von Beltz, a stunt ingenue paralyzed in a head-on collision during the making of *The Cannonball Run*, wrote a book and toured the talk-show circuit with the story of her courageous rehabilitation efforts.

The big-budget action films of the eighties and nineties provided unparalleled opportunities for the stunt field, but in recent years the increase in computer graphics and digital effects has created an industry "buzz" about a day in the near future when the stunt performer may become obsolete. There was a similar fear in the late sixties when the television networks eliminated all series with excessive violence, a move that temporarily put many stunt performers out of work. In all likelihood, audiences will demand to see real people doing real feats of derring-do, and the stunt profession will continue to thrive.

I have included as many stunt personnel as possible in this guide, over 600 names in all, using durability, notoriety, and work in at least ten major theatrical releases as my criteria. Ten films may seem a minuscule requirement, but simply to get into the business at all is a feat in itself. To continue to work and prosper is an accomplishment worth recognizing.

Hollywood
Stunt Performers

MICHAEL ADAMS

A stunt coordinator and bit player, Adams is a member of the Stuntmen's Association of Motion Pictures. He has doubled for Jim Belushi.

*Films—***1978:** The Manitou. **1979:** Concorde, Airport '79; Prophecy; Charleston (tv). **1980:** Heaven's Gate. **1982:** The Sword & the Sorcerer; P.K. & the Kid. **1983:** War Games; Spacehunter. **1984:** Bachelor Party; Rhinestone. **1985:** Mask; Commando; Pale Rider; Avenging Angel. **1986:** Ratboy; Raw Deal; Blue City; Nobody's Fool. **1987:** Nadine; Shy People; No Way Out. **1988:** Little Nikita; Red Heat; The Dead Pool; Out of the Dark. **1989:** K-9; Blind Fury; Lords of the Deep. **1990:** Problem Child; Mr. Destiny; Robocop 2; Wild at Heart. **1991:** Out for Justice. **1992:** Thunderheart; Deep Cover; Out on a Limb; Under Siege; Sneakers; Wayne's World. **1993:** In the Line of Fire; Robocop 3; Geronimo. **1994:** Lassie. **1995:** Separate Lives; Destiny Turns on the Radio; Wild Bill; Chameleon.

PHIL ADAMS

A veteran small-part actor, Adams has worked as a stunt coordinator,

doubled for both Tab Hunter and Jeffrey Hunter, and was one of many stuntmen who stood in for William Shatner on the "Star Trek" series.

*Films—***1950:** Kill the Umpire. **1957:** Hot Rod Rumble. **1958:** Lafayette Escadrille; The Last Hurrah. **1959:** Battle of the Coral Sea. **1960:** Sergeant Rutledge; The Wackiest Ship in the Army. **1967:** First to Fight; Tobruk; In the Heat of the Night. **1968:** The Green Berets; Ice Station Zebra. **1969:** Hello, Dolly!; Che; The Great Bank Robbery. **1970:** Catch-22; Kelly's Heroes; The Phynx. **1972:** Conquest of the Planet of the Apes; Buck & the Preacher; The Poseidon Adventure. **1973:** The Don Is Dead; Battle for the Planet of the Apes; Blume in Love. **1974:** The Towering Inferno; Black Samson; Shanks; Freebie & the Bean. **1975:** Day of the Locust. **1976:** Logan's Run. **1977:** Stunts; The Christmas Coalmine Miracle (tv). **1978:** Thank God, It's Friday. **1979:** Chomps. **1980:** The Stunt Man; The Island. **1982:** My Favorite Year. **1983:** To Be or Not to Be; Fire & Ice; Mr. Mom. **1984:** Firestarter; Racing with the Moon. **1985:** Cloak & Dagger; Commando; Black Moon Rising; Silver Bullet. **1986:** Sweet Liberty; Choke Canyon; Hollywood Vice Squad; 52 Pick-Up; Raw Deal; Maximum Overdrive; Ruthless People. **1987:** Million Dollar Mystery; Blind Date; Brenda Starr. **1988:** Earth Girls Are Easy; The Seventh Sign. **1990:**

Crazy People. **1991:** The Naked Gun 2½; Nothing but Trouble; Deadlock. **1992:** Sleepwalkers. **1993:** The Temp. **1994:** I'll Do Anything; The Naked Gun 33⅓; Clean Slate; Body Shot. **1995:** 3 Ninjas Knuckle Up. *Television*—Star Trek; The Invaders; Tour of Duty.

GEORGE AGUILAR
(b. 1956)

A Michigan-born stunt coordinator of Yaqui/Apache descent, Aguilar had a notable supporting role in *The Scarlet Letter*.

Films—**1972:** Ulzana's Raid. **1974:** The Trial of Billy Jack. **1984:** The Mystic Warrior (tv). **1988:** Bagdad Cafe; Vice Versa. **1989:** See No Evil, Hear No Evil; Chances Are; Her Alibi. **1990:** Robocop 2; Marked for Death. **1991:** McBain; Out for Justice; The Hard Way; New Jack City; A Kiss Before Dying. **1992:** Lunatics, a Love Story; Folks; Under Siege; Hoffa; The Lightning Incident (tv). **1993:** Robocop 3; Shadowhunter; Carlito's Way. **1994:** Body Snatchers; The Cowboy Way; Army of One. **1995:** Jeffrey; Batman Forever; The Scarlet Letter; 12 Monkeys. **1996:** The Juror; Head Above Water. *Television*—Gunsmoke; Petrocelli; Grizzly Adams; Little House on the Prairie; Star Trek, The Next Generation; Mann & Machine.

DANNY AIELLO III
(b. 1957)

This Bronx-born stunt coordinator has often stood in as a double for his popular character actor father, as well as John Lithgow, Ron Perlman, and Tim Robbins. He's a member of Stunt Specialists.

Films—**1979:** The Wanderers. **1981:** Fort Apache, the Bronx. **1982:** Amityville 2;

Fighting Back. **1984:** The Natural; Splash; Rappin'. **1986:** Legal Eagles. **1987:** Ishtar; Outrageous Fortune; Good Morning, Vietnam; Deadly Illusion; The Squeeze; Return to Salem's Lot; China Girl. **1988:** Shakedown; Last Rites; Spike of Bensonhurst. **1989:** The January Man; Ghostbusters 2; Heart of Dixie; Do the Right Thing; The Dream Team; Family Business; New York Stories; Bloodhounds of Broadway; See No Evil, Hear No Evil; Lock Up; Last Exit to Brooklyn. **1990:** Blue Steel; The Lemon Sisters; Loose Cannons; Miller's Crossing; Tune in Tomorrow; Jacob's Ladder; State of Grace; Street Hunter. **1991:** Hudson Hawk; 29th Street; Ricochet; The Hard Way; New Jack City; The Last Boy Scout. **1992:** Ruby; Whispers in the Dark; Hoffa. **1993:** Mac; The Pickel; The Saint of Fort Washington. **1994:** Drop Zone; Nell. **1995:** Just Cause; Die Hard with a Vengeance. **1996:** Diabolique. *Television*—One Life to Live; All My Children; Loving; The Bride Wore Black; The Equalizer; Beauty & the Beast; True Blue; Kojak; Law & Order; Tribeca; The Untouchables; Watchers.

LAURA ALBERT

Model/leading lady of low-budget actioners, best served by a sexy turn in *Dr. Caligari*. She has performed stunts exclusively since the mid-nineties.

Films—**1988:** Angel 3; Bloodstone; Glitch; The Jigsaw Murders; Death by Dialogue; Party Plane; The Unnameable. **1989:** Dr. Alien; Dr. Caligari; Road House. **1990:** Blood Games. **1991:** Stone Cold. **1992:** The Unnameable 2. **1993:** Live by the Fist. **1994:** The Naked Gun 33⅓; Automatic; Double Dragon; Road Racers; Fist of the North Star. **1995:** Sudden Death. **1996:** Spy Hard; Escape from L.A. *Television*—Tales from the Crypt; Dream On.

JOHN ALDEN

Films—**1983:** Young Warriors. **1984:** Making the Grade. **1986:** Out of Bounds. **1987:** The Night Stalker; Assassination; Lethal Weapon; House 2. **1988:** Bulletproof; Shakedown; Crocodile Dundee 2; The Presidio. **1989:** Johnny Handsome; Pink Cadillac. **1990:** Another 48 HRS.; The Rookie. **1991:** The Taking of Beverly Hills. **1992:** Under Siege. **1993:** In the Line of Fire. **1994:** Clear & Present Danger; Zero Tolerance; Deep Red; Deadly Target. **1995:** 3 Ninjas Knuckle Up; Top Dog; Strange Days; Money Train; The Silencers; Suspect Device. **1996:** Norma Jean & Marilyn; Dark Breed. *Television*— Misfits of Science.

MICKEY ALZOLA

A bit player and vehicular expert, Alzola often works in tandem with stunt coordinator Everett Creach.

Films—**1972:** Gargoyles (tv). **1973:** Electra Glide in Blue. **1977:** The Car. **1978:** The Driver. **1979:** Sunnyside; The Dark. **1980:** Survival Run. **1981:** The Nashville Grab (tv). **1982:** Megaforce. **1983:** Breathless. **1985:** Trouble in Mind. **1987:** Near Dark; The Principal; Remote Control; Nasty Hero. **1988:** Young Guns; Bat 21. **1989:** Jacknife. **1990:** Impulse.

JAY AMOR

Films—**1983:** Spring Break; Blue Skies Again. **1985:** The Heavenly Kid; Invasion USA; The New Kids; Two Fathers' Justice (tv). **1986:** Band of the Hand; Vengeance (tv); Charley Hannah (tv). **1989:** Cat Chaser; Black Rain; Welcome to Spring Break. **1993:** Excessive Force. **1994:** True Lies. **1995:** Bad Boys; Fair Game. **1996:** The Substitute; Striptease; Fled; Curdled.

BILL ANAGNOS
(b. 1958)

The son of a stock-car racer, this Greek/Italian joined Joie Chitwood's Traveling Thrill Show at the age of 13. Now a member of Stunt Specialists, he has doubled for John Travolta, Ray Liotta, and Eric Roberts.

Films—**1977:** Saturday Night Fever. **1978:** King of the Gypsies; The Eyes of Laura Mars; Somebody Killed Her Husband. **1979:** The Wanderers; The Warriors. **1980:** The Exterminator; Can't Stop the Music; Times Square. **1981:** Fort Apache, The Bronx; Wolfen; Rollover. **1982:** Vigilante; The World According to Garp; The Soldier; Muggable Mary, Street Cop (tv). **1983:** Something Wicked This Way Comes. **1984:** Alphabet City; The Exterminator 2; Beat Street; Firstborn; The Pope of Greenwich Village; Splash. **1985:** Preppies. **1986:** Something Wild. **1987:** Eat the Rich; Raising Arizona; Dirty Dancing; China Girl. **1988:** Shakedown; Masquerade; Miles from Home. **1989:** Race for Glory; Tap; Jacknife; See No Evil, Hear No Evil. **1990:** Loose Cannons; Quick Change; State of Grace; Blue Steel; Miller's Crossing; King of New York; Street Hunter; The Ambulance. **1991:** New Jack City. **1992:** Whispers in the Dark; Malcolm X. **1993:** The Music of Chance. **1994:** Body Snatchers; The Cowboy Way. **1995:** Die Hard with a Vengeance; Kiss of Death; 12 Monkeys. **1996:** Daylight; Bullet; Everyone Says I Love You.

ED ANDERS

An independent stunt coordinator, Anders has worked extensively on films lensed overseas.

Films—**1988:** Mercenary Fighters; Captive Rage; White Ghost. **1989:** American Ninja 3. **1990:** Peacemaker; 9½ Ninjas; In the Cold of the Night. **1991:** Star Trek 6: Undiscovered Country; FX-2; Dragonfight; Alligator 2; House 4. **1993:** No Place to Hide; Rescue Me; Love, Cheat, & Steal. **1994:** The Naked Gun 33⅓; Pumpkinhead 2; Love Is a Gun; The Hard Truth; Sensation. **1995:** Bodycount; The Chain. **1996:** Black Day, Blue Night; Bad Love.

PETE ANTICO

A dark-haired, compact supporting player and independent stunt coordinator, Antico has played the role of a police officer or a military figure in several major action films.

Films—**1982:** Yes, Giorgio. **1985:** Black Moon Rising. **1986:** Streets of Gold; F/X; Playing for Keeps; Back to School. **1987:** Over the Top; Teen Wolf 2; Morgan Stewart's Coming Home; Night Force; Code Name Zebra. **1988:** The Beat; Elvira, Mistress of the Dark; The Presidio; Midnight Run. **1989:** Wired; Best of the Best; Road House; Tango & Cash; Riding the Edge. **1990:** The Hunt for Red October; The Hot Spot; Die Hard 2; Impulse; Mr. Destiny; Last of the Finest; Ragin' Cajun. **1991:** Out for Justice; Hudson Hawk; Ricochet; 29th Street; The Last Boy Scout; Martial Law; Kiss and Be Killed. **1992:** Rapid Fire; Lethal Weapon 3; 3 Ninjas; Mission of Justice. **1993:** Surf Ninjas; Full Eclipse; Hard Target; Demolition Man; Best of the Best 2. **1994:** The Getaway; Pentathalon; In the Army Now; Motorcycle Gang; A Low Down Dirty Shame; Bad Blood; Roadracers. **1995:** Just Cause; Candyman: Farewell to the Flesh; Crimson Tide; Jade. **1996:** Heaven's Prisoners; Executive Decision; Mulholland Falls; Eraser; The Rock; Courage Under Fire; An Occasional Hell. *Television*—The Flash; B.L. Stryker; L.A. Law.

BOB APISA
(b. 1946)

A native Hawaiian supporting player, Apisa was an all–American football player for Michigan State and briefly played for the Green Bay Packers. Serving as an aid to the governor of Hawaii when cast for background work on TV's "Hawaii Five-O," he began coordinating stunts for the show and later moved to Hollywood.

Films—**1980:** Waikiki (tv). **1986:** Odd Jobs. **1987:** Number One with a Bullet; Code Name Zebra; Night Force; Real Men; Three O'Clock High. **1988:** Grotesque. **1989:** Collision Course; Fists of Steel. **1990:** The Forbidden Dance; Heart Condition; Marked for Death; The Rookie; Another 48 HRS. **1991:** The Perfect Weapon; Ricochet. **1992:** Nemesis; Under Siege. **1993:** Streetknight; The Sandlot; Hard Target; The Sandman (tv). **1994:** The Specialist; A Low Down Dirty Shame. **1995:** Mallrats. **1996:** Executive Decision; The Nutty Professor; Fled; Courage Under Fire. Glimmer Man; Santa with Muscles. *Television*—Hawaii Five-O; Magnum P.I.; Airwolf; China Beach; Twin Peaks; Jake & the Fatman; Raven; Renegade; L.A. Law.

ANDY ARMSTRONG
(b. 1955)

British-born stunt coordinator, writer, producer, director, and younger brother of Vic Armstrong. He's a member of the Professional Driver's Association.

Films—**1976:** At the Earth's Core. **1981:** Ragtime. **1986:** Highlander. **1987:** Hope & Glory. **1988:** Rambo 3; The Unholy. **1989:** Hellbound: Hellraiser 2. **1990:** Nightbreed; Solar Crisis; Total Recall.

1991: Double Impact; Homicide; The Indian Runner. **1992:** Universal Soldier; Hoffa. **1993:** The Firm; Flesh & Bone; Rescue Me. **1994:** Army of One (p); Stargate. **1995:** Moonshine Highway (s/p/d). **1996:** Truman.

VIC ARMSTRONG
(b. 1948)

This British stunt coordinator/director was a teenage horse trainer when first asked to do stunts for a film. A member of the Professional Driver's Association, he has doubled for Harrison Ford on the *Indiana Jones* films.

Films—**1966:** Arabesque. **1967:** You Only Live Twice. **1969:** On Her Majesty's Secret Service. **1970:** Figures in a Landscape; Ryan's Daughter. **1972:** Young Winston. **1973:** Live & Let Die. **1977:** A Bridge Too Far. **1978:** Superman. **1979:** Escape to Athena; The Unidentified Flying Oddball. **1980:** Superman 2; Bear Island. **1981:** The Watcher in the Woods; Green Ice; Raiders of the Lost Ark. **1982:** Blade Runner. **1983:** Invitation to the Wedding; Krull; Never Say Never Again; Superman 3. **1984:** Slayground; Conan the Destroyer; Indiana Jones & the Temple of Doom. **1985:** Red Sonja; Brazil; Legend. **1986:** The Mission; Tai-Pan. **1987:** Empire of the Sun; Million Dollar Mystery; The Sicilian. **1988:** Rambo 3. **1989:** We're No Angels; Indiana Jones & the Last Crusade; Henry V. **1990:** Total Recall; Air America; Cover Up. **1991:** Double Impact; FX-2; Terminator 2. **1992:** Universal Soldier. **1993:** The Last Action Hero; Black Beauty. **1994:** Army of One (d). **1995:** Rob Roy; Johnny Mnemonic; Cutthroat Island. *Television*—Young Indiana Jones.

JAMES M. ARNETT

This Colorado-born stunt coordinator and second unit director has doubled for both Paul Newman and William Hurt. A member of Stunts Unlimited, his son Seth is also in the business.

Films—**1967:** Cool Hand Luke. **1969:** Butch Cassidy & the Sundance Kid. **1970:** Little Big Man. **1971:** Sometimes a Great Notion (aka Never Give an Inch). **1972:** Pocket Money; The Life & Times of Judge Roy Bean. **1973:** The MacKintosh Man. **1974:** The Towering Inferno; The Black Godfather. **1975:** The Man Who Would Be King. **1976:** Jackson County Jail. **1977:** Airport '77; Delta Fox. **1978:** Foul Play. **1979:** Nightwing; The Onion Field; Winter Kills. **1980:** Steel; Foxes; When Time Ran Out; 9 to 5; Smokey & the Bandit 2; Altered States. **1981:** Gas; Taps. **1982:** Annie; Shoot the Moon; Visiting Hours; Grease 2. **1983:** D.C. Cab; Doctor Detroit; Scarface. **1984:** Dreamscape; 2010; Birdy; Impulse; Where the Boys Are '84; Buckaroo Banzai. **1985:** A View to a Kill; My Man Adam. **1986:** Out of Bounds; Police Academy 3: Back in Training. **1987:** Burglar; Leonard Part 6; The Lost Boys; No Man's Land; Police Academy 4: Citizens on Patrol. **1988:** The Blob. **1989:** Listen to Me; Loverboy; Uncle Buck; Police Academy 6: City Under Siege; Tango & Cash. **1991:** Nothing But Trouble; Hook; The Rocketeer. **1992:** Basic Instinct; Nails; Toys. **1993:** Fatal Instinct. **1994:** Major League 2; Renaissance Man; Wolf; Mixed Nuts. **1995:** Congo; Fluke. **1996:** Barb Wire; That Thing You Do. *Television*—Voyage to the Bottom of the Sea.

BOB ARNOLD
Films—**1987:** Kidnapped. **1991:** Mobsters; Ricochet; Leather Jackets. **1992:** Rapid Fire. **1993:** Nat'l Lampoon's

Loaded Weapon; Surf Ninjas; Demolition Man; Fatherhood; Best of the Best 2. **1994:** A Low Down Dirty Shame. **1995:** Just Cause; Crimson Tide; Fair Game. **1996:** Marshal Law; The Fan.

DENNY ARNOLD

Films—**1974:** Chinatown; The California Kid (tv). **1975:** A Boy & His Dog. **1976:** Logan's Run; Leadbelly. **1978:** Blue Collar. **1982:** Wacko. **1983:** Fire & Ice; Deadly Force. **1985:** Volunteers; Stand Alone. **1987:** Party Camp. **1990:** Short Time; Narrow Margin; 9 1/2 Ninjas. **1991:** Dragonfight; Alligator 2. **1994:** The Surgeon (aka Exquisite Tenderness). **1995:** Bodycount. **1996:** Carpool. *Television*—Gunsmoke.

JOHN ASHBY

Films—**1970:** M*A*S*H. **1972:** J.W. Coop. **1975:** Mitchell. **1979:** The Villain; Charleston (tv). **1980:** The Blues Brothers; Stir Crazy. **1982:** The Entity; The Sword & the Sorcerer. **1983:** Under Fire. **1985:** Iron Eagle; Silverado. **1986:** Band of the Hand. **1989:** Glory. **1990:** Joe vs. the Volcano; The Rookie. **1991:** Grand Canyon.

JONI AVERY

Films—**1987:** Steele Justice. **1988:** The Blob; Vibes; Angel 3. **1991:** The Perfect Weapon. **1992:** Article 99; Single White Female; Innocent Blood; Danger Island (aka The Presence) (tv). **1993:** Streetknight; True Romance. **1994:** Stranger By Night; The Expert; Double Dragon; The Mask. **1995:** Money Train. **1996:** Broken Arrow; Chain Reaction.

RICK AVERY
(b. 1955)

A kenpo karate champ assigned to bodyguard John Travolta, Avery instead became his double. He has worked as a stunt coordinator, second unit director, and recently a director for his other double, martial artist Jeff Speakman. A member of the Stuntmen's Association, his wife Joni also performs stunts.

Films—**1978:** The End. **1981:** Blow Out. **1982:** Fighting Back. **1984:** Killpoint; The River; Savage Dawn. **1985:** Perfect. **1986:** The Naked Cage; Legal Eagles; Hollywood Vice Squad; Firewalker; Armed & Dangerous. **1987:** Allan Quartermain & the Lost City of Gold; Back to the Beach; Steele Justice; Assassination; Down Twisted; The Hidden. **1988:** Bulletproof; Elvira, Mistress of the Dark; The Blob; Vibes; Hero & the Terror; The Night Before; Feds; Permanent Record; They Live; Out of Time (tv). **1989:** Look Who's Talking; Time Trackers; Night of the Warrior; Riding the Edge. **1990:** Look Who's Talking Too; Mr. Destiny. **1991:** Shout; Lionheart; Hook; Oscar; The Perfect Weapon; Cool as Ice; Night Eyes 2; Soldier's Fortune. **1992:** Article 99; The Waterdance; The Lawnmower Man; Innocent Blood; Rapid Fire; 3 Ninjas; Aces: Iron Eagle 3; Danger Island (tv). **1993:** Streetknight; Extreme Justice; Quick. **1994:** Eyes of an Angel; At Home with the Webbers; Killing Zoe; The Expert (d); Scanners: The Showdown. **1995:** Higher Learning; 3 Ninjas Knuckle Up; Heat; Last Man Standing; Money Train; Casino; Ballistic; Black Scorpion. **1996:** Deadly Outbreak (d); The Stupids; Escape from L.A.; Pure Danger; Riot; Set It Off; Crash Dive. *Television*—Gavilan; Off Duty; Renegade.

CHUCK BAIL
(b. 1936)

This 6'4" stunt coordinator and supporting player graduated from Westerns and biker flicks to writing, producing, and directing his own films. A competitive boxer and swimmer while in the Navy, he also performed in a Far East Wild West show. Bail more or less played himself in Richard Rush's existential masterpiece *The Stunt Man* and gave a critically acclaimed lead performance in Gary Kent's *Rainy Day Friends*, but would mostly direct episodic television from the eighties on.

Films—**1959:** The Jayhawkers. **1963:** Ballad of a Gunfighter. **1964:** Taggart. **1965:** The Glory Guys. **1967:** Winchester '73 (tv); Hell's Angels on Wheels. **1968:** The Savage Seven; The Green Berets. **1969:** Cycle Savages; The Devil's Eight. **1970:** Getting Straight. **1971:** The Scavengers; The Last Movie; Werewolves on Wheels. **1973:** Cleopatra Jones. **1974:** Black Samson (d); Freebie & the Bean. **1975:** Cleopatra Jones & the Casino of Gold (d). **1976:** The Gumball Rally (d/p/s). **1977:** Greased Lightning. **1980:** The Stunt Man. **1982:** The Beastmaster. **1985:** Rainy Day Friends (aka L.A. Bad). **1986:** Choke Canyon (d). **1994:** Color of Night. **1995:** Streetcorner Justice (d). *Television*—Wanted, Dead or Alive; Target; Laredo; The Big Valley; Daniel Boone; The High Chaparral; Kung Fu; Bobby Parker & Company; CHiPs (d); Knight Rider (d); Baywatch Nights (d).

A.J. BAKUNAS

(b. 1951; d. 1978)

A former physical education teacher, this New Jersey-born high-fall specialist died on the set of *Steel* attempting to break a record fall set by Dar Robinson. He was a member of Stunts Unlimited.

Films—**1975:** Dog Day Afternoon. **1977:** The Car. **1978:** Go Tell the Spartans; Hooper; Return from Witch Mountain. **1979:** The Apple Dumpling Gang Rides

Again; The Warriors. **1980:** The Stunt Man; Steel. *Television*—McCloud; CHiPs.

MAX BALCHOWSKY

An expert driver and former star on the racing circuit, Balchowsky is best known for participating in *Bullit*'s famous chase scene. He was the driving partner of stunt ace Carey Loftin.

Films—**1963:** It's a Mad, Mad, Mad, Mad World. **1964:** Viva Las Vegas. **1966:** Grand Prix. **1968:** Speedway; Bullit. **1969:** The Love Bug. **1971:** Slaughterhouse Five; Vanishing Point. **1973:** Magnum Force. **1974:** The Sugarland Express; The Front Page. **1975:** Part 2, Walking Tall. **1978:** The Deer Hunter. **1979:** The Promise. **1986:** Eye of the Tiger.

BRUCE BARBOUR

A member of the Stuntmen's Association, Barbour has worked steadily as a stunt coordinator, bit player, and double for Leslie Nielsen.

Films—**1978:** Piranha. **1979:** Meteor; The Amityville Horror; The Electric Horseman; The Lady in Red. **1980:** Alligator; Where the Buffalo Roam; Seems Like Old Times; Smokey & the Bandit 2; Without Warning. **1981:** The Howling; The Nashville Grab (tv). **1982:** Fast Walking; Eating Raoul; The Sword & the Sorcerer; The Beastmaster; First Blood. **1983:** Under Fire; Uncommon Valor; Heart Like a Wheel; The Man Who Loved Women; Flicks (aka Loose Joints). **1984:** Surf 2; Children of the Corn. **1985:** Certain Fury; Space Rage; Commando; Gotcha. **1987:**

Nuts; Innerspace; Undercover; Made in Heaven; Desperado (tv). **1988:** The Naked Gun; Alien Nation; Rambo 3; Turner & Hooch. **1989:** Under the Gun; Weekend at Bernie's; Road House; Glory. **1990:** Total Recall; Robocop 2; My Blue Heaven; Re-possessed; Marked for Death; Dangerous Passion (tv); Fear (tv). **1991:** The Naked Gun 2 1/2; The Hard Way. **1992:** Deep Cover; Under Siege. **1993:** Hear No Evil; Another Stakeout; Weekend at Bernie's 2. **1994:** The Naked Gun 33 1/3; Silence of the Hams. **1995:** Batman Forever; Assassins; Leaving Las Vegas; Dracula, Dead & Loving It. **1996:** Set It Off; Spy Hard. *Television*—Midnight Caller.

RICK BARKER

This independent stunt coordinator and second unit director has doubled for both Nicolas Cage and Jim Carrey.

Films—**1982:** Savannah Smiles. **1983:** The Returning; Breathless; Get Crazy; Space Raiders. **1984:** Ninja 3: The Domination; Ghoulies; The Lost Empire; Repo Man. **1985:** Hellhole; Space Rage; Crimewave. **1986:** Hollywood Vice Squad; Stand By Me; Trick or Treat; Riders of the Storm. **1987:** Amazon Women on the Moon; My Demon Lover; A Nightmare on Elm Street 3: Dream Warriors; Walker; Dudes. **1988:** Dead Heat; A Nightmare on Elm Street 4: Freddy's Revenge; Tapeheads. **1989:** Pow Wow Highway; Lost Angels; Spontaneous Combustion; A Nightmare on Elm Street 5: Dream Child; Cartel. **1990:** Boris & Natasha. **1991:** Dead Women in Lingerie; White Fang; Howling 6: The Freaks; Freddy's Dead. **1992:** The Lawnmower Man; Honeymoon in Vegas; Trancers 3. **1993:** Red Rock West; Freaked; Man's Best Friend; Dead Connection. **1994:** Automatic; The Mask; The Client; Dumb & Dumber; American Yakuza. **1995:** Things to Do in Denver When You're Dead; Ace Ventura: When Nature Calls. **1996:** Independence Day;

Kingpin; Scorpion Spring. *Television*—The Greatest American Hero.

PERRY BARNDT

A member of the Stuntmen's Association, this stunt coordinator has doubled for character actor Robert Davi.

Films—**1987:** Dragnet. **1990:** Robocop 2; The Rookie; Predator 2. **1991:** Mobsters; Hook; Flight of the Intruder; Deadlock. **1992:** Sleepwalkers. **1993:** Wilder Napalm; The Vanishing; Full Eclipse; Passenger 57; Ghost in the Machine. **1994:** Blind Justice. **1995:** Waterworld; The Sweeper. **1996:** Exit; Eraser; Spy Hard; Last Man Standing; Mars Attacks!; Ravenhawk; Set It Off; Dear God.

GREGORY J. BARNETT

A stunt coordinator best known for his recurring role on TV's "Baywatch," Barnett is a member of both Stunts Unlimited and the Professional Driver's Association. He has doubled for Leonard Nimoy and Billy Zane.

Films—**1979:** Buck Rogers in the 25th Century; The Ultimate Imposter (tv). **1980:** The Stunt Man. **1985:** Into the Night; Rainy Day Friends (aka L.A. Bad). **1986:** Star Trek 4: The Voyage Home; Out of Bounds; Ruthless People; Back to School. **1987:** The Omega Syndrome; Code Name Zebra; Lethal Weapon; Predator; Real Men; Campus Man; No Safe Haven; Kidnapped. **1988:** Maniac Cop; Tequila Sunrise; Elvira, Mistress of the Dark; Freeway; They Live. **1989:** Johnny Handsome; Star Trek 5: The Final Frontier; Lethal Weapon 2; Black Rain; Nat'l

Lampoon's Christmas Vacation; Riding the Edge; Night Life; Crack House. **1990:** Heart Condition; The Gumshoe Kid; Funny About Love; Almost an Angel; Last of the Finest; Maniac Cop 2; Vietnam, Texas. **1991:** Switch; The Butcher's Wife; The Perfect Weapon; V.I. Warshawski; Dead Again; Thelma & Louise; Beethoven; The Last Boy Scout; Blood & Concrete; Shakes the Clown. **1992:** Lethal Weapon 3; Cool World; Patriot Games; Forever Young. **1993:** Nat'l Lampoon's Loaded Weapon; Falling Down; Made in America; The Last Action Hero; Demolition Man. **1994:** Midnight Ride; Puppetmasters. **1995:** Demon Knight; Waterworld. **1996:** Riot. *Television*—The Bionic Woman; Hart to Hart; Baywatch (reg.).

JOHN BARRETT

This martial artist/fight coordinator entered films as a double for Chuck Norris and has since portrayed an occasional action lead in low-budget fare.

Films—**1980:** The Octagon. **1981:** An Eye for an Eye. **1982:** Silent Rage; Forced Vengeance. **1983:** Lone Wolf McQuade. **1984:** Missing in Action. **1985:** Missing in Action 2; Volunteers; Gymkata. **1986:** The Patriot; P.O.W. the Escape. **1987:** Hunk; Steel Dawn. **1989:** Lights, Camera, Murder; Headhunter. **1991:** American Kickboxer. **1992:** Dead Center (aka Crazy Joe). **1993:** To the Death. **1996:** Black Silence.

STAN BARRETT
(b. 1943)

A former professional boxer, this stunt coordinator /second unit director doubled regularly for both Burt Reynolds and Paul Newman. He set the world land speed record and broke the sound barrier using a rocket car in 1979.

Films—**1968:** The Green Berets; Hellfighters. **1969:** The Undefeated; The Good Guys & the Bad Guys; The Great Bank Robbery; Sam Whiskey. **1970:** Suppose They Gave a War & Nobody Came; Little Big Man; Beneath the Planet of the Apes; Hunters Are for Killing (tv). **1971:** Run, Simon, Run (tv); Sometimes a Great Notion (aka Never Give an Inch). **1972:** The Life & Times of Judge Roy Bean. **1975:** Sky Heist (tv). **1977:** Airport '77. **1978:** Hooper; Lord of the Rings. **1979:** When a Stranger Calls. **1980:** Gorp. **1984:** Harry & Son. **1987:** Heat. **1989:** Physical Evidence; Terror on Highway 91 (tv). **1992:** Freejack; Last of the Mohicans. **1993:** Striking Distance. **1995:** Jumanji. **1996:** The Nutty Professor; Mars Attacks! *Television*—Hawk; Hondo; Star Trek; Dan August; B.L. Stryker.

DAN BARRINGER

A stunt coordinator and bit player, Barringer is a member of both the Stuntmen's Association and the Professional Driver's Association.

Films—**1985:** Police Academy 2: Their First Assignment. **1986:** Never Too Young to Die; Slow Burn. **1987:** Made in Heaven. **1988:** License to Drive. **1990:** The First Power; I Come in Peace; Love at Large; Taking Care of Business; Class of 1999; The Exorcist 3. **1991:** Stone Cold; Eve of Destruction; Hook; Billy Bathgate; Cape Fear; Son of Darkness: To Die For 2. **1992:** The Lawnmower Man; The Hand That Rocks the Cradle; Aces: Iron Eagle 3; A River Runs Through It; Chaplin. **1993:** In the Line of Fire; Robin Hood: Men in Tights; Undercover Blues; A Perfect World **1993:** CB4. **1994:** The Mask; The Shawshank Redemption; Color of Night;

Deep Red. **1995:** Avenging Angel; Murder in the First; Panther; Casino; Ballistic; Chameleon. **1996:** Down Periscope; The Crow: City of Angels; Mars Attacks!

BOBBY BASS
(b. 1947)

A member of Stunts Unlimited, this stocky supporting player, stunt coordinator, and second unit director choreographed the outstanding fight scene in *The Ninth Configuration*. He has doubled for both Jackie Gleason and Burt Young.

Films—**1968:** The Green Berets. **1969:** Che. **1973:** The Don Is Dead. **1974:** Thieves Like Us. **1977:** Smokey & the Bandit. **1978:** Corvette Summer; Who'll Stop the Rain; Hooper. **1979:** Starting Over. **1980:** The Ninth Configuration; The Blues Brothers; Tom Horn; Serial; Smokey & the Bandit 2; Wholly Moses; The Hunter. **1981:** Blood Beach; The Cannonball Run; The Incredible Shrinking Woman; Sharky's Machine; Cheech & Chong's Nice Dreams. **1982:** Megaforce; Lookin' to Get Out. **1983:** The Sting 2; Independence Day; The Osterman Weekend; Star 80; Scarface; The Star Chamber. **1984:** The River Rat. **1985:** The Legend of Billie Jean; Warning Sign; To Live & Die in L.A.; Love on the Run (tv). **1986:** 8 Million Ways to Die; The Wraith; Let's Get Harry; The Return of Mike Hammer (tv). **1987:** The Wild Pair; Mannequin; Lethal Weapon; Predator; Real Men; The Squeeze. **1988:** Action Jackson; Tequila Sunrise; Die Hard; Twins. **1989:** Gleaming the Cube; Black Rain; Fists of Steel; Sundown. **1990:** Heart Condition; Rocky 5. **1991:** Thelma & Louise; The Perfect Weapon; Beethoven. **1992:** Rampage; Lethal Weapon 3; Diggstown; Patriot Games; Bram Stoker's Dracula; The Bodyguard. **1993:** Falling Down; The Last Action Hero; Rising Sun; Excessive Force. **1994:** Pentathalon; The Crow; True Lies; Double Dragon; Terminal Velocity; Puppetmasters; Junior. **1995:** Village of the Damned; Jade. **1996:** Executive Deci-

Action from 1982's *Megaforce*, coordinated by Bobby Bass and directed by stuntman Hal Needham.

sion; Mulholland Falls; Eraser; My Fellow Americans. *Television*—Star Trek; The Barbary Coast; Vegas; The Twilight Zone; Spenser for Hire.

BILLY BATES

Films—**1983:** Young Warriors. **1984:** The Ice Pirates. **1985:** To Live & Die in L.A. **1987:** Hell Comes to Frogtown. **1988:** Mac & Me; Miracle Mile. **1989:** Chopper Chicks in Zombie Town; Hack 'o' Lantern. **1991:** Barton Fink; Mannequin 2. **1992:** Mom & Dad Save the World; Hero; Guncrazy; Interceptor. **1993:** Super Mario Bros.; Wind; Aspen Extreme. **1994:** The River Wild; Cobb. **1995:** The Usual Suspects. **1996:** The Quest.

KEN BATES
(b. 1958)

A member of Stunts Unlimited, this stunt coordinator and high-fall specialist started in Wild West shows. He mastered a tricky falling camera shot known as "the decelerator."

Films—**1981:** An Eye for an Eye. **1982:** 48HRS. **1985:** Turk 182; Gotcha!; Stick; To Live & Die in L.A. **1986:** The Money Pit; Sweet Liberty; King Kong Lives; Invaders from Mars. **1987:** Number One With a Bullet; Million Dollar Mystery; *batteries not included; Deadly Illusion; Night Force. **1988:** Bulletproof; Rambo 3; Die Hard; 976 Evil. **1989:** Short Circuit 2; See No Evil, Hear No Evil; Hit List; Far from Home; Star Trek 5: The Final Frontier; Night Life; Physical Evidence; Casualties of War; One Man Force. **1990:** The First Power; Die Hard 2; Another 48 HRS.; Maniac Cop 2; The Adventures of Ford Fairlane; Marked for Death; Predator 2; The Ambulance. **1991:** Mobsters; Hudson Hawk; Fast Getaway; Ricochet; The Last Boy Scout. **1992:** Trespass; Doppelganger; Cool World; Hero; Rage &

Honor. **1993:** Nat'l Lampoon's Loaded Weapon; Extreme Justice; Hear No Evil; True Romance; Sliver; Class of 1999; In the Line of Fire; Demolition Man; Maniac Cop 3. **1994:** Army of One; Class of 1999 2; The Crow; The Shadow; The Mask; A Low Down Dirty Shame. **1995:** Bad Boys; Fair Game. **1996:** Adrenaline; The Lawnmower Man 2; The Rock (p); Ravenhawk.

HANK BAUMERT

An independent stunt coordinator, Baumert has worked predominantly on Chuck Norris vehicles.

Films—**1985:** The Naked Face; Code of Silence. **1986:** Legal Eagles. **1988:** Bulletproof; Above the Law; Party Line; The Dead Pool; Vibes; Angel 3. **1989:** Transylvania Twist; Bill & Ted's Excellent Adventure. **1990:** Delta Force 2. **1991:** The Killing Floor; Martial Law. **1992:** Sunset Grill. **1993:** Sidekicks; Hellbound. **1994:** Eyes of an Angel. **1995:** Top Dog. **1996:** Forest Warrior; Overkill; Raven. *Television*—Walker, Texas Ranger.

CHRISTINE BAUR

A stunt coordinator and second unit director, Baur is a member of the United Stuntwoman's Association. She has doubled for Annie Potts.

Films—**1979:** Meteor. **1980:** In God We Trust. **1982:** Fast Walking. **1983:** Sudden Impact. **1984:** No Small Affair. **1985:** Hellhole; Silver Bullet; Fright Night; Moving Violations. **1986:** 8 Million Ways to Die; Maximum Overdrive; Eye of the Tiger; Never Too Young to Die. **1987:** Over The Top; The Witches of Eastwick; Assassination; Prince of Darkness; Down Twisted. **1988:** They Live; Unholy Matrimony (tv). **1989:** Who's Harry Crumb?; Grave Secrets. **1990:** Young Guns 2; Peacemaker; Robocop 2; Die Hard 2; Texasville; Problem Child; Masters of Menace. **1991:** Barton Fink; Rich Girl; Little Man Tate; Mannequin 2; Highway to Hell. **1992:** Mom & Dad Save the World; Hero. **1993:** In the Line of Fire. **1994:** Puppetmasters. **1995:** Separate Lives; Copycat; The Sweeper.

CRAIG BAXLEY
(b. 1950)

The son of Paul Baxley, Craig went from helming action on TV's "A-Team" to modest success as a motion picture director with the large-scale action films *I Come in Peace* and *Stone Cold*. He has doubled for Warren Beatty.

Films—**1972:** What's Up, Doc? **1973:** Charley Varrick; Welcome to Arrow Beach. **1974:** The Parallax View; Earthquake. **1975:** Rollerball; Shampoo. **1976:** Logan's Run; Drum. **1977:** Delta Fox. **1978:** Heaven Can Wait; Foul Play. **1979:** Nightwing; The Warriors; Mind Over Murder (tv). **1980:** The Long Riders; Wholly Moses. **1981:** Reds; Take This Job & Shove It. **1982:** The Seduction; Eddie Macon's Run. **1987:** Predator. **1991:** Action Jackson (d). **1992:** Revenge on the Highway (d) (tv). **1993:** A Family Torn Apart (d) (tv). **1994:** Deconstructing Sarah (d); Deep Red (d). **1995:** Avenging Angel (d); The Twilight Man (d). *Television*—The Night Stalker; The Dukes of Hazzard; Freebie & the Bean; The A-Team; Hardcastle & McCormick; Hunter; Raven.

GARY BAXLEY

A member of the Stuntmen's Association and brother of Craig Baxley,

Gary has worked as a stunt coordinator and double for Andrew Stevens.

Films—**1977:** The Island of Dr. Moreau; Delta Fox. **1979:** The Warriors. **1980:** The Stunt Man; Heart Beat; In God We Trust. **1981:** Charlie Chan & the Curse of the Dragon Queen; Death Hunt. **1982:** Night Warning; The Seduction; Eddie Macon's Run; Six Pack. **1986:** Born American; Armed Response. **1988:** Action Jackson. **1989:** Rooftops; See No Evil, Hear No Evil. **1990:** Dick Tracy; I Come in Peace; Death Warrant; Peacemaker; Delta Force 2; Total Recall; The Exorcist 3; The Rookie. **1991:** Stone Cold; Highway to Hell; Eve of Destruction; Star Trek 6: Undiscovered Country; Timebomb; Diplomatic Immunity; Night Eyes 2. **1992:** Class Act; Universal Soldier; Hoffa; Munchie. **1993:** Rescue Me; Sidekicks. **1994:** Army of One; Zero Tolerance; Color of Night; Illicit Dreams. **1995:** Blackout; The Silencers. **1996:** Skyscraper. *Television*—The Night Stalker; The Dukes of Hazzard; The A-Team; Beverly Hills 90210; Pacific Blue.

PAUL BAXLEY
(b. 1923)

A veteran stunt coordinator and bit player, Baxley was a Wyoming native who once played professional football with the 49'ers. A noted knife man, he doubled for the likes of Alan Ladd, Marlon Brando, and William Shatner, later staging the spectacular car crashes on "The Dukes of Hazzard."

Films—**1948:** Whiplash; The Black Arrow. **1949:** Knock on Any Door. **1950:** Between Midnight & Dawn. **1952:** The Crimson Pirate. **1954:** King Richard & the Crusaders. **1955:** Cell 2455, Death Row. **1956:** Around the World in 80 Days; 54 Washington Street. **1957:** Gunfight at the O.K. Corral; Bombers B-52; Baby Face Nelson. **1958:** The Badlanders. **1959:** All

Unidentified stunt from *The Stunt Man* (1980).

the Young Men. **1960:** Desire in the Dust; Spartacus; Guns of the Timberland. **1962:** Mutiny on the Bounty. **1963:** PT-l09 The Ugly American. **1964:** The Carpetbaggers. **1965:** Morituri. **1966:** The Appaloosa; Harper. **1967:** Tobruk; The Karate Killers. **1968:** Journey to Shiloh; Coogan's Bluff. **1969:** Eye of the Cat; The Great Bank Robbery. **1970:** Suppose They Gave a War and Nobody Came; Catch-22. **1971:** Diamonds Are Forever. **1972:** What's Up, Doc?; The Godfather. **1973:** Cleopatra Jones; Charley Varrick; The Boy Who Cried Werewolf; Nightmare Honeymoon. **1974:** The Parallax View; Mr. Majestyk. **1975:** Report to the Commissioner. **1976:** Rich Man, Poor Man (tv). **1977:** Citizen's Band (aka Handle with Care); Fun with Dick & Jane; The Late Show; Telefon. **1979:** Sunburn; The Champ; Friendly Fire (tv). **1980:** In God We Trust. **1981:** Death Hunt. **1982:** Night Warning. **1984:** The Bounty. **1985:** Getting Even; Pee Wee's Big Adventure. **1987:** Shy People; The Garbage Pail Kids. **1988:** Action Jackson. **1990:** The Exorcist 3; I Come in Peace;

Class of 1999. **1991:** Stone Cold; Timebomb. **1992:** The Mambo Kings. **1994:** Deconstructing Sarah. **1995:** Avenging Angel. *Television*—The Restless Gun; The Twilight Zone; Wagon Train; Hawaiian Eye; The Munsters; Laredo; The Man from U.N.C.L.E.; Maverick; The Virginian; Star Trek; The Night Stalker; The Dukes of Hazzard; The A Team.

PAM BEBERMEYER

A member of the United Stuntwoman's Association, Bebermeyer has doubled for Kay Lenz, Sally Field, and Genevieve Bujold.

Films—**1971:** Harold & Maude. **1974:** Freebie & the Bean. **1976:** Swashbuckler; Moving Violation. **1977:** Smokey & the Bandit. **1978:** Nat'l Lampoon's Animal House; Hooper; Bloodbrothers. **1979:**

Prophecy; Just You & Me Kid. **1980:** The Blues Brothers; Smokey & the Bandit 2; Carny. **1982:** Friday the 13th Part 3. **1983:** Heart Like a Wheel; Nightmares; Nat'l Lampoon's Vacation. **1984:** Friday the 13th: The Final Chapter. **1985:** Hellhole. **1988:** Defense Play; Mac & Me; Miracle Mile. **1990:** Tremors. **1991:** Diplomatic Immunity. **1992:** Hero. **1993:** Aspen Extreme.

DANA BERTOLETTE

Films—**1989:** See No Evil, Hear No Evil. **1991:** Out for Justice; Mannequin 2; The Hard Way. **1992:** Folks; Hoffa. **1993:** Robocop 3. **1994:** Body Snatchers; The Cowboy Way; Army of One. **1995:** Kiss of Death; Die Hard with a Vengeance; Batman Forever; Assassins. **1996:** Daylight.

SANDY BERUMEN

A member of the Professional Driver's Association, Berumen has doubled for both Kyra Sedgwick and Sharon Stone.

Films—**1985:** Into the Night; The Man with One Red Shoe; Just One of the Guys. **1986:** The Wraith. **1987:** The Lost Boys. **1988:** License to Drive. **1989:** After Midnight. **1990:** Ghost; Misery; The Adventures of Ford Fairlane; Kindergarten Cop; The Rookie; Prayer of the Rollerboys; A Girl to Kill For. **1991:** Ricochet; The Last Boy Scout; Pyrates; Shakes the Clown. **1992:** Basic Instinct; Wild Orchid 2; Lethal Weapon 3. **1993:** Demolition Man; Calendar Girl. **1994:** Silence of the Hams; Savate (aka The Fighter). **1995:** 3 Ninjas Knuckle Up; Destiny Turns on the Radio; Jade; Seven; Money Train. **1996:** Marshal

Law; Bordello of Blood. *Television*—Baywatch.

RAY BICKEL

Films—**1978:** Hooper. **1979:** The Villain. **1980:** The Blues Brothers; The Hunter; Smokey & the Bandit 2. **1982:** Blade Runner. **1985:** Moving Violations. **1986:** The Golden Child; Ruthless People. **1987:** Cyclone; Cold Steel; Deadly Intent. **1988:** I'm Gonna Git You Sucka; Messenger of Death; Rush Week. **1989:** Shocker; The Wizard. **1991:** Mobsters; Alligator 2; Deadlock. **1992:** Bram Stoker's Dracula; Guncrazy. **1996:** Dear God.

CHINO BINAMO

Films—**1990:** Basket Case 2; Street Hunter. **1991:** Mobsters; Delta Force 3. **1992:** Rapid Fire; Buffy, the Vampire Killer; Into the Sun; Martial Law 2: Undercover; Mission of Justice; Dr. Mordrid. **1993:** Private Wars; Robot Wars; Cyborg 2. **1994:** Ice; Direct Hit; Automatic; Stargate; American Yakuza. **1995:** Strange Days. **1996:** Executive Decision; Back to Back.

RICHARD BLACKWELL

A stunt coordinator, Blackwell is a member of both the Stuntmen's Association and the Professional Driver's Association.

Films—**1990:** Robocop 2; Class of 1999; Firebirds; Masters of Menace; Marked for Death; Prayer of the Rollerboys. **1991:** Stone Cold; Eve of Destruction; Son of Darkness: To Die For 2; Hook; Alligator 2; Beastmaster 2; Freddy's Dead; Shakes the Clown. **1992:** Aces: Iron Eagle 3; Under

Siege; Adventures in Dinosaur City; Mission of Justice; Live Wire. **1993:** Hot Shots Part Deux; Hear No Evil; The Last Action Hero; Another Stakeout; Robocop 3; Kalifornia; The Pelican Brief; Attack of the 50 Foot Woman. **1994:** Surviving the Game; The Naked Gun 33 1/3; Deadly Target; The Hard Truth; T-Force; Relentless 4; American Yakuza; Outbreak; Batman Forever. **1995:** Strange Days; Casino. **1996:** Independence Day; The Crow; City of Angels; Before & After. *Television—* The Flash.

CHUCK BORDEN

*Films—***1988:** Dr. Alien. **1989:** Curfew. **1990:** Firebirds; Darkman; Circuitry Man; Steel & Lace; Trancers 2; Red Surf; Puppetmaster 3. **1991:** Soldier's Fortune; Club Fed. **1992:** Mission of Justice; Guncrazy; Death Ring. **1994:** Ice; Direct Hit; Zero Tolerance; Deadly Target; CIA 2: Target Alexa; T-Force. **1995:** Digital Man; The Silencers; Suspect Device; Caged Hearts. **1996:** Skyscraper; Mercenary; Somebody to Love; Back to Back; Phoenix.

SIMONE BOISSEREE

A member of the United Stuntwoman's Association, Boisseree has doubled such dark-haired ladies as Rae Dawn Chong, Sonia Braga, Barbara Carrera, and Barbara Hershey.

*Films—***1982:** The Sword & the Sorcerer. **1983:** Lone Wolf McQuade. **1985:** Commando; Rambo 2; Avenging Angel. **1986:** 52 Pick-Up; Big Trouble in Little China; Jumpin' Jack Flash. **1987:** Steele Justice; Assassination; Million Dollar Mystery; Prince of Darkness; Innerspace. **1988:** Action Jackson; Alien Nation; They Live. **1989:** Gleaming the Cube; Road House; After Midnight. **1990:** Total Recall; The Guardian; Texasville; The Rookie; Masters of Menace; The Borrower. **1991:** Highway to Hell; Harley Davidson & the Marlboro Man; Delirious; Showdown in Little Tokyo. **1992:** White Men Can't Jump; Last of the Mohicans; Hero; Hoffa; Sunset Grill. **1993:** Cyborg 2; Man's Best Friend. **1994:** The Naked Gun 33 1/3; The Crow; Stargate; Deadly Target. **1995:** 3 Ninjas Knuckle Up. **1996:** Don't Be a Menace; Fled; The Crow: City of Angels; Set It Off. *Television—*Jake & the Fatman.

KEN JOHN BORLAND

*Films—***1988:** Action Jackson; They Live. **1990:** I Come in Peace; Class of 1999; Far Out Man; The Exorcist 3. **1991:** Stone Cold; The Doors; Timebomb; Neon City. **1992:** Wild Orchid 2; American Me. **1993:** Hard Target; Demolition Man; Cybertracker. **1994:** White Mile; Guardian Angel; Hologram Man; Bad Blood. **1995:** Avenging Angel. **1996:** The Phantom; Sunchaser.

CLAY BOSS

The stunt coordinator son of stuntwoman May Boss, clay is a member of the International Stunt Association. He has doubled for Christopher Walken.

*Films—***1974:** Freebie & the Bean. **1980:** The Blues Brothers; The Mountain Men. **1981:** The Legend of the Lone Ranger. **1983:** Lone Wolf McQuade; Brainstorm; Scarface. **1984:** The River. **1985:** Girls Just Want to Have Fun; Invasion USA; Silverado. **1986:** The Naked Cage; Radioactive Dreams; Dangerously Close; Ferris Bueller's Day Off; Firewalker; Legal Eagles. **1987:** Steele Justice. **1988:** Fright

Night 2; Rambo 3; Bad Dreams; Hero & the Terror. **1989:** The Abyss; L.A. Bounty. **1990:** Satan's Princess; Total Recall. **1991:** The Taking of Beverly Hills; Nothing But Trouble; Highway to Hell; Beastmaster 2; McBain; Leather Jackets; Soldier's Fortune. **1992:** Innocent Blood; Mistress; Out on a Limb. **1994:** American Cyborg: Steel Warrior; Body Shot; The Mask; American Yakuza; Heaven & Hell (tv). **1995:** Money Train.

MAY R. BOSS

A veteran member of the United Stuntwoman's Association, Boss was a trick rider on the rodeo circuit. She has doubled for Bette Davis.

Films—**1959:** Westbound. **1966:** A Big Hand for the Little Lady. **1972:** Bunny O'Hare. **1973:** Cleopatra Jones. **1974:** Blazing Saddles; Earthquake. **1976:** Logan's Run; Drum; Moving Violation. **1978:** Goin' South; Rabbit Test; Return from Witch Mountain. **1979:** Concorde, Airport '79. **1980:** The Blues Brothers; The Mountain Men; Wholly Moses; Die Laughing; The Hollywood Knights. **1981:** Deadly Blessing. **1983:** Brainstorm. **1985:** Commando; Silverado; Avenging Angel. **1986:** Murphy's Law. **1987:** The Lost Boys. **1988:** Dead Heat; The Dead Pool. **1990:** Total Recall. **1992:** Kuffs. **1994:** Puppetmasters. **1995:** Separate Lives; Money Train; Sudden Death. *Television*— The Outer Limits.

BRAD BOVEE

A member of the Stuntmen's Association and the Professional Driver's Association, Bovee has coordinated stunts and served as a double for both John Larroquette and James Caan.

Films—**1980:** The Fifth Floor; A Small

Circle of Friends. **1982:** Cat People; Ruckus. **1983:** Spacehunter. **1984:** Repo Man. **1985:** The Man With One Red Shoe; Rambo 2. **1986:** Cobra; Ruthless People. **1987:** The Night Stalker; Wanted: Dead of Alive; Death Wish 4; Masters of the Universe; Dragnet. **1988:** Alien Nation; They Live; Border Heat. **1989:** Second Sight; Night Children; From the Dead of Night (tv). **1990:** Madhouse; Maniac Cop 2; The Rookie. **1991:** Toy Soldiers. **1992:** Memoirs of an Invisible Man; Honeymoon in Vegas. **1993:** Flesh & Bone; The Philadelphia Experiment 2; Rescue Me. **1994:** The Naked Gun 33 1/3; Cabin Boy; Silence of the Hams; Pumpkinhead 2. **1995:** Panther; Die Hard with a Vengeance; Tank Girl; Devil in a Blue Dress. **1996:** Last Man Standing; Raven. *Television*—Contact.

STEVE BOYUM

A member of both the Professional Driver's Association and Stunts Unlimited, Boyum is best known for taking part in *Apocalypse Now*'s famous exploding chopper scene. He has directed second unit, coordinated stunts, and has also doubled for character actor Tim Thomerson.

Films—**1975:** Rollerball. **1979:** Apocalypse Now; Skatetown U.S.A. **1980:** The Blues Brothers; Carny; In God We Trust; Just Before Dawn; The Mountain Men; Used Cars; Wholly Moses; Foolin' Around; Herbie Goes Bananas. **1982:** Megaforce; The Beastmaster. **1983:** D.C. Cab. **1985:** Knights of the City. **1987:** Predator. **1988:** Action Jackson; Twins; Something Is Out There (tv). **1989:** Blind Fury; Lethal Weapon 2. **1990:** Days of Thunder; Last of the Finest; Maniac Cop 2; Vietnam, Texas. **1991:** The Butcher's Wife; Thelma & Louise; The Last Boy Scout; Thelma & Louise; Dead Again; The Last Boy Scout; Body Parts. **1992:** Kuffs; Lethal Weapon 3; Rapid Fire; Forever Young; Patriot Games; White Sands;

Buffy, The Vampire Slayer. **1993:** Falling Down; Groundhog Day; True Romance; Sliver; Airborne; Gettysburg; Maniac Cop 3. **1994:** D2: The Mighty Ducks; Beverly Hills Cop 3; True Lies; Heavyweights; Drop Zone. **1995:** Nine Months; The Big Green; Mighty Ducks 3; Sudden Death; Mr. Holland's Opus. **1996:** Crazy Horse. *Television*—The Night Stalker; Wiseguy; Stingray; Werewolf; Hardball.

DAN BRADLEY

An independent stunt coordinator and second unit director, Bradley was responsible for the large-scale action scenes in the blockbuster *Independence Day.*

Films—**1984:** The Executioner Part 2; 3:15; Hambone & Hillie; Lethal. **1985:** Girls Just Want to Have Fun; Hell Riders; Hellhole; Trancers; The Boys Next Door; Nightmare on Elm Street 2: Freddy's Revenge; Re-Animator. **1986:** House; The Supernaturals; Hollywood Vice Squad; Trick or Treat; KGB: The Secret War; Dangerously Close; Armed Response; Critters. **1987:** Dudes; Prettykill; My Demon Lover; Valet Girls; White of the Eye; Nightstick. **1988:** Critters 2. **1989:** Cage; Kinjite; The Mighty Quinn; Heathers; Society. **1990:** Deceptions; Prayer of the Rollerboys; Genuine Risk; Boris & Natasha. **1991:** Meet the Applegates; Freddy's Dead. **1992:** The Lawnmower Man; The Public Eye; Critters 4; Trancers 3. **1993:** A Dangerous Woman; Kalifornia; Blindside. **1994:** The Dark Wind; Dead Connection; Red Rock West; The Mask; Steel Frontier; Blue Tiger; Dumb & Dumber. **1995:** 3 Ninjas Knuckle Up; Top Dog; My Family; Jury Duty; The Prophecy; How to Make an American Quilt; Casino. **1996:** Independence Day; Scorpion Spring; Back to Back.

BUFF BRADY

A veteran western actor, rodeo performer, and member of the Stuntman's Association, Brady portrayed one of the rowdy sons in William Wyler's *The Big Country.*

Films—**1950:** The Golden Stallion. **1951:** The Rodeo King & the Senorita. **1952:** Rodeo. **1958:** The Big Country. **1959:** Yellowstone Kelly. **1960:** Spartacus; The Alamo. **1961:** El Cid. **1963:** Wall of Noise. **1964:** Bullet for a Badman. **1965:** The Rare Breed; The Hallelujah Trail. **1969:** MacKenna's Gold; Paint Your Wagon. **1970:** There Was a Crooked Man. **1972:** The Great Northfield Minnesota Raid. **1974:** The Towering Inferno; Mame; Earthquake. **1975:** The Great Waldo Pepper. **1976:** Dr. Black, Mr. Hyde. **1977:** Black Oak Conspiracy. **1979:** The Last Ride of the Dalton Gang (tv). **1981:** Escape from New York; Heartbeeps. **1983:** Christine. **1985:** Silverado. **1990:** Problem Child. **1992:** Sweet Justice. **1993:** Hexed. *Television*—Roy Rogers; Frontier Justice; Have Gun, Will Travel; The Legend of Jesse James; Laredo; Cimarron Strip; The Green Hornet; The Wild Wild West; Beauty & the Beast; Zane Grey; F-Troops.

JANET BRADY

The first female member of Stunts Unlimited, this stunt coordinator has distinguished herself as one of the top women in the field. She has doubled for Sally Field, Holly Hunter, and Jennifer Jason Lee.

Films—**1977:** Smokey & the Bandit; Airport '77. **1978:** Hooper. **1979:** Beyond the Poseidon Adventure; Prophecy. **1980:** The Blues Brothers; The Hunter; Smokey & the Bandit 2. **1981:** Butterfly. **1982:** Blade Runner; Star Trek 2: The Wrath of Khan. **1983:** The Osterman Weekend; Scarface;

The Star Chamber; D.C. Cab. **1984:** Beverly Hills Cop; The River Rat. **1985:** Into the Night; Explorers; Moving Violations; Iron Eagle; Vendetta. **1986:** The Hitcher; Big Trouble in Little China; Out of Bounds. **1987:** The Omega Syndrome; Burglar; Night Force; Masters of the Universe; Less Than Zero; The Lost Boys. **1988:** Action Jackson; Die Hard; The Blob; The Presidio. **1989:** Wired; Always; K-9; Lethal Weapon 2; Road House; Nat'l Lampoon's Christmas Vacation; Backtrack. **1990:** Die Hard 2; The Adventures of Ford Fairlane; Predator 2. **1991:** Point Break; Ricochet; Terminator 2; Beethoven; The Rocketeer; The Last Boy Scout. **1992:** Basic Instinct; Lethal Weapon 3; Patriot Games; Doppleganger. **1993:** The Last Action Hero; Rising Sun. **1994:** Pentathalon; Speed; In the Army Now; Drop Zone; Puppetmasters; Roadracers. **1995:** The Criminal Mind; Seven; Money Train. **1996:** Eye for an Eye; Eraser; The Rock; Escape from L.A.; Jingle All the Way.

BOBBY BRAGG

Primarily working on low-budget films, Bragg has served as the preferred stunt coordinator for cult directors Fred Olen Ray and Donald Jackson.

Films—**1984:** Savage Dawn. **1986:** Armed Response; Wired to Kill. **1987:** Cyclone; Cold Steel; Hell Comes to Frogtown. **1988:** Rollerblade Warriors: Taken By Force; Terminal Force; Terminal Entry; Waxwork. **1989:** Survival Quest; Trust Me; Alienator; Mob Boss; Sundown. **1990:** Leatherface 3; Zandalee. **1991:** Waxwork 2; Roots of Evil. **1992:** Hellraiser 3: Hell on Earth; Legend of the Rollerblade Seven. **1993:** No Place to Hide; Frogtown II (aka Return to Frogtown). **1995:** Cyberzone. **1996:** Nightshade.

BOB BRALVER

A stunt coordinator, second unit director, and television player who moved into directing, Bralver has since begun to make his own films. He's a member of Drivers Inc.

Films—**1974:** Earthquake. **1978:** Avalanche. **1979:** Beyond the Poseidon Adventure; Star Trek, The Motion Picture; Jaguar Lives. **1980:** The Nude Bomb. **1982:** The Sword & the Sorcerer. **1984:** The Joy of Sex; Savage Streets. **1987:** Timestalkers (tv). **1988:** Rush Week (d); Tapeheads. **1989:** CHUD 2; L.A. Bounty; Road House. **1990:** Lambada. **1991:** Beastmaster 2. **1994:** Midnight Ride (d/s). **1995:** American Ninja 5 (p); Deadly Outbreak; The Sweeper. **1996:** Deadly Games; Set It Off. *Television*—The Man from U.N.C.L.E; The Girl from U.N.C.L.E; I Spy; Star Trek; Mission: Impossible; Kung Fu; Emergency; Switch; Chase; The Bionic Woman; The Fall Guy; Knight Rider; (d); Riptide (d); Hunter (d); J.J. Starbuck (d); Father Dowling Mysteries (d); Renegade (d); Diagnosis Murder (d).

JOHN BRANAGAN

A stunt coordinator and bit player, Branagan is a member of the International Stunt Association. He has doubled for Art Garfunkel and Daniel Stern.

Films—**1983:** The Entity; Strangers Kiss. **1984:** Streetwalkin'; City Limits. **1986:** Good to Go (aka Short Fuse); The Boss's Wife. **1987:** Steele Justice; Stranded; Summer Camp Nightmare; Code Name Zebra. **1988:** Torch Song Trilogy; Border Heat; Not of This Earth; Vibes; The Prince of Pennsylvania; Angel 3; Twice Dead; They Live. **1989:** Time Trackers; Transylvania Twist; Masque of the Red Death; Brain Dead; Street Asylum; Ministry of Vengeance. **1990:** Watchers 2; Peacemaker; Streets; Cold Fire; Syngenor. **1991:** Dragonfight; The People Under the Stairs; Beastmaster 2; Future Kick; The Perfect Weapon; The Rocketeer; Leather Jackets; Soldier's Fortune; California Casanova; Double Trouble. **1992:** Poison Ivy; 3 Ninjas; The Waterdance. **1993:** Streetknight. **1994:** The Pagemaster; Ed Wood; Dumb & Dumber; Steel Frontier; Hologram Man; Silk Degrees. **1995:** Frank & Jesse; 3 Ninjas Knuckle Up; Things to Do in Denver When You're Dead; Under the Hula Moon. **1996:** Kingpin; Ravenhawk; Crazy Horse; Raven.

EDDIE BRAUN
(b. 1962)

A member of both the Stuntmen's Association and the Professional Driver's Association, this California native has coordinated stunts and directed second unit. He has doubled for Charlie Sheen, Matt Dillon, and Michael Pare.

Films—**1983:** Young Warriors; Deadly Force; Lies. **1985:** Stand Alone. **1986:** Born American; Nomads; Wisdom. **1987:** Allan Quartermain & the Lost City of Gold; Steele Justice; Survival Game. **1988:** Bulletproof; Jack's Back; Sunset; Dangerous Love; Feds; Hero & the Terror; Kansas. **1990:** Navy Seals; Peacemaker; Men at Work; Hollywood Hot Tubs 2; The Rookie; 9 1/2 Ninjas; Backstreet Dreams; Red Surf. **1991:** Out for Justice; Hot Shots; Star Trek 6: Undiscovered Country; Diplomatic Immunity; Alligator 2; Liquid Dreams; Not of This World (tv). **1992:** Final Analysis; Freejack; Deep Cover; Class Act; Unlawful Entry; Universal Soldier; Buffy, the Vampire Slayer; Sneakers; Hoffa; Guncrazy; Sunset Heat; Death Ring. **1993:** Robocop 3; Undercover Blues; Amos & Andrew; Fatal In-

stinct; Excessive Force; Cyborg 2; Excessive Force; Cyborg 2; Rescue Me. **1994:** The Chase; Major League 2; Terminal Velocity; American Yakuza. **1995:** Separate Lives; Panther; Jade. **1996:** Down Periscope; The Arrival; First Kid; The Tuskegee Airman.

GREG BRAZZELL

An independent stunt coordinator and martial arts fight choreographer, Brazzell has doubled for Marc Singer.

Films—**1984:** Places in the Heart. **1986:** Mountaintop Motel Massacre. **1988:** The Further Adventures of Tennessee Buck. **1989:** Cutting Class. **1990:** After Dark, My Sweet; Last Call. **1991:** Martial Law. **1992:** Delta Heat; Sweet Justice; Martial Law 2: Undercover. **1993:** Hexed; No Escape, No Return; Cybertracker; Firepower. **1994:** The Last Ride (aka F.T.W.); Hologram Man; Red Sun Rising; Witch Hunt; Savate (aka The Fighter); Fast Getaway 2; Guardian Angel; Bad Blood; Silk Degrees; Victim of Desire; Ripper Man. **1995:** Frank & Jesse; Soldier Boyz; To the Limit; Unknown Origin; One Man's Justice; Black Scorpion; Blackout; The Silencers; Suspect Device. **1996:** Skyscraper; Dark Breed. *Television*—Young Riders.

NICK BRETT

Films—**1988:** Die Hard. **1989:** Time Trackers. **1990:** Die Hard 2; The Adventures of Ford Fairlane. **1991:** Mobsters; Hook; Fast Getaway; Ricochet; Double Trouble. **1992:** Trespass; Cool World; Doppleganger. **1993:** Full Eclipse; In the Line of Fire; Maniac Cop 3. **1994:** Army of One; Streetfighter; A Low Down Dirty Shame. **1995:** Bad Boys; Fair Game; Nemesis 3. **1996:** Lawnmower Man 2; The Rock; The Chamber.

CHARLIE BREWER

Brother of the late Geof Brewer, Charlie is a member of the International Stunt Association. He has doubled for Stanley Tucci.

Films—**1986:** Murphy's Law; Never Too Young to Die. **1988:** Vibes; Hero & the Terror. **1989:** Shocker; Tango & Cash. **1990:** Another 48 HRS.; Hangfire. **1991:** The Taking of Beverly Hills; The Naked Gun 2 1/2; Star Trek 5: Undiscovered Country; Hook; Cool as Ice; Ricochet; Suburban Commando; Double Trouble. **1992:** Article 99. **1993:** The Last Action Hero; Undercover Blues; Trouble Bound. **1994:** The Getaway; Cabin Boy; Stargate; Puppetmasters; The Hard Truth. **1995:** Outbreak; Nine Months; Money Train; The Crossing Guard; Grumpier Old Men. **1996:** Broken Arrow.

GEOF BREWER

(b. 1958; d. 1989)

A stunt coordinator and second unit director, Brewer died in a helicopter crash on the film *Delta Force 2.*

Films—**1983:** The Lords of Discipline. **1984:** Mission Thunderbolt. **1985:** The Boys Next Door; Invasion USA. **1986:** Never Too Young to Die. **1987:** Allan Quartermain & the Lost City of Gold; Back to the Beach; Overboard; The Hidden. **1988:** Bulletproof; Elvira, Mistress of the Dark; Dead Heat; Midnight Run. **1989:** Hit List; Road House; L.A. Bounty; One Man Force; Crack House; Tarzan in Manhattan (tv). **1990:** The Gumshoe Kid; Boris & Natasha; Satan's Princess; Delta Force 2. *Television*—Remington Steele.

GREG BRICKMAN

Films—**1977:** The Incredible Rocky Mountain Race (tv). **1978:** Corvette Summer; Hooper; The Clonus Horror. **1980:** The Blues Brothers; Hangar 18. **1981:** The Boogens. **1985:** The Falcon & the Snowman; Sweet Dreams. **1987:** Teen Wolf 2; The Untouchables. **1988:** The Blob. **1989:** K-9; Staying Together. **1992:** Encino Man. **1994:** In the Army Now. **1995:** The Enemy Within; Showgirls. **1996:** Eye for an Eye.

ALEX BROWN

A member of Rawn Hutchinson's Precision Drivers, Brown has doubled for Yaphet Kotto.

Films—**1971:** Dirty Harry. **1972:** Across 110th Street. **1974:** Black Belt Jones; Blazing Saddles; Earthquake. **1976:** Emma Mae. **1977:** The Choirboys. **1978:** Hooper. **1980:** The Dogs of War; Brubaker. **1982:** White Dog; The Sword & the Sorcerer. **1983:** Under Fire. **1984:** Night of the Comet. **1985:** The Color Purple. **1988:** I'm Gonna Git You Sucka. **1989:** Glory; Crack House. **1990:** Liberty & Bash; Backstreet Dreams. **1993:** Trouble Bound. **1994:** Sugar Hill. **1995:** Devil in a Blue Dress; Vampire in Brooklyn.

BOBBY BROWN

Having emerged as one of the top fall specialists in the industry, Brown has also coordinated stunts. He's a member of Stunts Unlimited.

Films—**1987:** Allan Quartermain & the Lost City of Gold; Cold Steel; Back to the Beach; Creepozoids; The Hidden. **1988:** Hero & the Terror; Messenger of Death; Tapeheads; Night of the Demons. **1989:**

Survival Quest; Lady Avenger; 976 Evil. **1990:** Men at Work; Child's Play 2; Predator 2. **1991:** Harley Davidson & the Marlboro Man; Terminator 2; McBain; Soldier's Fortune. **1992:** Double Trouble; Nails; Nemesis. **1993:** Hot Shots Part Deux; Demolition Man; Gettysburg; Excessive Force; Brain Smasher; Knights. **1994:** The Crow; The Mask; Zero Tolerance. **1995:** Waterworld; Seven; Fair Game; Last Man Standing; Money Train; The Sweeper; Nemesis 3. **1996:** From Dusk Till Dawn; Marshal Law; Barb Wire; Eraser; Spy Hard; The Cable Guy; The Rock; Bulletproof; The Glimmer Man; Ravenhawk.

COURTNEY BROWN

This Florida-based stunt coordinator is best known for doubling Lloyd Bridges on TV's "Sea Hunt." He was the stunt partner of Ricou Browning.

Films—**1963:** Flipper. **1964:** Flipper's New Adventure. **1966:** Birds Do It; Around the World Under the Sea. **1967:** Island of the Lost. **1968:** Speedway; Daring Game. **1969:** Hello Down There. **1970:** Darker Than Amber. **1972:** Key West (tv). **1976:** Joe Panther. **1979:** Hot Stuff. **1981:** Porky's. **1983:** Jaws 3-D; Spring Break. **1984:** Where the Boys Are '84. **1985:** Invasion USA; The New Kids. **1986:** Band of the Hand. **1992:** Folks. **1993:** Ace Ventura, Pet Detective. *Television*—Sea Hunt; The Aquanauts; Flipper.

JOPHERY BROWN

A stunt coordinator and familiar thick-necked supporting player (*The Bingo Long Traveling All-Stars*),

Brown is a member of Stunts Unlimited. He arranged the stellar gun battles seen in *Scarface* and has doubled for both Carl Weathers and Yaphet Kotto.

Films—**1973:** Big Mo (aka Maurie). **1974:** Mixed Company. **1976:** The Bingo Long Traveling All-Stars; Swashbuckler; Drum. **1977:** Smokey & the Bandit. **1978:** Hooper; Convoy; Foul Play. **1980:** American Gigolo; The Blues Brothers; Serial; The Hunter; Smokey & the Bandit 2. **1981:** Cheech & Chong's Nice Dreams. **1982:** Fighting Back; The Sword & the Sorcerer; Annie; Lookin' to Get Out; Rocky 3. **1983:** Scarface; Sudden Impact; The Star Chamber; Nat'l Lampoon's Vacation; Stroker Ace. **1984:** The River; Against All Odds; Splash. **1985:** To Live & Die in L.A.; Commando; Moving Violations. **1986:** The Hitcher. **1987:** Over the Top; The Wild Pair; Lethal Weapon; Real Men; The Big Easy; Predator; The Squeeze; Alien from L.A. **1988:** Little Nikita; Action Jackson; Die Hard; The Presidio; Twins. **1989:** Hit List; Cyborg; Lethal Weapon 2; Kinjite; Ghostbusters 2; Tango & Cash. **1990:** Heart Condition; I Come in Peace; The Adventures of Ford Fairlane; Last of the Finest; Marked for Death; Heat Wave (tv). **1991:** Harley Davidson & the Marlboro Man; Stone Cold; The Fisher King; The Naked Gun 2 1/2; Hook; Flight of the Intruder. **1992:** Article 99; Stop! or My Mom Will Shoot; Universal Soldier. **1993:** Extreme Justice; Posse; Boiling Point; Hard Target; Jurassic Park; Nowhere to Run; Jailbait; Maniac Cop 3. **1994:** Pentathalon; Army of One; House Party 3; Speed; In the Army Now; The Expert. **1995:** Panther; Get Shorty; Money Train; Sudden Death. **1996:** Eye for an Eye; Broken Arrow; Heaven's Prisoners; Spy Hard; Pure Danger. *Television*—Matt Houston; Beekman's Place.

TROY BROWN

A member of Stunts Unlimited and former professional bull rider, Brown has doubled for Joe Pesci, Joe Mantegna, and Robin Williams.

Films—**1989:** The Package; Curfew. **1990:** Downtown; Die Hard 2; Home Alone; The Rookie. **1991:** Stone Cold; Showdown in Little Tokyo; Flight of the Intruder; Only the Lonely; Dutch; Curly Sue. **1992:** Memoirs of an Invisible Man; Home Alone 2; Innocent Blood. **1993:** Dennis the Menace; The Fugitive; Mrs. Doubtfire. **1994:** The Crow; Baby's Day Out; Double Dragon; The Last Word; Illicit Dreams. **1995:** The Quick & the Dead; Village of the Damned; Crimson Tide; Waterworld; Virtuosity; Money Train. **1996:** Mulholland Falls; Eraser; Bordello of Blood; The Long Kiss Goodnight; Jingle All the Way.

RICOU BROWNING

(b. 1930)

This aquatic specialist was a member of the Air Force Swim Team before donning the gill suit for the underwater scenes in *The Creature from the Black Lagoon.* He later became a writer, producer, and director of wholesome, Florida-lensed family fare.

Films—**1954:** The Creature from the Black Lagoon. **1955:** Revenge of the Creature. **1956:** The Creature Walks Among Us. **1963:** Flipper (s/p). **1964:** Flipper's New Adventure. **1965:** Thunderball. **1966:** Namu, the Killer Whale; Around the World Under the Sea. **1967:** Island of the Lost (d). **1968:** Lady in Cement; Daring Game. **1969:** Hello, Down There. **1975:** Lucky Lady; Salty (d/s/p).

1976: Joe Panther. **1979:** Hot Stuff. **1980:** Raise the Titanic; Caddyshack; Island Claws (s). **1981:** Nobody's Perfect. **1983:** Never Say Never Again. **1985:** The Heavenly Kid. **1987:** Opposing Force. **1988:** Police Academy 5: Assignment Miami Beach. *Television*—Sea Hunt; The Aquanauts; Flipper (p); Gentle Ben (d); Primus; The Six Million Dollar Man; The Bionic Woman.

TONY BRUBAKER

A former stableboy and college football player, Brubaker began doubling Greg Morris on TV's "Mission: Impossible" and then top black actors Jim Brown, Fred Williamson, and Sidney Poitier. A supporting player, stunt coordinator and member of the Stuntmen's Association, Brubaker has served as Danny Glover's double since the late eighties.

Films—**1970:** There Was a Crooked Man; Cotton Comes to Harlem. **1972:** Come Back, Charleston Blue; Conquest of the Planet of the Apes; Buck & the Preacher. **1973:** Westworld; The Soul of Nigger Charley; Slaughter's Big Rip-Off; Battle for the Planet of the Apes. **1974:** The Towering Inferno; Black Samson; Three Tough Guys; Sugar Hill; 99 & 44/100% Dead; Hang Up (aka Super Dude); Earthquake. **1975:** Friday Foster; Rollerball. **1976:** Dr. Black, Mr. Hyde; Drum; Breakheart Pass. **1978:** Return from Witch Mountain. **1979:** Buck Rogers in the 25th Century; Freedom Road (tv). **1980:** Smokey & the Bandit 2; Used Cars. **1981:** Charlie Chan & the Curse of the Dragon Queen; Escape from New York. **1982:** The Sword & the Sorcerer; Conan the Barbarian; White Dog; Rocky 3; Tron. **1983:** D.C. Cab; Under Fire; Blue Thunder; Fire & Ice. **1984:** Love Streams. **1985:** Into the

Ricou Browning as *The Creature from the Black Lagoon* (1954).

Night; Commando. **1986:** Invaders from Mars; Jumpin' Jack Flash; Hollywood Vice Squad; Fatal Beauty; Eye of the Tiger. **1987:** The Night Stalker; The Wild Pair; Predator; Remote Control; Masters of the Universe; The Running Man; Weeds; Desperado (tv). **1988:** Action Jackson; Midnight Run; Shoot to Kill; Red Heat; I'm Gonna Git You Sucka; They Live; Bail Out. **1989:** Back to the Future 2; Ghostbusters 2; Second Sight; Glory; Next of Kin; One Man Force. **1990:** I Come in Peace; Far Out Man; Total Recall; Marked for Death; Predator 2. **1991:** Out for Justice; A Rage in Harlem; Pure Luck; Backdraft; Driving Me Crazy. **1992:** Deep Cover; Trespass; Lethal Weapon 3; Class Act; Rapid Fire; Far & Away; Wayne's World; Adventures in Dinosaur City; Extreme Justice. **1993:** Amos & Andrew; Posse; Nowhere to Run; The Last Outlaw; Weekend at Bernie's; Laurel Avenue. **1994:** Pentathalon; Sugar Hill; Blown Away; Deconstructing Sarah; The Mask. **1995:** Die Hard with a Vengeance; Tank Girl; Operation Dumbo Drop; The Set Up; Devil in a Blue Dress; Heat; Ballistic. **1996:** Original Gangstas; First Kid. *Television*—The Outcasts; Mission: Impossible; Kung Fu; The Rockford Files; The Six Million Dollar Man; Baretta; The Bionic Woman; Wonder Woman; The Incredible

Hulk; The Fall Guy; Magnum P.I.; Matt Houston; Simon & Simon; In the Heat of the Night; Renegade.

JERRY BRUTSCHE

A motorcycle specialist, Brutsche appeared as one of Erich Von Zipper's Rat Pack in sixties Beach Party movies. He later became a member of the Stuntmen's Association.

Films—1963: Beach Party. 1964: Pajama Party. 1965: Beach Blanket Bingo; Sgt. Deadhead; How to Stuff a Wild Bikini. 1966: The Ghost in the Invisible Bikini; Harper. 1968: Finian's Rainbow. 1969: The Good Guys & the Bad Guys; The Great Bank Robbery; Five the Hard Way (aka Sidehackers); Hell's Belles. 1972: Conquest of the Planet of the Apes; What's Up, Doc? 1973: Electra Glide in Blue; Magnum Force; Battle for the Planet of the Apes. 1974: Earthquake. 1975: Rooster Cogburn. 1976: St. Ives. 1977: Herbie Goes to Monte Carlo. 1978: The Deer Hunter; Every Which Way But Loose; The Cat from Outer Space; Return from Witch Mountain; Over the Edge. 1980: Foolin' Around; Oh, God Book II; Up the Academy; The Hollywood Knights; Any Which Way You Can. 1982: Annie. 1983: Scarface. 1984: Body Double. 1985: Grandview USA; Teen Wolf; Cloak & Dagger; Commando; Cocoon; Explorers; Fright Night. 1986: 52 Pick-Up. 1987: Million Dollar Mystery; *batteries not included. 1988: License to Drive; Illegally Yours; Twins. 1993: Calendar Girl. *Television*—Honey West; Starsky & Hutch.

KURT BRYANT

A member of the International Stunt Association, Bryant has coordinated stunts and doubled for John Cusack.

Films—1985: Deadly Intruder. 1987: Million Dollar Mystery; No Safe Haven; Hot Pursuit; Down Twisted. 1988: Shakedown; Maniac Cop; Last Rites; Die Hard; Short Circuit 2; They Live. 1989: One Man Force; Riding the Edge; Grave Secrets; Far from Home. 1990: Bird on a Wire; Death Warrant; Miller's Crossing; Desire & Hell at Sunset Motel; Dollman; Watchers 2. 1991: The Taking of Beverly Hills; Teenage Mutant Ninja Turtles 2. 1992: Memoirs of an Invisible Man; Storyville; 3 Ninjas; Innocent Blood; Davinci's War; Night Eyes 3; Mission of Justice; The Double-O Kid; The Water Engine (tv); Danger Island (aka The Presence) (tv). 1993: Streetknight; No Escape, No Return; Best of the Best 2; Jailbait; Indecent Behavior 2; Meatballs 4; Eye of the Stranger; Cyborg 2; Cybertracker; Firepower. 1994: Wagons East; Leprechaun 2; Double Dragon; Steel Frontier; Open Fire; Hologram Man; The Stranger; Criminal Passion; Scanners: The Showdown. 1995: The Quick & the Dead; Village of the Damned; 3 Ninjas Knuckle Up; Mortal Kombat; Bad Blood; To the Limit; Chameleon; One Man's Justice; The Silencers; Suspect Device; Blackout. 1996: Bio-Dome; A Thin Line Between Love & Hate; Skyscraper; The Demolitionist; Dark Breed; The Dentist; Ravenhawk; Mercenary; Little Witches Rattled.

CHERIE BRYSON *SEE* RAE, CHERIE

PETER BUCOSSI

A stunt coordinator, supporting player, and double for Anthony Lapaglia, Bucossi is a member of Stunt Specialists. His brother Paul often works with him.

Films—1984: The Exterminator 2; Scream

for Help. **1986:** 9 1/2 Weeks; Legal Eagles; Quiet Cool; F/X; Streets of Gold; Crocodile Dundee. **1987:** My Demon Lover; Mannequin; China Girl; Deadly Illusion. **1988:** Shakedown; Stealing Home; Last Rites; Crocodile Dundee 2; Homeboy. **1989:** Ghostbusters 2; See No Evil, Hear No Evil; Weekend at Bernie's; Hell High; Lock Up; Black Rain. **1990:** Quick Change; State of Grace; Blue Steel; King of New York; GoodFellas; Street Hunter. **1991:** 29th Street; Highlander 2; The Hard Way; McBain. **1992:** Freejack; Night & the City; Light Sleeper; Hoffa. **1993:** The Night We Never Met. **1994:** Body Snatchers; Serial Mom; Fresh; The Cowboy Way; Trial by Jury; The Professional; Mixed Nuts; Nobody's Fool. **1995:** Kiss of Death; Die Hard with a Vengeance; The Jerky Boys. **1996:** Independence Day; Daylight.

BUZZ BUNDY

A member of the Professional Driver's Association, Bundy entered films after work as an auto daredevil.

Films—**1971:** Diamonds Are Forever. **1977:** Black Oak Conspiracy. **1980:** In God We Trust. **1982:** Lookin' to Get Out. **1984:** Police Academy. **1985:** D.A.R.Y.L. **1987:** The Omega Syndrome. **1988:** Tripwire; Twins. **1989:** One Man Force; Relentless. **1990:** The Gumshoe Kid; Maniac Cop 2; The Ambulance. **1991:** Fast Getaway; 976 Evil 2. **1992:** Encino Man. **1993:** Extreme Justice. **1995:** Last Man Standing. **1996:** Pure Danger; Riot.

JIM BURK

A member of Stunts Unlimited and veteran supporting player in Western fare, Burk portrayed one of the rugged brothers in Wyler's *The Big Country.* He has doubled for that film's co-stars Charlton Heston and Chuck Connors.

Films—**1947:** Lost Honeymoon. **1949:** Red, Hot, & Blue. **1951:** His Kind of Woman. **1952:** The Toughest Man in Arizona. **1953:** Pony Express; Arrowhead. **1955:** You're Never Too Young. **1956:** The Birds & the Bees. **1958:** The Big Country. **1959:** The Young Philadelphians; Alias Jesse James. **1962:** Geronimo. **1964:** Old Shatterhand. **1965:** The Hallelujah Trail. **1967:** The Way West. **1968:** The Green Berets; Hellfighters. **1969:** The Undefeated; True Grit. **1970:** Chisum. **1971:** Sometimes a Great Notion (aka Never Give an Inch); Big Jake; One More Train to Rob. **1972:** The Life and Times of Judge Roy Bean; The Cowboys. **1973:** Oklahoma Crude; The Train Robbers; Hijack (tv). **1974:** Chinatown; The Midnight Man. **1975:** Crazy Mama. **1976:** Leadbelly; Gator; Drum; Slumber Party '57. **1978:** Hooper; Convoy. **1979:** Prophecy. **1980:** Tom Horn; The Long Riders; The Mountain Men; Wholly Moses; Belle Starr (tv). **1982:** Conan the Barbarian; Star Trek 2: The Wrath of Khan; Airplane 2. **1983:** Brainstorm; Hysterical. **1984:** 2010. **1987:** Dragnet. **1988:** Action Jackson; Young Guns. **1989:** Johnny Handsome; Tango & Cash. **1990:** Far Out Man. **1991:** My Heroes Have Always Been Cowboys; Hook; K-9000 (tv). **1992:** Hero. *Television*—Tales of Wells Fargo; Wagon Train; Mission: Impossible; Mannix; The Magician; M*A*S*H; Guns of Paradise.

BOBBY BURNS

A member of the International Stunt Association, Burns has doubled for Richard Dreyfuss and Corey Haim.

Films—**1985** To Live & Die in L.A.; Moving Violations. **1987:** Death Wish 4; The Wild Pair. **1988:** The Blob; License to Drive; Border Heat. **1989:** Best of the Best; Riding the Edge; Time Trackers. **1990:** Men at Work; Last of the Finest;

Hangfire; Prayer of the Rollerboys. **1991:** The Naked Gun 2 1/2; Hook; The Doors; What About Bob? **1992:** The Lawnmower Man; Bram Stoker's Dracula; Trancers 3. **1993:** Conflict of Interest; Caroline at Midnight. **1994:** A Low Down Dirty Shame. **1995:** Frank & Jesse; 3 Ninjas Knuckle Up. **1996:** The Trigger Effect; Sunchaser.

BLAIR BURROWS

Films—**1977:** Which Way Is Up? **1978:** Hooper. **1979:** Escape from Alcatraz; Kate Bliss & the Ticker Tape Kid (tv). **1980:** The Blues Brothers; Smokey & the Bandit 2; Night of the Juggler. **1981:** Smokey Bites the Dust. **1983:** Timerider; D.C. Cab **1984:** The River. **1985:** Return of the Living Dead. **1988:** Midnight Run; Lucky Stiff. **1989:** K-9; Under the Gun; Old Gringo. **1991:** Diplomatic Immunity. **1993:** Robin Hood: Men in Tights.

BRIAN BURROWS

Films—**1987:** Wanted: Dead or Alive; Masters of the Universe. **1988:** Midnight Run; Lucky Stiff. **1989:** The Package. **1990:** Young Guns 2; Downtown; The Rookie. **1991:** City Slickers; Showdown in Little Tokyo. **1992:** Last of the Mohicans; Mr. Saturday Night. **1993:** Robin Hood: Men in Tights. **1994:** City Slickers 2. **1995:** Die Hard with a Vengeance; Top Dog. **1996:** Crazy Horse (tv).

POLLY BURSON
(b. 1919)

An Oregon-born rodeo performer and daughter of horseman Wayne Burson, Patty worked as a trick rider for Gene Autry and later doubled actresses Betty Hutton and Julie Adams. A member of the Stuntwoman's Association, she married stuntman Jerry Gatlin.

Films—**1946:** The Perils of Pauline; The Crimson Ghost; The Purple Monster Strikes. **1952:** Rodeo; Westward, The Women. **1953:** Gunsmoke. **1954:** Creature from the Black Lagoon. **1955:** Escape to Burma. **1957:** The Kettles on Old McDonald's Farm; Night Passage. **1959:** The Jayhawkers. **1960:** Spartacus. **1962:** How the West Was Won. **1969:** True Grit. **1974:** Earthquake. **1984:** Last of the Great Survivors (tv). **1985:** Black Moon Rising. **1992:** Hero. *Television*—The Outer Limits.

BILL BURTON

This much in-demand second unit director/stunt coordinator has doubled for the likes of Don Johnson, Sam Shepard, Jeff Bridges, and William Hurt. A member of both Stunts Unlimited and the Professional Driver's Association, Burton's sons and daughter are also in the business.

Films—**1968:** The Pink Jungle. **1969:** The Good Guys & the Bad Guys; The Great Bank Robbery; The Undefeated; Tell Them Willie Boy Is Here. **1970:** Beneath the Planet of the Apes; The Phynx; Angel Unchained; Little Big Man. **1971:** The Computer Wore Tennis Shoes; Star Spangled Girl. **1972:** Ulzana's Raid; Boxcar Bertha. **1974:** Three the Hard Way; Blazing Saddles; Earthquake; Strange Homecoming (tv). **1975:** A Boy & His Dog; Bite the Bullet; Crazy Mama; Posse. **1976:** Slumber Party '57. **1977:** Moonshine County Express; Heroes; Delta Fox; Maniac (aka Ransom). **1978:** The Driver; Comes a Horseman; Hooper; Centennial (tv). **1979:** Game of Death; Prophecy; A Time to Die; The 11th Victim (tv). **1980:** Eyewitness; Herbie Goes Bananas; The Long Riders; Smokey & the Bandit 2; Heaven's Gate. **1981:** Body Heat; Cutter's Way. **1982:** Wrong Is Right; The Entity; Lookin' to Get Out; Tron; Yes, Giorgio; The Blue & the Gray (tv). **1983:** The Sting 2; Nat'l Lampoon's Vacation; Octopussy. **1984:** The Cotton Club; Against All Odds; Romancing the Stone. **1985:** To Live & Die in L.A.; Year of the Dragon; Fever Pitch. **1986:** American Justice; Playing for Keeps. **1987:** The Wild Pair; Predator; Teen Wolf 2; Code Name Zebra. **1988:** Action Jackson. **1989:** K-9; Best of the Best; Lonesome Dove (tv). **1990:** Dick Tracy; Die Hard 2; Desperate Hours; Dances with Wolves; Days of Thunder. **1991:** Predator 2; Harley Davidson & the Marlboro Man; The Doors; Bugsy. **1992:** American Me; White Sands; Thunderheart; Patriot Games; Bram Stoker's Dracula; The Bodyguard. **1993:** The Last Action Hero; Hard Target; Nowhere to Run; Best of the Best 2. **1994:** The Getaway; Pentathlon; Lightning Jack; The Shadow; Wyatt Earp; Terminal Velocity; In the Army Now; A Low Down Dirty Shame; Puppetmasters; Night of the Running Man; Prophet of Evil (tv). **1995:** Bad Boys; Nine Months; White Mile; The Good Old Boys; Waterworld; Operation Dumbo Drop; Jade. **1996:** Eye for an Eye; From Dusk Till Dawn; Mulholland Falls; The Phantom; Eraser; Escape from L.A.; Sunchaser. *Television*—The Immortal; The Texas Wheelers; Knot's Landing; Simon & Simon; O'Hara; Jake & the Fatman; The Flash.

DAVID BURTON
(b. 1965)

The oldest son of Bill Burton, David is also a member of Stunts Unlimited. He has doubled for Brad Pitt.

Films—**1980:** In God We Trust; Pleasure Palace (tv). **1983:** Amityville 3-D; Breathless; Scarface. **1984:** Beverly Hills Cop; Against All Odds; The River Rat; Star Trek 3: The Search for Spock. **1985:** Into the Night; My Man Adam. **1986:** The Hitcher. **1987:** Let's Get Harry; Night Force; Teen Wolf 2; Code Name Zebra; The Lost Boys. **1988:** The Blob; They Live. **1989:** Star Trek 5: The Final Frontier; Lethal Weapon 2. **1990:** Solar Crisis; Joe vs. the Volcano; Edward Scissorhands; Last of the Finest; Predator 2. **1991:** My Heroes Have Always Been Cowboys; Harley Davidson & the Marlboro Man; Thelma & Louise. **1992:** American Me; Patriot Games; Gladiator; A River Runs Through It. **1993:** The Ballad of Little Jo. **1994:** Lightning Jack. **1996:** Ravenhawk.

HAL BURTON

A member of the Stuntmen's Association, Hal has done bits and coordinated stunts.

Films—**1985:** Rustler's Rhapsody; Invasion USA. **1986:** Murphy's Law; Wisdom. **1987:** Overboard; The Hidden. **1988:** Bulletproof; Feds; Hero & the Terror; Critters 2; The Night Before. **1989:** Halloween 5. **1991:** The Doors; Harley Davidson & the Marlboro Man; Deadlock; Star Trek 6: Undiscovered Country. **1992:** The Lawnmower Man; White Sands; The Double-O Kid. **1993:** The Fugitive; Tombstone; Bitter Harvest. **1994:** Blind Justice. **1995:** Village of the Damned; Die Hard with a Vengeance; Tank Girl. **1996:** A Very Brady Sequel; Ravenhawk; Set It Off; Dear God.

HEATHER BURTON

The daughter of Bill Burton, Heather has doubled for Alyssa Milano and Lori Petty.

Films—**1993:** Conflict of Interest; Free Willy; Hard Target; Fearless; Double Dragon; A Low Down Dirty Shame; The Good Old Boys; Apollo 13; Showgirls. **1996:** The Phantom; Pure Danger; Sunchaser.

DICK BUTLER

A veteran stunt coordinator and supporting player, Butler has doubled for Gene Hackman. He's a member of both the Stuntmen's Association and the Professional Driver's Association.

Films—**1968:** Fade-In. **1969:** The Great Bank Robbery. **1970:** Catch-22. **1971:** Mrs. Polifax-Spy. **1972:** Conquest of the Planet of the Apes; What's Up, Doc? **1973:** Battle for the Planet of the Apes. **1974:** The Towering Inferno. **1975:** Jaws; Matt Helm (tv). **1976:** A Matter of Wife & Death (tv). **1977:** Freaky Friday; Black Sunday; Stunts; Herbie Goes to Monte Carlo. **1978:** Love & the Midnight Auto Supply; Superman; The Big Fix. **1979:** The Prizefighter. **1980:** Up the Academy; Die Laughing; Melvin & Howard; Motel Hell; Wholly Moses. **1981:** Pennies from Heaven. **1982:** The High Country; E.T.; The Sword & the Sorcerer; Tron. **1983:** Independence Day; Angel. **1984:** Bachelor Party; The Cartier Affair (tv); More Than Murder (tv). **1985:** Back to the Future; Commando. **1986:** 52 Pick-Up. **1987:** The Omega Syndrome; Death Wish 4. **1988:** Maniac Cop; Midnight Run; Mississippi Burning; Criminal Act. **1989:** Three Fugitives; Hit List; Johnny Handsome; Kinjite; One Man Force; Night Life; Crack House. **1990:** Loose Cannons; Far Out Man; Total Recall; Masters of Menace; Popcorn; Marked for Death; Secret Agent 00-Soul; The Handmaid's Tale; Kindergarten Cop; Murder in Paradise (tv). **1991:** 976 Evil 2; Hook; Fast Getaway. **1992:** Honey, I Blew Up the Kid; Mo' Money; Love Field; Universal Soldier; Lake Consequence; Hoffa; Adven-

tures in Dinosaur City. **1993:** Rescue Me; Bound by Honor; Maniac Cop 3. **1994:** Clean Slate; Four Weddings & a Funeral; Little Giants; Ring of the Musketeers. **1995:** Angus; Casino; Last Man Standing; The Sweeper. **1996:** Spy Hard; The Rock; Pure Danger. *Television*—Maverick; Daniel Boone; Police Story; Policewoman; McClain's Law; Today's FBI; Mike Hammer; Scarecrow & Mrs. King; Hunter; Hull Street High.

JOHN CADE

An independent stunt coordinator, Cade has managed to operate on both coasts.

Films—**1982:** The Sword & the Sorcerer. **1984:** Splash. **1985:** My Science Project; Moving Violations. **1986:** Odd Jobs; F/X. **1987:** The Garbage Pail Kids. **1988:** Last Rites; Earth Girls Are Easy. **1989:** Dream a Little Dream. **1990:** Joe vs. the Volcano; Die Hard 2; Peacemaker; Darkman; The Adventures of Ford Fairlane; Maniac Cop 2; In the Cold of the Night; Payback. **1991:** Shattered; The Last Boy Scout; Shakes the Clown. **1992:** We're Talkin' Serious Money. **1993:** Demolition Man; Cyborg 2. **1994:** The Mask; Deadly Target; American Yakuza. **1995:** Just Cause; The Addiction; Bigfoot. **1996:** Broken Arrow; Raven; The Rock; Fast Money.

JEFF CADIENTE

A second generation stunt coordinator and second unit director, Cadiente has doubled for Bill Paxton and Lou Diamond Phillips. He's with the International Stunt Association.

Films—**1986:** The Golden Child. **1989:** Disorganized Crime; Cage; Renegades; One Man Force. **1990:** The First Power; Predator 2; Vietnam, Texas; Angel Town.

1991: Eve of Destruction; The Perfect Weapon; Ambition; Driving Me Crazy. 1992: Rapid Fire; Trespass; 3 Ninjas; One False Move; Innocent Blood; Munchie. 1993: Extreme Justice; Streetknight; Dragon; Dangerous Touch; No Escape, No Return; Quick. 1994: The Dark Wind; The Crow; Airheads; Double Dragon; Blue Tiger; Mr. Write; Sioux City; A Low Down Dirty Shame; Steel Frontier; Hologram Man; Bad Blood; The Stranger. 1995: 3 Ninjas Knuckle Up; The Prophecy; Fair Game; The Silencers; The Sweeper. 1996: Phenomenon; The Crow: City of Angels; Escape from L.A.; Mercenary. *Television*—Jake & the Fatman; Renegade; Above & Beyond.

JOHN DAVID CADIENTE

A veteran bit player of Spanish descent, Cadiente is the father of Jeff Cadiente.

Films—1963: Donovon's Reef. 1964: Ride the Wild Surf. 1965: King Rat. 1966: 7 Women; The Professionals; Harper; Gambit. 1968: The Green Berets; Stay Away, Joe. 1969: True Grit; Che; The Great Bank Robbery. 1970: There Was a Crooked Man. 1974: Blazing Saddles. 1979: Buck Rogers in the 25th Century. 1980: The Kidnapping of the President; Defiance; Borderline; The Baltimore Bullet. 1981: Charlie Chan & the Curse of the Dragon Queen; Cheech & Chong's Nice Dreams. 1982: The Sword & the Sorcerer; Rocky 3. 1983: The Sting 2; Scarface. 1984: Star Trek 3: The Search for Spock. 1985: Stick. 1986: The Golden Child; Big Trouble in Little China. 1987: Extreme Prejudice; Night Force. 1988: They Live; Bail Out. 1991: Beastmaster 2; Ambition. 1993: Quick. 1994: The Naked Gun 33 1/3; Sioux City. 1995: Fair Game. 1996: 3 Ninjas Knuckle Up; Phenomenon. *Television*—Adventures in Paradise; Hawaiian

Eye; The Gallant Men; Kraft Suspense Theater; Star Trek; The Rockford Files; Wonder Woman; Sword of Justice; Vegas: Buck Rogers; Voyagers; T.J. Hooker; The A-Team; Airwolf; Beauty & the Beast; Downtown.

HANK CALIA
(b. 1933)

A short-statured bit player, Calia is a member of the Stuntmen's Association.

Films—1966: The Appaloosa. 1968: The Green Berets. 1969: Che. 1970: Beneath the Planet of the Apes. 1972: Conquest of the Planet of the Apes. 1973: Bad Charleston Charlie; Battle for the Planet of the Apes. 1974: The Towering Inferno; Black Samson; Freebie & the Bean; Earthquake. 1978: FM; Lord of the Rings. 1980: The Stunt Man; Heaven's Gate. 1982: The Sword & the Sorcerer; The Beastmaster. 1984: City Heat; City Limits. 1985: Commando; My Science Project. 1987: The Night Stalker. 1988: Rambo 3; The Seventh Sign. 1989: The Package; Glory; Cartel; Nightmare on Elm Street 5: Dream Child. 1990: Pump Up the Volume. 1991: Mobsters. 1992: Hero; Hoffa. 1994: The Dark Wind. *Television*—The Virginian; The Night Stalker.

KEITH CAMPBELL

A member of both the Stuntmen's Association and the Professional Driver's Association, Cambell has doubled for Tom Cruise.

Films—1990: The First Power; Prayer of the Rollerboys. 1991: Eve of Destruction; Hook; The Addams Family; Driving Me Crazy. 1992: Patriot Games; Sneakers;

Toys; Chaplin; Adventures in Dinosaur City. **1993:** Hot Shots Part Deux; Full Eclipse; Red Rock West; True Romance; The Sandlot; Sidekicks; Demolition Man; Fatal Instinct. **1994:** Automatic; Forest Gump; Wolf; Terminal Velocity; Stargate. **1995:** 3 Ninjas Knuckle Up; Batman Forever; Last Man Standing. **1996:** Barb Wire; Spy Hard; Mission: Impossible; The Crow: City of Angels; Riot.

JOHN CANN

A nationally ranked freestyle wrestler, this Indiana-born actor is the author of *The Stunt Guide.*

Films—**1989:** Dr. Alien; Ghettoblaster. **1990:** Marked for Death; Predator 2; Trancers 2; Circuitry Man. **1991:** Child's Play 3; Puppetmaster 3. **1992:** Deep Cover; Sweet Justice. **1993:** Bound by Honor; The Philadelphia Experiment 2; Man's Best Friend. **1994:** Witch Hunt; American Yakuza. **1995:** My Family; Suspect Device; The O.J. Simpson Story (tv).

JOE CANUTT
(b. 1937)

This 6'4" stunt coordinator was the longtime double for Charlton Heston and the youngest son of Yak Canutt. A member of the Stuntmen's Association, he's most famous for bouncing around Heston's chariot in *Ben Hur* and for performing the cliff jump in *Butch Cassidy and the Sundance Kid.*

Films—**1955:** The Far Horizons. **1956:** The Swan. **1959:** Ben Hur. **1960:** Spartacus; The Alamo. **1961:** El Cid. **1965:** Major Dundee; The War Lord. **1966:** Khartoum. **1967:** Camelot. **1968:** Will Penny; Planet of the Apes; Bandolero. **1969:** The Wild Bunch; The Good Guys & the Bad Guys;

Butch Cassidy & the Sundance Kid. **1970:** Patton; Rio Lobo; Chisum. **1971:** The Omega Man. **1972:** Skyjacked; Across 110th Street. **1973:** Anthony & Cleopatra; Papillon; Soylent Green. **1974:** Earthquake; Airport '75. **1975:** Mandingo. **1976:** The Last Hard Men. **1977:** MacArthur. **1982:** Mother Lode. **1983:** The Golden Seal. **1990:** Treasure Island (tv). *Television*—Lost in Space.

TAP CANUTT
(b. 1932)

The eldest son of Yak Canutt, Edward "Tap" Canutt doubled for both Charlton Heston and Stephen Boyd. He's a lifetime member of the Stuntmen's Association.

Films—**1950:** The Devil's Doorway. **1953:** The Stranger Wore a Gun. **1954:** The Lawless Rider. **1960:** Spartacus; The Alamo. **1961:** El Cid. **1964:** The Fall of the Roman Empire. **1965:** The War Lord. **1966:** Khartoum. **1967:** Camelot. **1968:** Bandolero; Planet of the Apes. **1969:** The Wild Bunch; The Good Guys & the Bad Guys; The Undefeated. **1970:** Beneath the Planet of the Apes; Rio Lobo. **1971:** The Omega Man. **1972:** The Cowboys; Joe Kid. *Television*—26 Men; The Monroes.

YAKIMA CANUTT
(b. 1895; d. 1986)

Washington-born stunt legend was a rodeo champion and Wild West show performer when he got into Westerns and serials as a stuntman, villain, and rare lead. He hit his stride performing the action in *Stagecoach* and then moved into second unit directing, peaking with his fantastic staging of the chariot race in *Ben Hur.*

Charlton Heston and Stephen Boyd in *Ben Hur's* famous chariot race, coordinated by stunt legend Yakima Canutt (1959).

Over the years he developed many revolutionary stunt techniques and equipment, winning a special Oscar for his achievements in 1966. His autobiography, *Stunt Man,* was published in 1979.

Films—**1922:** Heart of a Texan. **1923:** The Forbidden Range. **1924:** The Desert Hawk; Ridin' Mad; Branded a Bandit; Sell 'Em Cowboy. **1925:** Romance & Rustlers; Scar Hanan; The Cactus Cure; Riding Comet; The Human Tornado; White Thunder; Wolves of the Road; The Strange Riders; A Two-Fisted Sheriff. **1926:** The Fighting Stallion; Desert Greed. **1927:** Hell Hound of the Plains; The Iron Riders. **1928:** Wild Horse Canyon; King of the Rodeo; A Texan's Honor. **1929:** Bad Men's Money; The Three Outcasts; Captain Cowboy; Rider of the Storm; The Vanishing West.

1930: Canyon Hawks; Firebrand Jordan; Ridin' Law; Lonesome Trail; Bar L Ranch. **1931:** Westward Bound; The Pueblo Terror; Cheyenne Kid; Hurricane Horseman; Lightning Warrior. **1932:** Two Fisted Justice; Riders of Golden Gulch; The Devil Horse; Cheyenne Cyclone; Wyoming Whirlwind; Telegraph Trail; Hurricane Express; Shadow of the Eagle. **1933:** Scarlet River; Fighting Texans; Sagebrush Trail; Law & the Lawless; Via Pony Express; The Three Mesquiters; Riders of Destiny. **1934:** Battling Buckaroo; Elinor Norton; Guns for Hire; The Man from Hell; Wild Gold; Lucky Texan; Texas Tornado; West of the Divide; Blue Steel; The Man from Utah; Randy Rides Alone; The Star Packer; Fighting Through; 'Neath Arizona Skies. **1935:** The Last Days of Pompeii; Lawless Frontier; Circle of Death; Paradise Canyon; Dawn Rider; Westward Ho; Branded a Coward; Cyclone of the Saddle; Dante's Inferno; Lawless Range;

Outlaw Rule; Pals of the Range; Rough Riding Ranger; Texas Terror; Welcome Home. **1936:** The Amazing Exploits of the Clutching Hand; Roarin' Lead; King of the Pecos; The Vigilantes Are Coming; Darkest Africa; San Francisco; Rose Marie; The Oregon Trail; Winds of the Wasteland; Wildcat Trooper; The Lonely Trail; Trouble in Texas. **1937:** Ghost Town Gold; Riders of the Dawn; Roarin' Legend; Come On, Cowboy; Riders of the Whistling Skull; Range Defenders; Gunsmoke Ranch; Rider of the Rockies; Conquest; Heart of the Rockies; Hit the Saddle; It Could Happen to You; Prairie Thunder. **1938:** Overland Stage Raiders; Riders of the Black Hills; Santa Fe Stampede; Ten Laps to Go; Mysterious Pilot; Army Girl. **1939:** Stagecoach; Wyoming Outlaw; The Kansas Terror; Cowboys from Texas; Gone with the Wind; Man of Conquest; Jesse James; The Light That Failed; The Night Rider; The Carson City Kid. **1940:** Oklahoma Renegades; Pioneers of the West; Ghost Valley Riders; The Ranger & the Lady; Under Texas Skies; Frontier Vengeance; Young Bill Hickock; Virginia City; Dark Command; Prairie Schooners. **1941:** The Great Train Robbery; Gauchos of El Dorado; They Died with Their Boots On; Idaho. **1942:** Gentleman Jim; Shadow on the Sage. **1943:** In Old Oklahoma; Pride of the Plains; Hidden Valley Outlaws. **1945:** Sheriff of Cimarron (d); Dakota; Sunset in El Dorado; The Untamed Breed. **1948:** G-Men Never Forget. **1949:** Red Stallion of the Rockies. **1950:** The Shadow; The Devil's Doorway; Rocky Mountain; The Great Missouri Raid. **1951:** Only the Valiant. **1953:** Ivanhoe; Mogambo; The Naked Spur; Battle Circus; Knights of the Round Table. **1954:** The Lawless Rider. **1955:** The Far Horizons; Westward Ho, The Wagons. **1956:** Helen of Troy; Zarak. **1957:** Old Yeller. **1958:** In Love & War. **1959:** Ben Hur. **1960:** Spartacus; Swiss Family Robinson. **1961:** El Cid. **1962:** Son of Captain Blood; How the West Was Won. **1964:** Fall of the Roman Empire. **1965:** Cat Ballou. **1966:** Khartoum. **1967:** The Flim Flam Man. **1968:** Blue. **1969:** Where Eagles Dare. **1970:** A Man Called Horse; Song of Norway; Rio Lobo. **1976:** Breakheart Pass; Equus.

ROCKY CAPELLA

A San Francisco based stunt coordinator and head of the Bay Area Stuntmen's Association, Capella has doubled for Treat Williams.

Films—**1985:** Smooth Talk. **1986:** Brotherhood of Justice (tv). **1987:** Wildfire; Burglar; Survival Game; Escapes. **1988:** Killer Klowns from Outer Space; Who Framed Roger Rabbit?; '68. **1989:** True Believer; Season of Fear. **1991:** Long Road Home (tv). **1992:** Basic Instinct. **1994:** Golden Gate; Made in America; Fist of the North Star; Angels in the Outfield; Milk Money. **1995:** Village of the Damned; Nine Months; Copycat; Jade **1996:** James & the Giant Peach. *Television*—Jesse Hawks.

JOHN "BUD" CARDOS
(b. 1929)

The Missouri-born Cardos began in the film business as a child performer and bird wrangler, eventually becoming an all-purpose man on many late sixties low-budgeters. It was not uncommon for him to be the production manager, second unit director, stunt coordinator, and F/X rigger on films in which he was also acting or doubling for the likes of Adam Roarke or Cameron Mitchell. He later moved into full-fledged directing.

Films—**1940:** The Return of Frank James. **1962:** The Manchurian Candidate; To Kill a Mockingbird; If a Man Answers. **1963:** The Birds. **1964:** Devil Wolf of Shadow Mountain. **1965:** Deadwood '76; Run Home Slow. **1967:** Rebel Rousers; Blood of Dracula's Castle; Hell's Angels on Wheels. **1968:** Five Bloody Graves; The Savage Seven; Killers Three; Lash of Lust; No Tears for the Damned; Road Hustlers; Psych-Out. **1969:** Nightmare in Wax; The Gun Riders; The Wild Bunch; Satan's Sadists; Bloodbath; The Female Bunch. **1970:** Hell's Bloody Devils (aka The Fakers). **1971:** The Incredible Two-Headed Transplant; Jud. **1972:** Soul Soldier (d); Death Dream (aka Dead of Night); House of Terror. **1973:** F.T.A. 1972 Domo Arigato. **1974:** Drag Racer (d). **1975:** It Seemed Like a Good Idea at the Time. **1976:** Won Ton Ton; Breaking Point; Vengeance Is Mine; Find the Lady. **1977:** Whale of a Tale; Kingdom of the Spiders (d). **1978:** Death Dimension (aka Kill Factor). **1979:** The Dark (d). **1980:** The Day Time Ended (d). **1983:** Mutant (d); Other Realms (d). **1984:** Buckeye. **1986:** Last Resort; Bullies. **1988:** Act of Piracy (d); Skeleton Coast (d). **1989:** Outlaw of Gor (d). **1992:** Legend of the West (d). *Television*—Sugarfoot; Maverick; Judge Roy Bean; Daniel Boone; The Monroes; The High Chapparal.

JIMMY CASINO

A veteran bit player and former boxer, Casino is a member of the Stuntmen's Association. He is the father of John Casino.

Films—**1948:** Trouble Preferred. **1949:** Counterpunch; Duke of Chicago. **1951:** Hollywood Story. **1952:** Meet Danny Wilson. **1955:** Foxfire. **1956:** I've Lived Before. **1957:** Untamed Youth. **1959:** And Ride a Tiger. **1970:** There Was a Crooked Man. **1973:** The Don Is Dead. **1978:** Movie, Movie; Paradise Alley. **1979:** Rocky 2. **1980:** The Island; Die Laughing.

1983: Brainstorm. **1985:** Cloak & Dagger. **1988:** They Live. **1990:** The Last Hour. *Television*—Cain's Hundred; Mission: Impossible.

JOHN J. CASINO

The chief double for Kurt Russell since the late eighties, Casino is a member of the Stuntmen's Association.

Films—**1985:** To Live & Die in L.A.; Runaway Train. **1987:** Teen Wolf 2; World Gone Wild; Programmed to Kill. **1988:** Miracle Mile; They Live. **1989:** Stepfather 2; Chopper Chicks in Zombie Town; After Midnight; Tango & Cash. **1990:** Tremors; Darkman. **1991:** Backdraft; Mannequin 2; Leather Jackets; The Naked Truth; Diplomatic Immunity. **1992:** Rapid Fire; Unlawful Entry; Captain Ron; Martial Law 2: Undercover. **1993:** Robocop 3; Super Mario Bros. **1994:** Stargate. **1995:** Destiny Turns on the Radio; Tank Girl; Baja; The Usual Suspects; Wild Bill. **1996:** Executive Decision; Broken Arrow; Escape from L.A.

DAVID CASS
(b. 1942)

A veteran Texas-born supporting player, stunt coordinator, and second unit director, Cass has doubled for both Kenny Rogers and Robert Mitchum. He actually had the heroic lead in the obscure *Disciples of Death,* an early seventies horror film which he also wrote and produced. His son David Jr., has gone into assistant directing.

Films—**1963:** McLintock. **1965:** Shenandoah. **1969:** The Good Guys & the Bad Guys; Heaven with a Gun; Young Billy

Young. **1970:** Dirty Dingus Magee; Suppose They Gave a War & Nobody Came. **1971:** Disciples of Death (aka Enter the Devil) (a/d/s/); Black Noon (tv). **1973:** The Boy Who Cried Wolf. **1974:** Earthquake. **1975:** Farewell, My Lovely; The Master Gunfighter; Winner Take All (tv). **1976:** Two Minute Warning; Trackdown; The Treasure of Matecumbe; From Noon Till Three; Law of the Land (tv). **1977:** The Island of Dr. Moreau; The Goodbye Girl; Blue Sunshine; Mr. Billion; Flight to Holocaust (tv); The Incredible Hulk (tv). **1978:** Hot Lead & Cold Feet; Wheels (tv); The Dark Secret of Harvest Home (tv); Centennial (tv). **1979:** The Apple Dumpling Gang Rides Again; The Jerk; More American Graffiti; The Lady in Red; The Golden Gate Murders (tv); The Concrete Cowboys (tv). **1980:** The Island; Heaven's Gate; More Wild Wild West (tv); The Gambler (tv). **1981:** Going Ape; All Night Long. **1982:** The Sword and the Sorcerer; Endangered Species; Six Pack; Tron; Savannah Smiles. **1983:** Heart Like a Wheel; Smokey & the Bandit 3; Get Crazy; Flicks (aka Loose Joints); The Gambler 2 (tv). **1984:** Uphill All the Way. **1985:** Wild Horses (tv); Command 5 (tv). **1986:** Down the Long Hills (tv); Assassin (tv); Dream West (tv). **1987:** Best Seller; My Demon Lover; Desperado (tv); The Gambler 3 (tv). **1988:** Tequila Sunrise; Case Closed (tv). **1990:** Revenge; Rio Diablo (tv). **1991:** Suburban Commando; Knight Rider 2000 (tv); The Gambler 4 (tv). **1993:** Queen (tv); Vestige of Kings (tv); Heaven & Hell (tv). **1994:** The Gambler 5 (tv); Scarlett (tv). **1995:** Buffalo Girls (tv). **1996:** Streets of Laredo (tv). *Television*—Mission: Impossible; The FBI; The Six Million Dollar Man; The Rockford Files; The Waltons; Policewoman; Royce; The Bionic Woman; Buck Rogers; The Greatest American Hero; Voyagers; Knight Rider; Simon & Simon; Misfits of Science

MIKE CASSIDY

A member of the Stuntmen's Association, this stunt coordinator has doubled for Michael Keaton. His sons Zane and Mickey are also in the business.

Films—**1977:** The Amazing Captain Nemo. **1979:** Buck Rogers in the 25th Century. **1980:** Up the Academy; Alligator; The Island. **1982:** Zapped; The Sword and the Sorcerer. **1983:** Hysterical; Mr. Mom; Metalstorm; Return of the Jedi; Yellowbeard. **1984:** City Heat; Romancing the Stone. **1985:** Teen Wolf; My Science Project; Avenging Angel; Deadly Messages (tv); The Battle for Endor (tv). **1986:** Blue City; Invaders from Mars; 8 Million Ways to Die; Critters. **1987:** Slamdance; Maid to Order; Remote Control; Hellraiser. **1988:** Pulse; Freeway; Out of the Dark; Beetlejuice. **1989:** The Abyss; Honey, I Shrunk the Kids; Nightmare on Elm Street 5: Dream Child. **1990:** Pacific Heights; Pump Up the Volume; Firebirds; After Dark. My Sweet; In the Cold of the Night. **1991:** Eve of Destruction; Flight of the Intruder; Silence of the Lambs. **1992:** Batman Returns; The Naked Truth; Roadside Prophets. **1993:** Hexed; The Beverly Hillbillies. **1994:** Speechless. **1995:** 3 Ninjas Knuckle Up. **1996:** Multiplicity. *Television*—The Best of Friends.

BILL "J.P." CATCHING
(b. 1926)

This veteran stunt coordinator, second unit director, and supporting player specialized in western work, doubling for Robert Stack, Efrem Zimbalist, Jr., Lee Majors, Glenn Ford, and Peter Lawford. His daughter Dottie also performed stunts.

Films—**1948:** The Man from Colorado. **1953:** The Nebraskan. **1955:** The Man from Laramie; Five Against the House. **1959:** North by Northwest. **1960:** Spartacus; Raymie. **1962:** Six Black Horses; Ride the High Country; Sergeants Three. **1964:** Gunfight at Commanche Creek. **1965:** Major Dundee; Operation CIA; The Great Race. **1966:** Ride Beyond Vengeance. **1967:** Hondo; The Corrupt Ones; A Time for Killing (aka Long Ride Home); The Last Challenge. **1968:** Guns for San Sebastian; Day of the Evil Gun. **1969:** Heaven with a Gun; The Great Bank Robbery; Run, Angel, Run! **1970:** Flap; The Phynx. **1972:** The Great Northfield Minnesota Raid; The Cowboys; The Poseidon Adventure. **1973:** Mean Streets; Westworld; Ordeal (tv). **1974:** Dirty Mary, Crazy Larry; Earthquake; The Hanged Man (tv); Fer de Lance (tv). **1975:** The Hindenburg; Sky Heist (tv); The New Original Wonder Woman (tv). **1976:** Mayday at 40,000 Feet (tv). **1977:** Hostage Heart (tv). **1978:** Avalanche; Terror Out of the Sky (tv); The Bastard (tv). **1979:** The Runner Stumbles; The Rebels (tv). **1980:** The Man with Bogart's Face; Motel Hell; Texas Legend. **1981:** High Risk; Chicago Story (tv). **1982:** Timerider. **1983:** Sadat (tv). **1985:** Salvador. **1986:** Stagecoach (tv). **1988:** Moon Over Parador. **1994:** The Getaway. *Television*—The Cisco Kid; Rough Riders; Sea Hunt; Wild Bill Hickock; Wyatt Earp; Rin Tin Tin; Brave Eagle; Zane Grey Theatre; Death Valley Days; Cheyenne; Bronco; Maverick; Bat Masterson; Law of the Plainsman; Tombstone Territory; Texas John Slaughter; Elfego Baca; The Untouchables; Lawman; Laramie; Wanted, Dead or Alive; Johnny Ringo; Target; Klondike; The Westerner; Wagon Train; Rawhide; The Outer Limits; Kraft Suspense Theatre; The Loner; Branded; Laredo; The Virginian; The Big Valley; Honey West; The Monroes; Hondo; Star Trek; Bonanza; The Wild Wild West; Gunsmoke; The FBI; The Name of the Game; The Mod Squad; The Men from Shiloh; McCloud; Kung Fu; Movin' On; Wonder Woman; Salvage One; The Fall Guy.

TONY CECERE

A stunt coordinator, second unit director, and fire specialist, Cecere is a member of the International Stunt Association. He's doubled for character actor Ray Wise.

Films—**1976:** Bobbie Jo & the Outlaw. **1981:** Dead & Buried; An Eye for an Eye. **1982:** Swamp Thing; Star Trek 2: The Wrath of Khan; The Soldier; The Thing. **1983:** Spacehunter; Metalstorm. **1984:** The Terminator; Ghostbusters; Nightmare on Elm Street; The Exterminator 2. **1985:** The Hills Have Eyes 2; House. **1986:** Deadly Friend. **1987:** Programmed to Kill; Allan Quartermain & the Lost City of Gold; House 2. **1988:** The Serpent & the Rainbow; Elvira, Mistress of the Dark; Bad Dreams; The Dead Pool; Child's Play; Phantom of the Ritz. **1989:** The Return of the Swamp Thing; Shocker; Chopper Chicks in Zombie Town; L.A. Bounty. **1990:** Death Warrant; Genuine Risk; Circuitry Man; Boris & Natasha. **1991:** The People Under the Stairs; Meet the Applegates; Mom; Deadlock; Diplomatic Immunity; Leather Jackets. **1992:** Mom & Dad Save the World; Hero; Sunset Grill. **1993:** Hard Target. **1994:** Body Shot; Wes Craven's New Nightmare; Steel Frontier. **1995:** Mindripper. *Television*—Baretta; The Incredible Hulk.

FERNANDO CELIS

Celis has worked as a stunt coordinator, supporting player, animal handler, and producer for the films of director Stewart Raffill.

Films—**1977:** Across the Great Divide. **1981:** High Risk. **1984:** The Ice Pirates; The Philadelphia Experiment. **1985:** Return of the Living Dead. **1987:** They Still

Call Me Bruce; Programmed to Kill. **1988:** Defense Play; Mac & Me; Miracle Mile. **1989:** Chopper Chicks in Zombie Town. **1990:** Tremors; Fear (tv). **1991:** Barton Fink. **1993:** Aspen Extreme. **1994:** Tammy & the T-Rex (p). **1995:** Showgirls; The Usual Suspects; Beastmaster 3.

JOHN CENATIEMPO

Films—**1988:** Shakedown. **1990:** Quick Change; State of Grace; Street Hunter. **1991:** Hudson Hawk; 29th Street; Ricochet; The Last Boy Scout. **1992:** Rapid Fire; Lethal Weapon 3; Whispers in the Dark. **1993:** True Romance. **1994:** North. **1995:** Die Hard with a Vengeance; Money Train. **1996:** Executive Decision; Eraser; Courage Under Fire; Maximum Risk.

AL CERULLO

A pilot based on the East Coast, Cerullo often handles helicopter assignments.

Films—**1982:** Night Shift; Tempest; The Soldier; The World According to Garp. **1984:** The Exterminator 2. **1985:** Heaven Help Us. **1986:** One Crazy Summer; The Manhattan Project. **1987:** Black Widow; Deadly Illusion. **1988:** Sweetheart's Dance; Crocodile Dundee 2; 1969. **1990:** Blue Steel; Funny About Love. **1991:** McBain; Boomerang. **1992:** Home Alone 2. **1993:** Romeo Is Bleeding; Carlito's Way; Taking the Heat. **1994:** The Cowboy Way; Trapped in Paradise. **1995:** Kiss of Death; Major Payne; The Jerky Boys. **1996:** The Juror; Down Periscope; Eraser; Daylight.

ERIC CHAMBERS

Films—**1988:** The Serpent & the Rainbow. **1989:** The Mighty Quinn; Chance;

Glory. **1990:** Joe vs. the Volcano; Taking Care of Business; Last of the Finest; Prayer of the Rollerboys. **1991:** Convicts; Neon City. **1992:** Dead Center (aka Crazy Joe). **1993:** The Pelican Brief; No Escape, No Return; Cybertracker. **1994:** The Last Seduction; Hologram Man; Bad Blood. **1995:** Outbreak; Soldier Boyz; Black Scorpion. **1996:** Skyscraper; Dark Breed. *Television*—Hard Time on Planet Earth.

R.J. CHAMBERS

Films—**1988:** Lucky Stiff. **1989:** Always. **1991:** Harley Davidson & the Marlboro Man; Showdown in Little Tokyo; The Rocketeer; Suburban Commando; Flight of the Intruder. **1992:** Last of the Mohicans; Bram Stoker's Dracula. **1993:** The Philadelphia Experiment 2. **1995:** The Quick & the Dead; Die Hard with a Vengeance. **1996:** Broken Arrow; The Fan; Ravenhawk.

STEVE CHAMBERS

A member of Stunts Unlimited, Steve is the son of fifties stuntman Stan Chambers. He's doubled for Michael Beck.

Films—**1969:** Butch Cassidy & the Sundance Kid. **1979:** The Villain; The Warriors. **1980:** The Long Riders; Smokey & the Bandit 2; The Mountain Men; Wholly Moses; Urban Cowboy. **1981:** Body Heat. **1982:** Megaforce; Parasite; Lookin' to Get Out. **1983:** Scarface; Jimmy the Kid; The First Turn-On. **1985:** Moving Violations. **1987:** Code Name Zebra; Predator. **1988:** Action Jackson. **1989:** Lethal Weapon 2; Her Alibi; Dead Bang; Tango & Cash. **1990:** Dick Tracy; Days of Thunder; Die Hard 2; Impulse; Dances With Wolves; Last of the Finest. **1991:** Hook; Warlock; Harley Davidson & the Marlboro Man; The Rocketeer. **1992:** Lethal Weapon 3;

Sister Act; Bram Stoker's Dracula; Under Siege; Forever Young. **1993:** Point of No Return; Gettysburg; Excessive Force; Nowhere to Run. **1994:** The Crow; Maverick; The Shadow; In the Army Now; Puppetmasters. **1995:** Village of the Damned; Waterworld; Showgirls; Jade. **1996:** Eraser; Fled; My Fellow Americans. *Television*—Kung Fu; Airwolf; Black Jack Savage.

DOC CHARBONEAU

A motorcycle specialist, Charboneau is a member of the International Stunt Association.

Films—**1985:** Explorers. **1986:** Ratboy; Hollywood Vice Squad. **1987:** The Lost Boys. **1988:** Nightmare on Elm Street 4: Dream Master; Border Heat; Tripwire. **1989:** Sonny Boy; Hit List; One Man Force; Night Life; Crack House. **1991:** Fast Getaway; Hook; Terminator 2; Shakes the Clown. **1992:** Munchie; Radio Flyer; Sleepwalkers; 3 Ninjas; Adventures in Dinosaur City. **1993:** The Last Action Hero; Maniac Cop 3. **1994:** Class of 1999 2. **1995:** 3 Ninjas Knuckle Up; The Sweeper. **1996:** Lawnmower Man 2; Pure Danger; Riot; Jingle All the Way.

ANN CHATTERTON

A bit actress, Chatterton is a member of the Stuntwoman's Association.

Films—**1979:** Rock 'n' roll High School; Gold of the Amazon Women (tv). **1980:** Up the Academy. **1981:** The Incredible Shrinking Woman. **1982:** Blade Runner; Star Trek 2: The Wrath of Khan. **1983:** Hysterical; Spacehunter. **1985:** Moving Violations; Hellhole. **1988:** Colors. **1990:** Total Recall. **1992:** Honeymoon in Vegas.

GEORGE KEE CHEUNG

This recognizable Asian supporting player and martial artist is best known as one of the villains in the second *Rambo*. A member of the Stuntmen's Association, Cheung has doubled for character actor James Hong.

Films—**1975:** The Killer Elite. **1976:** The Invisible Strangler (aka The Astral Factor). **1977:** The Amsterdam Kill; The Kentucky Fried Movie. **1982:** Beach Girls. **1983:** Going Berserk. **1985:** Rambo 2; Promises to Keep (tv). **1986:** Big Trouble in Little China; Who Is Julie? (tv). **1987:** The Night Stalker; Steele Justice; Opposing Force; Million Dollar Mystery; Return to Horror High. **1989:** Weekend at Bernie's. **1990:** Robocop 2; Another 48 HRS.; Guns. **1991:** One Good Cop; Showdown in Little Tokyo; The Perfect Weapon; Ricochet; The Hard Way; A Thousand Pieces of Gold. **1992:** Rapid Fire; Honeymoon in Vegas; Storyville; Sneakers; Under Siege; Final Judgment; Death Ring. **1993:** Robocop 3; Wayne's World 2; Curacao (aka Deadly Currents). Cooperstown (tv). **1994:** Fist of the North Star; Army of One; North; Deadly Target; American Yakuza. **1995:** Galaxis; New York Cop. **1996:** Escape from L.A.; Mars Attacks! *Television*—The Streets of San Francisco; SWAT; Policewoman; The Bionic Woman; Wonder Woman; Spiderman; M*A*S*H; The Rockford Files; Undercover; Salvage One; The Six O'Clock Follies (reg.); Magnum P.I.; The Fall Guy; Hart to Hart; Bring 'Em Back Alive (reg.); T.J. Hooker; Matt Houston; Whattleby by the Bay; Knight Rider; The A-Team; Airwolf; Riptide; Mike Hammer; McGyver; Jake & the Fatman; Alien Nation; Wiseguy; L.A. Law; China Beach; Thunder in Paradise; Walker, Texas Ranger.

PHIL CHONG

A prolific Asian small-part actor, often times essaying soldiers in Vietnam-era battle scenes, Chong is a member of the Stuntmen's Association.

Films—**1978:** Go Tell the Spartans. **1979:** Buck Rogers in the 25th Century. **1981:** Bustin' Loose. **1982:** Inchon; The Sword & the Sorcerer. **1983:** Breathless; Hysterical; Spacehunter; Girls of the White Orchid (tv). **1984:** Bachelor Party; Star Trek 3: The Search for Spock. **1985:** Missing in Action 2; To Live & Die in L.A.; Rambo 2; Avenging Angel. **1986:** The Golden Child; Big Trouble in Little China; Firewalker. **1987:** The Night Stalker; Wanted: Dead or Alive; Fatal Beauty; Night Force; Code Name Zebra. **1988:** Waxwork; The Presidio; They Live; Criminal Act; Bail Out. **1989:** Black Rain. **1990:** Robocop 2; Death Warrant; Come See the Paradise; Joe vs. The Volcano; The Rookie; Predator 2; Vietnam, Texas. **1991:** The Naked Gun 2 1/2; The Perfect Weapon; Showdown in Little Tokyo; Flight of the Intruder; Leather Jackets; Past Midnight; Not of This World (tv). **1992:** Deep Cover; Candy Man; Rapid Fire; Unlawful Entry; Nemesis; Hot Shots Part Deux; Live Wire. **1993:** Sidekicks; Teenage Mutant Ninja Turtles 3. **1994:** Double Dragon; In the Army Now; Color of Night; American Yakuza. **1995:** Top Dog; A Walk in the Clouds; Mallrats. **1996:** Escape from L.A.; Mars Attacks! *Television*—The Fall Guy; Beauty & the Beast.

CARL CIARFALIO

(b. 1956)

A former college wrestler and football player best known for beating up Tom Cruise in *Far and Away,* Ciarfalio worked at stunt shows for both Knot's Berry Farm and Universal Studios. A member of the Stuntmen's Association, he has doubled for Chris Penn and even dabbled in stand-up comedy.

Films—**1982:** Cannery Row. **1983:** D.C. Cab; The Osterman Weekend. **1984:** Against All Odds. **1985:** Commando; Police Academy 3: Back in Training; To Live & Die in L.A.; Runaway Train. **1986:** Black Moon Rising; Invaders from Mars. **1987:** Number One with a Bullet; Death Wish 4; Real Men; Night Force; Code Name Zebra. **1988:** Beetlejuice; Halloween 4; Criminal Act; The Incredible Hulk Returns (tv). **1989:** Johnny Handsome; Cage; Kinjite; No Holds Barred; Glory; Lock Up; License to Kill; Nick Knight (tv). **1990:** The Hunt for Red October; State of Grace; King of New York; Death Warrant; The Rookie. **1991:** 29th Street; Eve of Destruction; Out for Justice; Lionheart; The Perfect Weapon; Beastmaster 2; Leather Jackets; Shakes the Clown. **1992:** Freejack; Rapid Fire; Far & Away; Class Act; Sneakers; Wayne's World; Death Ring; Sweet Justice; Fatal Charm. **1993:** Private Wars; Streetknight; In the Line of Fire; Robocop 3; Excessive Force; Best of the Best 2; Trouble Bound; No Escape, No Return; The Fantastic Four; The Hit List; Bounty Tracker; The Fire Next Time (tv). **1994:** Natural Born Killers; The Specialist; Blankman; A Low Down Dirty Shame; Night of the Running Man; Zero Tolerance; Scanners: The Showdown; Direct Hit; CIA 2: Target Alexa; T-Force. **1995:** Mallrats; One Man's Justice; Chameleon; Excessive Force 2; The Rockford Files Blessing in Disguise (tv). **1996:** Spy Hard; The Trigger Effect; Feeling Minnesota. *Television*—Magnum, P.I.; Misfits of Science; Shadow Chasers; Spenser for Hire; MacGyver: Jake & the Fatman; Sledge Hammer; Baywatch; Walker, Texas Ranger.

ROYDON CLARK

A veteran stunt coordinator and second unit director, Clark has doubled James Garner for over 30 years. He's a member of both the Stuntmen's Association and the Professional Driver's Association.

Films—**1950:** Colt .45; The Rogues of Sherwood Forest. **1952:** Ride the Man Down. **1953:** Minnesota; Sea of Lost Ships. **1954:** Them. **1957:** Badlands of Montana. **1958:** Auntie Mame; Escape from Red Rock. **1959:** Born Reckless. **1964:** A Distant Trumpet. **1965:** Mirage. **1966:** Duel at Diablo; Not with My Wife You Don't. **1967:** Bonnie & Clyde; Hour of the Gun. **1968:** A Big Hand for the Little Lady; The Pink Jungle; Bandolero. **1969:** The Undefeated; Marlowe; The Great Bank Robbery; Support Your Local Sheriff. **1970:** Little Big Man. **1971:** Skin Game; Support Your Local Gunfighter. **1972:** They Only Kill Their Masters; Conquest of the Planet of the Apes. **1973:** Cleopatra Jones; One Little Indian; Battle for the Planet of the Apes. **1974:** The Castaway Cowboy; Foxy Brown; The Towering Inferno; Earthquake; The Rockford Files (tv). **1978:** FM. **1981:** Going Ape; Escape from New York. **1982:** The Sword & the Sorcerer. **1985:** Gotcha; D.A.R.Y.L.; Murphy's Romance. **1986:** Invaders from Mars; Promise (tv). **1987:** Number One With a Bullet; Death Wish 4; Best Seller; Nuts; Desperado (tv). **1988:** Sunset; Midnight Run; Alien Nation. **1989:** Indiana Jones & the Last Crusade; Cat Chaser; The Burbs. **1990:** Wild at Heart; The Rookie. **1991:** The Naked Gun 2 1/2; The Marrying Man; Not of This World (tv). **1992:** Stop! Or My Mom Will Shoot; Deep Cover; Unlawful Entry; Love Field. **1993:** In the Line of Fire. **1994:** The Naked Gun 33 1/3; The Chase; Army of One; Direct Hit. **1995:** Separate Lives; Panther. **1996:** The Rock; My Fellow Americans; Mercenary; Set It Off. *Television*—Maverick; Bat Masterson; The Green Hornet; Bonanza; Nichols; The Rockford Files; Bret Maverick; Hunter.

CLARK COLEMAN

Films—**1982:** Megaforce; Jekyll & Hyde, Together Again. **1983:** Get Crazy. **1984:** Lovelines. **1985:** To Live & Die in L.A.; Moving Violations. **1986:** Neon Maniacs. **1987:** Million Dollar Mystery; Night Force; Winners Take All. **1988:** Mac & Me; Tequila Sunrise. **1989:** The Karate Kid 3; Gleaming the Cube; Riding the Edge. **1990:** Joe vs. the Volcano; Days of Thunder; Arachnophobia; Angel Town. **1991:** Bill & Ted's Bogus Journey; Defending Your Life; Suburban Commando. **1992:** Kuffs; Universal Soldier; Patriot Games. **1994:** Double Dragon; Tammy & the T-Rex; Ripper Man. **1995:** Waterworld. **1996:** Eye for an Eye; Mulholland Falls. *Television*—Baywatch.

DOUG COLEMAN

A member of the Stuntmen's Association, this stunt coordinator has doubled for Robert De Niro and Elias Koteas. His wife Liza Sweeney is also in the industry.

Films—**1986:** Never Too Young to Die. **1987:** Death Before Dishonor; Predator; The Rosary Murders; Private Road: No Trespassing. **1988:** Action Jackson; Last Rites; Spellbinder. **1989:** K-9; To Die For. **1990:** I Come in Peace; Quick Change; Far Out Man; Total Recall; Class of 1999; Worth Winning; Desperate Hours; Secret Agent 00-Soul. **1991:** Cape Fear; Highway to Hell; The Dream Machine; Diplomatic Immunity; Delta Force 3. **1992:** The Night & the City; Consenting Adults. **1993:** A Bronx Tale; The Pelican Brief; The Hit List. **1994:** Blue Tiger; Automatic; Blankman; The Hard Truth. **1995:** Murder in the First; The Prophecy; Strange Days; Casino; Heat. **1996:** The Great White

Hype; Skyscraper; Independence Day; Crow: The City of Angels; Daylight; Back to Back; Up Close & Personal; Flipper.

EUGENE COLLIER

A member of the International Stunt Association, Collier has done bits and doubled for O.J. Simpson.

Films—**1988:** Action Jackson; Colors; Alien Nation; I'm Gonna Git You Sucka; Miracle Mile. **1989:** Crack House. **1991:** Future Kick; The Naked Gun 2 1/2; Cast a Deadly Spell. **1992:** Deep Cover; Unlawful Entry; Mission of Justice; Final Judgment. **1993:** Streetknight; Red Sun Rising; Rising Sun. **1994:** The Naked Gun 33 1/3; Beverly Hills Cop 3; A Low Down Dirty Shame; Hard Vice; Payback. **1995:** Village of the Damned; 3 Ninjas Knuckle Up; Panther; Operation Dumbo Drop; Showgirls; One Man's Justice. **1996:** Broken Arrow; The Nutty Professor; Escape from L.A.; The Trigger Effect; Riot.

GEORGE B. COLUCCI

Films—**1989:** Blind Fury. **1990:** Firebirds; Peacemaker; Circuitry Man; Puppetmaster 3; In the Cold of the Night. **1991:** Highway to Hell; Barton Fink; Diplomatic Immunity; Rich Girl; Mannequin 2. **1992:** Mom & Dad Save the World; Hero; Guncrazy; Dead Center (aka Crazy Joe). **1993:** Rescue Me. **1994:** Stargate; Zero Tolerance; Direct Hit; CIA 2: Target Alexa; Tammy & the T-Rex; Roadracers. **1995:** Digital Man. **1996:** Somebody to Love; Back to Back; Crash Dive.

GARY COMBS

A member of Stunts Unlimited, Combs is a veteran stunt coordinator and second unit director, having worked closely with director Sam Peckinpah on many great action sequences. He has doubled for Steve McQueen, Kirk Douglas, and Harrison Ford.

Films—**1966:** Nevada Smith. **1968:** Blue; Bandolero; Hellfighters. **1969:** The Wild Bunch; True Grit. **1970:** Norwood. **1971:** What's the Matter with Helen?; Shootout. **1972:** The Getaway; The Life & Times of Judge Roy Bean. **1973:** Pat Garrett & Billy the Kid. **1974:** Three the Hard Way. **1975:** A Boy & His Dog; Rooster Cogburn; Mitchell; The Killer Elite; Peeper. **1976:** Midway; Two Minute Warning; Drum. **1977:** Smokey & the Bandit. **1978:** FM; Hooper; Convoy. **1979:** Prophecy; The Muppet Movie; The Villain; Wanda Nevada. **1980:** Hero at Large; Tom Horn; Smokey & the Bandit 2; The Hunter; Stunts Unlimited (tv). **1981:** History of the World, Part One; Body Heat; Looker; The Pursuit of D.B. Cooper. **1982:** Star Trek 2: The Wrath of Khan; Blade Runner; Wrong Is Right; Night Shift; Hanky Panky. **1983:** Something Wicked This Way Comes; Max Dugan Returns; Independence Day; Under Fire; The Man Who Loved Women; Scarface; The Survivors; Stroker Ace. **1986:** Out of Bounds. **1987:** The Omega Syndrome; Over the Top; Robocop; The Rosary Murders. **1988:** They Live. **1989:** K-9; Road House; The Rocketeer. **1992:** Stop! Or My Mom Will Shoot; Stay Tuned; Toys. **1993:** Falling Down; Bound by Honor; Josh & S.A.M.; The Son-In-Law; Jailbait. **1994:** Legends of the Fall; Speed; The Road to Wellville. **1995:** The Enemy Within; Showgirls; Sudden Death; Dracula, Dead & Loving It. **1996:** Eye for an Eye; Riot; Eddie; Dear God. *Television*—Wagon Train; Star Trek; Mannix; Planet of the Apes; Hardcastle & McCormick; Hunter; Booker; 21 Jump Street; Unsub; Wiseguy; The Commish.

GILBERT COMBS

The much sought-after brother of Gary Combs, Gil is also a member of Stunts Unlimited. He has doubled for Nick Nolte, Jeff Bridges, and Chevy Chase.

Films—**1978:** Nat'l Lampoon's Animal House; Hooper. **1979:** Prophecy; The Villain. **1980:** The Blues Brothers; Wholly Moses; Tom Horn; Belle Starr (tv). **1981:** The Pursuit of D.B. Cooper. **1982:** Cannery Row; Blade Runner; Star Trek 2: The Wrath of Khan; Rocky 3. **1983:** The Sting; Star 80; Breathless; Under Fire; Scarface; Stroker Ace; Angel of H.E.A.T. **1984:** Bachelor Party; The River Rat; The Falcon & the Snowman. **1985:** Sweet Dreams; Promises to Keep (tv). **1986:** Wise Guys; Out of Bounds. **1987:** Over the Top; The Untouchables; Teen Wolf 2; The Rosary Murders; Less Than Zero; Kidnapped. **1988:** Freeway; The Blob; They Live; I'm Gonna Git You Sucka. **1989:** K-9; Loverboy; Staying Together; Lethal Weapon 2; Tango & Cash; Best of the Best. **1990:** Far Out Man; Dick Tracy; Die Hard 2; Taking Care of Business; Last of the Finest; Predator 2. **1991:** V.I. Warshawski; The Fisher King; Terminator 2; The Last Boy Scout; The Great Pretender (tv). **1992:** Stop! Or My Mom Will Shoot; Stay Tuned; Encino Man. **1993:** The Vanishing; American Heart; Bound by Honor; Hard Target; Fearless; Maniac Cop 3; Deadly Exposure; Conflict of Interest. **1994:** Legends of the Fall; Clean Slate; Blind Justice; Speed; Blankman; Puppetmasters; Steel Frontier. **1995:** Man of the House; Congo; Last Man Standing; Hourglass; Showgirls; Sudden Death; The Sweeper. **1996:** Eye for an Eye; Barb Wire; Spy Hard; Independence Day; Pure Danger; Crazy Horse; Riot; Mr. Wrong. *Television*—The Last Precinct; Jake & the Fatman; Father Dowling Mysteries.

JIM CONNORS

A member of Stunts Unlimited, Connors has been performing utility stunts and bits since the early seventies.

Films—**1971:** Star Spangled Girl. **1973:** Ssssss. **1975:** Sky Heist (tv). **1976:** Cannonball. **1978:** Blue Collar; Hooper. **1981:** The Boogens. **1982:** Star Trek 2: The Wrath of Khan. **1983:** Hysterical; Nat'l Lampoon's Vacation; Stroker Ace. **1984:** Reckless. **1985:** To Live & Die in L.A. **1986:** Out of Bounds. **1987:** Code Name Zebra; Nightforce. **1988:** Action Jackson; The Seventh Sign. **1991:** Hook. **1993:** Nat'l Lampoon's Loaded Weapon; Demolition Man. **1994:** Pentathalon. **1995:** The Road Killers. *Television*—The Six Million Dollar Man; Vegas.

SCOTT ALAN COOK

Films—**1982:** Chasing Dreams. **1985:** Trancers; Re-Animator; Nightmare On Elm Street 2: Freddy's Revenge. **1986:** Hollywood Vice Squad; Never Too Young to Die. **1987:** Dudes. **1988:** Dead Heat; Critters. **1989:** Disorganized Crime. **1990:** Prayer of the Rollerboys; Genuine Risk; Boris & Natasha. **1992:** The Lawnmower Man. **1993:** Red Rock West; Kalifornia; Dead Connection; Man's Best Friend. **1994:** Blue Tiger; The Mask; American Yakuza. **1995:** The Prophecy. **1996:** Back to Back.

ERIC CORD

A veteran bit player, action coordinator, and second unit director, Cord doubled for the likes of B-movie star Ross Hagen in the late sixties and early seventies. He would later stand

Erik Cord doubling Ross Hagen in *Angels' Wild Women* (1971).

in for the unlikely combination of Jerry Lewis and Richard Dawson. He's a member of the Stuntmen's Association.

Films—**1969:** Five the Hard Way (aka Sidehackers). **1971:** Angels' Wild Women. **1972:** Five Minutes to Freedom; Chandler; Conquest of the Planet of the Apes; Mean Mother; Hammer. **1973:** Bad Charleston Charlie; Superchick; Battle for the Planet of the Apes; Wonder Women (aka The Deadly and the Beautiful). **1974:** The Towering Inferno; Black Samson; Earthquake. **1975:** The Great Waldo Pepper; Nevada Smith (tv). **1976:** Midway; Deadly Hero. **1977:** Black Sunday; The Island of Dr. Moreau; Damnation Alley; Black Oak Conspiracy; Angela. **1978:** The Norseman; The Glove; Death Dimension (aka Kill Factor; Black Eliminator). **1979:** Buck Rogers in the 25th Century; The Prisoner of Zenda; Freedom Road (tv). **1980:** The Stunt Man; Up the Academy; The Island. **1981:** Bustin' Loose; Ghost Story; Agency. **1982:** Tron; The Sword & the Sorcerer; The Beastmaster; Night Shift; Slapstick of Another Kind. **1985:** Silver Bullet; Cloak & Dagger; Doin' Time; Code Name Foxfire (tv). **1986:** Pretty in Pink; Sweet Liberty; 52 Pick-Up. **1987:** The Omega Syndrome; The Running Man; The Bedroom Window; Brenda Starr. **1988:** Little Nikita; Perfect Victims; Midnight Run; Alien Nation; The Night Before; Twins; Turner & Hooch. **1989:** Collision Course; Night Children; Ghostbusters 2; Nat'l Lampoon's Christmas Vacation; One Man Force; Night Life. **1990:** Short Time; Robocop 2; Maniac Cop 2; Total Recall. **1991:** 976 Evil 2; FX-2; This Gun for Hire (tv). **1992:** Love Field; Hoffa. **1993:** Robin Hood: Men in Tights; Sidekicks. **1994:** When a Man Loves a Woman; It Runs in the Family; North; Zero Tolerance. **1995:** Separate Lives; Panther; Stuart Saves His Family; Last Man Standing; The Crossing Guard; The Sweeper. **1996:** The Lawnmower Man

2; Eraser; Pure Danger; Riot; Jingle All the Way. *Television*—The Virginian; Kung Fu; Gibbsville; Walking Tall; Blacke's Magic; Sledge Hammer; Star Trek, The Next Generation.

DANNY COSTA

An equestrian specialist, Costa has worked primarily in Westerns. He's a member of the Stuntmen's Association.

Films—1978: Comes a Horseman. 1980: Hide in Plain Sight. 1983: Spacehunter. 1984: All of Me; Beverly Hills Cop; Repo Man. 1985: Into the Night; Clue; Rambo 2. 1986: The Three Amigos; Ruthless People. 1987: Wanted: Dead or Alive; Over the Top; Dragnet; Night Force; Death Wish 4; Masters of the Universe; Code Name Zebra. 1988: Off Limits; Freeway;

Poltergeist 3; Border Heat. 1989: The Burbs; Old Gringo; Glory; Second Sight; Next of Kin; Kill Me Again. 1990: Impulse; Back to the Future 3; Young Guns 2; Dances with Wolves. 1991: 976 Evil 2. 1992: Far & Away; Honeymoon in Vegas; Four Eyes & Six Guns. 1993: Shadowhunter; Posse; Geronimo; Tombstone; The Fire Next Time (tv). 1994: The Last Ride (aka F.T.W.). 1995: The Good Old Boys; Wild Bill. 1996: The Cable Guy; Crazy Horse (tv).

BILL COUCH

A veteran bit player and stunt coordinator, Couch has doubled for James Farentino. His son Bill, Jr., also performed stunts.

Films—1957: The Young Stranger. 1959: Girls Town; The Flying Fontaines. 1960:

Action from 1968's *The Green Berets*.

Ma Barker's Killer Brood; Walking Target. **1966:** Not with My Wife You Don't; The Silencers. **1967:** The King's Pirate; The Scorpio Letters (tv). **1968:** The Green Berets; The Boston Strangler; The Split. **1969:** Butch Cassidy & the Sundance Kid; The Love Bug; The Undefeated; The Wrecking Crew; Marooned. **1970:** Flap; Norwood. **1971:** Dirty Harry. **1972:** Deliverance; Conquest of the Planet of the Apes. **1973:** Magnum Force; Battle for the Planet of the Apes. **1974:** The Towering Inferno; Blazing Saddles. **1975:** Russian Roulette; The Eiger Sanction; At Long Last Love. **1976:** King Kong; Logan's Run. **1978:** The Betsy; Mean Dog Blues; Thank God, It's Friday. **1979:** The Last Embrace; The Black Hole; Star Trek, The Motion Picture; Fast Break; Meteor. **1980:** The Island; The First Deadly Sin; A Change of Seasons; The Blues Brothers; The Final Countdown. **1981:** Going Ape; Earthbound; Dead & Buried. **1982:** Vice Squad; Barbarosa; Star Trek 2: The Wrath of Khan. **1983:** Brainstorm; Strange Brew; Twilight Zone: The Movie; The Women of San Quentin (tv). **1984:** Ghostbusters; The Exterminator 2. **1985:** Into the Night; Explorers; Fright Night. **1986:** Touch & Go; Stewardess School; Poltergeist 2; Running Scared. **1987:** Harry & the Hendersons; Hiding Out; Code Name Zebra; Police Story: The Freeway Killings (tv). **1988:** Big Top Pee Wee. **1990:** Satan's Princess. *Television*—Manhunt; Las Vegas Beat; The Virginian; The Munsters; The Man from U.N.C.L.E.; Mission: Impossible; The Wild Wild West; The Green Hornet; Emergency.

CHUCK COUCH

The brother of Bill Couch, this stunt coordinator doubled on television for both Martin Landau and Jack Lord.

Films—**1955:** Bobby Ware Is Missing. **1957:** Jeanne Eagles. **1959:** The Flying Fontaines. **1964:** Jumbo. **1965:** Zebra in the Kitchen. **1967:** The King's Pirate; The St. Valentine's Day Massacre. **1968:** The Green Berets; Chubasco. **1969:** The Undefeated. **1972:** Conquest of the Planet of the Apes. **1973:** Battle for the Planet of the Apes. **1974:** The Towering Inferno. **1975:** Dead Man on the Run (tv). **1981:** Dead & Buried. **1982:** Death Wish 2; Barbarosa. **1987:** Witchboard. *Television*—Wyatt Earp; Panic; Have Gun, Will Travel; Target; The Aquanauts; Voyage to the Bottom of the Sea; Lost in Space; Star Trek; Mission: Impossible; Honey West; The Girl From U.N.C.L.E.; Hawaii Five-O.

CHUCK COURTNEY

A lifetime member of the Stuntmen's Association, this blond stunt coordinator/supporting player enjoys some notoriety for having the lead in the campy *Billy the Kid vs. Dracula.* He has doubled for Robert Conrad and Richard Jaeckel.

Films—**1950:** The Asphalt Jungle; West Point Story. **1951:** Hit Parade of 1951; Flying Leathernecks. **1952:** It Grows on Trees; Francis Goes to West Point; Fearless Fagan; Bonzo Goes to College; Back at the Front; The Affairs of Dobie Gillis. **1953:** Born to the Saddle; Walking My Baby Back Home. **1954:** The Bamboo Prison; Two Guns & a Badge. **1955:** The Long Gray Line; Bring Your Smile Along; The Eternal Sea; Five Against the House; At Gunpoint. **1956:** Away All Boats; Battle Stations; Meet Me in Las Vegas; Tea & Sympathy; Friendly Persuasion. **1957:** The Young Rebels; Teenage Monster. **1958:** The Lineup. **1959:** Some Came Running. **1960:** Spartacus; Swiss Family Robinson. **1964:** Man's Favorite Sport. **1965:** The War Lord. **1966:** Incident at Phantom Hill; Billy the Kid vs. Dracula. **1967:** El Dorado; First to Fight. **1968:** The Green Berets; Hellfighters. **1970:** There Was a

Crooked Man; Rio Lobo; Did You Hear the One About the Traveling Saleslady. **1971:** The Omega Man. **1972:** Ulzana's Raid; The Cowboys. **1973:** Santee. **1975:** Murph the Surf (p); Sudden Death; Little Moon & Jud McGraw (aka Gone with the West). **1976:** The Gumball Rally; Food of the Gods. **1985:** Invasion USA. **1986:** Assassin (tv). **1989:** Pet Cemetery; Blind Fury. **1990:** Firebirds; Peacemaker; 9 1/2 Ninjas; The Rookie; Backstreet Dreams. **1991:** Mannequin 2; Rich Girl; Alligator 2; Mom & Dad Save the World. *Television*—The Lone Ranger (reg.); Playhouse 90; Tales of Wells Fargo; Laramie; Wagon Train; Laredo; Star Trek; Voyage to the Bottom of the Sea; The Wild Wild West; Mannix; It Takes a Thief; Get Smart; Mission: Impossible; The Invisible Man; Baa Baa Black Sheep.

MONTY COX
(b. 1940)

An animal trainer and acrobat, Cox has doubled for Kris Kristofferson and Bill Sadler. He's a member of the International Stunt Association.

Films—**1965:** Zebra in the Kitchen. **1967:** Tender Warrior; Gentle Giant. **1974:** Grizzly & the Treasure. **1977:** Day of the Animals. **1979:** Mountain Family Robinson. **1983:** The Gambler 2 (tv). **1984:** The Ice Pirates; The Philadelphia Experiment. **1985:** Black Moon Rising. **1986:** King Kong Lives. **1987:** Lethal Weapon; The Hidden; Down Twisted; Timestalkers (tv). **1988:** Bulletproof; Shakedown; Dead Heat; Elvira, Mistress of the Dark; A Tiger's Tale; Pair of Aces (tv). **1989:** Spontaneous Combustion. **1990:** The Hot Spot; The Hunt for Red October; Bird on a Wire; Die Hard 2; Mr. Destiny; Syngenor; Another Pair of Aces (tv). **1991:** Lionheart. **1991:** The Perfect Weapon; Bill & Ted's Bogus Journey; The Last Boy Scout; 3 Ninjas. **1992:** Innocent Blood; Sweet Justice. **1993:** Streetknight; Surf Ninjas;

Homeward; The Incredible Journey. **1994:** Chasers; North; In the Army Now; Roadracers. **1995:** Just Cause; 3 Ninjas Knuckle Up; Things to Do in Denver When You're Dead. **1996:** Solo; An Occasional Hell; Crazy Horse (tv). *Television*—Daktari; Cowboy in Africa; Gentle Ben; Lady Blue; Doctors Wilde.

EVERETT CREACH
(b. 1930)

A high school rodeo star, Creach was recruited to double for a youthful Roddy McDowall. He stuck in the business, becoming both a stunt coordinator and second unit director.

Films—**1943:** My Friend Flicka. **1945:** Thunderhead, Son of Flicka. **1948:** Black Midnight. **1949:** She Wore a Yellow Ribbon. **1950:** Rio Grand; Killer Shark; Blue Grass of Kentucky. **1959:** Atomic Submarine; The Horse Soldiers. **1961:** Twenty Plus Two. **1962:** Confessions of an Opium Eater; How the West Was Won. **1964:** A Distant Trumpet. **1967:** The Way West; The War Wagon. **1968:** The Green Berets; Bullit; Chubasco; Hellfighters. **1969:** The Love Bug; Tell Them Willie Boy Is Here; The Great Bank Robbery; The Good Guys & the Bad Guys. **1970:** Tora, Tora, Tora!; Soldier Blue. **1971:** Sometimes a Great Notion (aka Never Give an Inch); Big Jake; Dirty Harry. **1972:** Evel Knievel; Napoleon & Samantha; The Wrath of God. **1973:** Magnum Force; Blume in Love; The Last American Hero. **1974:** The Towering Inferno; The Take; Airport '75. **1976:** Marathon Man; Embryo. **1977:** Black Sunday; The Car. **1978:** The Driver; The Wiz; Straight Time. **1979:** Time After Time; Prophecy; The Dark. **1980:** The Man with Bogart's Face; Defiance; Motel Hell; Cheaper to Keep Her. **1981:** Trapped. **1982:** Six Pack. **1983:** Breathless; Off the Wall; Smokey & the Bandit 3; Get Crazy.

1984: Bachelor Party; Best Defense. 1985: Fraternity Vacation; D.A.R.Y.L. 1986: Howard the Duck. 1987: Nasty Hero; Near Dark; The Principal; My Demon Lover; Remote Control. 1988: Bat 21; Young Guns. 1989: Distant Thunder; Jacknife. 1990: Impulse; The First Power; Secret Agent 00-Soul. 1991: Eve of Destruction; Suburban Commando; The Marrying Man. 1993: Man's Best Friend; Arizona Dream. 1994: American Yakuza. *Television*—The Girl from U.N.C.L.E.; Kung Fu; The Six Million Dollar Man; Matt Helm.

ROGER CREED

A lifetime member of the Stuntmen's Association and one-time double for Frank Sinatra, Creed performed many bit parts before moving into coordinating action scenes. His daughter Leah has also done stunts.

Films—1943: Five Graves to Cairo. 1944: Miracle of Morgan's Creek. 1945: The Truth About Murder; Twice Blessed. 1946: Crack Up; Without Reservations; O.S.S.; Nocturne; Deadline at Dawn. 1947: Well Groomed Bride; Dick Tracy's Dilemma. 1948: The Velvet Touch; Berlin Express; Joan of Arc; Miracle of the Bells. 1949: Ghost of Zorro. 1950: Let's Dance; Armored Car Robbery. 1951: My Favorite Spy. 1952: Las Vegas Story; Aaron Slick from Punkin Crick. 1954: Living It Up. 1955: Tall Man Riding; East of Eden. 1956: The Ten Commandments. 1957: Omar Khayyem; Gunfight at the O.K. Corral; The Kettles on Old McDonald's Farm. 1958: The Buccaneer. 1959: The Trap. 1963: Come Blow Your Horn. 1964: Raiders from Beneath the Sea; Roustabout; Robin & the Seven Hoods. 1965: Harlow. 1966: Jesse James Meets Frankenstein's Daughter. 1967: The President's Analyst. 1968: Rosemary's Baby. 1970: The Delta Factor; The Molly Maguires; Which Way to the Front?; Darker Than

Amber; There Was a Crooked Man. 1973: Badge 373. 1974: The Towering Inferno; The Front Page; The Thief Who Came to Dinner. 1976: Death Game. 1978: Piranha. 1979: The North Avenue Irregulars; The Amityville Horror; The Lady in Red; Meteor. 1980: A Change of Seasons; Alligator; Hopscotch; Seems Like Old Times. 1981: The Howling; The Night the Lights Went Out in Georgia. 1982: Six Pack; Fast Walking; Endangered Species. 1983: Heart Like a Wheel. 1984: Tank. 1988: Little Nikita; Alien Nation. 1989: Ghostbusters 2; Weekend at Bernie's. 1990: Marked for Death. 1992: Folks. 1993: Robocop 3. 1995: Batman Forever. *Television*—Harry O.

DICK CROCKETT
(b 1915; d. 1979)

Prolific supporting player and stunt double for the likes of Jack Lemmon, Mickey Rooney, Tony Curtis, and Peter Sellers. Crockett, who often worked for filmmaker Blake Edwards, died of a heart attack.

Films—1938: Room Service. 1939: Bachelor Mother; The Hunchback of Notre Dame. 1941: The Adventures of Captain Marvel. 1944: Airship Squadron Number Four; Music for Millions. 1945: This Man's Navy; Weekend at the Waldorf; The Dark Horse. 1946: The Postman Always Rings Twice; A Letter for Eve; Blonde Alibi. 1948: Panhandle; Winner Take Nothing. 1949: Government Agents vs. the Phantom Legion. 1950: Wabash Avenue; The Milkman. 1951: Sealed Cargo; Gold Raiders; Flying Disc Men from Mars. 1952: Sound Off; The Lusty Men. 1953: All Ashore; Topeka; Jalopy; Cruisin' Down the River; Split Second; China Venture. 1954: Drive a Crooked Road; The Pushover; Superman Flies Again. 1955: Davy Crockett, King of the

Wild Frontier. **1956:** Davy Crockett & the River Pirates; Santiago; Around the World in 80 Days; A Cry in the Night; The Lady is Waiting; Overexposed. **1957:** Mister Cory; Baby Face Nelson; The Garment Jungle; Operation Mad Ball. **1958:** Escape from Red Rock; The Perfect Furlough; Seeds of Violence; Street of Darkness; Bell, Book, and Candle. **1959:** It Happened to Jane; Operation Petticoat. **1960:** High Time; Spartacus; Strangers When We Meet. **1961:** Breakfast at Tiffany's. **1962:** Experiment in Terror; The Notorious Landlady. **1963:** Twilight of Honor; Days of Wine & Roses; Soldier in the Rain. **1964:** The Pink Panther. **1965:** The Great Race. **1966:** What Did You Do in the War, Daddy?; Munster, Go Home; Harper; Batman. **1967:** Gunn; The Karate Killers. **1968:** The Party. **1969:** A Man Called Gannon. **1970:** Darling Lili; The Moonshine War. **1971:** Wild Rovers; Diamonds Are Forever; Dirty Harry. **1972:** Across 110th Street; The Getaway. **1973:** The Don is Dead. **1974:** The Towering Inferno; Blazing Saddles; Earthquake. **1975:** The Hindenburg. **1976:** The Pink Panther Strikes Again. **1978:** Revenge of the Pink Panther. **1979:** 10. *Television—* Superman; Zane Grey Theatre; December Bride; The Line-Up; Peter Gunn; One Step Beyond; The Man from U.N.C.L.E.; The Girl from U.N.C.L.E.; Batman; Star Trek; Tarzan; It Takes a Thief; Kung Fu; The Rookies; Matt Helm; Police Woman.

CHARLIE CROUGHWELL

A former engineering student, this New York-born stunt coordinator has doubled for Michael J. Fox since the mid-eighties.

*Films—***1985:** Back to the Future. **1986:** Quiet Cool; Ruthless People. **1987:** Cherry 2000; Masters of the Universe; Dudes. **1988:** Maniac Cop; Vibes; Who

Framed Roger Rabbit?; 18 Again; It Takes Two; Border Heat; Bail Out. **1989:** Second Sight; Relentless; Back to the Future 2; Next of Kin. **1990:** Back to the Future 3; Lambada; Maniac Cop 2; The Rookie. **1991:** Out for Justice; Shattered; Hook; The Hard Way; All I Want for Christmas. **1992:** Of Mice & Men; Noises Off; Rapid Fire; Batman Returns; Poison Ivy; Sleepwalkers; Innocent Blood. **1993:** Life with Mikey; For Love or Money; Dead On. **1994:** Reality Bites; Greedy. **1995:** Breach of Conduct; A Little Princess; Species. **1996:** The Frighteners; Michael.

WALLY CROWDER

A member of the Stuntmen's Association, Crowder also founded the Professional Driver's Association and published *The Stunt Directory*. His wife Lori also performs stunts.

*Films—***1976:** Deadly Harvest; Drum;. **1978:** Grease; Laserblast. **1983:** Losin' It. **1985:** The Man with One Red Shoe; To Live & Die in L.A. **1986:** Weekend Warriors. **1988:** Kansas. **1989:** I, Madman; She's Out of Control; Relentless; Night Game; Teen Witch; Ghostbusters 2; From the Dead of Night (tv). **1990:** Goddess of Love (tv); Maniac Cop 2; Last of the Finest; Blind Faith (tv). **1991:** Fast Getaway; 976 Evil 2; Shakes the Clown. **1993:** Extreme Justice; The Last Action Hero; Maniac Cop 3. **1994:** True Lies; Fist of the North Star; Guardian Angel. **1995:** Separate Lives; Jade; The Sweeper. *Television—*Dynasty; Heart of the City; Lois & Clark.

CLIFF CUDNEY

A veteran stunt coordinator and second unit director, Cudney formed the East Coast Professional Stunt-man's Association.

Films—**1971:** The French Connection. **1973:** Cops & Robbers. **1980:** The Exterminator; Friday the 13th, Part 2. **1981:** The Nesting; So Fine; Nighthawks. **1982:** Alone in the Dark; Night Shift. **1983:** Sleepaway Camp. **1984:** Unfaithfully Yours; Maria's Lovers; Ghostbusters; Once Upon a Time in America; The Muppets Take Manhattan; Scream for Help. **1986:** Running Scared; Off Beat. **1987:** Lady Beware; Deadly Illusion. **1988:** The House on Carrol Street; Masquerade; Homeboy. **1989:** Signs of Life; The Chair. **1990:** Cadillac Man; A Show of Force; The Ambulance. **1991:** A Kiss Before Dying. **1992:** Thunderheart; Malcolm X. **1994:** The Last Ride (aka F.T.W.). **1995:** Lord of Illusions; New York Cop. **1996:** Bound.

KERRIE CULLEN

A member of the United Stunt-woman's Association, Cullen has worked as a stunt coordinator and doubled for actresses such as Bernadette Peters, Nancy Allen, and Kelly Mc-Gillis.

Films—**1978:** The Ghost of Flight 401 (tv). **1980:** Stir Crazy. **1981:** Deadly Blessing; Heartbeeps; Hell Night; Honkytonk Freeway. **1982:** White Dog; The Beast-master; Endangered Species; Halloween 3. **1983:** Heart Like a Wheel; Under Fire; Get Crazy. **1984:** Angel; Nightmare on Elm Street; Children of the Corn; The Lonely Guy. **1985:** Pale Rider. **1986:** Murphy's Law; Nobody's Fool. **1987:** Made in Heaven. **1988:** Little Nikita; The Accused; Poltergeist 3; Die Hard; License to Drive. **1989:** Under the Gun; Weekend at Bernie's; Ghostbusters 2; Pink Cadillac.

1990: Robocop 2; Lisa; Taking Care of Business; The Adventures of Ford Fair-lane; Marked for Death; Dollman; I'm Dangerous Tonight (tv); Fear (tv). **1991:** V.I. Warshawski; Fried Green Tomatoes; The Naked Gun 2 1/2; The Hard Way. **1992:** Memoirs of an Invisible Man; Dr. Giggles. **1994:** Cabin Boy; Bad Girls. **1995:** Copycat; The Tie That Binds; Money Train. **1996:** Executive Decision. *Television*—Spiderman; The Greatest American Hero.

PHIL CULOTTA

A stunt coordinator and bit player, Culotta is a member of the Stuntmen's Association.

Films—**1985:** Remo Williams; Weird Science. **1986:** The Three Amigos; Tough Guys. **1987:** The Omega Syndrome; The Monster Squad. **1988:** Off Limits; Full Moon in Blue Water; Maniac Cop; Fright Night 2; Tripwire. **1989:** Hit List; Cage; One Man Force; Night Life; Crack House. **1990:** Cutting Class; Hider in the House; Satan's Princess; Maniac Cop; Rockula; The Rookie; Rainbow Drive; Prayer of the Rollerboys; I'm Dangerous Tonight (tv). **1991:** Eve of Destruction; The Taking of Beverly Hills. **1992:** Dr. Giggles; Adventures in Dinosaur City. **1993:** Extreme Justice; Forced to Kill. **1994:** Airheads. **1995:** Separate Lives; 3 Ninjas Knuckle Up; The Tie That Binds; The Sweeper. **1996:** The Lawnmower Man 2; Sgt. Bilko; Pure Danger; Riot; Mercenary. *Television*—Alien Nation.

BOB CUMMINGS

Films—**1980:** Borderline. **1984:** Star Trek 3: The Search for Spock. **1985:** Invasion USA. **1986:** Odd Jobs; Firewalker; Big Trouble in Little China. **1987:** Wanted: Dead or Alive; Code Name Zebra; Night Force; Nightmare on Elm Street: Dream

Warriors; The Hidden. **1988:** Bulletproof; Hero & the Terror; Pumpkinhead; Child's Play; Tripwire; They Live; Angel 3; The Abyss. **1989:** Cage; Old Gringo. **1990:** Ghost; Marked for Death; Predator 2; Boris & Natasha. **1994:** Airheads. *Television*—Matt Houston; Alien Nation.

HOWARD CURTIS
(b. 1927; d. 1979)

A stunt coordinator and aerial ace best known for an exciting fight scene with Tony Brubaker on the icy top of a moving train in *Breakheart Pass,* Curtis doubled for both Charles Bronson and Robert Shaw. He died in a plane crash.

Films—**1960:** La Marciano Del Demonio. **1962:** Hitler. **1964:** Viva Las Vegas; Goodbye, Charlie; Pajama Party; 36 Hours. **1966:** Not with My Wife You Don't. **1968:** A Big Hand for the Little Lady; The Split. **1969:** The Great Bank Robbery; Butch Cassidy & the Sundance Kid. **1970:** Lost Flight. **1971:** Star Spangled Girl. **1972:** The Poseidon Adventure. **1973:** Cleopatra Jones; Firehouse (tv). **1974:** The Towering Inferno; The Front Page; Airport '75. **1975:** The Great Waldo Pepper; The Hindenburg; Jaws. **1976:** Breakheart Pass; Swashbuckler. **1977:** Black Sunday; The Deep; The Choirboys; Killer on Board (tv). **1978:** The Deer Hunter. **1979:** The Black Hole; Moonraker; Stunt Seven (tv). *Television*—Ripcord; Voyage to the Bottom of the Sea; Honey West; Branded; It Takes a Thief; Mission: Impossible; The FBI; The Rockford Files; Hart to Hart.

PAUL DALLAS
(b. 1962; d. 1996)

A promising stunt artist, Dallas died while performing a high fall for a television show.

Films—**1990:** Opportunity Knocks; Circuitry Man. **1992:** Sweet Justice. **1993:** Firepower. **1994:** Blown Away; Stargate; Pumpkinhead 2; Hologram Man. **1995:** To the Limit; Blackout; The Silencers; Excessive Force 2; Bodycount; Major Payne; Sister Act 2. **1996:** Skyscraper; Mercenary. *Television*—L.A. Heat.

GREGG DANDRIDGE

Films—**1985:** To Live & Die in L.A. **1987:** The Principal; Nightmare on Elm Street 3. **1988:** Colors; Alien Nation; I'm Gonna Git You Sucka; Nightmare on Elm Street 4. **1989:** Glory; Crack House. **1990:** Wild at Heart; Predator 2; Marked for Death. **1992:** Deep Cover; Honeymoon in Vegas. **1995:** Panther; One Man's Justice. **1996:** Escape from L.A.; Riot.

LAURA DASH
(b. 1960)

Standing only 4'5" and weighing but 65 pounds, Dash has primarily doubled for child performers such as Danielle Harris.

Films—**1981:** Under the Rainbow. **1986:** Invaders from Mars. **1988:** The Great Outdoors; Halloween 4. **1989:** Pet Sematary; Shocker; Halloween 5; Blind Fury. **1990:** Robocop 2; Almost an Angel; Kindergarten Cop. **1991:** Fried Green Tomatoes; Hook. **1992:** Radio Flyer; The Lawnmower Man. **1993:** The Last Action Hero; Cop & a Half; Jurassic Park; A Perfect World. **1994:** Fist of the North Star; Interview with the Vampire; Flashfire. **1995:** Village of the Damned. **1996:** The Long Kiss Goodnight.

JEFF DASHNAW

This 6'4" stunt coordinator second unit director is best know as the chief double for action star Steven Seagal. A member of Stunts Unlimited, he is the husband of stuntwoman Tracy Keehn.

Films—**1980:** Smokey & the Bandit 2. **1981:** Amy. **1984:** The Terminator. **1985:** To Live & Die in L.A.; Summer Camp Nightmare. **1986:** Let's Get Harry. **1987:** Over the Top; Lethal Weapon; Dragnet; Mannequin; World Gone Wild; The Hidden. **1988:** License to Drive; My Stepmother Is an Alien. **1989:** Who's Harry Crumb?; Gleaming the Cube; Her Alibi; Road House; Dead Bang; Blind Fury; Backtrack. **1990:** Die Hard 2; Marked for Death. **1991:** Warlock; Out for Justice; Terminator 2; The Fisher King. **1992:** American Me; Lethal Weapon 3; Cool World; Patriot Games; Diggstown; Under Siege; The Bodyguard; Hoffa. **1993:** Fatherhood; The Last Action Hero; The Real McCoy; The Ballad of Little Jo. **1994:** Pentathalon; Army of One; The Chase; Blankman; Puppetmasters. **1995:** Waterworld; Jade; The Scarlet Letter; Houseguest; Money Train. **1996:** Mulholland Falls; Pure Danger; Riot; Bulletproof; The Rich Men's Wife. *Television*—In the Heat of the Night.

JADIE DAVID

A nurse prior to her doubling for actress Pam Grier, the statuesque David is a member of the United Stuntwoman's Association.

Films—**1972:** The Legend of Nigger Charley. **1973:** Coffy. **1974:** Foxy Brown. **1975:** Sheba, Baby; Friday Foster. **1976:** Drum. **1978:** Hooper; Convoy. **1979:** Time After Time. **1980:** The Blues Brothers. **1981:** Bustin' Loose. **1982:** White Dog; The Sword & the Sorcerer; Penitentiary 2. **1983:** The Star Chamber; Sudden Impact. **1985:** Trancers; The Boys Next Door. **1986:** The Naked Cage; Legal Eagles; Jumpin' Jack Flash. **1987:** The Wild Pair; Remote Control. **1988:** Above the Law; Colors; Poltergeist 3. **1990:** Keaton's Cop. **1991:** The Naked Gun 2 1/2. **1992:** Lethal Weapon 3. **1994:** The Naked Gun 33 1/3. **1996:** Escape from L.A.

B.J. (BEAU) DAVIS

In addition to supporting parts in many low-budgeters, this enterprising blond stunt coordinator turned to second unit work and full-fledged directing. Often working overseas, he's doubled for Michael Dudikoff and Reb Brown.

Films—**1980:** Lunch Wagon. **1981:** The Witch. **1982:** Fatal Games. **1983:** The Young Warriors; Chained Heat; Deadly Force; Fire & Ice; Lies. **1984:** Hardbodies; Hot Moves; Running Hot; Savage Streets. **1985:** Volunteers; Invasion USA; Stand Alone. **1986:** The Delta Force; Nomads; Avenging Force. **1987:** Programmed to Kill; American Ninja 2; House 2. **1988:** Quiet Thunder; Mercenary Fighters; White Ghost (d). **1989:** Transylvania Twist; Laser Mission (d); Clean Sweep (d). **1990:** Pump Up the Volume; Firebirds; Darkman; 9 1/2 Ninjas; Peacemaker; Circuitry Man; Red Surf; Sorority Girls & the Creature from Hell; Backstreet Dreams; Trancers 2; In the Cold of the Night. **1991:** Blood & Concrete; Diplomatic Immunity; Dragonfight; The Rapture; Liquid Dreams; Highway to Hell; Rich Girl; Star Trek 6:

A B.J. Davis-coordinated action scene in *Mercenary Fighters* (aka *Freedom Fighters*) (1988).

Undiscovered Country; Alligator 2; Lonely Hearts; Shakes the Clown. **1992:** The Hollywood Stuntman (d); Universal Soldier; Mom & Dad Save the World; To Protect & Serve; Guncrazy. **1993:** Surf Ninjas; Running Cool; Love, Cheat & Steal; Rescue Me. **1994:** Stickfighter (d); Threesome; Love Is a Gun; The Hard Truth; Sensation; Pumpkinhead 2. **1995:** Bodycount. *Television*—Star Trek, The Next Generation.

BUD DAVIS
(b. 1937)

A former radioman in the Navy, Davis has worked as a stunt coordinator, second unit director, and frequent bit player. He's a member of the International Stunt Association.

Films—**1974:** Policewomen. **1975:** Race with the Devil. **1976:** A Small Town in Texas; Scorchy; Futureworld; Winterhawk; Hollywood Man. **1977:** Speedtrap;

Dixie Dynamite; Stunts; The Town That Dreaded Sundown; Wishbone Cutter; Nowhere to Hide (tv). **1978:** Grayeagle; High-Ballin'; Thank God, It's Friday. **1979:** Klondike Fever; Mr. Horn (tv). **1982:** Jekyll & Hyde, Together Again. **1983:** Deadly Force. **1984:** Against All Odds. **1985:** Superstition; Black Moon Rising. **1986:** F/X; Manhunter; Transformers: The Movie; Miracles; King Kong Lives; Wisdom; Beverly Hills Madame (tv). **1987:** The Wild Pair; Malone; Who's That Girl?; House of the Rising Sun. **1988:** The Blob; Child's Play; The Seventh Sign; Hero & the Terror. **1989:** Who's Harry Crumb?; War Party; Chattahoochee; Tango & Cash. **1990:** Navy Seals; Men at Work. **1991:** The Naked Gun 2 1/2; Nothing But Trouble; Deadlock; A Cop for the Killing (tv). **1992:** Sleepwalkers; Keeper of the City; A Woman Scorned (aka Till Murder Do Us Part) (tv). **1993:** The Temp; Sliver; So I Married an Axe Murderer; Wayne's World 2; Conflict of Interest. **1994:** Clifford; Forest Gump; Wagons East; Star Trek Generations. **1995:** Across the Moon. **1996:** Andersonville (tv). *Television*—The Six

Million Dollar Man; CHiPs; Knot's Landing.

GARY DAVIS
(b. 1952)

An Arizona-raised motocross racer and daredevil cyclist, Davis set a world record in 1972 by jumping 21 cars. He later doubled for Peter Fonda and Evel Knievel, the man who had previously held the record jump. A member of Stunts Unlimited, Davis has worked as a stunt coordinator and second unit director.

Films—1970: C.C. and Company. 1974: The Front Page. 1975: Race with the Devil. 1976: A Small Town in Texas; Futureworld. 1977: Stunts; Outlaw Blues; Sidewinder One; Viva Knievel; The Choirboys. 1978: Coming Home; High-Ballin'; Return from Witch Mountain; Thank God, It's Friday; Every Which Way But Loose. 1979: Blood Barrier; Captain America (tv); Captain America 2 (tv). 1980: Smokey & the Bandit 2; The Hollywood Knights. 1981: Knightriders; Roar. 1982: Megaforce; Grease 2. 1983: Blue Thunder; Stroker Ace. 1984: Against All Odds; Reckless. 1985: Black Moon Rising; Hellhole. 1986: F/X; 8 Million Ways to Die; Wisdom. 1987: The Wild Pair; Dragnet; Return of the Living Dead 2; The Lost Boys. 1988: Everybody's All-American; Bagdad Cafe; They Live. 1989: Gleaming the Cube; K-9; Lethal Weapon 2; Road House; Black Rain; Cartel. 1990: Men at Work; Ghost; Predator 2. 1991: Suburban Commando; FX-2; Terminator 2; Deadlock. 1992: Far & Away; Encino Man; Cool World. 1993: Bound by Honor; The Adventures of Huck Finn; Conflict of Interest (d). 1994: Speed; Blankman; The Shawshank Redemption; Stranger By Night; Ray Alexander: A Taste for Justice (tv). 1995: Murder in the First; Dolores Clairborne; Sudden Death. 1996: Independence Day; Escape from L.A.; Riot. *Television*—Charlie's Angels; Vegas; Fantasy Island; The Greatest American Hero; The Fall Guy; The A Team; Scarecrow & Mrs. King; The Master; Private Eye; Paradise; Tour of Duty.

SONJA DAVIS
(b. 1965; d. 1994)

Stunt ingenue had become the double for Angela Bassett when she died performing a much-publicized high fall for the movie *Vampire from Brooklyn*.

Films—1992: Deep Cover; Live Wire; Class Act. 1993: Poetic Justice; What's Love Got to Do with It?; Taking the Heat. 1994: Timecop; Blankman; A Low Down Dirty Shame. 1995: Panther; Ballistic; Strange Days; A Vampire in Brooklyn.

STEVE DAVISON

A member of Stunts Unlimited, Davison has worked as a stunt coordinator and directed second unit. He has doubled for Charlie Sheen and both Matt and Kevin Dillon.

Films—1980: Carny; Herbie Goes Bananas; Serial; Smokey & the Bandit 2. 1982: Megaforce; Parasite. 1983: The Osterman Weekend; The Outsiders; Scarface; Risky Business. 1984: The Joy of Sex; Beverly Hills Cop; No Small Affair. 1985: To Live & Die in L.A.; Into the Night. 1986: The Wraith. 1987: The Omega Syndrome; The Wild Pair; Critical Condition; Burglar; La Bamba; Teen Wolf 2; Mannequin; Less Than Zero; Code Name Zebra. 1988: The Blob; The Kiss. 1989: Gleaming the Cube; Great Balls of Fire. 1990: Impulse; Days of Thunder; Last of the Finest; The Godfather 3. 1991:

Point Break. **1992:** Kuffs; Patriot Games; Under Siege; A Midnight Clear. **1993:** Falling Down; Gettysburg. **1994:** Beyond the Law; Serial Mom; The Chase; True Lies; The Shadow; In the Army Now; Puppetmasters. **1995:** S.F.W.; Waterworld; Copycat; Jade; Desperado; Money Train; Houseguest; Body Language. **1996:** From Dusk Till Dawn; Mulholland Falls; The Long Kiss Goodnight; Jingle All the Way.

TIM DAVISON

Like his brother Steve, Tim is also a member of Stunts Unlimited. He has coordinated stunts, directed second unit, and doubled for Matt and Kevin Dillon.

Films—**1982:** Megaforce. **1983:** Rumble Fish; Scarface. **1984:** No Small Affair. **1985:** To Live & Die in L.A.; Moving Violations. **1986:** Invaders from Mars. **1987:** Critical Condition; Burglar; The Untouchables; Less Than Zero; Night Force; Code Name Zebra. **1988:** The Presidio; The Blob; They Live. **1989:** Gleaming the Cube; Johnny Handsome; Nat'l Lampoon's Christmas Vacation. **1990:** Die Hard 2; The Fourth War; Last of the Finest; Everybody Wins; Circuitry Man. **1992:** Kuffs; American Me; Thunderheart; Lethal Weapon 3; Rapid Fire; Patriot Games; A Midnight Clear; A Few Good Men. **1993:** Full Eclipse; Demolition Man; Body of Evidence. **1994:** Blink; My Father, The Hero; The Jungle Book; In the Army Now; Blankman; Puppetmasters. **1995:** The Road Killers; The Brady Bunch Movie; Copycat; Seven; Money Train. **1996:** From Dusk Till Dawn; Broken Arrow; Eraser; The Phantom; Bordello of Blood; Bulletproof; Jingle All the Way.

VINCE DEADRICK

A veteran member of the Stuntmen's Association, Deadrick has performed many bits, coordinated stunts, and doubled for Lee Majors on television's *The Six Million Dollar Man.*

Films—**1957:** The Enemy Below. **1959:** Operation Petticoat. **1961:** The Honeymoon Machine. **1963:** Love with the Proper Stranger. **1964:** Fate Is the Hunter. **1969:** The Great Bank Robbery. **1971:** The Skin Game; Dirty Harry. **1972:** Conquest of the Planet of the Apes. **1973:** Blume in Love; Battle for the Planet of the Apes; Set This Town on Fire (tv). **1974:** The Towering Inferno. **1978:** The Norseman. **1979:** The Apple Dumpling Gang Rides Again; H.O.T.S.; Beyond the Poseidon Adventure; The Lady in Red. **1980:** Used Cars; Any Which Way You Can. **1982:** The Beastmaster; Tron. **1983:** Heart Like a Wheel; Spacehunter. **1984:** Angel; Romancing the Stone; Beverly Hills Cop; Thief of Hearts; Ninja 3: The Domination; Breakin 2: Electric Boogaloo. **1985:** D.A.R.Y.L.; Commando; Avenging Angel. **1986:** Raw Deal; The Golden Child; Ruthless People. **1987:** Throw Momma from the Train; Million Dollar Mystery; Dragnet; Cop; Made in Heaven. **1988:** Young Guns; Colors; The Dead Pool; Two Moon Junction. **1989:** Indiana Jones & the Last Crusade; Glory; Nightmare on Elm Street 5: Dream Child. **1990:** Solar Crisis; Total Recall; Secret Agent 00-Soul; Dangerous Passion (tv). **1992:** Aces: Iron Eagle 3; Universal Soldier. **1994:** Blown Away; Blankman. **1995:** Separate Lives. **1996:** Broken Arrow; Mercenar; Set It Off. *Television*—Wanted, Dead or Alive; Gunsmoke; Voyage to the Bottom of the Sea; The Man from U.N.C.L.E.; Mission: Impossible; Star Trek; Batman; The Wild Wild West; The Big Valley; The Six Million Dollar Man; The Man from Atlantis; The Fall Guy; MacGyver.

An explosive action scene in 1994's *Blown Away*, action coordinated by Vince Deadrick, Jr.

VINCE DEADRICK, JR.

Best known for participating in *Romancing the Stone*'s comic mudslide, this stunt coordinator/second unit director is a member of the Stuntmen's Association. He's doubled for Michael Douglas and Jeff Bridges.

Films—**1979:** Sunnyside; Concorde, Airport '79. **1980:** The Island. **1981:** Charlie Chan & the Curse of the Dragon Queen. **1982:** The Sword & the Sorcerer; Zapped; Cat People. **1983:** Hysterical; Spacehunter. **1984:** Romancing the Stone; Ninja 3: The Domination; City Heat; Streets of Fire; Thief of Hearts. **1985:** Avenging Angel; The Jewel of the Nile; Tuff Turf. **1987:** The Zero Boys; Throw Momma from the Train; Return to Horror High. **1988:** Twins. **1989:** CHUD 2; Ghostbusters 2. **1993:** Striking Distance; Best of the Best 2; Judgment Night. **1994:** Clean Slate; Blown Away; T-Force; Bionic Breakdown (tv). **1995:** The Set Up; Devil in a Blue Dress; Wild Bill; Heat. **1996:** White Squall; The Ghost & the Darkness. *Television*—MacGyver; The Hat Squad.

MARK DEALLASANDRO

Sylvester Stallone's primary double for a number of years, Deallasandro is a member of the Professional Driver's Association. He married stuntwoman Lisa McCullough.

Films—**1985:** Rambo 2. **1986:** Cobra. **1987:** Over the Top; Dragnet. **1988:** Rambo 3. **1989:** The Vineyard; Tango & Cash. **1990:** Rocky 5. **1991:** Lionheart; Mannequin 2; The Rocketeer. **1992:** Stop! Or My Mom Will Shoot; Rapid Fire;

Under Siege; Toys. **1993:** Hot Shots Part Deux; Cliffhanger; Demolition Man. **1994:** The Client; The Specialist; Stargate. **1995:** Showgirls; Assassins; Last Man Standing; Deadly Outbreak; Hard Justice; The Sweeper. **1996:** Daylight; Riot.

LEON DELANEY

A stunt coordinator and second unit director, Delaney has doubled for Daniel Stern and Tommy Chong.

Films—**1979:** The Warriors. **1985:** Commando. **1987:** Predator. **1988:** Action Jackson. **1989:** Road House. **1990:** Far Out Man; Die Hard 2; Total Recall; Home Alone; Dangerous Passion (tv). **1991:** Stone Cold; Highway to Hell; Cape Fear. **1992:** Hoffa. **1993:** Excessive Force. **1994:** Radioland Murders; Army of One; Stargate.

ANTHONY DE LONGIS

A supporting player in martial arts fare, De Longis has occasionally worked as a stuntman. His most notable assignment was doubling Frank Langella in *Masters of the Universe.*

Films—**1979:** Circle of Iron; Jaquar Lives. **1980:** In Search of Historic Jesus. **1982:** The Sword & the Sorcerer. **1983:** The Warrior & the Sorceress. **1984:** Starchaser: The Legend of Orin. **1986:** Dangerously Close. **1987:** Masters of the Universe; The Chipmunk Adventure. **1989:** Road House. **1992:** Far & Away; Final Round. **1994:** Bad Girls; CIA 2: Target Alexa. **1995:** Expect No Mercy. *Television*—Logan's Run; Battlestar Galactica; "V"; MacGyver; Sledge Hammer; Renegade.

MICHAEL DELUNA
(b. 1951)

A Las-Vegas born stunt coordinator and aerial specialist, Deluna was especially active during the eighties.

Films—**1980:** Smokey & the Bandit 2. **1982:** Megaforce; Lookin' to Get Out; Nat'l Lampoon's Class Reunion. **1983:** Strangers Kiss; Scarface. **1984:** Friday the 13th: The Final Chapter; The River; Buckaroo Banzai. **1985:** Cloak & Dagger; D.A.R.Y.L.; Invasion USA. **1986:** The Delta Force; Radioactive Dreams; Thunder Run; Firewalker. **1987:** Lethal Weapon; Police Academy 4: Citizens on Patrol. **1988:** Bulletproof; The Seventh Sign; Hero & the Terror; The Blob. **1989:** Riding the Edge; The Abyss; Tango & Cash. **1990:** Almost an Angel; Predator 2; Genuine Risk. **1991:** Mobsters; Hook; Soldier's Fortune; The Rocketeer; Beastmaster 2. **1992:** Basic Instinct; Innocent Blood. **1993:** Falling Down. **1994:** Clear & Present Danger. **1995:** The Sweeper. **1996:** Barb Wire. *Television*—Alien Nation.

JUSTIN DeROSA

Films—**1977:** The Amazing Captain Nemo. **1979:** Beyond the Poseidon Adventure. **1980:** Smokey & the Bandit 2. **1983:** The Osterman Weekend; Scarface; D.C. Cab. **1984:** Fear City; Buckaroo Banzai. **1985:** Into the Night; The Falcon & the Snowman; Commando; To Live & Die in L.A.; Vendetta. **1986:** Odd Jobs; Out of Bounds; Back to School. **1987:** Prince of Darkness; Burglar; The Untouchables; Night Force; Code Name Zebra; Laguna Heat. **1988:** Midnight Run; The Presidio; Masque of the Red Death. **1989:** K-9; Tango & Cash. **1990:** Hard to Kill; Die Hard 2; Internal Affairs. **1991:** One Good Cop; Hook; The Rocketeer. **1992:** Stop!

Or My Mom Will Shoot; Basic Instinct; Sister Act; Nails. **1993:** Man's Best Friend. **1994:** The Naked Gun 33 1/3; Flashfire.

YANNICK DERRIEN

Films—**1987:** Blind Date; Death Feud; Death Wish 4. **1991:** Hook; Intimate Stranger. **1992:** Live Wire. **1993:** Cyber-tracker; Firepower. **1994:** Bad Blood; Hologram Man; The Last Ride (aka F.T.W.); Automatic; The Fighter (aka Savate); Steel Frontier. **1995:** Frank & Jesse; The Silencers; Black Scorpion; Blackout. **1996:** Public Enemies; Mercenary.

THOMAS DEWIER

A member of the International Stunt Association, this martial arts expert has doubled for Ralph Macchio in the *Karate Kid* films.

Films—**1984:** The Karate Kid. **1985:** Gotcha. **1986:** The Karate Kid 2; Welcome to 18. **1988:** Bulletproof; Dr. Hackenstein; L.A. Crackdown; Emperor of the Bronx. **1989:** The Karate Kid 3; CHUD 2; Time Trackers; Street Asylum. **1990:** Streets. **1991:** Teenage Mutant Ninja Turtles 2; Highlander 2; Ricochet. **1992:** Poison Ivy. **1993:** The Fugitive; Cybertracker; Cyborg 2. **1994:** Body Shot; Double Dragon; Hologram Man; Criminal Passion; Scanners: The Showdown; Bad Blood; The Stranger. **1995:** The Temptress; The Quick & the Dead; Village of the Damned; Mortal Kombat; One Man's Justice. **1996:** Bio-Dome; The Demolitionist; Dark Breed; Piranha; Rattled; Hellraiser—Bloodline. *Television*—Beauty & the Beast.

DICK DIAL
(d. 1993)

Predominantly active in the sixties and seventies as a bit player and stunt coordinator, Dial doubled for David Janssen in "The Fugitive" and William Shatner on "Star Trek."

Films—**1956:** Autumn Leaves. **1959:** Girls Town. **1964:** Goodbye, Charlie. **1965:** Zebra in the Kitchen. **1966:** The Glass Bottom Boat; Murderer's Row. **1967:** In Like Flint. **1968:** The Boston Strangler. **1969:** Hello, Dolly. **1970:** Lost Flight. **1974:** Earthquake; Airport '75. **1975:** The Hindenburg; The Eiger Sanction; Breakout. **1985:** Cloak & Dagger. **1991:** Shakes the Clown. **1992:** Mom & Dad Save the World. *Television*—The Fugitive; The Man from U.N.C.L.E.; Star Trek; Time Tunnel; Voyage to the Bottom of the Sea; The Green Hornet; Mission: Impossible; The Mod Squad; Star Trek, The Next Generation; Felony Squad.

NICK DIMITRI
(b. 1935)

Instantly recognizable supporting player of Greek parentage, often seen as mob enforcers or cops. The 6'2" square-jawed Dimitri doubled for Sean Connery early in his career, though he is best known for his classic fight scene opposite Charles Bronson in *Hard Times.* Other memorable moments include his baiting Eddie Murphy in *48HRS.,* his challenging Steven Seagal in *Out for Justice,* and his doubling Andreas Katsulas, "The Fugitive's" one-armed man. He's a member of the Stuntmen's Association.

Films—**1963:** Island of Love; Palm Springs Weekend. **1965:** Harlow. **1966:** The

Top: A large-scale stunt scene from 1974's *Earthquake*, action coordinated by John Daheim. *Bottom:* Nick Dimitri reacts to Bronson's sledgehammer punches, as Strother Martin and James Coburn look on in *Hard Times* (1975).

Last Moment; Murderer's Row. **1967:** In Cold Blood. **1968:** Planet of the Apes; The Ambushers. **1970:** Darker Than Amber; The Molly Maguires; Beneath the Planet of the Apes. **1971:** Diamonds Are Forever. **1972:** Conquest of the Planet of the Apes; Grave of the Vampire. **1973:** The Don Is Dead; Cleopatra Jones; Sweet Jesus, Preacher Man; The Student Teachers; Battle for the Planet of the Apes; The Norlis Tapes (tv). **1974:** The Towering Inferno; Black Samson; Earthquake; The Rockford Files (tv). **1975:** The Master Gunfighter; Hard Times; Adios Amigo. **1976:** St. Ives; Death Journey; No Way Back; Scorchy; Futureworld. **1977:** The World's Greatest Lover. **1978:** The Driver; F.I.S.T. **1979:** Stunt Seven (tv). **1980:** The Nude Bomb; For The Love of It (tv); Any Which Way You Can. **1981:** Bustin' Loose. **1982:** The Sword & the Sorcerer; 48HRS. **1983:** They Call Me Bruce; Sudden Impact. **1984:** City Heat. **1985:** Commando; Rainy Day Friend (aka L.A. Bad). **1986:** The Longshot; Raw Deal; Eye of the Tiger. **1987:** Million Dollar Mystery. **1988:** Twins; Turner & Hooch; Nitti: The Enforcer (tv). **1989:** Cage; Glory; Kill Me Again; Original Sin (tv). **1990:** Total Recall; Masters of Menace; Dangerous Passion (tv). **1991:** Out for Justice; Toy Soldiers; Stone Cold Mobsters. **1992:** Aces: Iron Eagle 3; Rapid Fire; Unlawful Entry. **1993:** The Last Action Hero; The Fugitive; Fist of Honor. **1994:** Ice; Direct Hit. **1995:** Panther. **1996:** Back to Back; Flipping. *Television*—77 Sunset Strip; Route 66; Branded; Laredo; Daniel Boone; Voyage to the Bottom of the Sea; The Rockford Files; The Six Million Dollar Man; Matt Helm; Switch; Grandpa Goes to Washington; BJ & the Bear; Hart to Hart; When the Whistle Blows; Love, Sidney; The Fall Guy; The A Team; Knight Rider; MacGyver; Cheers; Beauty & the Beast; Hardball; Midnight Caller; Young Indiana Jones.

SHANE DIXON

A former mechanical engineer, this Oklahoma-born stunt coordinator/second unit director has doubled for Wings Hauser, Rutger Hauer, and Gary Busey. The husband of stunt-woman Cheryl Wheeler, Dixon is a member of both Stunts Unlimited and the Professional Driver's Association.

Films—**1979:** Night of the Demon. **1984:** Lovelines. **1985:** Fandango; Moving Violations. **1986:** Let's Get Harry; Eye of the Tiger. **1987:** The Night Stalker; Lethal Weapon; Raising Arizona; No Safe Haven; Dead Man Walking. **1988:** Bulletproof; Rambo 3; They Live; Act of Piracy. **1989:** Street Asylum; Far From Home; Hider in the House; Blind Fury. **1990:** Vietnam, Texas; The Hunt for Red October; Ghost; Another 48 HRS.; Pacific Heights; Death Warrant; Bad Influence; Last of the Finest; The Adventures of Ford Fairlane; Maniac Cop 2. **1991:** Point Break; The Butcher's Wife; True Identity; The Last Boy Scout; Past Midnight. **1992:** Ruby; Memoirs of an Invisible Man; Lethal Weapon 3; Adventures in Dinosaur City; Universal Soldier; Radio Flyer. **1993:** Point of No Return; Full Eclipse; Rising Sun; Maniac Cop 3. **1994:** Maverick; The Little Rascals; Night of the Demons 2; Drop Zone. **1995:** The Road Killers; Village of the Damned; Demonknight; Outbreak; Nine Months; Virtuosity; Copycat; Last Man Standing; Nick of Time; One Man's Justice. **1996:** The Lawnmower Man 2; Black Sheep; Bordello of Blood; Jingle All the Way. *Television*—The Greatest American Hero; The Antagonists; Tales from the Crypt.

BENNIE DOBBINS
(b. 1931; d. 1988)

Once a baseball player in the Boston Red Sox organization, Dobbins entered stunts initially as a horse wrangler and television double for Van

Williams. He moved up to coordinating stunts and directing second unit before dying of a heart attack on the set of the film *Red Heat*. He served as the president of the Stuntmen's Association during the mid-seventies.

Films—**1959:** Ride Lonesome. **1966:** Not with My Wife You Don't. **1967:** A Covenant with Death; Bonnie & Clyde. **1968:** Planet of the Apes; The Boston Strangler. **1969:** Che; The Great Bank Robbery; The Pigeon (tv). **1970:** Barquero; Soldier Blue. **1971:** Wild Rovers; Sometimes a Great Notion (aka Never Give an inch); Dirty Harry. **1972:** The Life & Times of Judge Roy Bean; Conquest of the Planet of the Apes. **1973:** Emperor of the North; Magnum Force; Battle for the Planet of the Apes. **1974:** 99 & 44/100% Dead; The Towering Inferno; Blazing Saddles; Earthquake. **1975:** Little Moon & Jud McGraw (aka Gone with the West). **1976:** The Duchess & the Dirtwater Fox. **1977:** The White Buffalo. **1978:** F.I.S.T. **1979:** Love & Bullets; The In-Laws; Over the Edge; The Great Santini. **1980:** The Mountain Men; A Change of Seasons; Used Cars. **1981:** The Legend of the Lone Ranger; Southern Comfort. **1982:** Ruckus; Cat People; E.T.; First Blood; The Sword & the Sorcerer; Split Image; Tron; 48 HRS. **1983:** Spacehunter; Streets of Fire. **1985:** Brewster's Millions; Commando; Weird Science. **1986:** Blue City; Jumpin' Jack Flash; Ferris Bueller's Day Off. **1987:** Extreme Prejudice; The Running Man; Planes, Trains, & Automobiles. **1988:** Red Heat. *Television*—Bourbon Street Beat; Hawaiian Eye; Surfside Six; The Green Hornet; Custer; Mission: Impossible; Gunsmoke; Kung Fu; Nichols.

J. MARK DONALDSON

Films—**1986:** Baby: Secret of the Lost Legend. **1987:** Walk Like a Man; The Monster Squad; Remote Control. **1988:** Nightmare on Elm Street 5: Dream Child. **1990:** Payback. **1991:** Eve of Destruction; The Marrying Man; Highway to Hell; Into the Badlands. **1993:** Boiling Point. **1994:** The Mask. **1995:** Casino. **1996:** The Crow: City of Angels; Mars Attacks!

EDDY DONNO

This stocky supporting player, stunt coordinator, and second unit director is most closely associated with the films of his friend Dennis Hopper. A member of Stunts Unlimited, his wife Kathryn and son Tony are also in the business. He's doubled for Bob Hoskins.

Films—**1966:** Hold On!; The Last of the Secret Agents. **1968:** The Savage Seven; The Green Berets. **1970:** Getting Straight; Beneath the Planet of the Apes; Chisum. **1971:** The Last Movie. **1972:** Conquest of the Planet of the Apes. **1973:** Kid Blue; Cleopatra Jones; The Train Robbers; Battle for the Planet of the Apes. **1974:** Freebie & the Bean; Big Bad Mama; Black Samson. **1975:** The Killer Elite; Cleopatra Jones & the Casino of Gold; Flash & the Firecat. **1976:** Harry & Walter Go to New York; The Gumball Rally; Trackdown; The Van. **1977:** Ruby. **1978:** Foul Play; Long Journey Back (tv). **1979:** North Avenue Irregulars; A Time to Die; Flesh & Blood (tv). **1980:** The Blues Brothers; Hide in Plain Sight. **1982:** The Entity; The Beastmaster; I'm Dancing as Fast as I Can; Star Trek 2: The Wrath of Khan; Yes, Giorgio. **1983:** Independence Day; Twilight Zone: The Movie; Scarface; The Star Chamber; The Osterman Weekend. **1984:** Love Streams; Beverly Hills Cop; Star Trek 3: The Search for Spock; Chattanooga Choo Choo. **1985:** Into the Night; To Live & Die in L.A.; Bad Guys. **1986:** The Hitcher; Invaders from Mars; Out of Bounds; Big Trouble in Little China. **1987:** The Omega Syndrome; The

Wild Pair; Over the Top; Code Name Zebra; Night Force; Real Men; The Untouchables. **1988:** Action Jackson; Grotesque. **1989:** The Winter People; Lethal Weapon 2; Backtrack. **1990:** The Hot Spot; Last of the Finest; Mr. Destiny. **1991:** Shattered; The Perfect Weapon; 29th Street; Point Break. **1992:** Article 99; Rapid Fire; Nails; Passed Away. **1993:** Fist of Honor. **1994:** Chasers; In the Army Now. **1995:** Nine Months; Waterworld; Money Train. **1996:** Executive Decision; The Arrival; The Rock; Fled; Crazy Horse; Jingle All the Way; An Occasional Hell; Star Trek, First Contact. *Television*—The Munsters; Daniel Boone; Mannix; The Magician; Vegas; Knight Rider; Hunter.

NORMAN DOUGLAS

Films—**1987:** Dirty Dancing; China Girl; Deadly Illusion. **1988:** Shakedown; Homeboy. **1989:** See No Evil, Hear No Evil; Penn & Teller Get Killed; Hell High. **1990:** State of Grace; Miller's Crossing; Two Evil Eyes; Goodfellas; Street Hunter. **1991:** Mortal Thoughts; New Jack City. **1992:** Whispers in the Dark; Malcolm X. **1993:** Romeo Is Bleeding; Daybreak. **1994:** Handgun; The Cowboy Way; The Professional. **1995:** Kiss of Death. **1996:** Independence Day; Bullet.

CHRIS DOYLE

A member of the Stuntmen's Association, Doyle has doubled for James Russo and worked as a stunt coordinator for Stephen J. Cannell's television productions.

Films—**1979:** The Streets of L.A. (tv). **1980:** The Island. **1982:** Swamp Thing;

The Sword & the Sorcerer. **1985:** Trancers; Nightmare on Elm Street 2: Freddy's Revenge. **1986:** The Naked Cage; Hollywood Vice Squad. **1987:** Murphy's Law; The Omega Syndrome; Private Investigations; The All-Nighter; Down Twisted; Timestalkers (tv). **1988:** Bulletproof; Dead Heat; Bad Dreams; The Blue Iguana; Critters 2; Tapeheads. **1989:** Return of Swamp Thing; No Holds Barred; Blind Fury. **1990:** Joe vs. The Volcano; Darkman; Firebirds; Circuitry Man; Masters of Menace; Kindergarten Cop; 9 1/2 Ninjas; Backstreet Dreams; In the Cold of the Night; The Last Hour; Peacemaker; Puppetmaster 3; Red Surf. **1991:** Rich Girl; Hot Shots; Alligator 2; Blood & Concrete; Intimate Stranger; Shakes the Clown. **1992:** Mom & Dad Save the World; Live Wire. **1993:** Army of Darkness; Another Stakeout; Trouble Bound; Attack of the 50 Foot Woman; Bounty Tracker; Danger of Love (tv). **1994:** Silence of the Hams; Automatic; Pulp Fiction; Wes Craven's New Nightmare; Midnight Ride; Zero Tolerance; CIA 2: Target Alexa. **1995:** Galaxis; Casino; Last Man Standing; Deadly Outbreak. **1996:** The Lawnmower Man 2; Multiplicity; The Crow: City of Angels; Last Man Standing; Forest Warrior; Back to Back. *Television*—Riptide; Sonny Spoon; J.J. Starbuck; Midnight Caller; Star Trek, The Next Generation; The Hat Squad.

RICK DROWN

This diminutive stunt performer has doubled for Danny Devito and Dudley Moore since the early eighties.

Films—**1980:** Wholly Moses. **1981:** Going Ape. **1984:** Romancing the Stone; Unfaithfully Yours; City Heat; Micki & Maude. **1985:** Avenging Angel; The Jewel of the Nile. **1986:** Ruthless People. **1987:** Throw Momma from the Train. **1992:** Batman Forever; Hoffa. **1993:** Jack the Bear. **1996:** Truman.

DOC DUHAME

Films—1985: To Live & Die in L.A.; Runaway Train; Iron Eagle. **1987:** The Omega Syndrome; Monster in the Closet; World Gone Wild; Kidnapped. **1989:** The Karate Kid Part 3; Pink Cadillac; Lock Up; Hider in the House. **1990:** Narrow Margin; The Gumshoe Kid; The Borrower; Psycho 4: The Beginning (tv). **1991:** Warlock; V.I. Warshawski. **1993:** The Sandman (tv). **1994:** Maverick; Dropzone. **1995:** The Quick & the Dead; Get Shorty; Tyson. *Television*—Sledge Hammer; Swamp Thing; Baywatch.

TED DUNCAN

A veteran bit player and stunt coordinator, Duncan's specialty is car stunts.

Films—1963: Palm Springs Weekend. **1969:** The Love Bug. **1972:** What's Up, Doc? **1973:** The Last American Hero; Magnum Force. **1974:** Freebie & the Bean; The Sugarland Express. **1976:** Crash; Sweet Revenge. **1977:** Greased Lightning; Stunts. **1978:** The Deer Hunter; Return from Witch Mountain. **1979:** Meteor; Aunt Mary (tv). **1980:** The Stunt Man; The Exterminator. **1981:** Bustin' Loose; Charlie Chan & the Curse of the Dragon Queen; Night School (aka Terror Eyes). **1982:** Cannery Row; Swamp Thing; The Sword & the Sorcerer; The Soldier. **1983:** Timerider; Christine. **1984:** The Exterminator 2. **1985:** Police Academy 2: Their First Assignment. **1994:** Major League 2.

JOE DUNNE

This stunt coordinator/second unit director doubled Peter Sellers for a number of years. He works primarily with director Blake Edwards.

Films—1975: Return of the Pink Panther. **1976:** The Pink Panther Strikes Again. **1978:** Revenge of the Pink Panther. **1979:** The Prisoner of Zenda. **1980:** The Fiendish Plot of Dr. Fu Manchu. **1982:** S.O.B.; Trail of the Pink Panther; Victor/Victoria; Fast Walking. **1983:** Curse of the Pink Panther; Flashdance; The Man Who Loved Women; The Man with Two Brains; Mr. Mom; Missing Pieces (tv). **1985:** Cloak & Dagger; D.A.R.Y.L.; Police Academy 2: Their First Assignment. **1986:** A Fine Mess; North & South Book 2 (tv); Stark: Mirror Image (tv). **1988:** License to Drive. **1989:** Three Fugitives; Skin Deep; Hollywood Detective (tv); Peter Gunn (tv). **1990:** Taking Care of Business. **1991:** L.A. Story; Pure Luck. **1992:** Storyville; Chaplin. **1993:** Son of the Pink Panther; Fearless. **1994:** Clifford; I.Q.; Scarlett (tv). **1995:** Born to Be Wild; Showgirls; The Usual Suspects. **1996:** Mars Attacks!

ANDY DUPPIN

Films—1986: Jumpin' Jack Flash. **1987:** Deadly Illusion. **1988:** Homeboy. **1989:** Black Rain; True Blood. **1990:** Ghost; Two Evil Eyes; King of New York; Street Hunter; The Ambulance. **1991:** New Jack City. **1992:** Freejack; Malcolm X. **1993:** Daybreak. **1994:** Body Snatchers; Sugar Hill. **1995:** Boys on the Side; Kiss of Death. **1996:** Girl 6.

LARRY DURAN
(b. 1925)

A lifetime member of the Stuntmen's Association, Duran was an amateur boxer in the military before befriending Marlon Brando, whom he began to double. He subsequently played many Mexicans and native Americans on screen.

Films—**1952:** Viva Zapata. **1954:** The Wild One. **1955:** Guys & Dolls. **1958:** The Young Lions; The Flame Barrier. **1959:** The Fugitive Kind. **1960:** The Magnificent Seven; The Mountain Road. **1961:** One Eyed Jacks. **1962:** Mutiny on the Bounty. **1963:** The Ugly American. **1965:** The Hallelujah Trail; The Cincinnati Kid. **1966:** The Last of the Secret Agents. **1967:** Good Times; The President's Analyst. **1968:** The Boston Strangler; Coogan's Bluff; Project X. **1969:** Che; The Great Bank Robbery. **1971:** The Omega Man; Dirty Harry. **1972:** Lady Sings the Blues; Conquest of the Planet of the Apes. **1973:** Lost Horizon; Battle for the Planet of the Apes; The Blue Knight (tv). **1974:** The Towering Inferno; Zandy's Bride; Earthquake; Hang Up (aka Super Dude). **1979:** Buck Rogers in the 25th Century; Meteor; Time After Time; The Champ; The Paradise Connection (tv). **1980:** The Kidnapping of the President; Escape (tv). **1981:** Charlie Chan & the Curse of the Dragon Queen. **1985:** My Science Project. **1986:** The Golden Child. **1987:** Extreme Prejudice; Remote Control; Brenda Starr. **1989:** Cage. **1990:** Solar Crisis; Boris & Natasha. **1992:** Rapid Fire. **1994:** The Naked Gun 33 1/3. *Television*—Gunsmoke; I Spy; The Wild Wild West; Mission: Impossible; The Invaders; Get Smart; Vegas; Buck Rogers; The Fall Guy.

RICHARD DURAN

The son of Larry Duran, Richard is a member of the Stuntmen's Association.

Films—**1973:** The Student Teachers. **1985:** Back to the Future; Stick; Commando. **1986:** Hollywood Vice Squad. **1987:** Extreme Prejudice. **1988:** Action Jackson; Off Limits; They Live; Border Heat; Bail Out. **1989:** K-9; Old Gringo; Tango & Cash; Crack House. **1990:** Young Guns 2;

Death Warrant; Marked for Death; The Rookie; Boris & Natasha; Keaton's Cop; Legal Tender; Drug Wars: The Camarena Story (tv). **1991:** Beastmaster 2; Deadly Game (tv). **1992:** Live Wire; Last of the Mohicans; Aces: Iron Eagle 3. **1993:** Demolition Man; Geronimo; Tombstone; Blindside; No Escape, No Return. **1994:** Blue Tiger; Stargate; The Hard Truth; Hologram Man. **1995:** Bad Boys. **1996:** Escape from L.A.; Mars Attacks! *Television*—Kung Fu, The Next Generation.

CHRIS DURAND

Films—**1989:** Hit List; One Man Force; Night Life. **1991:** Mobsters; The Doors; The Last Boy Scout; Fast Getaway; Past Midnight; 976 Evil 2. **1992:** Ruby; Encino Man; Trespass; Rapid Fire; Cool World; Rage & Honor; Adventures in Dinosaur City. **1993:** Demolition Man; Maniac Cop 3. **1994:** The Crow. **1994:** The Mask; Class of 1999 Part 2; Last Man Standing. **1995:** The Sweeper. **1996:** The Lawnmower Man 2; Skyscraper; Pure Danger; Riot; Ravenhawk.

DICK DUROCK
(b. 1940)

A former marine and computer programmer, this Indiana-born supporting player was already a recognizable face before gaining cult status as the *Swamp Thing*. At 6'5", with a trademark flattened nose, Durock got his start doubling for Guy Williams and Max Baer, Jr. In addition to his many sci-fi creature assignments, his most notable role was as Clint Eastwood's opening opponent in *Any Which Way You Can*. He's a member of the Stuntmen's Association.

Dick Durock as the *Swamp Thing* (1982).

Films—**1968:** The Man from the 25th Century. **1970:** Beneath the Planet of the Apes. **1972:** The Poseidon Adventure; Conquest of the Planet of the Apes; Hammer. **1973:** Westworld; Battle for the Planet of the Apes. **1974:** The Towering Inferno. **1975:** Doc Savage, The Man of Bronze. **1976:** The Enforcer. **1978:** F.I.S.T.; The Dark Secret of Harvest Home (tv). **1979:** Battlestar Galactica; 1941; Stunt Seven (tv). **1980:** Bronco Billy; Coast to Coast; The Nude Bomb; Any Which Way You Can. **1981:** History of the World Part One. **1982:** The Sword & the Sorcerer; Swamp Thing; They Call Me Bruce. **1983:** Return of the Man from U.N.C.L.E. (tv). **1985:** Silverado; Runaway Train; My Wicked, Wicked Ways (tv); Ewoks: The Battle for Endor (tv); Braker (tv). **1986:** Raw Deal; Stand By

Me; Howard the Duck. **1987:** Heat; Blind Date; The Monster Squad; Remote Control. **1988:** Mr. North; License to Drive; Border Heat; Bail Out; Something is Out There (tv). **1989:** The Return of the Swamp Thing; Street Justice. **1991:** Delirious. **1995:** Die Hard with a Vengeance. *Television*—Lost in Space; Star Trek; Time Tunnel; The Beverly Hillbillies; The Wild Wild West; The Six Million Dollar Man; Man Hunter; Joe Forrester; The Rockford Files; Quark; Battlestar Galactica (reg.); Buck Rogers; The Fall Guy; The Powers of Matthew Star; Knight Rider; The Quest; Cover Up; The Big Easy; Dynasty; Falcon Crest; Lime Street; Spenser for Hire; Hard Time on Planet Earth; Swamp Thing (reg.); Baywatch Nights; The Streets of San Francisco.

DAVE EFRON

Films—**1986:** Never Too Young to Die. **1987:** Predator; Brenda Starr. **1988:** Action Jackson; Hero & the Terror; License to Drive; Illegally Yours; Twins. **1989:** Fright Night 2; Physical Evidence; One Man Force. **1990:** I Come in Peace; Far Out Man; Another 48 HRS.; Darkman; Masters of Menace; Keaton's Cop. **1991:** Stone Cold; Barton Fink; Suburban Commando. **1992:** Universal Soldier; Wayne's World. **1993:** Hard Target; The Pelican Brief. **1994:** Wyatt Earp. *Television*—Something Is Out There; Renegade.

BUD EKINS

This expert motorcyclist entered films when his pal Steve McQueen asked him to do stunts in *The Great Escape.* Ekins wound up making the famous cycle jump that McQueen himself has often been credited with. He later did the chase sequence in *Bullit* and became a full-fledged stunt coordinator on motorcycle themed features. A member of the Stuntmen's Association, his brother Dave has also done stuntwork.

Films—**1963:** The Great Escape. **1965:** The Cincinnati Kid. **1968:** Speedway; Bullit; Coogan's Bluff. **1969:** Hell's Angels '69; The Love Bug. **1970:** Angel Unchained; Flap. **1971:** Chrome & Hot Leather. **1972:** The Thing with Two Heads. **1973:** Electra Glide in Blue. **1974:** The Towering Inferno; The Front Page; Earthquake. **1975:** Race with the Devil. **1976:** Dixie Dynamite; Scorchy. **1977:** Sorcerer. **1978:** Movie, Movie; Nat'l Lampoon's Animal House; Return from Witch Mountain. **1979:** Fast Charlie, The Moonbeam Rider. **1980:** The Blues Brothers. **1982:** Megaforce; Jekyll & Hyde, Together Again. **1983:** Deadly Force. **1984:** City Heat. **1985:** Black Moon Rising. **1988:** Mac & Me. **1990:** Pacific Heights. **1993:** Extreme Justice. **1994:** The Next Karate Kid; The Specialist. *Television*—The Mod Squad; Then Came Bronson; Barnaby Jones; CHiPs.

GREG ELAM

Elam grew up around the film business, often working as an extra in his youth. He went on to double both Richard Pryor and Gregory Hines, co-ordinate stunts, and father three stuntmen sons—Ouson, Kiante, and Kirk. A member of the Stuntmen's Association, he had a supporting role in the film *Hear No Evil.*

Films—**1976:** Drum. **1979:** Sunnyside; Concorde, Airport '79. **1980:** Inside Moves; The Nude Bomb. **1982:** Endangered Species; The Sword & the Sorcerer. **1983:** Fire & Ice; Superman 3. **1984:** A Soldier's Story; Breakin' 2: Electric Boogaloo; City Limits. **1985:** Trouble in Mind; Commando; Space Rage; Weird Science; The Color Purple. **1986:** Running Scared;

Jumpin' Jack Flash; The George McKenna Story (tv). **1987:** Robocop; Remote Control; Traxx; Date With an Angel. **1988:** Off Limits; Little Nikita; Midnight Run; Alien Nation; Mississippi Burning; Colors; License to Drive; Earth Girls Are Easy. **1989:** Collision Course; Cage; K-9; See No Evil, Hear No Evil; Glory; Back to the Future 2; Tap; Street Asylum. **1990:** Downtown. Robocop 2; Another 48 HRS.; Love at Large; Marked for Death; Talkin' Dirty After Dark. **1991:** Cool as Ice. **1992:** Deep Cover; Aces: Iron Eagle 3; Class Act; Unlawful Entry; Under Siege. **1993:** Hear No Evil; The Cemetery Club; Sister Act 2; Robocop 3; Weekend at Bernie's 2. **1994:** Silence of the Hams. **1995:** Top Dog; Major Payne. **1996:** The Chamber. *Television*—M*A*S*H; Roll Out; Walker, Texas Ranger.

KIANTE ELAM

Films—**1992:** Deep Cover; Class Act. **1993:** Hear No Evil; Streetknight; Full Eclipse; Undercover Blues; Man's Best Friend. **1994:** The Naked Bun 33 1/3; Double Dragon; A Low Down Dirty Shame. **1995:** Higher Learning; Just Cause; Batman Forever; Nick of Time; Money Train; Tyson. **1996:** Executive Decision; Don't Be a Menace; The Long Kiss Goodnight; Pure Danger.

OUSAN ELAM

The most prolific son of Greg Elam, this stunt coordinator has acted in bit parts and doubled for Denzel Washington. He's a member of the Stuntmen's Association.

Films—**1989:** Glory. **1990:** Pump Up the Volume; Taking Care of Business; Wild at Heart; Marked for Death. **1991:** Eve of Destruction; Ricochet; Boyz N the Hood; Cast a Deadly Spell. **1992:** Live Wire; Wild Orchid 2; Deep Cover; American

Me; Trespass; Class Act; Under Siege; Mo' Money; The Bodyguard. **1993:** Streetknight; Hear No Evil; Menace II Society; Full Eclipse; Demolition Man; Weekend at Bernie's. **1994:** Beverly Hills Cop 3; Airheads; Double Dragon; Mantis (tv). **1995:** Men of War; Panther; Batman Forever; Virtuosity; Vampire in Brooklyn; Things to Do in Denver When You're Dead; One Man's Justice. **1996:** Executive Decision; Don't Be a Menace .; The Great White Hype; Original Gangstas; Fled; The Glimmer Man; Broken Arrow.

LOUIS ELIAS

A veteran supporting player and stunt coordinator, most active on television, Elias is best known for the closing crash in the film *Vanishing Point.*

Films—**1960:** Spartacus. **1962:** The Spiral Road. **1965:** Tickle Me; Dr. Goldfoot & the Bikini Machine. **1969:** The Wild Bunch; Stiletto; True Grit. **1971:** Vanishing Point. **1973:** Sssssss; The Train Robbers. **1974:** Hang Up (aka Super Dude). **1975:** Posse; Night Moves. **1976:** The Next Man; The Treasure of Matecmbe; Law of the Land (tv). **1977:** Flight to Holocaust (tv). **1978:** The Norseman; Lord of the Rings. **1979:** The Apple Dumpling Gang Rides Again; Just You & Me, Kid. **1980:** Nightside (tv); My Kidnapper, My Love (tv). **1983:** Flashdance; The Man with Two Brains. **1987:** Return to Dodge (tv). **1989:** Riding the Edge; B.O.R.N.; Street Justice. **1990:** Dick Tracy. *Television*—The Twilight Zone; The Outer Limits; Combat; Gunsmoke; Voyage to the Bottom of the Sea; Mission: Impossible; Batman; I Spy; Star Trek; The FBI; Roll Out (reg.); The Six Million Dollar Man; Kojak; Baretta; Future Cop; Charlie's Angels; Dog & Cat; Logan's Run; M.A.S.H.; The Fall Guy; Airwolf; Knight Rider; Jake & the Fatman; K-9.

TOM ELLIOT

A member of the International Stunt Association, Elliot has done bits, coordinated stunts, and doubled for both Al Pacino and Matthew Broderick.

Films—**1978:** Hooper. **1979:** Sunnyside; The Dark Side of Terror (tv). **1980:** Heaven's Gate. **1981:** The Postman Always Rings Twice. **1982:** The Border; Fighting Back; Friday the 13th Part 3. **1983:** Wargames; Christine; Scarface. **1984:** Indiana Jones & the Temple of Doom; The Cannonball Run 2; The Joy of Sex; Red Dawn; The River. **1985:** Missing in Action 2; Girls Just Want to Have Fun. **1986:** Band of the Hand; Ferris Bueller's Day Off; Murphy's Law; Never Too Young to Die; The Three Amigos; Back to School; Thunder Run. **1987:** Over the Top; Less Than Zero; Three O'Clock High. **1988:** Rambo 3. **1989:** Cyborg; Always; Far From Home; Society. **1990:** Days of Thunder; Captain America; Last of the Finest; Pacific Heights; A Girl to Kill For. **1991:** The Perfect Weapon. **1992:** Article 99; Far & Away; Out on a Limb; Innocent Blood. **1993:** Streetknight; Geronimo; Gettysburg; Ghost in the Machine; Conflict of Interest. **1994:** Speed; Clear & Present Danger; Double Dragon. **1995:** The Criminal Mind; Tall Tale; Waterworld; Heat; Tremors 2. **1996:** Eraser; The Cable Guy; Jingle All the Way; Sunchaser. *Television*—Vegas; T.J. Hooker; Hill Street Blues; Knot's Landing.

ANNIE ELLIS

The sister of David Ellis, Annie has doubled for the likes of Glenn Close, Helen Hunt, and Madonna. She's a member of the United Stuntwoman's Association and the Professional Driver's Association.

Films—**1983:** Private School. **1984:** The River Rat. **1987:** Burglar; Fatal Attraction. **1989:** Dead Bang; After Midnight; Nat'l Lampoon's Christmas Vacation. **1990:** After Dark, My Sweet; Last of the Finest. **1991:** Warlock; Cast a Deadly Spell. **1992:** Kuffs; Whispers in the Dark; Patriot Games; A River Runs Through It; Forever Young. **1993:** Point of No Return; Sliver; Made in America; The Last Action Hero; The Beverly Hillbillies; Body of Evidence. **1994:** Chasers; Double Dragon; Puppetmasters; Wes Craven's New Nightmare. **1995:** Jade; Money Train. **1996:** Twister; Escape from L.A.; Homeward Bound 2. *Television*—Charlie's Angels.

DAVID ELLIS

A former professional surfer raised in Malibu, Ellis entered films as a protégé of Buddy Joe Hooker and double for Gary Busey. He graduated into stunt coordinating and second unit work, eventually becoming a bonified director. He's a member of both Stunts Unlimited and the Professional Driver's Association.

Films—**1974:** Superdad. **1976:** Baby Blue Marine. **1977:** Heroes; Smokey & the Bandit. **1978:** Deathsport; Hooper; Invasion of the Body Snatchers; Fast Charlie, the Moonbeam Rider; Game of Death; Carny; Smokey & the Bandit 2; Honeysuckle Rose; Foolin' Around. **1981:** Backroads; King of the Mountain; Cheech & Chong's Nice Dreams; Sharky's Machine. **1982:** Megaforce; Airplane 2: The Sequel; The Beastmaster; Fast Times at Ridgemont High; Lookin' to Get Out; Second Thoughts. **1983:** Gorky Park; Nat'l Lampoon's Vacation; Private School; Scarface. **1985:** To Live & Die in L.A. **1986:** The Wraith; Out of Bounds. **1987:** Critical Condition; Burglar; Real Men; Cold Steel; Fatal Attraction; Anna; Lethal Weapon. **1988:** The Rescue; Moving; The Presidio. **1989:** Gleaming the Cube; Beaches; Star

Trek 5: The Final Frontier; Road House; Dead Bang; Blind Fury; Backtrack. **1990:** Everybody Wins; The Freshman; Impulse; Days of Thunder; Flatliners; Joe vs. The Volcano; Misery; Last of the Finest. **1991:** Warlock; Wild Hearts Can't Be Broken; The Addams Family; Defending Your Life; Life Stinks. **1992:** Kuffs; Whispers in the Dark; Patriot Games; A League of Their Own; Forever Young; Thunderheart. **1993:** The Man Without a Face; Sliver; Beethoven's 2nd; Made in America; Body of Evidence. **1994:** Ironwill; My Father, the Hero; Clear & Present Danger; The Jungle Book. **1995:** Waterworld. **1996:** Homeward Bound 2: Lost in San Francisco (d). *Television*—Wonder Woman.

RICHARD ELLIS
(b. 1928)

The father of David Ellis, Richard broke into stuntwork when already well into his fifties. He's a member of the Professional Driver's Association.

Films—**1985:** To Live & Die in L.A. **1987:** Critical Condition; Burglar; Lethal Weapon. **1989:** Gleaming the Cube. **1990:** Impulse; Days of Thunder; Last of the Finest. **1991:** Warlock. **1992:** Kuffs; Thunderheart; Patriot Games; Forever Young. **1993:** Made in America; Attack of the 50 Foot Woman. **1994:** Maverick; Clear & Present Danger. **1995:** Waterworld. **1996:** Sunchaser. *Television*—Baywatch.

KENNY ENDOSO

A veteran bit player of Asian extraction, Endoso has worked as both a stunt coordinator and second unit director. He's a member of Stunts Unlimited.

Films—**1967:** The President's Analyst. **1968:** Project X. **1969:** The Great Bank Robbery. **1974:** Freebie & the Bean; Blazing Saddles; Earthquake. **1977:** Zebra Force. **1978:** Go Tell the Spartans. **1979:** Buck Rogers in the 25th Century; The Electric Horseman; Meteor; A Time to Die. **1980:** The Stunt Man; Alligator; The Blues Brothers; Serial; In God We Trust; Herbie Goes Bananas. **1982:** The Entity; The Sword & the Sorcerer. **1983:** Fire & Ice; Private School; The Star Chamber; Girls of the White Orchid (tv). **1984:** The Ice Pirates; Beverly Hills Cop; The Joy of Sex; Star Trek 3: The Search for Spock. **1985:** Into the Night; Cloak & Dagger; To Live & Die in L.A. **1986:** The Hitcher; Streets of Gold; Big Trouble in Little China. **1987:** Over the Top; The Hanoi Hilton; No Man's Land; Real Men; Kidnapped. **1988:** Die Hard; The Presidio; I'm Gonna Git You Sucka. **1989:** Kinjite; Lethal Weapon 2; Black Rain. **1990:** Die Hard 2; Total Recall; Death Warrant; Vietnam, Texas. **1991:** Mobsters; Dead Again; The Perfect Weapon; Thelma & Louise; Ricochet; The Last Boy Scout; K-9000 (tv); Rapid Fire. **1992:** Nemesis; Patriot Games. **1993:** Point of No Return; Hot Shots Part Deux; Robot Wars; Full Eclipse; The Last Action Hero; Demolition Man. **1994:** The Getaway; Pentathalon; Chasers; The Shadow; True Lies; Clear & Present Danger; In the Army Now; A Low Down Dirty Shame; Puppetmasters; Deadly Target. **1995:** The Criminal Mind; Just Cause; Bad Boys; Waterworld; Devil in a Blue Dress; Seven; Heat. **1996:** Executive Decision; Fled. *Television*—Daniel Boone; Kung Fu; The Six Million Dollar Man.

ANDY EPPER

Films—**1974:** Phantom of the Paradise; Blazing Saddles; Earthquake. **1976:** Death Trap. **1977:** Delta Fox. **1978:** Tilt. **1980:** Smokey & the Bandit 2; Wholly Moses. **1981:** Cutter's Way; Legend of the Lone Ranger. **1982:** Fighting Back; The Sword & the Sorcerer. **1985:** Baby: Secret of the Lost Legend. **1986:** Never Too Young to Die. **1987:** Heat; Million Dollar Mystery;

Summer Camp Nightmare; The Hidden; Survival Game. **1988:** Bulletproof; Action Jackson; Big Business; Dead Heat; Vibes; Rambo 3; Die Hard. **1990:** Boris & Natasha. **1991:** The Perfect Weapon. **1992:** Deep Cover; Toys. **1993:** The Last Action Hero; Striking Distance. **1994:** The Mask. **1996:** The Glimmer Man. *Television*—My Friend Flicka; Knight Rider.

DANNY EPPER

Films—**1985:** Vendetta. **1987:** Night Force. **1988:** Rambo 3; Nightmare on Elm Street 4: Dream Master. **1989:** Road House; Lock Up. **1990:** I Come in Peace; Megaville; Rocky 5; The Exorcist 3; Prayer of the Rollerboys. **1991:** Stone Cold; Beethoven; Deadlock; Driving Me Crazy. **1992:** American Me; Cool World; Out on a Limb; Nemesis. **1993:** Falling Down; Demolition Man; Excessive Force; Jailbait; Best of the Best 2. **1994:** Pentathalon; Terminal Velocity; The Mask; In the Army Now; Puppetmasters; Dumb & Dumber; American Yakuza. **1995:** Waterworld; Showgirls; Strange Days; Money Train. **1996:** Lawnmower Man 2; Eraser; The Rock; Kingpin; Escape from L.A.; 2 Days in the Valley; Jingle All the Way. *Television*—Renegade.

EURLYNE EPPER
(b. 1961)

Films—**1979:** 1941. **1980:** Die Laughing. **1982:** Fighting Back. **1983:** Scarface; The Man with Two Brains. **1984:** Romancing the Stone. **1986:** The Naked Cage; Dangerously Close; Legal Eagles; Murphy's Law; Slow Burn. **1987:** Hot Pursuit. **1988:** Elvira, Mistress of the Dark; They Live. **1989:** Grave Secrets. **1991:** Bill & Ted's Bogus Journey. **1992:** Article 99; Breaking the Rules. **1995:** Money Train.

GARY EPPER

The middle son of John Epper, Gary has directed second unit, done bits, and coordinated stunts. He and son Danny are members of Stunts Unlimited. Gary has doubled for Don Stroud and David Soul.

Films—**1953:** Law & Order. **1959:** Westbound. **1969:** A Man Called Gannon. **1970:** Beneath the Planet of the Apes. **1971:** The Omega Man. **1972:** Conquest of the Planet of the Apes; The Cowboys. **1973:** Magnum Force; Battle for the Planet of the Apes; Soylent Green. **1974:** The Towering Inferno; Mame; Blazing Saddles; Earthquake. **1975:** The Hindenburg; Rollerball. **1976:** Futureworld; Death Trap. **1977:** Delta Fox. **1978:** Hooper; Return from Witch Mountain; Tilt. **1979:** 1941; Nightwing. **1980:** The Ninth Configuration; The Blues Brothers; In God We Trust. **1981:** The Night the Lights Went Out in Georgia. **1982:** Megaforce; Tron; The Beastmaster; Blade Runner. **1983:** Scarface; The Man with Two Brains. **1984:** Bachelor Party. **1985:** Into the Night; Witness. **1986:** Top Gun; Back to School. **1987:** The Untouchables; Code Name Zebra. **1988:** Shakedown; Rambo 3; The Blob; The Seventh Sign; They Live. **1989:** K-9; The Burbs; Lethal Weapon 2; Road House; Dead Bang; One Man Force. **1990:** The Hunt for Red October; Pacific Heights; Last of the Finest. **1991:** V.I. Warshawski; Hook; The Rocketeer. **1992:** Basic Instinct; Unlawful Entry. **1993:** Demolition Man; Fatherhood; Jailbait. **1994:** Speed; The Shadow; The Mask; Night of the Running Man; In the Army Now; American Yakuza. **1995:** The Enemy Within; 3 Ninjas Knuckle Up; Money Train; Sudden Death. **1996:** Eye for an Eye; Broken Arrow; Eraser; Crazy Horse (tv); Star Trek, First Contact. *Television*—Lassie; Fury; Voyage to the Bottom of the Sea; Here Come the Brides; Hawaii Five-O; Kung Fu; Wonder Woman; Starsky & Hutch; Charlie's Angels; Vegas; From Here to Eternity; 240 Robert; Voyagers; The Fall Guy; T.J. Hooker; Airwolf; Magnum P.I.; Something Is Out There; Combat; The Gallant Men; Rat Patrol; Mod Squad.

JEANNIE EPPER
(b. 1941)

The daughter of John Epper, Jeannie is herself the mother of Eurlyne, Richard and Kurtis Epper. A member of the United Stuntwoman's Association, she has worked as a stunt coordinator and doubled for Melinda Dillon, Farrah Fawcett, Shelly Long, and Lynda Carter on television's "Wonder Woman."

Films—**1951:** Elopement. **1969:** Hello, Dolly!; MacKenna's Gold. **1972:** The Life & Times of Judge Roy Bean. **1973:** The Don Is Dead; Soylent Green. **1974:** Foxy Brown; The Towering Inferno; Blazing Saddles; Earthquake. **1976:** Death Trap; Drum. **1977:** Close Encounters of the 3rd Kind. **1979:** 1941; Return of the Mod Squad (tv). **1980:** The Blues Brothers; The Ninth Configuration; Melvin & Howard; Smokey & the Bandit 2; Used Cars; Silent Scream. **1981:** Caveman; The Terror. **1982:** The Beastmaster; Blade Runner; The Sword & the Sorcerer; Poltergeist. **1983:** The Man with Two Brains; Terms of Endearment. **1984:** Romancing the Stone; Ghost Warrior (aka Swordkill). **1985:** Clue; Warning Sign; Fletch; Vendetta. **1986:** The Naked Cage; Legal Eagles; Extremities; Murphy's Law. **1987:** Outrageous Fortune; Million Dollar Mystery. **1988:** Elvira, Mistress of the Dark; Patty Hearst. **1989:** K-9; Road House; The Package; Nat'l Lampoon's Christmas Vacation. **1990:** Come See the Paradise; Total Recall; Don't Tell Her It's Me; The Rookie. **1991:** Dead Again; Mobsters. **1992:** Article 99; Honey, I Blew Up the Kid; Innocent Blood. **1993:** Demolition Man; The Fugitive. **1994:** Beverly Hills Cop 3; Blown Away; Night of the Running Man. **1995:** Die Hard with a Vengeance; Separate Lives; Money Train. **1996:** Sgt. Bilko; Spy Hard; A Very Brady Sequel; High School High. *Television*—Lancer; Emergency; Wonder Woman; The Bionic Woman; Charlie's Angels; Dynasty.

JOHN EPPER
(b. 1906; d. 1992)

Born in Switzerland, Epper was a master horseman who originally broke into films as a trainer and riding instructor. Doubling for Errol Flynn, Gary Cooper, Ronald Reagan, Randolph Scott, and Henry Fonda, he was the patriarch of a stunt dynasty. His sons Tony, Gary, and Andy all entered the business, as did daughters Margo, Jeannie, and Stephanie.

Films—**1936:** Charge of the Light Brigade. **1938:** The Cowboy & the Lady. **1940:** The Westerner; Santa Fe Trail. **1943:** They Came to Blow Up America. **1945:** They Were Expendable; Frontier Gal. **1946:** The Bride Wore Boots. **1948:** The Winner's Circle; Fort Apache; Joan of Arc. **1949:** She Wore a Yellow Ribbon. **1952:** At Sword's Point; Springfield Rifle. **1953:** Son of Paleface. **1954:** King Richard & the Crusaders; Broken Lance. **1956:** Never Say Goodbye; Love Me Tender; Friendly Persuasion. **1959:** Westbound; These Thousand Hills. **1960:** Spartacus. **1962:** The Spiral Road; How the West Was Won. **1964:** Cheyenne Autumn. **1965:** The War Lord. **1968:** The Scalphunters. *Television*—The Big Valley.

KURTIS EPPER (SANDERS)
(b. 1970)

Films—**1979:** 1941; Return of the Mod Squad (tv). **1980:** Used Cars. **1982:** Annie. **1990:** The Rookie. **1992:** Buffy, The Vampire Slayer. **1994:** Beverly Hills Cop 3; Airheads; Blown Away; Double Dragon. **1995:** Across the Moon; Die Hard with a Vengeance; One Man's Justice. **1996:** The Rock; The Chamber.

RICHARD EPPER
(b. 1960)

Films—1980: The Blues Brothers; Smokey & the Bandit 2; Used Cars. 1982: Megaforce; Grease 2; Penitentiary 2. 1984: The River. 1985: Silverado; The Protector. 1986: Dangerously Close; Cobra; The Three Amigos; Back to School; Slow Burn; Radioactive Dreams; Thunder Run. 1987: Winners Take All. 1988: Shakedown; Crocodile Dundee 2. 1989: Far from Home. 1990: Days of Thunder; Impulse. 1991: The Taking of Beverly Hills; Highway to Hell; Lionheart; The Perfect Weapon; Cool as Ice; Beastmaster 2; McBain. 1992: Into the Sun; 3 Ninjas; Innocent Blood. 1993: Streetknight; Hard Target; Wayne's World 2. 1994: The Expert; Airheads; A Low Down Dirty Shame; Scanners: The Showdown. 1995: 3 Ninjas Knuckle Up; Tall Tale; Money Train; Things to Do in Denver When You're Dead; The Sweeper. 1996: The Lawnmower Man 2; The Phantom; The Rock; The Fan; Pure Danger; Sunchaser.

STEPHANIE EPPER

Yet another child of John Epper, Stephanie served as both Amanda Blake's double on television's "Gunsmoke" and Barbara Bain's on "Mission: Impossible."

Films—1965: The Rare Breed; The War Lord. 1969: Once You Kiss a Stranger; Hello, Dolly! 1970: There Was a Crooked Man; Little Big Man. 1974: Foxy Brown; The Towering Inferno; Mame; Earthquake. 1975: Satan's Triangle. 1980: The Blues Brothers; Smokey & the Bandit 2. 1981: Cheech & Chong's Nice Dreams; Deadly Blessing. 1984: Beverly Hills Cop. 1985: Commando; Silverado. 1987: Teen Wolf 2; Walk Like a Man. 1988: Twins. 1989: Nightmare on Elm Street 5:

Dream Child. 1990: Total Recall; The Rookie. 1991: Nothing But Trouble. *Television*—Gunsmoke; Mission: Impossible.

TONY EPPER
(b. 1938)

This veteran supporting player, stunt coordinator, and second unit director is the oldest son of John Epper. He made his film debut at the age of nine months and later played juvenile roles in the Ma and Pa Kettle films. As an adult he doubled regularly for Burt Lancaster and Slim Pickens. In 1992 he formed the National League of Screen Actor's Guild Stunt Performers in an effort to unite all of the stunt organizations. He himself is a member of Stunts Unlimited.

Films—1938: The Thin Man. 1951: Elopement. 1952: Carbine Williams. 1954: Ma & Pa Kettle at Home. 1964: Mail Order Bride. 1965: The Hallelujah Trail; The War Lord. 1966: The Professionals. 1968: The Scalphunters. 1969: The Wild Bunch; Paint Your Wagon; The Good Guys & the Bad guys; The Gay Deceivers. 1970: Beneath the Planet of the Apes. 1971: Lawman; Valdez is Coming; The Omega Man. 1972: Ulzana's Raid; Conquest of the Planet of the Apes; The Great Northfield Minnesota Raid; The Cowboys. 1973: Battle for the Planet of the Apes. 1974: The Towering Inferno; Blazing Saddles. 1975: Doc Savage, The Man of Bronze; The Master Gunfighter. 1977: The Island of Dr. Moreau. 1978: Corvette Summer; Hooper; FM; Tilt. 1979: 1941; Beyond the Poseidon Adventure. 1980: Cattle Annie & Little Britches; Just Before Dawn; More Wild Wild West (tv); For the Love of It (tv). 1981: Cutter's Way; Sizzle (tv). 1982: The Sword & the Sorcerer; The Beastmaster. 1983: Nat'l Lampoon's Vacation. 1984: Beverly Hills Cop; The Wild

Life. **1985:** To Live & Die in L.A.; Runaway Train; Vendetta. **1986:** Thrashin'; Hamburger; Condor (tv). **1987:** Outrageous Fortune; Shy People; Night Force; Kidnapped; Return to Dodge (tv). **1988:** Alien from L.A. **1989:** Lethal Weapon 2; Nat'l Lampoon's Christmas Vacation; Road House; Lonesome Dove (tv). **1990:** Dick Tracy; Don't Tell Her It's Me; Homer & Eddie; Kid. **1991:** My Heroes Have Always Been Cowboys; Servants of Twilight; Suburban Commando; Thelma & Louise; Driving Me Crazy. **1992:** Freejack; American Me; White Sands; Lethal Weapon 3; Patriot Games; Bram Stoker's Dracula; Forever Young. **1993:** Nowhere to Run; Excessive Force; Trouble Bound. **1994:** The River Wild; In the Army Now; Army of One; Maverick. **1995:** Waterworld; The Good Old Boys; Money Train. **1996:** Executive Decision; Heaven's Prisoners; Spy Hard; The Rock; The Glimmer Man; Jingle All the Way; Sunchaser. *Television*—Lassie; Fury; Daniel Boone; Gunsmoke; Batman; The Green Hornet; I Spy; Cimarron Strip; The High Chaparral; Kung Fu; Kodiak; The Night Stalker; The Manhunter; The Six Million Dollar Man; The Rockford Files; The Man from Atlantis; Charlie's Angels; Vegas; Buck Rogers; A Man Called Sloane; CHiPs; The Fall Guy; Voyagers; Knight Rider; Airwolf; MacGyver; Hunter; Paradise.

JON EPSTEIN

An independent stunt coordinator, Epstein doubled for Chuck Norris during the mid–1980's.

Films—**1984:** The Ice Pirates; The Philadelphia Experiment. **1985:** Invasion USA. **1986:** The Delta Force; Firewalker. **1987:** Allan Quartermain & the Lost City of Gold; Dudes. **1988:** Bulletproof; Hero & the Terror; License to Drive; They Live. **1989:** The Abyss; Kinjite. **1991:** The Perfect Weapon; Mom; Soldier's Fortune. **1992:** Basic Instinct; Nails. **1993:** Streetknight; Full Eclipse; Sliver; Brain

Smasher; Knights. **1994:** The Mask. **1995:** Village of the Damned; The Brady Bunch Movie; Things to Do in Denver When You're Dead; Nemesis 3. **1996:** Barb Wire; Ravenhawk; Adrenaline; Saints and Sinners. *Television*—Walker, Texas Ranger.

WILLIAM ERICKSON

Films—**1977:** Herbie Goes to Monte Carlo. **1979:** The Apple Dumpling Gang Rides Again. **1982:** Swamp Thing. **1987:** Cold Steel; The Lost Boys; Cyclone; Deadly Intent. **1988:** Big Business; The Rescue; Beaches. **1989:** Survival Quest; Lady Avenger; Action USA. **1990:** Flatliners; Joe vs. the Volcano. **1991:** Disaster in Time; Neon City. **1992:** Big Girls Don't Cry, They Get Even. **1994:** Bad Girls; The Last Seduction. **1995:** 3 Ninjas Knuckle Up; Evolver.

JOHN ESCOBAR

An independent stunt coordinator of Hispanic descent, Escobar has doubled for Esai Morales.

Films—**1978:** Hooper. **1979:** Boulevard Nights; The Streets of L.A. (tv)). **1980:** Borderline. **1982:** Star Trek 2: The Wrath of Khan. **1983:** D.C. Cab. **1985:** Appointment with Fear; Gotcha. **1986:** The Boys Next Door; Band of the Hand; Hollywood Vice Squad; 8 Million Ways to Die. **1987:** Private Investigations. **1988:** Bulletproof; The Blue Iguana; Critters 2; Tapeheads. **1989:** K-9; Cage; Bill & Ted's Excellent Adventure; Blind Fury; One Man Force. **1990:** Maniac Cop 2; Darkman; Boris & Natasha; Prayer of the Rollerboys; Drug Wars: The Camarena Story (tv). **1991:** Harley Davidson & the Marlboro Man; Ever of Destruction; Meet the Applegates. **1994:** Blue Tiger. **1995:** My Family; The Sweeper. **1996:** Escape from L.A.; Scorpion Spring. *Television*—Renegade.

COREY EUBANKS

The son of game show host Bob Eubanks, Corey was at one time reported to be the highest paid stuntman in the business. He moved from coordinating stunts and doing second unit work to starring in low-budget action films and directing low-budget family fare.

Films—**1983:** The Sting 2. **1986:** Cobra; Wisdom. **1987:** The Night Stalker; The Omega Syndrome; Wanted: Dead or Alive; No Man's Land; Dragnet; Innerspace; Planes, Trains & Automobiles; Independence Day (tv). **1988:** Freeway; Maniac Cop; Midnight Run; Earth Girls Are Easy; Poltergeist 3; Vice Versa; Tripwire. **1989:** Cage; One Man Force; Collision Course; Night Life; Relentless; Chances Are. **1990:** The First Power; The Gumshoe Kid; Payback. **1991:** Backdraft; Bright Angel; The Indian Runner; The Marrying Man. **1992:** Dr. Giggles; Far & Away; The Gun in Betty Lou's Handbag; Out on a Limb. **1993:** Forced to Kill; Bound by Honor. **1995:** Separate Lives; The Tie That Binds; Hourglass; The Set Up; Bigfoot: The Unforgettable Encounter (d); Two Bits & Pepper (d). **1996:** Barb Wire; Mars Attacks! *Television*—Sonny Spoon; Renegade.

DEBBIE EVANS
(b. 1959)

A champion motorcyclist, Debbie was recruited to double Claudia Jennings in *Deathsport* and quickly became one of the most in-demand women in the business. A member of both the Professional Driver's Association and the United Stuntwoman's Association, she later married stuntman Lane Leavitt.

Films—**1978:** Deathsport. **1979:** Rock 'n' Roll High School; The Jerk; 1941; Concorde, Airport '79. **1980:** Smokey & the Bandit 2; Airplane; Heaven's Gate. **1982:** Fighting Back. **1983:** Private School. **1984:** Friday the 13th: A New Beginning; Surf 2; City Limits. **1985:** Moving Violations; Black Moon Rising; Rainy Day Friends (aka L.A. Bad). **1986:** The Naked Cage; Cobra; Murphy's Law; The Three Amigos; Never Too Young to Die. **1987:** Prince of Darkness; Burglar; Death Wish 4; Assassination; Hunter's Blood; Private Road: No Trespassing. **1988:** Halloween 4; Messenger of Death; Critters 2; They Live; Twins. **1989:** To Die For; Ghostbusters 2; Grave Secrets. **1990:** Kindergarten Cop; The Borrower; Class of 1999; I'm Dangerous Tonight (tv). **1991:** Eve of Destruction; Terminator 2; Beastmaster 2. **1992:** Poison Ivy; Nails; Sweet Justice. **1993:** Jack the Bear; The Last Action Hero; Cliffhanger; Demolition Man; The Beverly Hillbillies; Cyborg 2. **1994:** Puppetmasters; Midnight Ride. **1995:** Just Cause; Destiny Turns on the Radio; Fair Game; The Tie That Binds; Showgirls; Last Man Standing. **1996:** Marshal Law; Barb Wire. *Television*—CHiPs.

DONNA EVANS

A member of the United Stuntwoman's Association, Evans has doubled for Sharon Stone, Jessica Lange, Sean Young, and Sandra Bullock.

Films—**1983:** Christine; D.C. Cab. **1984:** Bachelor Party. **1985:** Trancers. **1986:** Legal Eagles; Radioactive Dreams; Thunder Run; Hollywood Vice Squad. **1987:** The Witches of Eastwick; Lethal Weapon; Assassination; Down Twisted. **1988:** Critters 2; Alien from L.A. **1989:** Night Game; Road House; The Package; Dead Bang. **1990:** The Guardian; Die Hard 2; Total Recall; Firebirds; Wild at Heart; Pump Up the Volume; The Adventures of Ford Fairlane; Marked for Death; The Rookie; Boris & Natasha; The Ambulance. **1991:**

Shattered; Highway to Hell; Showdown in Little Tokyo; Hook; Cape Fear; A Kiss Before Dying; Maze. **1992:** Basic Instinct; Nails; Pet Sematary 2; Poison Ivy; Universal Soldier; Hero; Hoffa. **1993:** Fatal Instinct. **1994:** Past Tense; Speed; The Specialist; Automatic; Illicit Dreams. **1995:** Destiny Turns on the Radio; Nine Months; Species; The Net; Showgirls; Houseguest; The Tie That Binds; Casino; Body Language; Mirage. **1996:** Barb Wire; Diabolique; A Very Brady Sequel; Bordello of Blood; Fast Money.

DANA DRU EVENSON

Films—**1985:** Gotcha. **1986:** Invaders from Mars; Poltergeist 2. **1987:** Million Dollar Mystery; Throw Momma from the Train; Remote Control; Private Road: No Trespassing. **1988:** Colors. **1990:** Total Recall; The Ambulance. **1991:** Not of This World (tv). **1992:** Universal Soldier; Out on a Limb. **1993:** The Beverly Hillbillies. **1996:** The Demolitionist; Ravenhawk.

ROY FARFEL

A member of Stunt Specialists, this stunt coordinator has doubled for Joe Pesci.

Films—**1985:** Remo Williams. **1987:** China Girl. **1988:** Shakedown; Last Rites; Homeboy. **1989:** See No Evil, Hear No Evil; Penn & Teller Get Killed. **1990:** Blue Steel; State of Grace; Miller's Crossing; King of New York; Goodfellas. **1991:** New Jack City; The Butcher's Wife. **1992:** My Cousin Vinny; The Public Eye; Malcolm X. **1993:** The Pelican Brief. **1994:** The Cowboy Way; The Professional. **1995:** Little Odessa; Search & Destroy; Dead Presidents. **1996:** Daylight.

"DIAMOND" HILL FARNSWORTH
(b. 1950)

A member of the Stuntmen's Association, the son of Richard Farnsworth has coordinated stunts, directed second unit, and doubled for both Sylvester Stallone and Scott Bakula.

Films—**1969:** Paint Your Wagon. **1978:** Piranha; F.I.S.T.; The Norseman. **1979:** 10; The Lady in Red. **1980:** Alligator; The Big Brawl; Humanoids from the Deep. **1981:** Charlie Chan & the Curse of the Dragon Queen; Ghost Story; Heartbeeps; Halloween 2. **1982:** The Beastmaster; The Sword & the Sorcerer. **1983:** Fire & Ice. **1984:** Rhinestone; The Terminator; City Limits. **1985:** Rambo 2; Commando. **1986:** Ruthless People. **1987:** The Big Easy; Nadine; No Way Out; Three on a Match (tv). **1988:** Shakedown; Last Rites; The Dead Pool; They Live. **1989:** Fletch Lives; Pink Cadillac; Weekend at Bernie's. **1990:** Pump Up the Volume. **1991:** Harley Davidson & the Marlboro Man. **1993:** The Fugitive. **1994:** Color of Night. **1995:** Batman Forever; The Usual Suspects; Last Man Standing. **1996:** Ransom. ***Television***—Quantum Leap; Walker, Texas Ranger; Jag.

RICHARD FARNSWORTH
(b. 1920)

Farnsworth was a stuntman and bit player for 40 years before it was decided that he might have the right look for a supporting role in the film *Comes a Horseman*. He was so right that he got an Oscar nomination and a new career as a reliable character

Richard Farnsworth takes a fall in 1955's *Desert Sands*.

actor (*The Grey Fox, The Two Jakes, Misery*). A former rodeo rider and archery expert, he doubled for Montgomery Clift, Henry Fonda, Kirk Douglas, Steve McQueen, and Roy Rogers. In all, he worked anonymously on nearly 300 films.

Films—**1937:** A Day at the Races. **1938:** The Adventures of Marco Polo. **1943:** This Is the Army. **1947:** Stallion Road. **1948:** Red River. **1952:** The Lusty Men. **1953:** Arena; Arrowhead. **1954:** The Caine Mutiny; The Wild One. **1955:** Man Without a Country; The Indian Fighter. **1956:** Pardners. **1957:** The Tin Star; The Hard Man. **1960:** Spartacus. **1962:** Six Black Horses. **1965:** Major Dundee; Cat Ballou; The War Lord. **1966:** Duel at Diablo; Texas Across the River; Chamber of Horrors. **1969:** The Good Guys & the Bad Guys; Paint Your Wagon; The Stalking Moon. **1970:** Monte Walsh. **1971:** The Omega Man; The Skin Game; Shootout. **1972:** The Cowboys; Pocket Money; Ulzana's Raid; The Life & Times of Judge Roy Bean. **1973:** Papillon; The Soul of Nigger Charley; High Plains Drifter. **1974:** The Front Page. **1975:** Rooster Cogburn; Strange New World (tv). **1976:** The Outlaw Josey Wales; The Duchess & the Dirtwater Fox. **1977:** Another Man, Another Chance; Roots (tv). **1978:** Comes a Horseman. **1980:** Tom Horn; Resurrection. **1981:** The Legend of the Lone Ranger. **1982:** The Grey Fox; Waltz Across Texas. **1983:** Independence Day; Travis McGee (tv); Ghost Dancing (tv). **1984:** The Natural; Rhinestone. **1985:** Into the Night; Sylvester; Space Rage; Wild Horses (tv); Anne of Green Gables (tv). **1989:** Red Earth, White Earth; Desperado, The Outlaw Wars (tv). **1990:** Havana; The Two Jakes; Misery. **1991:** Highway to Hell. **1993:** The Fire Next Time (tv). **1994:** The Getaway; Lassie. **1995:** The Magic Forest. *Television*—Wild Bill Hickok; Roy Rogers; Wanted, Dead or Alive; The

Outer Limits; Bonanza; The Big Valley; Cimarron Strip; The High Chaparral; Mission: Impossible; Little House on the Prairie; Cherokee Trail; The Texas Rangers; The Boys of Twilight (reg.).

DANE FARWELL

A member of the International Stunt Association, Farwell has doubled for Tom Hanks and Joe Regalbuto.

Films—**1987:** The Wild Pair. **1988:** Bad Dreams. **1989:** Hit List; After Midnight; Shocker; Crack House. **1990:** Child's Play 2. **1990:** Repossessed; The Gumshoe Kid; Predator 2; Prayer of the Rollerboys; Genuine Risk; Beastmaster 2. **1991:** Late for Dinner; The People Under the Stairs; Writer's Block (tv). **1992:** 3 Ninjas; Dead Center (aka Crazy Joe); Davinci's War; Sweet Justice. **1993:** Streetknight; Dragon; Hard Target; Knights. **1994:** Blue Tiger; Cabin Boy; Cops & Robbersons; Forrest Gump; White Mile; Killing Zoe. **1995:** 3 Ninjas Knuckle Up; Get Shorty; Vampire in Brooklyn; Last Man Standing; One Man's Justice; Things to Do in Denver When You're Dead; The Sweeper. **1996:** Broken Arrow; Lawnmower Man 2; The Phantom; Pure Danger; Riot; Ravenhawk.

EDDIE FERNANDEZ

A member of the Mid-West Stunt Association, Fernandez has worked predominantly on Chicago-lensed fare.

Films—**1985:** The Naked Face; Code of Silence. **1986:** Raw Deal. **1988:** Above the Law; Child's Play; Vice Versa. **1989:** Next of Kin. **1991:** V.I. Warshawski; Backdraft; Three Days to a Kill. **1992:** Folks; Rapid Fire; Hoffa. **1993:** Excessive Force; Judgment Night. **1994:** Blink. **1994:** Richie Rich; Blankman; Chain Reaction. **1996:** Normal Life.

DEAN FERRANDINI

This independent stunt coordinator, second unit director, and producer has worked on many films as a double for Chuck Norris, even directing Norris' brother Aaron in *Overkill*. He's married to actress/stuntwoman Keefe Millard.

Films—**1979:** Beyond the Poseidon Adventure; Orphan Train (tv). **1980:** Smokey & the Bandit 2. **1982:** Silent Rage; Fighting Back; The Sword & the Sorcerer. **1983:** Nat'l Lampoon's Class Reunion; White Water Rebels (tv). **1984:** The Ice Pirates; Breakin'; Missing in Action; Indiana Jones & the Temple of Doom. **1985:** Code of Silence; Invasion USA; Blade in Hong Kong (tv). **1986:** Firewalker. **1987:** Street Justice. **1988:** Innerspace; Above the Law; Platoon Leader; Braddock: Missing in Action 3; Critters 2; Nightmare on Elm Street 4: Dream Master; Glitz (tv). **1989:** The Mighty Quinn; L.A. Bounty. **1990:** Boris & Natasha; Delta Force 2; The Exorcist 3. **1991:** The Hitman (p); The Naked Truth; Relentless 2: Dead On; A Time to Die. **1992:** Trancers; Overkill (tv). **1993:** Sidekicks (p); Cybertracker. **1994:** Hellbound (p) 1993; Army of One; Midnight Ride; Squanto; Zero Tolerance; Hologram Man; Deadly Target. **1995:** Top Dog; The Silencers. **1996:** Forest Warrior; Overkill (d).

FRANK FERRARA

A stunt coordinator and supporting player who has stood in for both Sean

Connery and Terence Stamp, Ferrara is the head of the East Coast group Stunts, Inc. His son Frank, Jr., has also done stunts.

Films—**1979:** The Wanderers; The Warriors. **1980:** Atlantic City. **1981:** Ragtime. **1982:** Wrong Is Right; Hanky Panky; Tempest. **1984:** The Executioner 2; Firstborn; Scream for Help. **1985:** Turk 182; Stick; Remo Williams; The Last Dragon. **1986:** 9 1/2 Weeks; Sweet Liberty; The Money Pit; F/X; Raw Deal; The Manhattan Project; Wise Guys; Out of Bounds. **1987:** Orphans; The Untouchables; Mannequin; Deadly Illusion. **1988:** Shakedown; Last Rites; Married to the Mob; Big Business; Working Girl. **1989:** Ghostbusters 2; A Shock to the System; Black Rain. **1990:** Quick Change; King of New York; The Rookie. **1991:** Stone Cold; Mobsters; Out for Justice; One Good Cop; Hook; Ricochet; Hudson Hawk; Betsy's Wedding; The Hard Way; The Prince of Tides; The Last Boy Scout. **1992:** Rapid Fire; Hoffa. **1993:** Rising Sun; The Real McCoy. **1994:** Sugar Hill; The Cowboy Way; The Professional. **1995:** Just Cause; Kiss of Death; Die Hard with a Vengeance. **1996:** Independence Day; Maximum Risk; Bullet; Marvin's Room.

LINDA FETTERS (HOWARD)

A Memphis-born physical education major, Fetters is a member of the Stuntwoman's Association. She's married to actor Ken Howard.

Films—**1988:** Sunset; Bad Dreams. **1989:** Star Trek V: The Final Frontier; After Midnight; L.A. Bounty. **1990:** Disturbed; Peacemaker. **1991:** Mom; The Rocketeer; Alligator 2; Intimate Stranger. **1993:** Boiling Point. **1995:** Die Hard with a Vengeance.

RANDY FIFE

A member of the Stuntmen's Association, the Texas-raised Fife has worked as a stunt coordinator, second unit director, special effects technician, and as a double for Dennis Hopper.

Films—**1979:** The Evictors. **1982:** Silent Rage; Split Image. **1983:** Tender Mercies; Ellie. **1984:** Places in the Heart; Not for Publication. **1986:** Play Dead. **1987:** O.C. & Stiggs; Robocop; End of the Line; Square Dance; The Dirtbike Kid; The Man Who Broke 1,000 Chains (tv). **1988:** D.O.A.; The Tracker; Paramedics. **1989:** Pow Wow Highway; Damned River. **1990:** Flashback; Problem Child; Robocop 2. **1991:** Graveyard Shift 2; Daddy's Dyin'. Who's Got the Will; Problem Child 2. **1992:** Wild Orchid 2; Deep Cover; Wayne's World; Sunset Heat. **1993:** CB4. **1994:** Monkey Trouble; Silent Fall; The Chase. **1995:** The Walking Dead; Dark Dealer. **1996:** Multiplicity; Last Dance.

LILA FINN
(b. 1911; d. 1996)

A champion diver and swimmer, the Los Angeles-born Finn began a long and distinguished career by doubling for Dorothy Lamour, Vivian Leigh, and Donna Reed. She also competed in the 1959 Pan Am Games for the U.S. Women's Volleyball team.

Films—**1937:** Hurricane. **1939:** Gone with the Wind. **1946:** It's a Wonderful Life. **1947:** Unconquered. **1959:** Scarlet Angel; A Summer Place. **1962:** Incident in an Alley. **1972:** The Poseidon Adventure. **1974:** The Towering Inferno; Blazing Saddles; Earthquake. **1976:** Drum. **1981:** Heartbeeps; Goliath Awaits (tv). **1984:** Surf 2. **1986:** Cobra; Legal Eagles; Out of

Bounds; Armed & Dangerous. **1987:** Private Investigations. **1988:** License to Drive. **1989:** Tango & Cash. **1990:** Robocop 2; Repossessed; Predator 2. **1991:** The Naked Gun 2 1/2; The Rocketeer; Suburban Commando. **1992:** Folks. **1994:** True Lies; Army of One.

JOE FINNEGAN

A veteran small-part actor, Finnegan has worked in tandem with stuntman Mickey Gilbert for a number of years. He was one of the men in the famous exploding chopper shot in *Apocalypse Now.*

Films—**1963:** Operation Bikini. **1964:** The Patsy. **1965:** Young Fury. **1966:** Duel at Diablo. **1968:** The Green Berets. **1969:** The Wild Bunch; Che; The Good Guys & the Bad Guys; The Great Bank Robbery; Butch Cassidy & the Sundance Kid. **1970:** Little Big Man. **1971:** Dirty Harry. **1973:** The Don Is Dead. **1974:** Mame. **1978:** The Fury. **1979:** Apocalypse Now. **1980:** Just Before Dawn; The Mountain Men; Coast to Coast; Smokey & the Bandit 2; Heaven's Gate; Gorp. **1981:** Raggedy Man; The Legend of the Lone Ranger; The Intruder Within (tv). **1982:** Zapped. **1984:** Romancing the Stone; Ghost Warrior (aka Swordkill). **1986:** Cobra; Band of the Hand; The Golden Child; The Three Amigos; Eye of the Tiger. **1987:** Robocop; Programmed to Kill; Traxx. **1988:** Above the Law. **1989:** Old Gringo; Johnny Handsome; Renegades. **1990:** Another 48 HRS.; Problem Child; Young Guns 2. **1991:** Shattered; Dogfight. **1992:** Last of the Mohicans. **1993:** Ghost in the Machine. **1994:** City Slickers 2. **1995:** Apollo 13. **1996:** The Nutty Professor. *Television*—The Girl from U.N.C.L.E.

GLORIA (GLORY) FIORAMONTI

A stunt coordinator and double for actress Susan Sarandon, Fioramonti is a member of the International Stuntwoman's Association.

Films—**1975:** Sky Heist (tv). **1981:** Honkytonk Freeway. **1983:** Chained Heat. **1984:** The Philadelphia Experiment. **1985:** To Live & Die in L.A. **1986:** Wisdom; Choke Canyon; Radioactive Dreams; Trick or Treat. **1987:** The Hidden; Dudes. **1988:** Above the Law; Dead Heat; Maniac Cop; Mac & Me; Child's Play; Alien Nation; Tapeheads. **1989:** The Abyss; Kinjite; L/A. Bounty; Spontaneous Combustion; See No Evil, Hear No Evil; Night Life. **1990:** Tremors; Maniac Cop 2; Child's Play 2; Marked for Death; Masters of Menace; Fear (tv). **1991:** Highway to Hell; Thelma & Louise; Deadlock; Beastmaster 2; Future Kick; Soldier's Fortune; K-9000 (tv)); Knight Rider 2000 (tv). **1992:** Love Field; Raising Cain; Out on a Limb; Sneakers; Innocent Blood. **1993:** Striking Distance; Streetknight; Man's Best Friend; Ghost in the Machine. **1994:** Clean Slate; The Client; The Mask; The Last Seduction; Killing Zoe; Dumb & Dumber; Criminal Passion. **1995:** Safe Passage; Batman Forever; Showgirls; Sudden Death; Things to Do in Denver When You're Dead; Indictment: The McMartin Trial; Deadly Outbreak. **1996:** The Craft. *Television*—Lady Blue.

SUZANNE FISH *SEE* RAMPE, J. SUZANNE

GEORGE FISHER

A veteran supporting player and stunt coordinator, the burly, red-haired Fisher is a longtime member of the Stuntmen's Association. He has doubled for Jack Weston.

Films—**1966:** Cyborg 2027. **1968:** Pretty Poison; The Boston Strangler. **1972:** Lady Liberty; Conquest of the Planet of the Apes; Melinda; Portnoy's Complaint. **1973:** The Don Is Dead; Badlands; Battle for the Planet of the Apes. **1974:** The Towering Inferno; Blazing Saddles. **1975:** Mr. Ricco. **1976:** Hawmps. **1977:** The Domino Principle; The 3,000 Mile Chase (tv). **1978:** Movie, Movie. **1980:** The Island; How to Beat the High Cost of Living; The Big Brawl; The Baltimore Bullet. **1981:** The Four Seasons. **1982:** The Sword & the Sorcerer. **1983:** Heart Like a Wheel; Flashdance; The Man with Two Brains; Under Fire. **1984:** City Heat; Firestarter; Red Dawn; Oh, God! You Devil; P.K. & the Kid; The Vindicator. **1985:** Cloak & Dagger; Commando; Rambo 2; Gotcha; Space Rage. **1986:** Sweet Liberty; The Morning After; The Golden Child; Raw Deal; Hollywood Vice Squad. **1987:** Million Dollar Mystery; The Omega Syndrome; Return to Horror High; Heat; Programmed to Kill; Brenda Starr. **1988:** Above the Law; Alien Nation; The Blob; Freeway; They Live. **1989:** Catch Me If You Can; 976 Evil; UHF; Bill & Ted's Excellent Adventure; Glory; CHUD 2; Fists of Steel. **1990:** Genuine Risk. **1991:** Hangfire; Hook; Son of Darkness: To Die For 2; The Lawnmower Man. **1992:** Deep Cover; Aces: Iron Eagle 3; Love Field; Unlawful Entry; Hoffa. **1993:** Nat'l Lampoon's Loaded Weapon; Posse; Robin Hood: Men in Tights; Conflict of Interest. **1994:** Surviving the Game; Silence of the Hams; Beverly Hills Cop 3; One Woman's Courage (tv). **1995:** Panther; Money Train; The Crossing Guard. **1996:** The Glimmer Man; Mars Attacks!; Jingle All the Way; Set It Off. *Television*—Mission: Impossible; The Rockford Files; The Invisible Man; Mork & Mindy; Hawaii Five-O; Boston & Kilbride; The Fall Guy; Knight Rider; Young Indiana Jones.

CINDY FOLKERSON
(b. 1956)

The daughter of stuntman Robert Folkerson, Cindy is a member of the United Stuntwoman's Association. She has doubled for Rosanna Arquette and Samantha Mathis.

Films—**1982:** Poltergeist. **1984:** Red Dawn. **1985:** Clue; Silverado. **1986:** 8 Million Ways to Die. **1988:** Sunset. **1990:** The Adventures of Ford Fairlane; The Rookie. **1991:** The Naked Gun 2 1/2; Mobsters; The Borrower; Timebomb. **1992:** Ruby; Honey, I Blew Up the Kid; Whispers in the Dark; Sleepwalkers. **1994:** Wolf. **1995:** The Stars Fell on Henrietta. **1996:** Broken Arrow; Norma Jean & Marilyn; Poison Ivy—The New Seduction.

BOBBY FOXWORTH

An independent stunt coordinator and second unit director, Foxworth has performed stunts for Don Johnson.

Films—**1982:** Megaforce. **1985:** Invasion USA. **1986:** Band of the Hand. **1988:** Sweetheart's Dance. **1989:** Let It Ride. **1990:** Pacific Heights. **1991:** Harley Davidson & the Marlboro Man; Mission of the Shark (tv); The Take (tv); Red Wind (tv). **1992:** Honey, I Blew Up the Kids; Pure Country. **1993:** Sniper. **1994:** Army of One; Night of the Running Man;

Speed; The Specialist. **1995:** The Criminal Mind; Just Cause; Houseguest. **1996:** Eye for an Eye; Spy Hard; Public Enemies. *Television*—CHiPs; Miami Vice; Wiseguy.

RICHIE GAONA

Onetime trainer for the "Circus of the Stars," Gaona's son Alex has also performed stunts.

Films—**1989:** Back to the Future 2. **1990:** Kindergarten Cop. **1991:** Hook. **1992:** American Me; Poison Ivy; Out on a Limb; Mission of Justice. **1993:** Falling Down; Surf Ninjas; Coneheads. **1994:** The Naked Gun 33 1/3; North; Clear & Present Danger; The Mask; Wes Craven's New Nightmare; Ice. **1995:** Desperado. **1996:** Spy Hard; Fled; Raven.

DONNA GARRETT
(b. 1944)

A former physical education major and wife of stuntman Ralph Garrett, Donna doubled actress Raquel Welch for a number of years. She has also stood in for the likes of Barbra Streisand, Karen Black, Jackie Bisset, Kate Jackson, and Angie Dickinson.

Films—**1966:** Fantastic Voyage. **1967:** Fathom. **1968:** Bandolero. **1969:** Flare-Up; 100 Rifles. **1970:** Airport; Myra Breckinridge. **1971:** Star Spangled Girl; Diamonds Are Forever. **1972:** What's Up, Doc?; Portnoy's Complaint; Kansas City Bomber; The Poseidon Adventure; The Getaway. **1974:** Earthquake; Wonder Woman (tv). **1976:** Mother, Jugs, & Speed; Death Trap; Dr. Black, Mr. Hyde; Drum; Logan's Run. **1977:** Blue Sunshine; Out-law Blues; Opening Night. **1978:** Comes a Horseman. **1980:** How to Beat the High Cost of Living; Melvin & Howard; The Gong Show Movie; Midnight Madness. **1981:** Charlie Chan & the Curse of the Dragon Queen; All Night Long; Deadly Blessing; Halloween 2. **1982:** Tron; Poltergeist. **1983:** The Osterman Weekend. **1984:** Footloose; Her Life as a Man (tv). **1986:** Blue City; Invaders from Mars; Wildcats; The Golden Child. **1987:** Blind Date; Throw Momma from the Train; Private Investigations. **1988:** Maniac Cop; Twins; Freeway. **1989:** CHUD; Pet Sematary; Ghostbusters 2. **1990:** Megaville; Kindergarten Cop. **1992:** Hero. **1994:** Puppetmasters. **1995:** The Tie That Binds. *Television*—Lassie; Lost in Space; The Green Hornet; Star Trek; Mission: Impossible; Dan August; Policewoman; Charlie's Angels; The Man from Atlantis; Cagney & Lacey; Scarecrow & Mrs. King.

RALPH GARRETT
(b. 1937)

A stunt coordinator and bit player who got into stunts after service in the Army, Garrett has doubled for Jon Voigt and Ryan O'Neal.

Films—**1972:** Deliverance. **1973:** Soylent Green. **1974:** Earthquake. **1979:** The Electric Horseman. **1980:** How to Beat the High Cost of Living. **1982:** Partners; The Sword & the Sorcerer. **1985:** Moving Violations. **1986:** Raw Deal; Ruthless People; Jumpin' Jack Flash. **1987:** Million Dollar Mystery; Remote Control. **1988:** Rambo 3; Alien Nation; Two Moon Junction; In Dangerous Company. **1989:** Glory; Casualties of War. **1990:** Wild at Heart. **1993:** No Place to Hide. *Television*—Voyage to the Bottom of the Sea; Land of the Giants; Chopper One; The Rockford Files; Nancy Drew.

Jerry Gatlin takes a fall for Tab Hunter in 1956's *The Burning Hills*.

JERRY GATLIN
(b. 1933)

This Colorado-born supporting player and stunt coordinator entered films after time on the rodeo circuit and service in the Army's Mountain Ski Troop. A double for Tab Hunter and Earl Holliman, Gatlin eventually became a recognizable face in Westerns, giving his best role as one of John Wayne's partners in *The Train Robbers*. Married to stuntwoman Patti Burson, he's a member of the Stuntmen's Association.

Films—**1956:** The Burning Hills. **1957:** Gunfight at the O.K. Corral. **1959:** Last Train from Gun Hill. **1960:** The Magnificent Seven. **1961:** Posse from Hell. **1964:** Cheyenne Autumn. **1965:** Major Dundee; The Hallelujah Trail; The Sons of Katie Elder. **1966:** Nevada Smith; An Eye for and Eye. **1968:** Run, Appaloosa, Run; Blue; Five Card Stud; Bandolero; Will Penny. **1969:** The Good Guys & the Bad Guys; The Undefeated. **1970:** Little Big Man; Dirty Dingus Magee. **1971:** Big Jake; Shootout. **1972:** Buck & the Preacher; The Cowboys; The Culpepper Cattle Company; The Honkers; The Legend of Nigger Charley; Ulzana's Raid. **1973:** The Don Is Dead; The Train Robbers; Cahil, U.S. Marshal. **1974:** Mame; Blazing Saddles. **1975:** Bite the Bullet; Rooster Cogburn; The Hindenburg; Nevada Smith (tv). **1976:** The Duchess & the Dirtwater Fox; The Great Scout & Cathouse Thursday. **1978:** F.I.S.T.; Convoy; Wolf Lake. **1979:** Prophecy. **1980:** Coast to Coast; The Mountain Men; Cattle Annie & Little Britches. **1981:** The Legend of the Lone Ranger. **1982:** Ruckus. **1983:** Spacehunter; Sudden Impact; Cowboy (tv). **1984:** George Washington (tv). **1985:** Pale Rider; Silverado; Sylvester. **1986:** Band of the Hand; The Three Amigos; Poltergeist 2. **1987:** Wanted: Dead or Alive. **1988:** Ernest Saves Christmas; Blood Red; Lucky Stiff. **1989:** Glory. **1990:** Lord of the Flies; Sibling Rivalry. **1991:** City Slickers. **1992:** Far & Away. **1993:** Jack the Bear. **1994:** The Shawshank Redemption; Cobb. **1996:** Ruby Jean & Joe. *Television*—Have Gun, Will Travel; Hotel de Paree; Hondo; Gunsmoke; The FBI; Bonanza.

GREG GAULT

A member of the International Stunt Association, Gault has coordinated stunts and performed bit parts.

Films—1976: The Capture of Bigfoot. 1981: Butterfly. 1982: Megaforce. 1983: Under Fire. 1985: Black Moon Rising; Invasion USA. 1986: The Delta Force; King Kong Lives. 1987: Back to the Beach; The Hidden; House of the Rising Sun. 1988: Bulletproof; Hero & the Terror; Feds; A Tiger's Tale; Body Beat. 1989: Shocker; Spontaneous Combustion; L.A. Bounty. 1991: The Taking of Beverly Hills; The Perfect Weapon; McBain; Soldier's Fortune. 1992: 3 Ninjas; Live Wire; Dead Center (aka Crazy Joe). 1993: Sniper. 1994: Robin Cook's Virus (tv); Come Die with Me (tv). 1996: Eraser. *Television*—FBI, the Untold Story.

JAMES GAVIN
(b. 1932)

Ace chopper pilot flew evac missions during the Korean War and later for the U.S. Forest Service, where his skills were recruited for a film. He became a supporting player and member of the Stuntmen's Association, often listing himself as Gavin James when given dialogue.

Films—1956: The Werewolf. 1959: The Gazebo; Face of a Fugitive. 1960: Key Witness. 1961: The Misfits. 1963: Rampage. 1965: My Blood Runs Cold. 1968: Coogan's Bluff. 1969: A Man Called Gannon. 1970: The Other Man (tv). 1971: Wild Rovers; Vanishing Point; Escape From the Planet of the Apes. 1972: Hickey & Boggs. 1973: The All-American Boy; Hijack (tv); Set This Town on Fire (tv); The President's Plane Is Missing (tv); Birds of Prey (tv); Chase (tv). 1974: The Towering Inferno; Dirty Mary, Crazy Larry; Earthquake; Airport '75; Nightmare (tv). 1975: Breakout. 1977: Black Sunday; Heroes; The Domino Principle; Airport '77; Mr. Billion; Rollercoaster; The Gauntlet; Fire (tv). 1978: Who'll Stop the Rain. 1979: Concorde, Airport '79; Hanging By a Thread (tv); Disaster on the

Coastliner (tv). 1980: The Nude Bomb; When Time Ran Out; Raise the Titanic; Seems Like Old Times; The Return of Frank Cannon (tv); The Great Cash Giveaway Getaway (tv). 1982: The Border; Night Crossing; Hanky Panky. 1983: Blue Thunder; Uncommon Valor; Get Crazy. 1986: Short Circuit. 1987: Number One with a Bullet. 1988: Mac & Me; Alien Nation; Tequila Sunrise; The Blob; The Dead Pool. 1989: Always; Lethal Weapon 2. 1990: Bird on a Wire; Die Hard 2; Taking Care of Business; Last of the Finest; The Adventures of Ford Fairlane; The Rookie. 1991: Toy soldiers; True Identity; Doublecrossed. 1992: Radio Flyer; Folks. 1993: A Perfect World; The Pelican Brief. 1995: Assassins. 1996: Mulholland Falls; Chain Reaction. *Television*—Jane Wyman; Kraft Theatre; Zane Grey Theatre; Tales of the Texas Rangers; Cheyenne; Tales of Wells Fargo; Rawhide; Suspicion; The Lineup; Dragnet; Two Faces West; Cain's Hundred; M Squad; The Big Valley; The Wild Wild West; Mission: Impossible; The High Chaparral; The Name of the Game; Night Gallery; Adam-12; Emergency; Chase; Chopper One; The Rockford Files; The Six Million Dollar Man; McCloud; SWAT; The Bionic Woman; Baa Baa Black Sheep; Blue Thunder.

STEVE GERAY

An independent stunt coordinator and aerial expert, Geray has worked on several top-drawer action films.

Films—1987: Nadine; Desperado (tv). 1988: Alien Nation; Made in U.S.A.; The Dead Pool; The Nest. 1989: Under the Gun; Pink Cadillac. 1990: Robocop 2. 1991: The Naked Gun 2 1/2; The Doors. 1992: Class Act; Universal Soldier. 1993: In the Line of Fire. 1994: The Last Ride (aka F.T.W.); A Low Down Dirty Shame. 1995: Die Hard with a Vengeance; Mad Love.

ALAN GIBBS
(b. 1941; d. 1988)

A former bartender and motorcyclist, Gibbs became a Hal Needham protégé and developed into a top stunt coordinator and second unit director, performing the famous car jump in *Smokey and the Bandit,* Dustin Hoffman's horse transfer in *Little Big Man,* and a magnificently timed two-story fall into a moving wagon for *Judge Roy Bean.* He doubled for the likes of Burt Reynolds, Charles Bronson, and Jack Nicholson before succumbing to cancer.

Films—**1968:** The Green Berets; Chubasco; Hellfighters; The Savage Seven. **1969:** The Undefeated; The Great Bank Robbery; The Good Guys & the Bad Guys. **1970:** Little Big Man; C.C. & Co.; Beneath the Planet of the Apes; Angel Unchained. **1971:** Sometimes a Great Notion (aka Never Give an Inch); The Jesus Trip. **1972:** Ulzana's Raid; The Life & Times of Judge Roy Bean; Conquest of the Planet of the Apes; The Mechanic. **1973:** The Man Who Loved Cat Dancing; Electra Glide in Blue; Scorpio; The Stone Killer; Battle for the Planet of the Apes. **1974:** Chinatown; The Midnight Man; Death Wish; Crazy Mama; Three the Hard Way; One Flew Over the Cuckoo's Nest. **1975:** Mitchell; Cleopatra Jones & the Casino of Gold. **1976:** Massacre at Central High; Cannonball; Nickelodeon; Jigsaw John (tv). **1977:** Smokey & the Bandit. **1978:** Straight Time; Convoy; The Bermuda Triangle (tv). **1980:** Heaven's Gate; Hangar 18. **1981:** The Postman Always Rings Twice; The Pursuit of D.B. Cooper; The Cannonball Run. **1982:** The Border; Fighting Back. **1983:** Lone Wolf McQuade; Nat'l Lampoon's Class Reunion; Terms of Endearment; Scarface. **1984:** The Ice Pirates; The Cannonball Run 2; The River. **1985:** The Protector. **1986:** Armed & Dangerous. **1987:** Big Shots; Down Twisted; Ironweed; The Witches of Eastwick. **1988:** The Wrong Guys; Shakedown; Crocodile Dundee 2. *Television*— The Girl from U.N.C.L.E.; Mannix; The Immortal; Mission: Impossible; Vegas; CHiPs; 240 Robert; Alex & the Dobermans; Beauty & the Beast.

BEAU GIBSON

Films—**1975:** Race with the Devil; The Runaway Barge (tv). **1976:** A Small Town in Texas; Hollywood Man; Ode to Billy Joe. **1977:** Stunts. **1978:** Return from Witch Mountain; Steel Cowboy (tv). **1985:** Black Moon Rising. **1986:** Wisdom. **1987:** The Wild Pair; The Hidden. **1988:** Bulletproof. **1991:** Soldier's Fortune.

LANCE GILBERT

A stunt coordinator and member of Stunts Unlimited, Lance often works on films in which his father Mickey is in charge. He has doubled for Stephen Baldwin.

Films—**1988:** Above the Law; Freeway. **1989:** Old Gringo; Renegades. **1990:** Tremors; Problem Child; Young Guns 2. **1991:** Barton Fink; Driving Me Crazy; Point Break; City Slickers; Cool as Ice; Beastmaster 2; Diplomatic Immunity. **1992:** Last of the Mohicans; Hero; Under Siege. **1993:** Striking Distance; The Last Action Hero; Cop & a Half; Ghost in the Machine. **1994:** True Lies; Double Dragon; Puppetmasters; The Cisco Kid (tv). **1995:** The Road Killers; Waterworld; Virtuosity. **1996:** From Dusk Till Dawn; Heaven's Prisoners; The Nutty Professor; Fled; A Time to Kill; The Long Kiss Goodnight; Pure Danger. *Television*—The Fall Guy; Baywatch; The Flash; Baywatch Nights; Paradise.

Top: Alan Gibbs jumps a car in 1976's *Cannonball. Bottom:* Action scenes in *Cannonball* coordinated by Alan Gibbs.

MICKEY GILBERT

Top stunt coordinator and second unit director, Gilbert was a rodeo cowboy before committing himself to stunts full-time in the late sixties. The son-in-law of Joe Yrigoyen, he doubled regularly for the likes of Robert Redford and Gene Wilder, as well as Lee Majors on the television series "The Fall Guy." We saw him jumping from a moving train to an overhead signal in *Silver Streak,* immortalized weekly on the Majors show. His three sons often work with him.

Films—**1959:** Ben Hur. **1967:** Africa, Texas Style. **1969:** The Wild Bunch; The Undefeated; Butch Cassidy & the Sundance Kid. **1970:** Little Big Man; The Ballad of Cable Hogue; Beneath the Planet of the Apes. **1971:** Sometimes a Great Notion (aka Never Give an Inch). **1972:** Joe Kidd; Pocket Money; When Legends Die; Junior Bonner. **1973:** The Don Is Dead; The Sting; Cleopatra Jones; Westworld. **1974:** The Towering Inferno; Mame; Blazing Saddles; Earthquake. **1975:** The Wind & the Lion; The Great Waldo Pepper; Rooster Cogburn. **1976:** Silver Streak; Return of a Man Called Horse. **1977:** The World's Greatest Lover; Fire Sale. **1978:** FM; The Fury; Who'll Stop the Rain; Hooper; Our Winning Season; Stranger in Our House (tv). **1979:** The Apple Dumpling Gang Rides Again; The Promise; Concorde, Airport '79; Buck Rogers in the 25th Century; The Electric Horseman; The Frisco Kid; The Prisoner of Zenda. **1980:** The Blues Brothers; Brubaker; Stir Crazy; Little Miss Marker; Gorp; Stunts Unlimited (tv). **1981:** All the Marbles; Hard Country; Honkytonk Freeway; The Intruder Within (tv). **1982:** Swamp Thing; Fast Times at Ridgemont High. **1983:** Blue Thunder. **1985:** Wild Horses (tv). **1986:** The Golden Child; Night of the Creeps; Eye of the Tiger. **1987:** Harry & the Hendersons. **1988:** Little Nikita; Above the Law; Moving; Freeway; The Milagro Beanfield War. **1989:** Kinjite; Listen to Me; Old Gringo; Renegades. **1990:** We're No Angels; Young Guns 2; Problem Child; Coup de Ville. **1991:** Barton Fink; City Slickers. **1992:** Freejack; Last of the Mohicans; Brain Donors; Hero. **1993:** Striking Distance; Fire in the Sky; The Ghost in the Machine; Blindsided (tv). **1994:** When a Man Loves a Woman; City Slickers 2; Wes Craven's New Nightmare. **1995:** Forget Paris; Waterworld; Apollo 13; Last Man Standing. **1996:** Spy Hard; The Nutty Professor; Little Panda; A Time to Kill. *Television*— The Man & the Challenge; The Man from U.N.C.L.E.; Cowboy in Africa; The Night Stalker; Wonder Woman; The Quest; Gemini Man; Vegas; The Fall Guy; Baywatch.

TIM GILBERT

Films—**1985:** Invasion USA; Fletch. **1986:** Sweet Liberty; Legal Eagles; Never Too Young to Die; Stagecoach (tv). **1987:** Morgan Stewart's Coming Home; Heat; Less Than Zero; Timestalkers (tv). **1988:** Shakedown; Crocodile Dundee 2; Above the Law; Tequila Sunrise. **1989:** Old Gringo; Renegades; Cyborg. **1990:** Problem Child. **1991:** City Slickers. **1992:** Last of the Mohicans; Hero. **1993:** Striking Distance; Full Eclipse; Ghost in the Machine. **1994:** Beverly Hills Cop 3; Clean Slate; City Slickers 2; Killing Zoe; The Expert; Dead Badge. **1996:** The Nutty Professor.

TROY GILBERT

A stunt coordinator son of Mickey Gilbert, Troy has doubled regularly for Kiefer Sutherland. He's a member of Stunts Unlimited.

Films—**1986:** Legal Eagles. **1988:** Above the Law. **1989:** Old Gringo; Renegades;

We're No Angels. **1990:** Young Guns 2; Pump Up the Volume; Problem Child; Coup de Ville. **1991:** Highway to Hell; Career Opportunities; City Slickers. **1992:** Last of the Mohicans. **1993:** Striking Distance; The Vanishing; The Ghost in the Machine. **1994:** When a Man Loves a Woman; True Lies; City Slickers 2; The Cowboy Way; Double Dragon; Puppetmasters. **1995:** Class of '61. **1995:** Waterworld; Virtuosity; The Sweeper; Eye for an Eye. **1996:** From Dusk Till Dawn; The Nutty Professor; Freeway; Fled; A Time to Kill; Crazy Horse.

JOE GILBRIDE

Films—**1984:** The Exterminator 2. **1985:** Invasion USA. **1986:** Hollywood Vice Squad; King Kong Lives; The Boss's Wife. **1987:** No Safe Haven; Steele Justice; The Untouchables; Nightmare on Elm Street 3: Dream Warriors; Dudes; The Hidden. **1988:** Bulletproof; Bad Dreams; The New Adventures of Pippi Longstocking; Child's Play; Fright Night 2; They Live; Heartbreak Hotel. **1989:** Sonny Boy; L.A. Bounty; Tango & Cash; The Revenge of Al Capone (tv). **1990:** Satan's Princess; Chattahoochee.

ANDY GILL

A stunt coordinator and younger brother of Jack Gill, Andy is a member of the Professional Driver's Association.

Films—**1985:** Invasion USA. **1986:** Legal Eagles; Firewalker; Never Too Young to Die; Radioactive Dreams. **1987:** Assassination; Down Twisted. **1988:** Maniac Cop; Bulletproof; Dead Heat; Tequila Sunrise; The Dead Pool; They Live; Tripwire. **1989:** Hit List; Cohen & Tate; One Man Force; Night Game; Night Life; Pink Cadillac. **1990:** Almost an Angel; Delta Force 2; Satan's Princess; Rainbow Drive;

Maniac Cop 2; The Ambulance. **1991:** The Taking of Beverly Hills; Highlander 2; Hook; McBain; Beastmaster 2; Fast Getaway; 976 Evil 2; Highway to Hell; Cool as Ice; Driving Me Crazy. **1992:** Sleepwalkers; Innocent Blood. **1993:** Striking Distance; Hot Shots Part Deux; The Temp; In the Line of Fire; Calendar Girl; A Perfect World; Maniac Cop 3. **1994:** The Naked Gun 33 1/3; Sioux City; Airheads; Streetfighter; A Low Down Dirty Shame; Dead Badge. **1995:** 3 Ninjas Knuckle Up; Tall Tale; Congo; Species; Money Train; Last Man Standing; Nemesis 3; The Sweeper. **1996:** Lawnmower Man 2; The Rock; Pure Danger.

JACK GILL
(b. 1952)

A stunt coordinator, second unit director, and member of the Professional Driver's Association, this Georgia-native and former motocross racer/thrill circus performer has doubled for television stars John Schneider and David Hasselhoff. He is married to actress Morgan Brittany.

Films—**1976:** Gator. **1979:** Rock 'n' Roll High School; The Jerk; 1941; Samurai (tv). **1980:** In God We Trust; The Exterminator; Just Before Dawn. **1981:** The Gangster Chronicles (tv). **1982:** Megaforce; Fighting Back; First Blood; Masada (tv). **1983:** The Loveless. **1984:** The Joy of Sex. **1987:** Assassination. **1988:** Shakedown; Crocodile Dundee 2; Tequila Sunrise; Elvira, Mistress of the Dark; A Time of Destiny; Turner & Hooch. **1989:** L.A. Bounty; One Man Force; Easy Wheels. **1990:** Stella; Stanley & Iris; Almost an Angel; Robocop 2; Rainbow Drive; Maniac Cop 2. **1991:** The Taking of Beverly Hills; Hook; 976 Evil 2; Highway to Hell; Cool as Ice; McBain. **1992:** Mo' Money. **1993:** Extreme Justice; Streetknight; Untamed Heart; In the Line of Fire; Rising Sun; Calendar Girl; The Good Son; Maniac

Cop 3; Nowhere to Run; The Fire Next Time (tv). **1994:** A Gnome Named Norm; Getting Even with Dad; Richie Rich; I Love Trouble; Puppetmasters; Dead Badge. **1995:** 3 Ninjas Knuckle Up; Money Train; Last Man Standing; The Sweeper. **1996:** The Rock; The First Wives Club; Riot; Jack. *Television*—Battlestar Galactica; The Love Boat; The Dukes of Hazzard; The Fall Guy; Knight Rider.

JOHN GILLESPIE

A former law enforcement officer and Navy veteran, Gillespie has worked as an animal trainer, aerial stunt coordinator, weapons specialist, and double for Fred Ward.

Films—**1974:** Cro-Magnon (tv). **1977:** The Island of Dr. Moreau. **1978:** Savage Journey (aka Brigham Young); Ziegfield (tv); Greatest Heroes of the Bible (tv). **1981:** Savage Harvest. **1984:** The Ice Pirates. **1987:** They Still Call Me Bruce; Commando Squad; Hell Comes to Frogtown; Programmed to Kill; Defense Play. **1988:** Mac & Me; Miracle Mile; I Saw What You Did (tv). **1989:** Chopper Chicks in Zombie Town; Checkered Flag; Riding the Edge. **1990:** Tremors. **1991:** Mannequin 2; Barton Fink; The Grifters; Diplomatic Immunity. **1992:** Hero. **1993:** Aspen Extreme; Super Mario Bros.; The Last Mafia Marriage (tv). **1994:** The River Wild. **1995:** The Usual Suspects; Beastmaster 3; Spirit. **1996:** Livers Ain't Cheap. *Television*—The Rockford Files; The Six Million Dollar Man; The Incredible Hulk; CHiPs; M*A*S*H; "V"; The Rousters; Remington Steele; Crazy Like a Fox; Alfred Hitchcock; Amazing Stories; Perry Mason.

SANDY GIMPEL

A member of the United Stuntwoman's Association, Gimpel has co-ordinated stunts and directed second unit. She has doubled for Kate Mulgrew.

Films—**1966:** A Fine Madness. **1967:** The Gnome-Mobile. **1977:** Sixth & Main. **1978:** Avalanche. **1979:** Battlestar Galactica; Prophecy; Tourist Trap. **1980:** Resurrection; Inside Moves; Survival Run; Airplane; Brave New World (tv). **1981:** Honkytonk Freeway. **1982:** The Escape Artist. **1984:** Night of the Comet. **1985:** Hellhole; Commando; Moving Violations. **1986:** Reform School Girls; KGB: The Secret War. **1987:** The Lost Boys; My Demon Lover; The Killing Time; Death Spa. **1988:** Seven Hours to Judgment; Above the Law; Elvira, Mistress of the Dark; Waxworks; Twins. **1989:** The Burbs; Nat'l Lampoon's Christmas Vacation. **1990:** Joe vs. the Volcano; The Adventures of Ford Fairlane; Keaton's Cop. **1991:** The People Under the Stairs; Disaster in Time. **1992:** Stop! Or My Mom Will Shoot. **1994:** The Stand (tv). **1996:** The Rock; Jingle All the Way. *Television*—Lost in Space; Battlestar Galactica; Kate Loves a Mystery; Otherworld; Harts of the West.

AL GOTO

A member of the International Stunt Association, this Asian actor has played a number of bit parts in a relatively short period of time.

Films—**1989:** Cage; Street Asylum; Black Rain. **1990:** Vietnam, Texas; Hard to Kill; Come See the Paradise; Circuitry Man; The Rookie; Prayer of the Rollerboys; The Chinatown Connection. **1991:** The Naked Gun 2 1/2; Showdown in Little Tokyo; The Perfect Weapon; Flight of the Intruder; Leather Jackets; Border of the Tong; Intimate Stranger. **1992:** Kuffs; Rapid Fire; Buffy, The Vampire Slayer; 3 Ninjas; Inside Edge; Mission of Justice; Davinci's War. **1993:** Hot Shots Part Deux;

Dragon; Another Stakeout; No Escape, No Return. **1994:** Fist of the North Star; Army of One; The Naked Gun 33 1/3; The Crow; The Shadow; Clear & Present Danger; 3 Ninjas Kick Back; Double Dragon; American Yakuza; Scanners: The Showdown; Hard Vice; Deadly Target. **1995:** Village of the Damned; 3 Ninjas Knuckle Up; The Walking Dead; Blood for Blood; To the Limit; The Immortals. **1996:** Don't Be a Menace.; Escape from L.A.; Back to Back. *Television*—Renegade.

Roughness. **1992:** Trespass; Wayne's World; Universal Soldier; Trancers 3; Wild Orchid 2; Lake Consequence. **1993:** Kiss of a Killer (tv). **1994:** The Last Ride (aka F.T.W.); Blankman; The Specialist; Rise & Walk: The Dennis Byrd Story (tv). **1995:** Destiny Turns on the Radio; Wild Bill; Chameleon. **1996:** Broken Arrow; Independence Day; Last Man Standing; Jerry Maguire. *Television*—Blue Thunder; Mike Hammer; Airwolf; Half Nelson; Misfits of Science.

ALLAN GRAF

A burly supporting player, stunt coordinator, second unit director and member of the Stuntmen's Association, this former football player is most closely associated with action director Walter Hill. Best known for flipping a bus in *Another 48 HRS.*, he has doubled for both Dick Butkus and Randall "Tex" Cobb.

Films—**1976:** Moving Violation. **1978:** The Driver. **1980:** The Long Riders; Roadie; For the Love of It (tv). **1981:** Southern Comfort; The Cannonball Run. **1982:** Fighting Back; Penitentiary 2; I Ought to Be in Pictures; Poltergeist; Star Trek 2: The Wrath of Khan. **1983:** D.C. Cab; White Water Rebels (tv). **1984:** Surf 2; City Heat; Impulse. **1985:** Brewster's Millions; Space Rage; Braker (tv). **1986:** Blue City; Crossroads; Never Too Young to Die; Hamburger, The Motion Picture; Out of Bounds; Back to School; Radioactive Dreams; Assassin (tv). **1987:** Over the Top; Real Men; Raising Arizona; Dragnet; Code Name Zebra; Extreme Prejudice. **1988:** Action Jackson; Sunset; The Presidio; Red Heat; The Wizard of Speed & Time; License to Drive; They Live. **1989:** K-9; Johnny Handsome; The Cover Girl & the Cop (tv). **1990:** Flashback; Come See the Paradise; The Fourth War; Another 48 HRS.; Total Recall. **1991:** Fever; The Butcher's Wife; Necessary

DAVID M. GRAVES

Films—**1985:** Silverado; My Science Project; Rainy Day Friends (aka L.A. Bad). **1987:** The Omega Syndrome; Remote Control; Brenda Starr. **1988:** Maniac Cop; Fright Night 2; Border Heat. **1989:** Night Children; Night Life; Hit List; One Man Force; Relentless. **1990:** The Gumshoe Kid; Die Hard 2; Maniac Cop 2; The Ambulance. **1991:** Mobsters; Fast Getaway. **1993:** Maniac Cop 3. **1996:** Pure Danger; Riot. *Television*—Star Trek, the Next Generation.

MARIAN GREEN

Green has doubled for the likes of Demi Moore, Tyne Daly, and Dana Delaney.

Films—**1982:** The Sender. **1984:** The Terminator. **1987:** Cold Steel; Night Force. **1988:** Night of the Demons; Pumpkinhead. **1989:** L.A. Bounty. **1990:** Hangfire; Predator 2. **1991:** Nothing But Trouble; The Rocketeer; The People Under the Stairs; Freddy's Dead. **1992:** Basic Instinct; Aces: Iron Eagle 3; Reservoir Dogs; Innocent Blood. **1993:** For Their Own Good (tv). **1994:** The Naked Gun 33 1/3; North; Blown Away; Exit to Eden; The Hard Truth. **1995:** Nick of Time. **1996:** Broken Arrow; Spy Hard; The

Nutty Professor; Chain Reaction. *Television*—Cagney & Lacey; L.A. Law.

TED GROSSMAN

This veteran stunt coordinator is most closely associated with the block-buster films of Steven Spielberg and George Lucas. A member of the Stuntmen's Association, he often doubled for Roy Scheider.

Films—**1959:** Compulsion. **1964:** John Goldfarb, Please Come Home. **1969:** Che. **1970:** The Only Game in Town. **1972:** What's, Up Doc?; Conquest of the Planet of the Apes. **1973:** The Don Is Dead; Sssssss; Magnum Force; Battle for the Planet of the Apes. **1974:** The Towering Inferno; The Thief Who Came to Dinner; The Girl from Petrovka; The Sugarland Express. **1975:** Jaws; Night Moves. **1976:** Swashbuckler. **1978:** Jaws 2. **1979:** The Last Embrace; Freedom Road (tv); H.O.T.S. **1980:** Up the Academy; The Island. **1981:** Raiders of the Lost Ark; Charlie Chan & the Curse of the Dragon Queen; Deadly Blessing. **1982:** The Sword & the Sorcerer; E.T. **1983:** Return of the Jedi; Hysterical; Mr. Mom; Flashdance; Two of a Kind. **1984:** Body Double; Oh, God! You Devil; Indiana Jones & the Temple of Doom; Racing with the Moon. **1985:** Cloak & Dagger; The Goonies; Cocoon. **1986:** Sweet Liberty; 52 Pick-Up; Gung Ho; Raw Deal; 8 Million Ways to Die. **1987:** Brenda Starr. **1989:** Indiana Jones & the Last Crusade; Always. **1991:** The Naked Gun 2 1/2; Rush. **1994:** The Naked Gun 33 1/3; Clean Slate. *Television*—Police Woman; Starsky & Hutch; Today's FBI; Dallas.

JEFF HABBERSTAD

A parachutist and skydiving specialist, Habberstad has also coordinated stunts.

Films—**1984:** Nightmare on Elm Street. **1987:** Russkies; The Lost Boys. **1988:** Braddock: Missing in Action 3; Bad Dreams. **1989:** Shocker. **1990:** Delta Force 2. **1991:** The People Under the Stairs; Freddy's Dead. **1992:** Sunset Grill. **1993:** Hot Shots Part Deux; Sidekicks; Dead On; Cyborg 2. **1994:** Sugar Hill; It Could Happen to You; Stargate. **1995:** Tank Girl; Top Dog; Congo; Sudden Death; Steal Big, Steal Little.

RANDY HALL

A supporting player and karate black belt, Hall has doubled for Patrick Swayze. He's a member of the International Stunt Association.

Films—**1985:** Black Moon Rising. **1986:** American Justice (aka Jackals); Never Too Young to Die; King Kong Lives. **1987:** The Wild Pair; Prince of Darkness; The Lost Boys; Kidnapped. **1988:** Die Hard; They Live. **1989:** Road House. **1990:** Navy Seals; Dick Tracy; Die Hard 2; Desperate Hours; Predator 2. **1991:** Eve of Destruction; The Doors; Ambition; Deadlock; The Servants of Twilight; The Last Boy Scout. **1992:** Thunderheart. **1993:** Hard Target; Free Willy; Demolition Man. **1994:** Renaissance Man; Wagons East; A Low Down Dirty Shame; Star Trek Generations; Night of the Running Man. **1995:** Tank Girl; Congo; One Man's Justice. **1996:** From Dusk Till Dawn; Barb Wire; Bulletproof; Ravenhawk; Sunchaser.

JAMES M. HALTY

A member of Stunts Unlimited, Halty has directed second unit and worked as a stunt coordinator. He's doubled for both Don Johnson and Bill Paxton.

Films—**1970:** Little Big Man. **1975:** Crazy Mama. **1976:** Drum. **1977:** The Choirboys. **1978:** Nat'l Lampoon's Animal House; Casey's Shadow; Corvette Summer. **1980:** The Blues Brothers; Smokey & the Bandit 2. **1981:** Caveman; Body Heat. **1982:** The Border; Blade Runner; Fighting Back. **1983:** D.C. Cab; Stroker Ace; Scarface; The Star Chamber. **1984:** Star Trek 3; The Search for Spock; 2010; Ghost Warrior (aka Swordkill). **1985:** To Live & Die in L.A.; Secret Admirer; Moving Violations. **1987:** The Wild Pair; Over the Top; Number One with a Bullet; The Untouchables; Night Force; Code Name Zebra. **1988:** The Seventh Sign; Patty Hearst; I'm Gonna Git You Sucka; License to Drive; Alien from L.A. **1989:** Star Trek 5: The Final Frontier; Caddyshack 2; K-9; Lethal Weapon 2; The Wizard; Road House; Dead Bang; Tango & Cash. **1990:** The Hot Spot; Almost an Angel; Impulse; Heart Condition; Die Hard 2; Last of the Finest; Dollman; Predator 2; A Girl to Kill For. **1991:** Bill & Ted's Bogus Journey; Hook; Don't Tell Mom the Babysitter's Dead; Ricochet. **1992:** Memoirs of an Invisible Man; Radio Flyer; American Me; Patriot Games; Captain Ron. **1993:** Full Eclipse; The Last Action Hero; Demolition Man; The Ballad of Little Jo. **1994:** Midnight Ride. **1995:** Bye Bye Love; Apollo 13; Waterworld; Virtuosity. **1996:** Twister; The Rock; Courage Under Fire.

DICK HANCOCK

A Texas-born stunt coordinator and former auto racer, Hancock is a member of the Stuntmen's Association.

Films—**1982:** Split Image. **1983:** Heart Like a Wheel; Revenge of the Ninja. **1984:** Surf 2. **1985:** Space Rage. **1986:** Pretty in Pink; Tough Guys. **1987:** *batteries not included; Born in East L.A.; Remote Control; Cyclone; Cold Steel. **1988:** Little Nikita; Alien Nation; License to Drive; Turner & Hooch. **1989:** See No

Evil, Hear No Evil; Weekend at Bernie's; Glory; CHUD 2; Phantom of the Mall. **1990:** Robocop 2; Marked for Death; Fear (tv). **1991:** Out for Justice; The Hard Way. **1992:** Deep Cover; Under Siege. **1993:** Hear No Evil; Hard Target; Robocop 3; Weekend at Bernie's 2. **1994:** The Naked Gun 33 1/3; The Cowboy Way; The Shawshank Redemption; Silence of the Hams. **1995:** Batman Forever; Assassins; Devil in a Blue Dress; Strange Days; Casino; Leaving Las Vegas; Ballistic. **1996:** The Crow: City of Angels; Mars Attacks!

TABBY HANSON

This bit-part actress and stunt performer has served as a double for Julia Roberts.

Films—**1991:** The Doors; Hook; Bill & Ted's Bogus Journey. **1993:** Demolition Man; Calendar Girl; The Pelican Brief; Wayne's World 2; Attack of the 50 Foot Woman; Conflict of Interest. **1994:** I Love Trouble; Killing Zoe. **1995:** Destiny Turns on the Radio; Money Train; The Crossing Guard. *Television*—Hunter.

CLIFF HAPPY

A Western specialist and member of the Stuntmen's Association, Happy is the son of stuntman Don Happy. He's doubled for Kevin Costner, Tommy Lee Jones, Dennis Quaid, and Armand Assante.

Films—**1978:** Hooper; Nat'l Lampoon's Animal House; Movie, Movie. **1979:** The Villain. **1980:** The Long Riders. **1981:** Charlie Chan & the Curse of the Dragon Queen. **1983:** Christine; Spacehunter. **1984:** Red Dawn; City Limits. **1985:** Pale Rider; Silverado; Promises to Keep (tv). **1986:** Band of the Hand; Raw Deal; Blue City; The Three Amigos. **1987:** Innerspace. **1988:** Midnight Run; Earth Girls Are Easy. **1989:** Collision Course; Ghostbusters 2; Glory; Pink Cadillac. **1990:** Come See the Paradise; Taking Care of Business; Dangerous Passion (tv). **1992:** Far & Away; Nemesis; Under Siege. **1993:** Posse; Hard Target; Geronimo; Aspen Extreme. **1994:** Lightning Jack; Bad Girls; Blind Justice; Blown Away; Cobb. **1995:** The Good Old Boys. **1996:** Mulholland Falls.

MARGUERITE HAPPY

A member of the United Stuntwoman's Association and sister of Cliff Happy, Marguerite has doubled for Geena Davis, Glenne Headly, and Suzy Amis.

Films—**1983:** Wargames. **1984:** Starman. **1986:** The Three Amigos. **1987:** Wanted: Dead or Alive; Throw Momma from the Train; Remote Control; Dudes. **1988:** Purple People Eater; Twins; Bonanza: The Next Generation (tv). **1990:** Die Hard 2; The Adventures of Ford Fairlane. **1991:** Mortal Thoughts; Thelma & Louise; Cool as Ice. **1992:** Far & Away; Chaplin. **1993:** The Ballad of Little Jo; The Hit List. **1994:** Bad Girls. **1995:** The Set Up.

TOM HARPER

Films—**1982:** The Sender. **1985:** Invasion USA; The Annihilators. **1987:** Death Wish 4. **1989:** Riding the Edge; No Holds Barred. **1990:** Blood Salvage. **1991:** Bill & Ted's Bogus Journey; Point Break; Beethoven. **1992:** Under Siege. **1993:** Robocop 3; The Real McCoy; Gettysburg. **1994:** Maverick; Clear & Present Danger; Puppetmasters. **1995:** Separate Lives; The Road Killers; Waterworld. **1996:** Executive Decision; Freeway; Star Trek, First Contact; The Nutty Professor; Fled; Escape from L.A.; The Glimmer Man.

BOB HARRIS
(b. 1930)

Veteran supporting player and stunt driver, specializing in motorcycle and car stunts. A member of the Stuntmen's Association, he was a regular on the late fifties television show "Troubleshooters," a series that emphasized fast driving.

Films—**1960:** The Alamo; The Crowded Sky. **1965:** Dr. Goldfoot & the Bikini Machine. **1967:** Bonnie & Clyde; Jack of Diamonds. **1968:** Angels from Hell; Speedway; Bullit. **1969:** The Arrangement; The Love Bug; Hell's Angels '69. **1971:** Dirty Harry. **1972:** Evel Knievel; Hit Man; Conquest of the Planet of the Apes; What's Up, Doc? **1973:** Dillinger; The Student Teachers; Magnum Force; I Escaped from Devil's Island; Battle for the Planet of the Apes. **1974:** The Towering Inferno; Truck Turner; The Sugarland Express. **1977:** Herbie Goes to Monte Carlo. **1978:** The Deer Hunter; The Cat from Outer Space; Return from Witch Mountain. **1979:** The China Syndrome. **1982:** The Sword & the Sorcerer. **1984:** Grandview USA; A Flash of Green. **1985:** Commando. **1986:** 52 Pick-Up; The Defiant Ones (tv). **1987:** Wanted: Dead or Alive. **1989:** Second Sight. *Television*—Troubleshooters (reg.); Mannix; Barnaby Jones; Bonanza.

BILL HART

Veteran supporting player and member of the Stuntmen's Association, chiefly seen in Western fare like *The Wild Bunch*. A former rodeo cowboy, he played exactly that on the television series "Stoney Burke."

Films—**1962:** Hero's Island. **1964:** A Distant Trumpet. **1966:** Duel at Diablo. **1967:** Hurry Sundown. **1968:** The Last Challenge; Firecreek. **1969:** The Wild Bunch. **1970:** There Was a Crooked Man. **1972:** The Getaway. **1973:** Pat Garrett & Billy the Kid. **1976:** Drum. **1979:** The Apple Dumpling Gang Rides Again; The Frisco Kid; The Sacketts (tv). **1980:** Tom Horn; The Hunter; Seems Like Old Times; Heaven's Gate. **1981:** Legend of the Lone Ranger; Escape from New York. **1982:** The Beastmaster; The Sword & the Sorcerer. **1983:** Deadly Force; Flicks; The Gambler 2 (tv). **1984:** City Heat. **1985:** Cloak & Dagger. **1986:** Raw Deal; No Mercy. **1987:** Outrageous Fortune; The Bedroom Window; Hell Comes to Frogtown. **1988:** Young Guns; Sunset; Midnight Run; Tequila Sunrise; Scrooged; Dangerous Love; The Wizard of Speed & Time. **1989:** Glory. **1990:** Solar Crisis; Peacemaker; Keaton's Cop. **1991:** Mobsters; Suburban Commando. **1992:** Lethal Weapon 3; Live Wire; Dr. Giggles. **1995:** Separate Lives; The Prophecy. *Television*—Wanted, Dead or Alive; Stoney Burke (reg.); The Outer Limits; Laredo; Gunsmoke; Riding High; The Rockford Files.

STEVE HART

Films—**1988:** They Live. **1989:** Riding the Edge; Tango & Cash. **1990:** Misery; Last of the Finest; Legal Tender. **1991:** The Naked Gun 2 1/2; Hook; Leather Jackets; Double Trouble. **1993:** Sexual Response; Matinee; Cop & a Half. **1995:** Just Cause; Fair Game. **1996:** The Substitute; Dark Breed; First Kid. *Television*—Alien Nation; Walker, Texas Ranger.

GENE HARTLINE

A member of the Stuntmen's Association, Hartline has worked steadily

as a stunt coordinator, supporting player, and big rig specialist. He married stuntwoman Cindy Wills.

Films—**1977:** Grand Theft Auto. **1978:** Deathsport. **1979:** Sunnyside; Fast Charlie, the Moonbeam Rider; Buck Rogers in the 25th Century; Hometown USA; Time After Time; A Time to Die. **1980:** Urban Cowboy; Motel Hell. **1981:** Separate Ways; Four Friends; Smokey Bites the Dust. **1982:** Megaforce; Parasite; Android; The Soldier; Timerider. **1983:** Nightmares. **1984:** Grandview USA; Firestarter; Loveliness; The Terminator; Ghost Warrior (aka Swordkill). **1985:** Friday the 13th: A New Beginning; Certain Fury; Pale Rider; Silverado; Space Rage; Death Wish 3; Return of the Living Dead; Police Academy 2: Their First Assignment; Avenging Angel. **1986:** Maximum Overdrive; Raw Deal; The Three Amigos; That's Life; Eye of the Tiger; Ruthless People; Jumpin' Jack Flash. **1987:** Cherry 2000; Wanted: Dead or Alive; Over the Top; Raising Arizona; Traxx; Innerspace; Code Name Zebra; Remote Control; Made in Heaven. **1988:** Above the Law; Midnight Run; The Blob; The Dead Pool; Ernest Saves Christmas; Miracle Mile. **1989:** Harlem Nights; Next of Kin; The Cover Girl & the Cop (tv). **1990:** Predator 2. **1991:** Stone Cold; Dogfight; Mannequin 2; V.I. Warshawski. **1992:** Thunderheart; Hero. **1993:** The Vanishing; Posse; Wilder Napalm; Ghost in the Machine; Jailbait. **1994:** The Specialist; Cobb; Lakota Woman (tv). **1995:** Tommy Boy; Bad Boys; Mad Love. **1996:** Fled; The Crow: City of Angels; Last Man Standing; Pure Danger; Maximum Risk. *Television*—The Fall Guy.

ORWIN HARVEY

Barrel-chested stunt coordinator and bit player Harvey was a former high diver in the circus before becoming a member of the Stuntmen's

Association. He doubled for the likes of Claude Akins, Lorne Greene, and Leif Erikson.

Films—**1970:** Beneath the Planet of the Apes; Which Way to the Front? **1971:** Diamonds Are Forever. **1972:** Conquest of the Planet of the Apes; The Poseidon Adventure. **1973:** Battle for the Planet of the Apes. **1974:** The Towering Inferno; Earthquake. **1975:** The Eiger Sanction; The Hindenburg. **1976:** Silent Movie; Swashbuckler. **1978:** Every Which Way But Loose; F.I.S.T. **1979:** The Prisoner of Zenda; Stunt Seven (tv). **1980:** The Final Countdown; The Island; The Last Flight of Noah's Ark; Any Which Way You Can. **1982:** The Toy. **1983:** Smokey & the Bandit 3; Women of San Quentin (tv). **1984:** Firestarter. **1985:** D.A.R.Y.L.; The Goonies; To Live & Die in L.A. **1986:** Ratboy; The Golden Child; Slow Burn. **1987:** Amazing Grace & Chuck; Throw Momma from the Train. **1988:** Colors; Midnight Run; The Dead Pool. **1989:** Glory. **1990:** Loose Cannons; Repossessed; Wild at Heart; The Rookie; Secret Agent 00-Soul. **1991:** Eve of Destruction; The Marrying Man; Cast a Deadly Spell. **1992:** Aces: Iron Eagle 3; Sneakers. **1993:** Boiling Point; In the Line of Fire; A Perfect World. **1994:** Cabin Boy. **1995:** Panther. *Television*—Voyage to the Bottom of the Sea; Lost in Space; Time Tunnel; Mannix; Here's Lucy; The High Chaparral; The FBI; Nichols; McMillan & Wife; Kung Fu; Lobo; BJ & the Bear; Hart to Hart; Daniel Boone.

JOHN HATELY

A member of the Stuntmen's Association, Hately is a car and motorcycle specialist.

Films—Deathsport **1978:** Rock 'n' Roll High School **1979:** Megaforce **1982:** Ruckus **1982:** Timerider **1983:** Streets of Fire **1984:** City Limits **1984:** Raw Deal **1986:** Eye of the Tiger **1986:** Innerspace

1987: Defense Play **1988:** Pumpkinhead **1988:** Indiana Jones & the Last Crusade **1989:** The Burbs **1989:** Black Rain **1989:** Robocop 2 **1990:** Another 48 HRS. **1990:** Harley Davidson & the Marlboro Man **1991:** The Butcher's Wife **1991:** Wayne's World **1992:** hard Target **1993:** Speed **1994:** A Low Down Dirty Shame **1994:** Cobb **1994:** The Brady Bunch Movie **1995:** Sudden Death **1995:** Last Man Standing **1995:** The Sweeper **1995:** Eye for an Eye **1996:** The Lawnmower Man 2 **1996:** The **Crow:** City of Angels **1996:** Escape from L.A. **1996:** Bulletproof **1996:** Riot **1996:** Sunchaser 1996

KENT HAYES

A lifetime member of the Stuntmen's Association, Hayes has worked as a bit player and horse wrangler.

Films—**1965:** Young Fury. **1968:** Planet of the Apes. **1969:** The Undefeated; The Good Guys & the Bad Guys; The Great Bank Robbery. **1970:** Beneath the Planet of the Apes; Little Big Man. **1971:** Skin Game. **1972:** The Cowboys. **1979:** The Villain; Butch & Sundance: The Early Days; Concorde, Airport '79. **1981:** Escape from New York. **1982:** The Thing. **1985:** Police Academy 2: Their First Assignment. **1986:** Raw Deal 1986; Maximum Overdrive; Big Trouble in Little China. **1987:** Number One with a Bullet; Innerspace; Planes, Trains, & Automobiles; Remote Control. **1988:** Midnight Run; Halloween 4.

MICHAEL HAYNES
(b. 1944)

A former model for seventies cigarette ads, Haynes entered films as a double for Fabian and was initially ambitious enough to script the biker

Michael Haynes on the lead motorcycle in 1971's *Chrome & Hot Leather.*

flick *Chrome and Hot Leather.* He's a member of the International Stunt Association.

Films—**1967:** Moroc 7. **1968:** Mary Jane. **1969:** The Devil's Eight. **1970:** Scorpio '70; Zigzag; The Dunwich Horror; A Bullet for Pretty Boy. **1971:** Wild Rovers; Chrome & Hot Leather (a/s). **1972:** Hot Summer Week. **1973:** The Girl Who Came Gift Wrapped (tv). **1985:** Black Moon Rising. **1986:** Manhunter; Wisdom; Stagecoach (tv). **1987:** House of the Rising Sun. **1988:** Tripwire. **1990:** Chattahoochee; Ski School. **1991:** Servants of Twilight; True Colors; Deadlock; Writer's Block (tv). **1993:** Cop & a Half; The Temp; Conflict of Interest. **1994:** Wagons East; Star Trek Generations. **1995:** 3 Ninjas Knuckle Up. **1996:** Mohave Moon; Thinner. *Television*—Time Tunnel; CHiPs; Off Duty.

CHUCK HAYWARD

A lifetime member of the Stuntmen's Association, Hayward was one of director John Ford's stock stuntmen/supporting player, labeled "Good Chuck" by the master in comparison to Chuck Roberson's "Bad Chuck." A horsefall specialist, he went on to become a stunt coordinator and second unit director.

Films—**1950:** Wagonmaster; Rio Grande; Tripoli; Rock Island Trail; The Fargo Phantom; Tales of the West. **1951:** Apache Drums. **1952:** Buffalo Bill in Tomahawk Territory; Fort Osage; The World in His Arms. **1953:** Arena; Fair Wind to Java; Hondo; San Antone; The Sun Shines Bright. **1954:** Jubilee Trail; Man with the Steel Whip. **1955:** The Road to Denver. **1956:** The Searchers; Desperados of the West; Red Sundown. **1957:** Run of the Arrow; The Wings of Eagles; Forty Guns; Gun for a Coward; The Unholy Wife. **1958:** The Big Country. **1959:** The Horse Soldiers; Pork Chop Hill; Escort West. **1960:** Spartacus; The Alamo; Sergeant Rutledge. **1961:** Two Rode Together; The Deadly Companions. **1962:** Taras Bulba; Merrill's Marauders; The Man Who Shot Liberty Valance; How the West Was Won.

1963: McLintock. 1964: Cheyenne Autumn. 1965: Major Dundee; The Sons of Katie Elder; The Great Race. 1966: Nevada Smith. 1968: Blue; Five Card Stud; Villa Rides. 1969: True Grit; The Good Guys & the Bad Guys. 1970: Rio Lobo; Chisum. 1971: The Horsemen. 1972: Joe Kidd; Buck & the Preacher; Night of the Lepus. 1973: The Train Robbers; High Plains Drifter. 1974: The Longest Yard; Mame; Blazing Saddles. 1975: Rooster Cogburn; Hustle; Little Moon & Jud McGraw (aka Gone With the West). 1977: March or Die; Airport '77. 1978: Who'll Stop the Rain; The Swarm; Lord of the Rings; The Clonus Horror. 1979: The Frisco Kid. 1980: Tom Horn; The Blues Brothers; Wild Times (tv). 1981: Legend of the Lone Ranger. 1985: Stark (tv). *Television*—Zane Grey Theatre; Doc Holliday; Wagon Train; Black Saddle; Maverick; Wichita Town; Wanted, Dead or Alive; The Outer Limits; Bonaza; Gunsmoke; The men from Shiloh; Kung Fu; Little House on the Prairie; Have Gun, Will Travel.

DANA HEE
(b. 1962)

A former airline hostess, this Louisiana native was a Tae-Kwondo champion at the 1988 Olympics in Seoul. She has doubled for Penelope Ann Miller, Lori Singer, and Pam Anderson.

Films—1993: Undercover Blues; Full Eclipse; Demolition Man. 1994: The Last Ride (aka F.T.W.); The Shadow; Terminal Velocity; Deadly Target. 1995: The Brady Bunch Movie; Last Man Standing; Species; Batman Forever; Jade. 1996: The Lawnmower Man 2; Barb Wire; Independence Day; The Long Kiss Goodnight.

ROBERT B. (BUZZ) HENRY
(b. 1931; d. 1971)

A former child star in Western serials, this rodeo performer wound up as a bit player and stuntman, doubling for the likes of Glenn Ford, Frank Sinatra, and James Coburn. Moving into second unit work, he's best known for laying out the famous bridge stunt in *The Wild Bunch*. He died in a motorcycle accident.

Films—1935: Western Frontier. 1936: The Unknown Ranger. 1937: Rio Grande Ranger; Ranger Courage. 1940: Buzzy Rides the Range. 1941: Buzzy & the Phantom Pinto. 1942: Mr. Celebrity. 1943: Calling Wild Bill Elliot; Chatterbox; Three of a Kind. 1944: Trail to Gunsight; Trigger Trail; The Great Mike. 1945: Her Lucky Night; The Virginian. 1946: Dragonwyck; Danny Boy; Hop Harrigan; Son of the Guardsman; Wild Beauty; Wild West. 1947: King of the Wild Horses; Last of the Redmen; Moonrise. 1948: Tex Grange; Prairie Outlaws; Wild Beauty. 1950: Rocky Mountain; The Blue Grass of Kentucky. 1951: Heart of the Rockies. 1952: Against All Flags. 1953: The Homesteaders; Last of the Pony Riders. 1954: Jubilee Trail; Bamboo Prison; Man with the Steel Whip; The Outcast. 1955: Hell's Outpost; The Indian Fighter; The Road to Denver. 1956: Jubal; Duel at Apache Wells; 54 Washington Street. 1957: The Lawless Eighties; 3:10 to Yuma. 1958: Tonka; The Sheepman; Cowboy; Imitation General. 1959: Face of a Fugitive. 1960: The Rise & Fall of Legs Diamond. 1962: The Manchurian Candidate. 1963: Captain Newman, M.D.; Spencer's Mountain. 1964: Seven Days in May. 1965: Major Dundee; The Rounders; Shenandoah; Von Ryan's Express. 1966: Our Man Flint; Texas Across the River. 1967: El Dorado; In Like Flint; Tony Rome; Waterhole #3. 1969: MacKenna's Gold; The Wild Bunch.

1970: Macho Callahan; Skullduggery. *Television*—The Outer Limits.

BOB HERRON

A member of the Stuntmen's Association, this veteran supporting player and former race car driver doubled Tony Curtis for years. He also stood in for Robert Conrad and later tutored the actor in the screen fights that made him such a popular performer on "The Wild Wild West." Herron remains best known for making a spectacular car jump through the roof of a barn in the film *Convoy*.

Films—**1952:** Cattle Town. **1953:** Gun Fury; Invaders from Mars. **1954:** Four Guns to the Border; Saskatchewan. **1955:** The Far Horizons; The Man from Bitter Ridge. **1956:** Away All Boats; Pillars of the Sky; The Ten Commandments; The Rawhide Years; The Mole People; The Burning Hills. **1957:** The Big Land; Man Afraid. **1959:** Rio Bravo; Westbound. **1960:** Spartacus; Seven Ways from Sundown; The Rise & Fall of Legs Diamond. **1961:** The Great Impostor; The Outsider; Love in a Goldfish Bowl; Portrait of a Mobster. **1962:** The Spiral Road. **1963:** The Slime People. **1964:** A Distant Trumpet; Bullet for a Badman; Gunfight at Comanche Creek. **1965:** Major Dundee; The Great Race. **1966:** An American Dream; Not with My Wife You Don't; Harper. **1967:** Chuka. **1969:** Paint Your Wagon; The Great Bank Robbery; The Wild Bunch. **1970:** Zigzag; There Was a Crooked Man. **1971:** $. **1972:** Joe Kidd; The Groundstar Conspiracy; The Great Northfield Minnesota Raid. **1973:** The Don Is Dead; Cleopatra Jones; Oklahoma Crude. **1974:** Black Samson; Blazing Saddles; Earthquake. **1975:** The Hindenburg; Lepke. **1977:** The Domino Principle; Mr. Billion.

Robert Herron makes a famous car jump through the top of a barn in 1978's *Convoy*, action coordinated by Gary Combs.

1978: Movie, Movie; Convoy; Local Color. 1979: The Black Hole; The Frisco Kid; Flatbed Annie & Sweetie Pie (tv); Stunt Seven (tv). 1980: The Island; Melvin & Howard; The Fifth Floor. 1982: Poltergeist; The Sword & the Sorcerer. 1983: Cujo; Hysterical. 1984: City Heat. 1985: Pale Rider; Explorer. 1986: 52 Pick-Up; The Three Amigos. 1987: The Untouchables; Betrayed; Prince of Darkness. 1988: Sunset; The Seventh Sign; License to Drive; Messenger of Death. 1989: Pet Sematary; Johnny Handsome; Grave Secrets. 1990: I Come in Peace. 1991: Child's Play 3. 1992: Sneakers. *Television*— Hawaiian Eye; Laredo; The Wild Wild West; I Spy; Star Trek; Gunsmoke; Mission: Impossible; Kung Fu.

DON HEWETT

Films—1988: Shakedown. 1989: The January Man; Jacknife. 1990: Night of the Living Dead; Q & A; Blue Steel; Street Hunter. 1991: Mannequin 2; Betsy's Wedding; FX-2; The Hard Way. 1992: Malcolm X; Bob Roberts. 1993: The Music of Chance; The Dark Half; Daybreak. 1994: Body Snatchers; The Hudsucker Proxy; The Professional. 1995: Boys on the Side; Kiss of Death. 1996: Diabolique; Maximum Risk; First Kid; Daylight.

JERRY HEWETT

A member of Stunt Specialists, Hewett has worked as a stunt coordinator and special effects man. He's the brother of Don.

Films—1979: H.O.T.S.; The Wanderers; The Warriors. 1980: Simon; The Exterminator. 1981: The Nesting; Rollover; Wolfen. 1982: The Soldier; Vigilante; Tempest. 1983: The Survivors. 1984: The Exterminator 2; Alphabet City; Firstborn; Preppies; Splash. 1985: Remo Williams; The Stuff. 1986: F/X; Raw Deal; Legal

Eagles; Sid & Nancy; Playing for Keeps; Crocodile Dundee; Fat Guy Goes Nutzoid; Quiet Cool. 1987: Broadcast News; Raising Arizona; My Demon Lover; Deadly Illusion. 1988: Five Corners; Shakedown; Last Rites; Arthur 2: On the Rocks; Miles from Home; Spike of Bensonhurst; Sticky Fingers; Call Me; Internal Affairs (tv). 1989: Cookie; Family Business; Hell High; Ghostbusters 2; Penn & Teller Get Killed; Rude Awakening; See No Evil, Hear No Evil; Bloodhounds of Broadway. 1990: Last Exit to Brooklyn; State of Grace; Cry Baby; Blue Steel; The Lemon Sisters; Miller's Crossing. 1991: The Hard Way; New Jack City; A Kiss Before Dying. 1992: Whispers in the Dark; Light Sleeper; Bob Roberts; Boomerang; Malcolm X; Hoffa. 1993: Ethan Fromme; Romeo Is Bleeding; Mr. Wonderful. 1994: Car 54, Where Are You?; Guarding Tess; The Hudsucker Proxy; The War; Nell. 1995: Safe Passage; Hackers. 1996: Fargo; Independence Day; Sleepers.

EDDIE HICE

A member of the Stuntmen's Association, this veteran stunt coordinator and second unit director was married to the late stuntwoman Patti Elder. He has doubled for Robert Duvall.

Films—1965: Young Fury. 1967: Bonnie & Clyde; First to Fight. 1968: Planet of the Apes; Countdown. 1969: Hell's Belles. 1970: M*A*S*H; Beneath the Planet of the Apes. 1972: The Mad Bomber; Conquest of the Planet of the Apes; The Night Stalker (tv). 1973: The Soul of Nigger Charley; Battle for the Planet of the Apes. 1974: The Towering Inferno; The Front Page; Mame; Earthquake. 1978: Corvette Summer; Lord of the Rings. 1979: Walk Proud. 1980: Borderline; Cheech & Chong's Next Movie. 1981: Charlie Chan & the Curse of the Dragon Queen; True Confessions; Escape from New York. 1982: Vice Squad; The Best Little Whorehouse in Texas; The Sword & the Sorcerer; The Beastmaster. **1983:** Heart Like a Wheel; Deal of the Century; Get Crazy; The Lost Empire. **1984:** Hard to Hold; Repo Man; Ghost Warrior (aka Swordkill). **1985:** Silverado; Crimewave; Hellhole; Avenging Angel. **1986:** Ratboy; Star Trek 4: The Voyage Home; Eye of the Tiger. **1987:** The Night Stalker; Night Force; Wanted: Dead or Alive; Traxx; Survival Game; Remote Control. **1988:** Midnight Run; They Live; Alien from L.A. **1989:** Collision Course; The Burbs; Glory; Always; Nightmare on Elm Street 5: Dream Child. **1990:** Robocop 2; The Rookie. **1991:** Out for Justice. **1992:** Sweet Justice. **1996:** The Cable Guy. *Television*—Gunsmoke; Get Smart; The Mod Squad; The Night Stalker; SWAT; Joe Forrester; The Texan Combat.

FRED HICE
(B. 1957)

The son of Eddie Hice and Patti Elder, Fred has worked as both a stunt coordinator and a second unit director. A member of Stunts Unlimited, he doubled for River Phoenix.

Films—**1974:** Earthquake. **1976:** Dogs; Two Minute Warning. **1978:** Avalanche; Hooper; Animal House. **1979:** Fast Charlie, The Moonbeam Rider; Rocky 2. **1980:** The Blues Brothers; Carny; The Long Riders; Detour to Terror (tv). **1981:** Hell Night. **1982:** Megaforce; Night Shift; The Beastmaster; Grease 2; Rocky 3. **1983:** Heart Like a Wheel; Rumble Fish; Scarface; The Star Chamber. **1984:** Beverly Hills Cop; The Falcon & the Snowman; 2010. **1985:** Into the Night. **1986:** The Hitcher; The Wraith. **1987:** Burglar; Robocop; Lethal Weapon; Beverly Hills Cop 2. **1988:** Maniac Cop; Off Limits; Rambo 3; Tequila Sunrise; The Blob; The Dead Pool; They Live; Alien from L.A. **1989:** Indiana Jones & the Last Crusade; Gleaming the Cube; Lethal Weapon 2; Riding

the Edge; One Man Force; To Die For; Star Trek 5: The Final Frontier; Casualties of War; Dead Bang; Tango & Cash; Lonesome Dove (tv). **1990:** Total Recall; Home Alone; Impulse; Last of the Finest. **1991:** Curly Sue; Only the Lonely; Highway to Hell; Point Break. **1992:** Kuffs; American Me; Rapid Fire; Buffy, the Vampire Slayer; Home Alone 2. **1993:** Dennis the Menace. **1994:** Baby's Day Out; Miracle on 34th Street. **1995:** Bushwhacked; Jade; Nick of Time; Money Train; Grumpier Old Men. **1996:** From Dusk Till Dawn; The Cable Guy; My Fellow Americans. *Television*—Sam.

BILL HICKMAN
(b. 1920; d. 1986)

An expert stunt driver and second unit director, Hickman got his start in "Our Gang" shorts. Best known for his vehicular work in both *Bullit* and *The French Connection,* he was a member of the Stuntmen's Association.

Films—**1943:** Salute to the Marines. **1947:** The Beginning of the End. **1950:** To Please a Lady. **1951:** Angels in the Outfield. **1952:** Fixed Bayonets. **1957:** The Joker Is Wild; Jailhouse Rock. **1958:** Houseboat. **1959:** Don't Give Up the Ship. **1966:** A Fine Madness. **1967:** Point Blank. **1968:** Bullit. **1969:** The Wrecking Crew. **1970:** Daughter of the Mind (tv) 1969; Patton. **1971:** The French Connection. **1972:** What's Up, Doc?; The War Between the Tates; Hickey & Boggs. **1973:** Electra Glide in Blue; The Seven-Ups. **1974:** The Thief Who Came to Dinner. **1975:** The Hindenburg. *Television*—The Twilight Zone; The Fugitive; Voyage to the Bottom of the Sea; The FBI; Klondike; Branded.

CHUCK HICKS
(b. 1927)

Burly, instantly recognizable supporting player has been playing thickheaded toughs for five decades. A former school teacher, Hicks has served as the double for both Aldo Ray and Brian Dennehey.

Films—1952: The Rose Bowl Story; She's Working Her Way Through College; Francis Goes to West Point; Bonzo Goes to College. 1953: Gentlemen Prefer Blondes. 1954: Casanova's Big Night. 1955: Battle Cry; Rebel Without a Cause. 1956: The Girl He Left Behind. 1957: Gunfire at Indian Gap; Designing Woman. 1958: Onionhead; Home Before Dark; The Last Hurrah. 1959: Up Periscope. 1960: The Ice Palace; The Bramble Bush; Sunrise at Campobello. 1961: A Fever in the Blood. 1962: Hell Is for Heroes; The Chapman Report; Merrill's Marauders. 1963: Days of Wine & Roses; PT 109; Wives & Lovers; Shock Corridor; Black Gold. 1965: The Third Day; The Great Race; Johnny Reno; This Property Is Condemned. 1966: A Fine Madness; Not with My Wife You Don't; The Silencers; Our Man Flint; Murderer's Row. 1967: Point Blank; Cool Hand Luke; In Like Flint. 1968: Planet of the Apes; Rogue's Gallery; The Split. 1969: Paint Your Wagon; Where Were You When the Lights Went Out? 1970: The Molly Maguires; There Was a Crooked Man. 1971: Wild Women (tv). 1972: Hound of the Baskervilles (tv). 1973: Slaughter's Big Rip-Off; Magnum Force; Dillinger. 1975: Night Moves; Hard Times. 1976: The Enforcer; Scott Free (tv). 1978: Movie, Movie; Every Which Way But Loose. 1979: Star Trek, the Motion Picture; The Jericho Mile (tv); Stunt Seven (tv); Flesh & Blood (tv). 1980: Hide in Plain Sight; In God We Trust; Bronco Billy; Raging Bull; The Nude Bomb; Cheaper to Keep Her; Beyond Evil; Pleasure Palace (tv); Top of the Hill (tv). 1981: Blood Beach; Blow Out; All the Marbles. 1982: The Sword & the Sorcerer; Star Trek 2: The Wrath of Khan. 1984: City Heat; Johnny Dangerously; Star Trek 3: The Search for Spock; The River Rat. 1985: Runaway Train; George Washington 2 (tv). 1986: Odd Jobs; Legal

Eagles; Native Son. 1987: Best Seller; The Assassin; Programmed to Kill. 1988: Everybody's All-American. 1990: Dick Tracy; Last of the Finest. 1991: Servants of Twilight; FX-2; Bride of Re-Animator; Deadlock. 1992: Article 99; The Double-0 Kid; Sweet Justice. 1993: Streetknight; Bitter Harvest. 1994: The Naked Gun 33 1/3. 1995: The Enemy Within. *Television*—The Untouchables; Cheyenne; Rawhide; The Twilight Zone; Alfred Hitchcock Presents; Gunsmoke; 77 Sunset Strip; The Rogues; Branded; The Man from U.N.C.L.E.; Honey West; The Green Hornet; Mannix; Hogan's Heroes; Mission: Impossible; Nichols; Kung Fu; The Magician; The Manhunter; The Rockford Files; The Six Million Dollar Man; Baretta; Wonder Woman; Starsky & Hutch; Vegas; M*A*S*H; When the Whistle Blows; Fantasy Island; The Powers of Matthew Star; CHiPs; Voyagers; Wizards & Warriors; The Fall Guy; Matt Houston; Blue Thunder; Manimal; Airwolf; Hunter; Star Trek, The Next Generation; In the Heat of the Night; The Flash; Dallas.

JOHN HOCK

A member of the Stuntmen's Association, John is the son of stuntman Peter Hock. He has doubled for Gregory Peck.

Films—1979: The Darker Side of Terror (tv). 1980: The Blues Brothers; Smokey & the Bandit 2; Cattle Annie & Little Britches. 1984: Friday the 13th, a New Beginning; The River; City Limits. 1985: Commando; Band of the Hand; The Journey of Natty Gann. 1986: Blue City; Dangerously Close. 1988: Elvira, Mistress of the Dark; Rambo 3; Blood Red; Earth Girls Are Easy. 1989: Chances Are; Old Gringo; Glory; Next of Kin. 1990: Eternity; Total Recall; Arachnophobia. 1991: Backdraft; Beastmaster 2. 1992: Deep Cover; Far & Away; Four Eyes & Six Guns. 1993: Posse; Tombstone; Weekend at Bernie's 2; Conflict of Interest. 1994:

Lightning Jack; The Cowboy Way. **1995:** Showgirls. **1996:** Riders of the Purple Sage; Crazy Horse; Raven.

PETER HOCK

This East Coast stunt coordinator has frequently worked with director Larry Cohen. He's the father of John Hock and stuntwoman Bonnie Hock.

Films—**1966:** A Man Called Adam. **1967:** Fitzwilly. **1968:** Lady in Cement. **1972:** Across 110th Street. **1976:** God Told Me To (aka Demon). **1982:** Q. **1983:** Trading Places. **1984:** Scream for Help. **1985:** The Stuff. **1986:** F/X. **1987:** Deadly Illusion; My Demon Lover; Return to Salem's Lot. **1988:** Shakedown; Call Me; Masquerade; Homeboy. **1989:** Vampire's Kiss; Black Rain; Jacknife. **1990:** Ghost; The Ambulance. **1993:** The Dark Half.

KANE HODDER
(b. 1955)

Cult favorite supporting player/ stunt coordinator thanks to his donning of Jason's hockey mask in the Friday the 13th films. A fire specialist, Hodder also played Leatherface in the third Texas Chainsaw film. He grew up in the South Pacific.

Films—**1983:** Lone Wolf McQuade. **1984:** Hardbodies; Volunteers; City Limits. **1986:** Nomads; House; Avenging Force; Born to Race; Dream West (tv). **1987:** Prison; House 2; Open House. **1988:** Friday the 13th Part 7: The New Blood; Silent Assassins; Ghost Town; Wax Works. **1989:** Horror Show; Deep Star Six; Best of the Best; Time Trackers. **1989:** Friday the 13th Part 8: Jason Takes Manhattan. **1990:** Leatherface: The Texas Chainsaw Massacre 3; Zandalee; 9 1/2

Ninjas; Backstreet Dreams. **1991:** Roots of Evil; Wax Works 2; House 4; The Rapture; Alligator 2; Out for Justice; Double Trouble. **1992:** Under Siege. **1993:** Best of the Best 2; Demolition Man; Jason Goes to Hell: The Final Friday; Fatherhood; No Place to Hide; Rubdown (tv). **1994:** Pumpkinhead 2; Steel Frontier; A Low Down Dirty Shame; Scanners: The Showdown. **1995:** Just Cause; Seven; Fair Game; Four Rooms; Best of the Best 3. **1996:** Marshal Law; The Fan. *Television*—Emergency: The Dukes of Hazzard; Hill Street Blues; Days of Our Lives; Santa Barbara; Who's the Boss?; The Adventures of Brisco County, Jr.

STEVE HOLLADAY

A member of the Professional Driver's Association, Holladay has coordinated stunts.

Films—**1980:** Smokey & the Bandit 2. **1982:** Megaforce; Grease 2. **1985:** To Live & Die in L.A. **1986:** Out of Bounds; Top Gun; Peggy Sue Got Married. **1987:** Burglar; The Untouchables; The Lost Boys. **1988:** The Seventh Sign; The Blob. **1989:** Tango & Cash. **1990:** Days of Thunder; Last of the Finest. **1992:** Kuffs. **1993:** Full Eclipse. **1994:** The Shadow; Clear & Present Danger. **1995:** The Road Killers; Body Language. **1996:** From Dusk Till Dawn; The Glimmer Man; Bulletproof.

MARCIA HOLLEY

A member of the United Stuntwoman's Association, Holley has doubled for Debra Winger and Juliette Lewis.

Films—**1977:** Damnation Alley. **1980:** Heaven's Gate; Just Before Dawn. **1981:** Hell Night. **1983:** Timerider. **1984:** City Limits. **1985:** Avenging Angel. **1986:** Blue City; Ferris Bueller's Day Off; Legal Eagles; Jumpin' Jack Flash. **1987:** Burglar; Black Widow. **1988:** The Seventh Sign; Illegally Yours; They Live. **1989:** The Abyss; Her Alibi. **1990:** Total Recall. **1991:** My Heroes Have Always Been Cowboy; Cape Fear; The Chase (tv). **1992:** Sweet Justice; Reservoir Dogs; Beyond the Law. **1993:** Wilder Napalm. **1994:** Army of One; Blown Away; Pulp Fiction. **1995:** Showgirls. **1996:** Broken Arrow; The Lawnmower Man 2; The Phantom; Sunchaser.

LARRY HOLT

A member of the Stuntmen's Association, Holt has coordinated stunts and doubled for Roddy McDowall.

Films—**1972:** The Poseidon Adventure; Conquest of the Planet of the Apes. **1973:** Battle for the Planet of the Apes. **1974:** The Towering Inferno; Earthquake. **1975:** Lucky Lady. **1976:** Swashbuckler. **1977:** Rollercoaster; The Man from Atlantis (tv). **1978:** The Manitou; The Norseman. **1979:** The Prisoner of Zenda. **1980:** The Island; Seems Like Old Times; Any Which Way You Can. **1981:** Ghost Story. **1982:** Fast Times at Ridgemont High; The Sword & the Sorcerer. **1982:** The Thing; Tron. **1983:** Return of the Jedi; Class; Sudden Impact. **1984:** Bachelor Party; Firestarter; The Exterminator 2. **1985:** Fandango; Commando; D.A.R.Y.L.; Fright Night; To Live & Die in L.A.; Avenging Angel; Rainy Day Friends (aka L.A. Bad). **1986:** Ratboy; Raw Deal; The Texas Chainsaw Massacre 2; The Golden Child; That's Life; No Mercy; Slow Burn. **1987:** Stacking; The Monster Squad; Best Seller; Traxx; Remote Control; Throw Momma from the Train. **1988:** Colors; Midnight Run; The Dead Pool. **1989:** Collision Course; Ghostbusters 2; Pink Cadillac.

1990: The First Power; Pump Up the Volume; Maniac Cop 2; The Rookie; Secret Agent 00-Soul. **1991:** Eve of Destruction; The Marrying Man; A Rage in Harlem. **1992:** Freejack; Unlawful Entry; Sneakers. **1993:** Amos & Andrew; In the Line of Fire; Undercover Blues; CB4; Robin Hood: Men in Tights. **1994:** Cops & Robersons; Blown Away; Silence of the Hams. **1995:** Separate Lives; Panther; The Tie That Binds; The Crossing Guard. **1996:** Down Periscope; Last Man Standing; Set It Off. *Television*—The Man from Atlantis.

BILLY HANK HOOKER

This son of stuntman Hugh Hooker began his career at the age of nine, often working in tandem with his brother Buddy Joe. A member of Stunts Unlimited, he has also coordinated stunts.

Films—**1977:** Saturday Night Fever; Delta Fox; Empire of the Ants. **1978:** Hooper; Nat'l Lampoon's Animal House. **1979:** Buck Rogers in the 25th Century; Prophecy; Skatetown USA. **1980:** Heaven's Gate; Smokey & the Bandit 2. **1981:** Amy; King of the Mountain; The Incredible Shrinking Woman. **1982:** The Beastmaster; Tron; Lookin' to Get Out. **1983:** Scarface; Rumble Fish; D.C. Cab; Fire & Ice; Private School. **1984:** Beverly Hills Cop. **1985:** Into the Night; Moving Violations; Secret Admirer. **1986:** The Longshot; 8 Million Ways to Die; The Wraith; Out of Bounds; Back to School. **1987:** The Wild Pair; Burglar; Lethal Weapon; Mannequin; Code Name Zebra. **1989:** Lethal Weapon 2; Casualties of War. **1990:** The Guardian; Days of Thunder; Last of the Finest; The Adventures of Ford Fairlane. **1991:** Out for Justice; Thelma & Louise; Terminator 2; Beethoven. **1992:** American

Top: **Jan-Michael Vincent (left) and Burt Reynolds ponder an auto leap in** *Hooper* **(1978).** *Bottom:* **Buddy Joe Hooker makes a world record rocket-propelled car jump for the film** *Hooper.*

Me; Lethal Weapon 3; Rapid Fire; Honey, I Blew Up the Kid. **1993:** The Last Action Hero; Gettysburg. **1994:** Gunmen; Pentathalon; The Chase; The Shadow; Terminal Velocity; In the Army Now; Puppetmasters. **1995:** The Road Killers; Demon Knight; Waterworld; Jade; Houseguest. **1996:** From Dusk Till Dawn; Executive Decision; The Arrival; Eraser; The Rock; The Glimmer Man; Star Trek, First Contact. *Television*—Rin Tin Tin.

BUDDY JOE HOOKER

Top stunt coordinator, second unit director, and supporting player began his career as a child on "Leave It to Beaver." A member of Stunts Unlimited, Buddy Joe doubled regularly for

Jan-Michael Vincent and won an all-around stunt competition in the late seventies. He set a world record for a rocket car jump in the film *Hooper*.

Films—**1969:** Hello, Dolly!; Hell's Angels '69. **1970:** Like It Is. **1971:** Clay Pigeon; Harold & Maude. **1972:** Melinda. **1973:** White Lightning. **1974:** Blazing Saddles; The Castaway Cowboy; The Conversation; Three the Hard Way. **1975:** Trained to Kill, USA (aka No Mercy Man); Rafferty & the Gold Dust Twins; The Strongest Man in the World; Take a Hard Ride; White Line Fever. **1976:** Bound for Glory; Gus; The Treasure of Matecumbe; Vigilante Force; Shadow of the Hawk. **1977:** Close Encounters of the Third Kind; Empire of the Ants; Heroes. **1978:** Hooper; Corvette Summer; The Evil; Paradise Alley; Hot Lead & Cold Feet; KISS Meets the Phantom of the Park (tv). **1979:** The Odd Angry Shot; Game of Death; Prophecy; Hot Rod (tv). **1980:** Defiance; Herbie Goes Bananas; Carny; Serial; Stunts Unlimited (tv). **1981:** Cheech & Chong's Nice Dreams; Search & Destroy; King of the Mountain; The Hand; Sharky's Machine. **1982:** The Entity; First Blood; Tex; Lookin' to Get Out; Parasite; Night Shift. **1983:** D.C. Cab; Beyond the Limit; The Outsiders; The Right Stuff; Rumble Fish; Scarface; To Be or Not to Be. **1984:** Against All Odds. **1985:** Into the Night; To Live & Die in L.A.; Moving Violations; The Zoo Gang. **1986:** F/X.; 8 Million Ways to Die; The Wraith. **1987:** Critical Condition; Burglar; Gardens of Stone; Mannequin; Nowhere to Hide. **1988:** The Presidio; Tucker: The Man & His Dream. **1989:** Gleaming the Cube; Who's Harry Crumb?; Lethal Weapon 2; Road House; Backtrack. **1990:** The Godfather 3; The Guardian; Hard to Kill; Days of Thunder. **1991:** Miami Blues; Beethoven; Thelma & Louise. **1992:** American Me; Lethal Weapon 3; School Ties; Cool World; Jennifer 8; Beyond the Law. **1993:** The Last Action Hero; Demolition Man; Rising Sun; The Ballad of Little Jo; Carlito's Way. **1994:** Gunmen; The Crow; The Chase; The Shadow; Terminal Velocity; Pentathalon. **1995:** The Road Killers; The Hunted; Waterworld; Jade; The Scarlet Letter. **1996:** From Dusk Till Dawn; Executive Decision; Mulholland Falls; The Arrival; Sunchaser; Star Trek, First Contact. *Television*—Leave It to Beaver; The Wild Wild West; Mission: Impossible; The Immortal; Mannix; The Mod Squad; Charlie's Angels; T.J. Hooker; Something Is Out There; Guns of Paradise.

HUGH HOOKER
(b. 1909; d. 1987)

A horse and stagecoach specialist, Hooker doubled for such stars as Gene Autry, John Derek, and Richard Basehart. He also produced the film *The Littlest Hobo,* which won an award at Cannes.

Films—**1945:** Texas Panhandle. **1946:** Gallant Journey; Meet Me on Broadway. **1947:** Dead Reckoning. **1948:** Fighting Mustang. **1950:** The Texan Meets Calamity Jane; Bandit Queen. **1951:** King of the Bullwhip; Gold Raiders; Cattle Drive; Fort Defiance. **1958:** The Littlest Hobo (p). **1961:** The Devil's Partner. **1977:** Empire of the Ants. **1978:** Corvette Summer; Hooper. **1980:** Herbie Goes Bananas. **1981:** Cutter's Way; The Incredible Shrinking Woman. **1982:** Parasite. **1983:** Nat'l Lampoon's Vacation; Scarface. **1985:** To Live & Die in L.A. **1986:** Back to School. **1987:** Mannequin.

RED HORTON

Horton has worked chiefly as a stunt coordinator and second unit director for the low-budget action outfit PM Entertainment.

Films—**1979:** A Time to Die. **1987:** L.A. Crackdown. **1988:** Outlaw Force; L.A. Heat; L.A. Crackdown 2; Emperor of the Bronx. **1989:** Midnight Warrior; L.A. Vice. **1990:** Delta Force 2. **1991:** The Last Riders; A Time to Die. **1992:** Intent to Kill; Maximum Force; CIA, Code Name Alexa; Alien Intruder. **1993:** Private Wars; Fist of Honor; Street Crimes; Sidekicks. **1994:** Ice; Direct Hit; CIA 2: Code Name Alexa; Zero Tolerance; Deadly Target; T-Force. **1995:** Blood for Blood; Top Dog; To the Limit; The Crossing Guard. **1996:** Forest Warrior; Somebody to Love.

CHRIS HOWELL

A former rodeo rider and member of the Stuntmen's Association, this stunt coordinator is the father of actor C. Thomas Howell. He has doubled for Jeff Bridges.

Films—**1972:** The Poseidon Adventure. **1974:** Zandy's Bride. **1978:** The Driver; Deathsport. **1979:** Sunnyside; The In-Laws; The Jazz Singer; A Time to Die. **1980:** Defiance; Motel Hell; Night of the Juggler; Urban Cowboy; Survival Run. **1981:** Cutter's Way; Smokey Bites the Dust. **1982:** Parasite; The Entity; The Sword & the Sorcerer. **1983:** Amityville 3-D; Cujo. **1984:** Up the Creek; Red Dawn; Ghost Warrior (aka Swordkill). **1985:** Into the Night; Iron Eagle. **1986:** Soul Man. **1987:** Teen Wolf 2. **1988:** Miracle Mile; Clean & Sober; Ladykillers (tv). **1989:** K-9; Road House; Backtrack; Out Cold. **1990:** Impulse; Robocop 2; Kid. **1991:** My Heroes Have Always Been Cowboys; The Fisher King; Hook; Diplomatic Immunity. **1992:** Honeymoon in Vegas. **1993:** The Vanishing; American Heart; Wilder Na-palm; Fearless; Jailbait. **1994:** Blind Justice; Speed. **1995:** Showgirls; Hour Glass; Blackout; The Silencers; The Sweeper. **1996:** Set It Off; House Arrest; Barb Wire; Skyscraper; Independence Day; Kingpin; Pure Danger; Sunchaser. *Television*—The Mod Squad; Moonlighting.

NORMAN HOWELL
(b. 1957)

The brother of Chris Howell, Norman was competing in junior rodeos at the age of seven. A member of Stunts Unlimited, he has coordinated stunts and doubled regularly for Kevin Costner and Mark Harmon. He is the father of Shawn Howell.

Films—**1972:** The Cowboys. **1975:** The Boy in the Plastic Bubble (tv). **1982:** My Favorite Year; Yes, Giorgio. **1983:** Christine; The Osterman Weekend; Octopussy; Girls of the White Orchid (tv). **1984:** Foot-loose; Sheena. **1986:** The Wraith. **1987:** Wanted: Dead or Alive; The Wild Pair; Over the Top; Night Force; Predator. **1988:** Action Jackson; Vice Versa; Sunset; Die Hard; The Presidio; I'm Gonna Git You Sucka; They Live. **1989:** Worth Winning; Gleaming the Cube; Lethal Weapon 2; Her Alibi; Road House; Next of Kin. **1990:** Far Out Man; Dances with Wolves; Days of Thunder; Last of the Finest; Vietnam, Texas. **1991:** Backdraft; Ricochet; Hook; Terminator 2; Thelma & Louise; The Last Boy Scout; Shakes the Clown. **1992:** Radio Flyer; American Me; Rapid Fire; A Midnight Clear; Under Siege; The Bodyguard. **1993:** Nat'l Lampoon's Loaded Weapon; Falling Down; The Last Action Hero; A Perfect World. **1994:** Army of One; Wyatt Earp; True Lies; The Shadow; Junior; Puppetmasters; Dumb & Dumber. **1995:** Waterworld; Heat. **1996:** Eraser; The Rock; The Cable Guy; Kingpin; Escape from L.A.; Jingle All the Way. *Television*—Jake & the Fatman; Johnny Bago.

SHAWN HOWELL

Films—**1988:** Bat 21. **1990:** Dances with Wolves. **1993:** The Ballad of Little Jo.

1994: Bad Girls; Wyatt Earp. 1995: Tank Girl; Die Hard with a Vengenance; Wild Bill. 1996: Chain Reaction; Escape from L.A.; Crazy Horse; Ruby Jean & Joe.

ROBERT HOY
(b. 1927)

A lifetime member of the Stuntmen's Association and former double for Audie Murphy, Hoy gained recognition as a supporting player on the television shows "Steve Canyon" and "The High Chaparral." He was frequently cast as a television heavy.

Films—1949: Ambush. 1952: The Lawless Breed. 1954: Destry; A Star Is Born; Four Guns to the Border; Taza, Son of Cochise; Border River; The Silver Chalice; Bengal Brigade; The Black Shield of Falworth. 1955: One Desire; The Long Gray Line; Francis in the Navy; Kiss of Fire; Revenge of the Creature; To Hell & Back. 1956: Raw Edge; Four Girls in Town; Away All Boats; Behind the High Wall; The Mole People. 1957: Tammy & the Bachelor; Gun for a Coward. 1958: Lafayette Escadrille; No Time for Sergeants; Twilight for the Gods; The Defiant Ones; Live Fast, Die Young. 1959: Operation Petticoat. 1960: Spartacus. 1962: The Spiral Road. 1963: The Ugly American. 1965: The Great Race; Tickle Me; The Slender Thread; Harlow. 1966: Nevada Smith; Assault on a Queen. 1967: Tobruk; First to Fight. 1968: Rogue's Gallery; Five Card Stud; Nobody's Perfect. 1969: The Love Bug; Che. 1971: Earth 2 (tv). 1973: The Don Is Dead; Scream, Blacula, Scream; Call to Danger (tv). 1974: A Cry in the Wilderness (tv). 1975: The Master Gunfighter; Bite the Bullet; The Barbary Coast (tv). 1976: The Duchess & the Dirtwater Fox; The Outlaw Josey Wales; The Enforcer; The Invisible Strangler (aka The Astral Factor); Helter Skelter (tv). 1977: The Gauntlet; Flight to Holocaust (tv). 1978: Desperate Women (tv); Steel Cowboy (tv); The Other Side of Hell (tv). 1980: Bronco Billy; Alcatraz, The Whole Shocking Story (tv). 1981: Legend of the Lone Ranger. 1983: The Gambler 2 (tv). 1984: Last of the Great Survivors (tv). 1985: Promises to Keep (tv). 1986: Choke Canyon; Legal Eagles; A Fine Mess; Houston, the Legend of Texas (tv); Assassin (tv). 1987: Desperado (tv); Return of the Six Million Dollar Man (tv). 1988: Border Heat; Bail Out; Bonanza, the Next Generation (tv). *Television*—Zane Grey Theatre; Steve Canyon (reg.); Have Gun, Will Travel; Laramie; The Virginian; Combat; Branded; Laredo; The Man from U.N.C.L.E.; Mission: Impossible; The Guns of Will Sonnett; The Green Hornet; The High Chaparral (reg.); The FBI; Mannix; The Mod Squad; Night Gallery; Cade's County; Kung Fu; Hawkins; The Magician; Kodiak; The Six Million Dollar Man; The Rockford Files; Cannon; Bronk; Bert D'Angelo, Superstar; Police Woman; Hawaii Five-0; Switch; The Quest; Future Cop; Wonder Woman; Quincy; Sword of Justice; Vegas; Salvage One; Dallas; The Fall Guy; Magnum P.I.; Simon & Simon; Airwolf; Beauty & the Beast; The Young Riders; Our House; Zorro; The Three Musketeers.

JOHN "BEAR" HUDKINS
(b. 1918)

A veteran bit player and burly double for the likes of Spencer Tracy and George C. Scott, Hudkins is a member of the Stuntmen's Association. He is the son of horse trainer Dick Hudkins.

Films—1939: Jesse James. 1945: Code of the West. 1948: Fort Apache. 1955: The Prodigal. 1956: One Mask Too Many. 1959: Westbound. 1962: Hero's Island. 1963: It's a Mad, Mad, Mad, Mad World. 1964: The Quick Gun; Iron Collar; A Distant Trumpet. **1967:** Guess Who's Coming to Dinner. **1968:** Bandolero. **1969:** The Undefeated; Tell Them Willie Boy Is Here; Run, Shadow, Run; Paint Your Wagon. **1970:** Monte Walsh. **1971:** Dirty Harry. **1972:** The Life & Times of Judge Roy Bean; Something Evil (tv). **1973:** Oklahoma Crude; Cleopatra Jones; High Plains Drifter. **1977:** Fire Sale; The Domino Principle. **1978:** Movie, Movie. **1979:** The Prisoner of Zenda; The In-Laws; Flesh & Blood (tv). **1980:** The Island; The Mountain Men; Heaven's Gate. **1981:** Going Ape. **1983:** Two of a Kind. **1987:** The Monster Squad. **1988:** Young Guns; Miracle Mile. **1990:** Dick Tracy. *Television*—The Lone Ranger; The Outer Limits; Gunsmoke; Cimarron Strip.

Heart Condition; Last of the Finest; The Adventures of Ford Fairlane. **1991:** Highlander 2; The Rocketeer; Star Trek 6: Undiscovered Country. **1992:** Basic Instinct; White Sands; Lethal Weapon 3; Rapid Fire; Bram Stoker's Dracula; Beyond the Law. **1993:** Falling Down; Made in America; The Last Action Hero; Hard Target; Gettysburg; No Place to Hide. **1994:** Pentathalon; The Getaway; Speed; In the Army Now; Puppetmasters. **1995:** Houseguest; The Good Old Boys; Waterworld; Jade; Money Train. **1996:** From Dusk Till Dawn; Twister; Eraser; Kingpin; The Long Kiss Goodnight. *Television*—The Wild Wild West; Mission: Impossible; Vegas; Buck Rogers; CHiPs.

TOM HUFF

A member of Stunts Unlimited, Huff has worked steadily as a supporting player, utility stuntman, and occasional stunt coordinator.

Films—**1971:** The D.A.: Conspiracy to Kill (tv). **1974:** Black Samson; The Front Page; Freebie & the Bean; Earthquake; Dirty O'Neil. **1975:** Crazy Mama. **1976:** Two Minute Warning. **1977:** The Farmer; Joyride; Delta Fox. **1978:** Convoy; Corvette Summer; Hooper; Tilt. **1979:** Buck Rogers in the 25th Century; The Prizefighter; The Warriors; Just You & Me Kid. **1980:** The Blues Brothers; Steel. **1982:** The Entity; The Beastmaster; Star Trek 2: The Wrath of Kahn; Yes, Giorgio. **1983:** Brainstorm; The Osterman Weekend; The Star Chamber; Scarface; Windy City. **1984:** The Woman in Red; Buckaroo Banzai. **1985:** Into the Night; To Live & Die in L.A. **1986:** F/X; Out of Bounds; Wisdom. **1987:** Over the Top; Kidnapped; Night Force; Code Name Zebra. **1988:** Action Jackson; Elvira, Mistress of the Dark; The Blob. **1989:** Gleaming the Cube; Lethal Weapon 2; Star Trek 5: The Final Frontier; Road House; Dead Bang; Lock Up; Tango & Cash; Backtrack. **1990:**

ROBERT "WHITEY" HUGHES

Standing only 5'6" this veteran blond-haired stunt coordinator often doubled for women and children in the days when female stunt performers were few. He also tried his hand at producing low-budget films and worked closely with Sam Peckinpah on a number of classic action scenes.

Films—**1951:** Crazy Over Horses. **1953:** Son of the Renegade. **1958:** No Place to Land. **1962:** The Pleasure of His Company; Ole Rex; Stakeout; Geronimo; Night Rider; Airborne. **1965:** Major Dundee. **1968:** Sol Madrid. **1969:** The Wild Bunch. **1970:** Beneath the Planet of the Apes. **1971:** The Omega Man; Smoke in the Wind (p). **1972:** Conquest of the Planet of the Apes. **1973:** Pat Garrett & Billy the Kid; Dillinger; Battle for the Planet of the Apes. **1974:** Black Samson; Bring Me the Head of Alfredo Garcia. **1975:** Doc Savage, The Man of Bronze; Flash & the Firecat; The Killer Elite; Summer School

Unidentified stunt from *The Stunt Man* (1980).

Teachers. **1976:** The Gumball Rally; Logan's Run; Train Ride to Hollywood. **1977:** Kingdom of the Spiders. **1978:** Convoy; Harper Valley PTA; The Bees. **1980:** The Stunt Man; The Baltimore Bullet. **1981:** Demonoid. **1982:** Death Valley. **1984:** Country. **1985:** Lost in America; Rainy Day Friends (aka L.A. Bad); Blackout (tv). **1987:** Million Dollar Mystery. **1988:** Biloxi Blues; Messenger of Death. **1990:** Chattahoochie; Bill & Ted's Excellent Adventure. **1994:** Color of Night. *Television*—The Westerner; The Wild Wild West; Gunsmoke.

STEVE HULIN

Films—**1981:** An Eye for an Eye. **1983:** Lone Wolf McQuade. **1986:** Avenging Force. **1987:** House 2; Teen Wolf 2; Banzai Runner. **1988:** Elvira, Mistress of the Dark; Silent Assassins. **1989:** Wired; Best of the Best. **1990:** The Hunt for Red October; Taking Care of Business. **1991:** House 4; The Rapture; Martial Law. **1992:** Innocent Blood. **1993:** True Romance;

Bounty Tracker; Best of the Best 2; Jailbait. **1994:** Pentathalon; Hologram Man. **1995:** Best of the Best 3. **1996:** Mulholland Falls; Crazy Horse.

RAWN HUTCHINSON

This stunt coordinator is the head of Rawn Hutchinson's Precision Drivers, specializing in crashes, jumps, and rollovers.

Films—**1979:** Institute for Revenge (tv). **1985:** The Man with One Red Shoe. **1987:** Hunter's Blood. **1988:** Lady in White; In Dangerous Company; Midnight Cabaret. **1989:** True Blood; Silent Night, Deadly Night 3. **1990:** Almost an Angel; Disturbed; Liberty & Bash. **1992:** The Runestone. **1993:** Hexed; Trouble Bound; The Philadelphia Experiment 2; Attack of the 50 Foot Woman. **1995:** Waiting to Exhale; Crosscut. *Television*—Charlie's Angels;

Vegas; Matt Houston; Highway to Heaven; Beauty & the Beast; Dynasty.

Damned. **1996:** Escape from L.A. *Television*—Beauty & the Beast.

GARY HYMES

Voted multiple times the top stuntman by his peers for his expert driving skills, Hymes has worked as a stunt coordinator and second unit director on such blockbuster assignments as *Speed* and *Jurassic Park*. A member of Stunts Unlimited, he has also doubled for Richard Gere.

Films—**1982:** Megaforce; Grease 2; Shoot the Moon. **1983:** Scarface. **1984:** Buckaroo Banzai. **1985:** To Live & Die in L.A. **1986:** F/X; Out of Bounds; Back to School. **1987:** Less Than Zero; The Untouchables. **1988:** The Blob; Police Academy 5: Assignment Miami Beach; The Seventh Sign; Sweet Hearts Dance; Shoot to Kill. **1989:** K-9; Loverboy; Tango & Cash; Speedzone. **1990:** Impulse; Internal Affairs; Days of Thunder; White Palace. **1991:** Bonfire of the Vanities; One Good Cop; Hook. **1992:** Raising Cain. **1993:** Addams Family Values; Alive; Bound By Honor; Jurassic Park; Mr. Jones. **1994:** Speed; The Flintstones. **1995:** Casper; Sudden Death. **1996:** Broken Arrow; Barb Wire. *Television*—T.J. Hooker; Hardcastle & McCormick; Stingray; Sunset Beat; Mighty Morphin Power Rangers.

BRIAN IMADA

Films—**1985:** Better Off Dead. **1986:** Big Trouble in Little China. **1987:** Steele Justice. **1988:** They Live. **1989:** Kinjite; Black Rain. **1991:** Showdown in Little Tokyo; The Perfect Weapon. **1992:** Rapid Fire; Inside Edge. **1993:** Hot Shots Part Deux; Rising Sun. **1994:** Army of One; The Crow; Double Dragon; Deadly Target; American Yakuza. **1995:** Village of the

JEFF IMADA

A member of Stunts Unlimited, this former karate champ and martial arts author has coordinated the action for several John Carpenter films. He's the father of Brian Imada.

Films—**1981:** Cheech & Chong's Nice Dreams. **1982:** Blade Runner; Massarati & the Brain (tv); Renegades (tv). **1983:** Breathless; Blue Thunder; Fire & Ice; Uncommon Valor; Going Berserk. **1985:** Missing in Action 2; Rambo 2. **1986:** Hollywood Vice Squad; House; Police Academy 3: Back in Training; Gung Ho; Big Trouble in Little China. **1987:** The Night Stalker; Steele Justice; Winners Take All; Prince of Darkness; Lethal Weapon; Private Investigations. **1988:** The Presidio; Patty Hearst; They Live; The Dead Pool. **1989:** Bill & Ted's Excellent Adventure; Gleaming the Cube; Kinjite; Road House; Tango & Cash; One Man Force. **1990:** Come See the Paradise; Tremors; Death Warrant; Captain America; Last of the Finest; Marked for Death; The Rookie; Kindergarten Cop; Vietnam, Texas; Angel Town. **1991:** V.I. Warshawski; Showdown in Little Tokyo; The Perfect Weapon; Flight of the Intruder; Highlander 2; Point Break; Star Trek 6: Undiscovered Country; Driving Me Crazy; Leather Jackets; K-9000 (tv). **1992:** Kuffs; Memoirs of an Invisible Man; Rapid Fire; Patriot Games; Martial Law 2: Undercover. **1993:** Falling Down; Hot Shots Part Deux; Robot Wars; Showdown. **1994:** Army of One; The Naked Gun 33 1/3; Even Cowgirls Get the Blues; The Crow; Double Dragon; Puppetmasters; The Last Word. **1995:** The Criminal Mind; Village of the Damned; Free Willy 2; Waterworld; Mortal Kombat; Mighty Morphin Power Rangers; In the Mouth of Madness; Jade; Money Train; To the Limit; One Man's Justice.

1996: From Dusk Till Dawn; Marshal Law; Spy Hard; Escape from L.A.; The Glimmer Man. *Television*—Renegades; Matt Houston; Call to Glory; Beauty & the Beast; O'Hara; Spenser for Hire.

STEVE ITO

Films—1988: Outlaw Force. 1989: Black Rain. 1990: Come See the Paradise; The Rookie. 1991: Flight of the Intruder; Showdown in Little Tokyo. 1992: Rapid Fire. 1993: Rising Sun; Cyborg 2. 1994: Army of One; Blue Tiger; Cage 2; Deadly Target. 1995: Best of the Best 3. 1996: Escape from L.A.; Mars Attacks! *Television*—Beauty & the Beast.

BOB IVY

An independent stunt coordinator and action director, Ivy is most closely associated with the direct-to-video outfit Action International.

Films—1985: Star Slammer. 1986: Armed Response; Wired to Kill. 1987: Near Dark; The Phantom Empire; Hell Comes to Frogtown; Zombie High; Nightmare at Noon; Night Wars. 1988: Deep Space; Deadly Reactor; Hell on the Battleground. 1989: The Bounty Hunter; Action USA; Lady Avenger; Cohen & Tate; Warlords; Future Force; Jungle Assault. 1990: Soultaker; Future Zone; Deadly Dancer; The Final Sanction. 1991: Hangfire; Dark Rider (d/s); Raw Nerve; Mind, Body, & Soul. 1992: Dead Center (aka Crazy Joe); Center of the Web; Mardi Gras for the Devil; Double Threat. 1994: Raw Justice. 1995: Fall Time; Destiny Turns on the Radio; Evolver. 1996: Flipping; The Late Shift.

TERRY JACKSON

A member of the Stuntmen's Association, this stunt coordinator has doubled regularly for Bruce Willis.

Bob Ivy makes the first successful flip of a schoolbus for the 1992 film *Center of the Web.*

Films—**1976:** Hawmps. **1984:** Red Dawn. **1985:** Runaway Train; Gotcha. **1986:** Cobra; Invaders from Mars; Never Too Young to Die. **1987:** Cherry 2000; Death Before Dishonor; Dragnet; Private Road: No Trespassing. **1988:** Who Framed Roger Rabbit?; Alien Nation. **1989:** Farewell to the King; The Package; Hit List; Glory; One Man Force; Night Life. **1990:** Downtown; The First Power; Satan's Princess; Robocop 2; Maniac Cop 2; The Rookie; Masters of Menace; The Borrower. **1991:** Eve of Destruction; Iron Maze; Mobsters; Delirious; The Taking of Beverly Hills; Showdown in Little Tokyo; Another You; Flight of the Intruder. **1992:** Unlawful Entry; Pet Sematary 2; Buffy, the Vampire Slayer; Under Siege. **1993:** Hot Shots Part Deux; In the Line of Fire; The Fugitive; Robocop 3; Undercover Blues; Slaughter of the Innocents. **1994:** Past Tense; The River Wild; Pulp Fiction; Silence of the Hams; Steel Frontier. **1995:** Die Hard with a Vengeance; Mad Love; Money Train; 12 Monkeys; Ballistic. **1996:** Last Man Standing.

STEVE JAMES
(b. 1953; d. 1994)

Popular New York-born action star got his start in films with Stunt Specialists. The charismatic, smooth-talking actor subsequently played second fiddle to Chuck Norris and Michael Dudikoff in several eighties martial arts films before breaking into starring roles. He died of cancer.

Films—**1974:** The Education of Sonny Carson. **1978:** The Wiz; Oliver's Story; Slow Dancing in the Big City. **1979:** The Warriors; The Wanderers. **1980:** The Exterminator; Dressed to Kill. **1981:** Wolfen; Fort Apache, The Bronx; He Knows You're Alone; Ragtime. **1982:** Hanky Panky; Vigilante; The Soldier; Muggable Mary, Street Cop (tv). **1984:** The Brother from Another Planet; The Exterminator 2; Fatal Vision (tv). **1985:** To Live & Die in L.A.; Weird Science; Mask; The Atlanta Child Murders (tv). **1986:** American

Actor/stuntman Steve James (left), here shown with David Bradley enjoyed popularity as the co-star of the *American Ninja* films.

Ninja; P.O.W The Escape; The Delta Force; C.A.T. Squad (tv). **1987:** American Ninja 2; Hollywood Shuffle. **1988:** Hero & the Terror; Johnny Be Goode; I'm Gonna Git You Sucka; Python Wolf (tv). **1989:** American Ninja 3; Riverbend. **1990:** Street Hunter (a/s/p). **1991:** McBain; Mister Johnson. **1992:** The Player. **1993:** Weekend at Bernie's 2. **1994:** Bloodfist 5: Human Target. *Television*—The Dukes of Hazzard; T.J. Hooker; E/R; Hotel; Moonlighting; Pee Wee's Playhouse; Hammer, Slammer & Slade; Mantis.

TERRY JAMES

A member of both the Stuntmen's Association and Rawn Hutchinson's Precision Drivers, James has coordinated stunts and doubled for Cliff DeYoung.

Films—**1980:** Those Lips, Those Eyes. **1981:** Stripes. **1984:** Revenge of the Nerds. **1985:** Fright Night. **1987:** Night Force. **1988:** In Dangerous Company; Dangerous Love. **1989:** Glory; Blind Fury. **1990:** Liberty & Bash; Darkman; Disturbed. **1991:** Blood & Concrete. **1992:** The Runestone; Sneakers; The Double-O Kid. **1993:** Trouble Bound; Bitter Harvest; The Philadelphia Experiment 2. **1994:** Relentless 4; Steel Frontier; Jericho Fever (tv). **1995:** Panther; Suspect Device; The Immortals; Excessive Force 2.

LOREN JANES
(b. 1931)

The founding president of the Stuntmen's Association, Janes competed in swimming, gymnastics, and water polo, even entering the U.S. Olympic trials in the pentathalon twice. He had been teaching trigonometry when asked to perform a high-dive for a

film, going on to double for Kirk Douglas and Steve McQueen and becoming a top stunt coordinator. He's best known for the "cactus jump" in *How the West Was Won*.

Films—**1954:** Jupiter's Darling. **1958:** High School Confidential. **1959:** The Mating Game; Darby O'Gill & the Little People. **1960:** Spartacus; Flaming Star; The Magnificent Seven; Swiss Family Robinson. **1961:** Snow White & the Three Stooges; Everything's Ducky. **1962:** How the West Was Won; Hell Is for Heroes. **1965:** A Patch of Blue; The Sons of Katie Elder. **1966:** Wild, Wild Winter; Nevada Smith; The Sand Pebbles. **1967:** The King's Pirate; The Graduate. **1968:** Planet of the Apes; Bullit. **1969:** The Reivers; The Good Guys & the Bad Guys; The Great Bank Robbery; Paint Your Wagon. **1970:** I Love My Wife; Beneath the Planet of the Apes. **1972:** What's Up, Doc?; Conquest of the Planet of the Apes. **1973:** The Don Is Dead; Battle for the Planet of the Apes. **1974:** The Terminal Man; The Towering Inferno; Blazing Saddles; Earthquake. **1975:** The Other Side of the Mountain. **1976:** Logan's Run; Call of the Wild (tv). **1978:** Goin' South; F.I.S.T.; Lord of the Rings. **1979:** Butch & Sundance: The Early Days; Players. **1980:** Melvin & Howard; The Big Brawl; Raise the Titanic; Wholly Moses; The Hunter. **1981:** The Four Season; Force Five; Escape from New York; Raggedy Man. **1982:** The Sword & the Sorcerer; Zapped; Halloween 3. **1983:** The Dead Zone; Fire & Ice; Hysterical; Yellowbeard. **1984:** Beverly Hills Cop; Repo Man. **1985:** Back to the Future; Rambo 2; Runaway Train; Fright Night; To Live & Die in L.A.; Death of an Angel. **1986:** Raw Deal; The Three Amigos; Ruthless People. **1987:** Masters of the Universe; Stacking. **1988:** Dead Heat. **1989:** The Abyss; Weekend at Bernie's; CHUD 2; Prancer. **1990:** Wild at Heart. **1991:** Hook. **1992:** Man Trouble. **1993:** Jack the Bear; In the Line of Fire; Robin Hood: Men in Tights. **1994:** Silence of the Hams. **1995:** Casino. **1996:** Spy Hard.

Television—Wanted, Dead or Alive; El Coyote; Kentucky Jones; The Fugitive; Gemini Man; The Rifleman; Cisco Kid.

BOB JAUREGUI

A third generation stuntman, horse trainer, and double for Steve Martin, Jauregui is a member of the Stuntmen's Association. His father is Ed Jauregui.

Films—1984: Starman. 1985: Silverado; Rambo 2. 1986: Band of the Hand; The Three Amigos. 1987: Roxanne; Planes, Trains, & Automobiles. 1988: Ernest Saves Christmas; Blood Red; Bonanza: The Next Generation (tv). 1989: Indiana Jones & the Last Crusade; Always. 1990: Back to the Future 3; Total Recall; My Blue Heaven. 1991: Backdraft. 1992: Far & Away; Hoffa. 1993: Posse; Judgment Night. 1994: Bad Girls; Blind Justice; Night of the Running Man. 1995: Tank Girl. 1996: Eye for an Eye; Sgt. Bilko; Chain Reaction.

ANTHONY JEFFERSON

A skiing expert, this stunt coordinator broke into the business as a protégé of Max Kleven.

Films—Crisis in Sun Valley (tv) 1978: Ruckus 1982: Hot Dog, the Movie 1984: Cherry 2000 1987: Dead Man Walking; Border Heat. 1988: Tripwire; The Purple People Eater. 1990: Ski Patrol; Payback. 1991: Suburban Commando. 1993: Jack the Bear. 1994: The Chase; The River Wild; Come Die with Me (tv). 1995: Species. 1996: The Lawnmower Man 2; Bound.

DEAN JEFFRIES

This auto stylist and specialized car-maker has coordinated stunts for a few auto-themed films.

Films—1971: Diamonds Are Forever. 1973: Charley Varrick. 1974: Freebie & the Bean. 1975: Flash & the Firecat; Death Race 2000. 1977: Damnation Alley. 1980: The Blues Brothers. 1981: Honkytonk Freeway. 1983: Bad Boys. 1984: Romancing the Stone. 1985: Fletch. 1987: The Believers. 1988: Who Framed Roger Rabbit? 1990: The Rookie. 1993: The Fugitive. 1995: Die Hard with a Vengeance. 1996: The Lawnmower Man 2. *Television*—Logan's Run; Vegas.

GARY JENSEN

The brother of Jeff Jensen, this independent stunt coordinator has doubled for Kevin Bacon and Greg Evigan.

Films—1976: Drum. 1978: Lord of the Rings. 1980: Motel Hell; Survival Run. 1981: The Nashville Grab (tv). 1982: Tron; The Beastmaster. 1983: Independence Day; Timerider; Nightmares; Lust in the Dust. 1985: Private Resort; Hellhole; Return of the Living Dead. 1986: Eye of the Tiger. 1987: The Evil Dead 2; Hell Comes to Frogtown; Programmed to Kill; Defense Play. 1988: Mac & Me; Miracle Mile; I Saw What You Did (tv). 1989: Shocker; Chopper Chicks in Zombie Town; Blind Fury; Think Big; Stepfather 2. 1990: Tremors; Peacemaker; Problem Child; Young Guns 2; Under the Boardwalk; The Rookie. 1991: Barton Fink; The Grifters; Mannequin 2; Rich Girl; Diplomatic Immunity. 1992: Mom & Dad Save the World; Hero; That Night. 1993: Super Mario Bros.; In the Line of Fire; Aspen Extreme. 1994: The Air Up There; The River Wild. 1995: The Usual Suspects; Baja. *Television*—BJ & the Bear; The

Greatest American Hero; Alfred Hitchcock Presents; Amazing Stories; Perry Mason; Star Trek, The Next Generation; Loose Cannon.

JEFF JENSEN

A member of the Stuntmen's Association, Jensen has coordinated stunts, directed second unit, and doubled for the likes of Dolph Lundgren, John Candy, and John Goodman.

Films—1983: Lone Wolf McQuade; The Lost Empire. 1984: Star Trek 3: The Search for Spock. 1985: Commando; Mask; Weird Science. 1986: Sweet Liberty; Blue City; The Money Pit; Eye of the Tiger; No Mercy. 1987: The Night Stalker; Number One with a Bullet; Million Dollar Mystery; Real Men; Raising Arizona; The Untouchables; Planes, Trains, & Automobiles. 1988: Jack's Back; Rambo 3; License to Drive; The Great Outdoors. 1989: Indiana Jones & the Last Crusade; The Blood of Heroes; Always; Casualties of War; Glory. 1990: Robocop 2; Joe vs. the Volcano; Total Recall; Genuine Risk; Keaton's Cop; Neon City. 1991: Harley Davidson & the Marlboro Man; Star Trek 6: Undiscovered Country; Convicts; The Indian Runner; Martial Law. 1992: Ruby; Universal Soldier; Honey, I Blew Up the Kid; Buffy, the Vampire Slayer; Under Siege; Hoffa; Sunset Grill; Sunset Heat; Martial Law 2: Undercover; Ladykiller (tv). 1993: Rising Sun; Best of the Best 2; Three of Hearts; Tainted Blood (tv). 1994: Army of One; Surviving the Game; Dangerous Heart; The Flintstones; Speed; Puppetmasters; Salmonberries; Jack Reed: A Search for Justice (tv). 1995: Kingfish. 1996: The Arrival. *Television*—Unsolved Mysteries; Walker, Texas Ranger.

ROY JENSON
(b. 1930)

Popular Canadian-born character actor was a former star football player for UCLA and both the Calgary Stampeders and the Vancouver Alouettes. The 6'2" 230-pounder broke into films as a stuntman and stayed active in that capacity even after his parts grew in size and stature (*Harper, The Getaway, Chinatown*). Noted as a top fight-man, Jenson delivered some of the most brutal punches ever seen on film.

Films—1952: Operation Secret; Westward, the Women. 1954: River of No Return. 1956: The Harder They Come. 1957: Hell on Devil's Island; Operation Mad Ball. 1958: Buchanan Rides Alone; The Missouri Traveler; The Last Hurrah. 1959: Al Capone; Ride Lonesome; Warlock; Career. 1960: North to Alaska; Flaming Star; The Rise & Fall of Legs Diamond; Let No Man Write My Epitaph; Bells Are Ringing; 13 Ghosts; The Wackiest Ship in the Army. 1961: Atlantis, the Lost Continent; Marines, Let's Go; The George Raft Story; The Fiercest Heart. 1962: How the West Was Won; Confessions of an Opium Eater; Five Weeks in a Balloon. 1964: Law of the Lawless; Stage to Thunder Rock; 36 Hrs. 1965: Morituri; Black Spur; Baby, the Rain Must Fall; The Great Race. 1966: Our Man Flint; Harper; Apache Uprising; Blindfold. 1967: The Helicopter Spies; Hostile Guns; Red Tomahawk; Waterhole #3; The Bandits; Stranger in the House. 1968: The Ambushers; Will Penny; Jigsaw; The Thomas Crown Affair; Five Card Stud. 1969: Number One; Paint Your Wagon. 1970: Fools; Halls of Anger. 1971: Big Jake; Sometimes a Great Notion (aka Never Give an Inch); Powderkeg (tv); A Tattered Web (tv). 1972: The Life & Times of Judge Roy Bean; The Getaway; Journey Through Rosebud; Cry for Me, Billy; Brute Corps; Kung Fu (tv); The Glass House (tv). 1973: The Outfit; Deadly Honeymoon (aka Nightmare Honeymoon); Dillinger; The Way We Were; Soylent Green; Call to Danger (tv); The Red Pony (tv). 1974: Chinatown; Thunderbolt & Lightfoot; 99 & 44/100 % Dead; Hit Lady

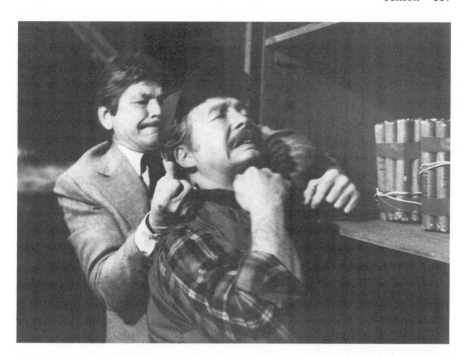

Top: Charles Bronson strangles Roy Jenson in 1977's *Telefon. Bottom:* Roy Jenson (rear) staggers away from Joe Don Baker during a brutal fight in 1975's *Framed.*

(tv). **1975:** Framed; Breakout; The Wind & the Lion; The Abduction of St. Anne (tv); Force Five (tv). **1976:** The Duchess & the Dirtwater Fox; Breakheart Pass; Rich Man, Poor Man (tv); Helter Skelter (tv). **1977:** The Gauntlet; Telefon; The Car. **1978:** Every Which Way But Loose; King (tv). **1980:** Tom Horn; The Mountain Men; Foolin' Around; Any Which Way You Can; The Gambler (tv); Nightside (tv). **1981:** Bustin' Loose; Demonoid. **1982:** Honkytonk Man. **1984:** Red Dawn; Last of the Great Survivors (tv). **1986:** Kung Fu, the Movie (tv). **1987:** The Night Stalker; Day of the Survivalist; Cherry 2000. **1988:** Border Heat. **1989:** Bail Out. **1990:** Solar Crisis. **1992:** The Osceola Sheriff's Office. **1995:** The Set Up. *Television*—Shirley Temple Storybook; Schlitz Playhouse; Not for Hire; Wagon Train; Rawhide; The Law & Mr. Jones; Peter Gunn; Hong Kong; Bob Cummings; Checkmate; The Outer Limits; Bob Hope Chrysler Theatre; Kraft Suspense Theatre; Honey West; Batman; Voyage to the Bottom of the Sea; I Spy; Daniel Boone; 12 O'Clock High; The Fugitive; T.H.E. Cat; The Wild Wild West; Gunsmoke; The Monroes; The Invaders; Cimarron Strip; The Man from U.N.C.L.E.; The Big Valley; Hondo; Andy Griffith; Tarzan; Mission: Impossible; The Virginian; Star Trek; The High Chaparral; The Outcasts; Bonanza; Lancer; The Silent Force; Sarge; Nichols; Mannix; Search; Kung Fu; Toma; New Perry Mason; Chase; The Magician; The Man Hunter; The Streets of San Francisco; Baretta; Barnaby Jones; The Quest; Gibbsville; Little House on the Prairie; Kojak; The Rockford Files; Rafferty; Quincy; Charlie's Angels; How the West Was Won (reg.) Hunter's Moon; Vegas; Fantasy Island; The Dukes of Hazzard; Father Murphy; Bret Maverick; Simon & Simon; Hardcastle & McCormick; Magnum P.I.; The A Team; Knight Rider; Police Story.

BEN JOHNSON
(b. 1918; d. 1996)

A modern cowboy legend and Oscar-winning character actor (*The Last Picture Show*), Johnson was cherished for his consistently honest portrayals. Originally recruited by Howard Hughes as a horse wrangler, he moved into stuntwork to double for Wild Bill Elliot, Joel McCrae, Fred MacMurray, Henry Fonda, and John Wayne. His skills attracted the attention of director John Ford, who subsequently starred him in *Wagon Master*. Johnson returned to the rodeo, however, winning the 1953 World Championship in Steer Roping, and was content to continue as a horse specialist until a strong role in Sam Peckinpah's *The Wild Bunch* brought him a new level of prestige. He also had a memorable fight scene with Alan Ladd in *Shane*.

Films—**1943:** The Outlaw; Red Riders; Riders of the Rio Grande; Border Town Gunfighters. **1944:** Nevada. **1945:** The Naughty Nineties; California Gold Rush. **1946:** Smoky; Badman's Territory. **1947:** Wyoming; Ramrod. **1948:** Gallant Legion; Red River; Fort Apache. **1949:** 3 Godfathers; She Wore a Yellow Ribbon; Mighty Joe Young. **1950:** Rio Grande; Wagon Master. **1951:** Fort Defiance. **1952:** Wild Stallion. **1953:** Hondo; Shane. **1955:** Oklahoma. **1956:** Rebel in Town. **1957:** Slim Carter; War Drums. **1958:** Fort Bowie. **1959:** Warlock; The Horse Soldiers. **1960:** Ten Who Dared. **1961:** One-Eyed Jacks; Tomboy & the Champ. **1962:** Ride the High Country. **1964:** Cheyenne Autumn. **1965:** Major Dundee. **1966:** The Rare Breed. **1967:** El Dorado; The War Wagon. **1968:** Hang 'Em High; Will Penny. **1969:** The Wild Bunch; The Undefeated; Ride a Northbound Horse (tv). **1970:** Chisum.

Veteran character actor/stuntman Ben Johnson in 1978's *The Swarm*.

1971: The Last Picture Show; Something Big. **1972:** Corky; The Getaway; Junior Bonner. **1973:** Dillinger; Kid Blue; The Train Robbers; Bloodsport (tv); Runaway (tv); The Red Pony (tv); Locusts (tv). **1974:** The Sugarland Express. **1975:** Bite the Bullet; Hustle. **1976:** Breakheart Pass; The Savage Bees (tv). **1977:** The Greatest; The Town That Dreaded Sundown; Grayeagle. **1978:** The Swarm. **1979:** The Sacketts (tv). **1980:** The Hunter; Terror Train; Wild Times (tv). **1981:** Soggy Bottom USA. **1982:** Ruckus; Tex; The Shadow Riders (tv). **1984:** Champions; Red Dawn. **1986:** Wild Horses (tv). **1987:** Cherry 2000. **1988:** Dark Before Dawn; Stranger on My Land (tv). **1989:** Back to Back. **1991:** My Heroes Have Always Been Cowboys; The Chase (tv). **1992:** Radio Flyer. **1993:** Bonanza: The Return (tv). **1994:** Angels in the Outfield. **1995:** Outlaws. **1996:** The Evening Star. *Television*—Laramie; Have Gun, Will Travel; Bonanza; The Virginian; Gunsmoke; Ozzie & Harriet; Alfred Hitchcock Presents; Route 66; Bob Hope Chrysler Theatre; The Monroes (reg.); Branded.

GRAY JOHNSON
(b. 1939)

A Native American stunt coordinator and second unit director, Johnson often served as Alan Arkin's double.

Films—**1971:** The Last Movie; The Hired Hand; Werewolves on Wheels. **1974:** Freebie & the Bean; Black Samson; Black Starlet. **1975:** The Ultimate Warrior; The Killer Elite; Flash & the Firecat. **1976:** Rocky; The Gumball Rally. **1977:** Punishment Park. **1978:** The Defection of Simas Kudirka (tv). **1979:** Fish & Tails; Having Fun; Love at First Bite; The In-Laws. **1980:** The Stunt Man; Nothing Personal. **1981:** Chu Chu & the Philly Flash. **1982:** That Championship Season; The Beastmaster; Zapped. **1983:** Bad Boys. **1985:** Big Trouble.

An unidentified stunt from 1980's *The Stunt Man.*

JOHN MICHAEL JOHNSON

Films—**1980:** The Stunt Man; The Island. **1981:** East of Eden (tv). **1984:** Firestarter. **1985:** Hellhole; Commando; Rambo 2; Avenging Angel. **1986:** Cobra. **1987:** The Night Stalker; Cherry 2000; Remote Control. **1988:** Two Moon Junction; They Live. **1989:** Blind Fury. **1990:** Secret Agent 00-Soul. **1992:** Aces: Iron Eagle 3. **1993:** Another Stakeout.

KEII JOHNSON

A regular double for Bruce Willis, this stunt coordinator is a member of the Stuntmen's Association.

Films—**1985:** Gotcha; Iron Eagle. **1987:** Blind Date. **1988:** Sunset; Die Hard. **1989:** Under the Gun. **1990:** The Hunt for Red October; Die Hard 2; Mr. Destiny; Bonfire of the Vanities. **1991:** Harley Davidson &

the Marlboro Man; Hook; The Last Boy Scout. **1992:** Nails; 3 Ninjas; Death Becomes Her; Innocent Blood. **1993:** Striking Distance. **1994:** North; Speed; Wolf; In the Army Now. **1995:** Frank & Jesse; Just Cause; 3 Ninjas Knuckle Up; Die Hard with a Vengeance; The Indian in the Cupboard; Under the Hula Moon; Sudden Death; Things to Do in Denver When You're Dead. **1996:** Broken Arrow; Barb Wire; Mulholland Falls.

LEROY JOHNSON

Johnson was a veteran horseback specialist and bit Western player, especially active during the fifties and sixties. A member of the Stuntmen's Association, he doubled for Barry Sullivan.

Films—**1948:** Challenge of the Range. **1950:** Colt .45. **1951:** Al Jennings of Oklahoma; Smoky Canyon. **1952:** The Hawk of Wild River; Bronco Buster; The Lusty Men. **1953:** Pony Express; Arrowhead. **1955:** The Far Horizons. **1956:** Friendly Persuasion; Texas Lady. **1957:** Dragon Wells Massacre; Gun for a Coward; Forty Guns. **1960:** The Alamo; Seven Ways from Sundown. **1962:** The Magic Sword; How the West Was Won. **1965:** Major Dundee; Shenandoah. **1966:** Duel at Diablo. **1968:** Buckskin. **1969:** The Good Guys & the Bad Guys. **1970:** Monte Walsh. **1972:** The Life & Times of Judge Roy Bean. **1974:** The House on Skull Mountain. **1980:** Heaven's Gate. *Television*—Tales of Wells Fargo; The Tall Man; Bonanza.

MIKE JOHNSON

A fire specialist, Johnson is a member of the Stuntmen's Association. His most notable gag was doubling for a burning Robert Wagner in *The Towering Inferno.*

Films—**1972:** The Poseidon Adventure. **1974:** Homebodies; The Towering Inferno. **1978:** The Norseman. **1979:** The In-Laws; Stunt Seven (tv). **1980:** Borderline. **1981:** An Eye for an Eye; Escape from New York. **1982:** Silent Rage; The Sword & the Sorcerer. **1983:** Lone Wolf McQuade; Fire & Ice; Sudden Impact. **1984:** Beverly Hills Cop. **1985:** Runaway Train; Porky's Revenge; To Live & Die in L.A. **1986:** Ratboy; Raw Deal; Invaders from Mars; Eye of the Tiger; Jumpin' Jack Flash; Firewalker. **1987:** Death Before Dishonor; Wanted: Dead or Alive; Near Dark; Innerspace; Traxx; The Untouchables; Return to Horror High; Laguna Heat. **1988:** Midnight Run; Alien Nation; Evil Altar. **1989:** The Abyss; Lethal Weapon 2; Glory. **1990:** Loose Cannons; Popcorn; Problem Child; Wild at Heart; Masters of Menace. **1991:** Highlander 2; Mobsters; Backdraft. **1992:** Live Wire; Lethal Weapon 3; Radio Flyer; Rapid Fire; Cool World; Buffy, the Vampire Slayer;

Toys; Sidekicks. **1993:** Robocop 3; Man's Best Friend; Judgment Night. **1994:** Pumpkinhead 2; Even Cowgirls Get the Blues; Blown Away; Flashfire. **1995:** Tank Girl; A Walk in the Clouds; Soldier Boyz. **1996:** Don't Be a Menace…; Chain Reaction.

PAT E. JOHNSON
(b. 1939)

This martial arts champ, teacher, and writer got into films through his friendships with Chuck Norris and Steve McQueen. He works chiefly as a karate coordinator.

Films—**1973:** Enter the Dragon. **1974:** Golden Needles; Black Belt Jones. **1975:** The Ultimate Warrior. **1978:** Good Guys Wear Black. **1979:** Little Dragons; A Force of One (a/s). **1980:** Tom Horn; The Big Brawl; The Hunter. **1981:** Force Five. **1984:** The Karate Kid. **1985:** To Live & Die in L.A. **1988:** Mac & Me; Python Wolf. **1989:** The Karate Kid Part 3. **1990:** Teenage Mutant Ninja Turtles. **1991:** Showdown in Little Tokyo; Teenage Mutant Ninja Turtles 2. **1992:** Buffy, The Vampire Slayer. **1993:** Teenage Mutant Ninja Turtles 3. **1994:** The Next Karate Kid. **1995:** Mortal Kombat.

MATT JOHNSTON

Films—**1981:** An Eye for an Eye. **1984:** Beverly Hills Cop. **1985:** To Live & Die in L.A.; Porky's Revenge; Just One of the Guys; Vendetta. **1987:** The Wild Pair; Night Force; World Gone Wild; Code Name Zebra; Kidnapped. **1988:** They Live. **1989:** Riding the Edge; Speed Zone; Road House; Lock Up. **1990:** Impulse. **1991:** Stone Cold; Highlander 2; Hook; The Last Boy Scout. **1992:** Stop! Or My

Mom Will Shoot; Radio Flyer; Cool World; Beyond the Law. **1993:** Full Eclipse. **1994:** The Crow. **1995:** Waterworld; Nick of Time. **1996:** From Dusk Till Dawn; Eraser; Escape from L.A.

AL JONES

A stunt coordinator, second unit director, and supporting player, Jones is a member of the International Stunt Association. He's doubled for Christopher Lloyd.

Films—**1973:** Scream, Blacula, Scream. **1978:** The Bees. **1980:** The Stunt Man. **1981:** Demonoid; The Pursuit of D.B. Cooper. **1982:** Megaforce; The Beastmaster; Fighting Back; Tron. **1983:** Lone Wolf McQuade; Wargames; Scarface; Get Crazy. **1984:** The Ice Pirates; Country; Star Trek 3: The Search for Spock; Purple Rain; The Joy of Sex; Savage Streets. **1985:** Girls Just Want to Have Fun; Invasion USA. **1986:** The Naked Cage; Hollywood Vice Squad; Never Too Young to Die; Radioactive Dreams. **1987:** Assassination; Dudes; Independence (tv). **1988:** Dead Heat; Messenger of Death; Bad Dreams; Critters 2; Salsa; Hero & the Terror; Pumpkinhead. **1989:** Bill & Ted's Excellent Adventure; Disorganized Crime; Cohen & Tate; Heathers; Cage; L.A. Bounty. **1990:** Child's Play 2; Delta Force 2; Satan's Princess. **1991:** The Perfect Weapon; Beastmaster 2; Freddy's Dead. **1992:** The Lawnmower Man; The Waterdance; One False Move; Innocent Blood; Davinci's War; Sweet Justice. **1993:** Streetknight; The Temp; Calendar Girl; Cybertracker. **1994:** Midnight Ride; Body Shot; 3 Ninjas Kick Back; Steel Frontier; Killing Zoe. **1995:** 3 Ninjas Knuckle Up; The Four Diamonds; Last Man Standing. **1996:** Dead Man; Mr. Ice Cream Man; Ravenhawk. *Television*—Riptide.

BRETT JONES

A member of the International Stunt Association, Jones has doubled for Robert Patrick and Corbin Bernsen.

Films—**1985:** Invasion USA. **1989:** The Abyss; L.A. Bounty. **1990:** Joe vs. The Volcano; Child's Play 2; Prayer of the Rollerboys. **1991:** Grand Canyon; The Art of Dying; Cool as Ice; Beastmaster 2; Driving Me Crazy. **1992:** The Lawnmower Man; Inside Edge. **1993:** Streetknight; Calendar Girl; Demolition Man; Dead Connection. **1994:** Body Shot; Double Dragon; Wagons East; Killing Zoe; Steel Frontier; Scanners: The Showdown. **1995:** Showgirls; The Prophecy; Temptress; One Man's Justice. **1996:** Marshal Law; Sgt. Bilko; The Trigger Effect; Saints & Sinners; The Dentist; Riot; Mercenary.

HAROLD JONES

Films—**1971:** The Omega Man. **1974:** Blazing Saddles. **1976:** Drum; Leadbelly. **1978:** Hooper. **1979:** The Fish That Saved Pittsburgh. **1980:** The Blues Brothers; Smokey & the Bandit 2. **1982:** I'm Dancing as Fast as I Can; The Sword & the Sorcerer; Zapped. **1983:** Under Fire. **1984:** Beverly Hills Cop. **1985:** Commando. **1986:** Band of the Hand. **1988:** Miracle Mile. **1989:** Glory; Nat'l Lampoon's Christmas Vacation.

MELVIN JONES
(b. 1946)

A paratrooper during the Vietnam War, Jones has doubled for Samuel L. Jackson and T.K. Carter.

Films—**1973:** Cleopatra Jones. **1979:** Concorde, Airport '79; The Black Hole. **1980:** Inside Moves; Xanadu. **1981:**

Bustin' Loose; Southern Comfort. **1982:** Fast Times at Ridgemont High; The Sword & the Sorcerer; The Thing; Penitentiary 2. **1983:** Fire & Ice; Spacehunter. **1984:** A Soldier's Story; Ghost Warrior (aka Swordkill). **1985:** City Limits; Baby: Secret of the Lost Legend; Big Trouble. **1986:** Eye of the Tiger. **1987:** Allan Quartermain & the Lost City of Gold; American Ninja 2. **1988:** Mercenary Fighters; I'm Gonna Git You Sucka. **1989:** Under the Gun; Glory. **1990:** Marked for Death. **1991:** The People Under the Stairs. **1992:** Article 99; Deep Cover; Sneakers. **1993:** Amos & Andrew; Extreme Justice; CB4; Weekend at Bernie's 2; No Place to Hide. **1994:** The Naked Gun 33 1/3; Pulp Fiction; Automatic; The Hard Truth. **1995:** 3 Ninjas Knuckle Up; Candyman: Farewell to the Flesh; Panther; Things to Do in Denver When You're Dead. **1996:** The Nutty Professor; Yesterday's Target.

KIM KAHANA
(b. 1929)

A paratrooper during the Korean War, this Hawaiian-born martial artist opened the Kahana Stunt School in the mid-seventies, one of the first specialized training grounds for prospective stunt people. His sons Rick and Kim and daughter Debbie have also worked in the industry.

Films—**1954:** The Wild One. **1963:** Fun in Acapulco. **1966:** Paradise Hawaiian Style. **1969:** Che. **1970:** Move; Brother, Cry for Me. **1971:** The Omega Man. **1974:** The Castaway Cowboy; Earthquake; Airport '75. **1975:** The Killer Elite. **1976:** Up! **1979:** Buck Rogers in the 25th Century. **1980:** Smokey and the Bandit 2. **1983:** The Thorn Birds (tv). **1984:** The Exterminator 2. **1988:** Silent Assassins. **1990:** Revenge. **1991:** Street Soldiers. **1993:** Wilder Napalm; Matinee; Passenger 57. **1996:** Don't Be a Menace. *Television*—The Man from U.N.C.L.E.; The Girl from U.N.C.L.E.;

Mission: Impossible; The Six Million Dollar Man; Starsky & Hutch; The Fighting Nightengales.

RICK KAHANA

Films—**1987:** Kidnapped. **1988:** The Milagro Beanfield War; Emperor of the Bronx; Nightmare on Elm Street 4: Dream Master. **1989:** Blind Fury. **1990:** Predator 2; Angel Town. **1991:** Toy Soldiers. **1993:** Private Wars; Sidekicks; Best of the Best 2; Martial Outlaw; Cyborg 2. **1994:** Airheads; A Low Down Dirty Shame; Zero Tolerance. **1995:** Top Dog. **1996:** Forest Warrior; Overkill.

DONNA KEEGAN
(b. 1960)

Best known for doubling Jamie Lee Curtis in *True Lies,* this New Jersey-born swimming/diving champion and former beauty contest winner got into films originally as a double for Kate Capshaw and Cybill Shepherd.

Films—**1983:** Scarface. **1984:** Indiana Jones & the Temple of Doom. **1985:** Trancers; To Live & Die in L.A. **1986:** Top Gun; Spacecamp; Legal Eagles. **1987:** Outrageous Fortune; Robocop; Private Investigations. **1993:** Hot Shots Part Deux; Sliver; Man's Best Friend. **1994:** Mother's Boys; True Lies; The Mask. **1995:** Money Train. **1996:** Kingpin; Set It Off. *Television*—Moonlighting.

TRACY KEEHN-DASHNAW
(b. 1960)

The wife of stuntman Jeff Dashnaw, this former rodeo performer has doubled regularly for Kim Basinger and Melanie Griffith.

Films—**1984:** All of Me; Ghost Warrior (aka Swordkill). **1986:** Cobra; The Three Amigos; Ruthless People; Never Too Young to Die. **1987:** Cherry 2000; Over the Top; Death Before Dishonor; Dragnet; Walk Like a Man; Private Road: No Trespassing. **1988:** The Blob; The Presidio; Poltergeist 3; My Stepmother Is an Alien. **1989:** Johnny Handsome; Stepfather 2; Chopper Chicks in Zombie Town. **1990:** Pacific Heights; Impulse; Robocop 2; The Guardian. **1991:** Warlock; Suburban Commando. **1992:** Final Analysis; Cool World. **1993:** The Real McCoy. **1994:** The Getaway; Cobb; Night of the Running Man. **1995:** Houseguest. **1996:** Spy Hard; Bulletproof; Dear God.

MARIA KELLY

A former magazine model, Kelly is a member of both the Stuntwoman's Association and Rawn Hutchinson's Precision Drivers. She has doubled for Meg Ryan, Julia Roberts, Tracy Scoggins, Joan Severance, and Teri Hatcher.

Films—**1988:** Beetlejuice; Fright Night 2; The Dead Pool; Bad Dreams. **1989:** 976 Evil; Crackhouse; Tango & Cash. **1990:** Liberty & Bash; Satan's Princess; Watchers 2. **1991:** Mobsters; Sleeping with the Enemy; Nothing But Trouble; The Rocketeer; Deadlock; Prey of the Chameleon. **1992:** Basic Instinct; Cool World; The Runestone; Toys; The Double-0 Kid; Sweet Justice; Lake Consequence. **1993:** No Place to Hide; Dead On; The Philadelphia Experiment 2; Kalifornia; Bitter Harvest; Brain Smasher; Attack of the 50 Foot Woman. **1994:** Sugar Hill; The Naked Gun 33 1/3; When a Man Loves a Woman; Wes Craven's New Nightmare; Steel Frontier; Fast Getaway 2; Flashfire. **1995:** The Set Up; Showgirls; Nick of Time; Black Scor-

pion. **1996:** Heaven's Prisoners; Norma Jean & Marilyn; Spy Hard; Bordello of Blood; 2 Days in the Valley; Maximum Risk; Fast Money; Riot. *Television*—Lois & Clark.

STEVE KELSO

A member of the Stuntmen's Association, Kelso has worked as both a stunt coordinator and second unit director.

Films—**1982:** Megaforce. **1984:** City Limits. **1985:** Commando; Rambo 2; Murphy's Romance; Weird Science. **1986:** Quicksilver; Ratboy; Blue City; Eye of the Tiger. **1987:** The Night Stalker; *batteries not included; The Big Easy; Shy People; No Way Out; Cop. **1988:** Mississippi Burning. **1989:** Indiana Jones & the Last Crusade; Nightmare on Elm Street 5: Dream Child; Glory; Pink Cadillac; Mob Boss. **1990:** The Handmaid's Tale; Last Call; Wild at Heart; The Adventures of Ford Fairlane; Maniac Cop 2. **1991:** Mobsters; Out for Justice; The Doors; Harley Davidson & the Marlboro Man; Late for Dinner; Fast Getaway; The Last Riders; Dead On: Relentless 2; Knight Rider 2000 (tv). **1992:** Deep Cover; Cool World; Trespass; Wayne's World. **1993:** Cybertracker. **1994:** Dead Man's Revenge; Airheads; Guardian Angel; Steel Frontier; Hologram Man; Bad Blood. **1995:** Destiny Turns on the Radio; Top Dog; Cybertracker 2; Cyborg 3; Last Man Standing. **1996:** The Rock; Courage Under Fire; The Crow: City of Angels. *Television*—Misfits of Science; Columbo.

GARY KENT

A supporting actor in very low-budget exploitation films during the sixties and early seventies, Kent worked on all levels of film production, including the coordinating of stunts. Best known as the hero in *Satan's Sadists,* reputed to be one of the most depraved films ever made, Kent would later turn sensitive as the author behind the critically acclaimed *Rainy Day Friends.*

Films—1959: Battle Flame; Stallion Road. 1964: The Devil Wolf of Shadow Mountain (d). 1965: Run Home Slow; The Thrill Killers. 1967: Hell's Angels on Wheels. 1968: A Man Called Dagger; The Savage Seven; Psych-Out; Targets; Hell's Chosen Few; Sinthia: the Devil's Doll; Body Fever. 1969: The Mighty Gorga; Satan's Sadists; The Fabulous Bastard from Chicago. 1970: Hell's Bloody Devils (aka The Fakers); Sondra, The Making of a Woman; The Hard Road; Machismo; The Psycho Lover. 1971: Dracula vs. Frankenstein; Blood Mania; Angels' Wild Women 1973: Let's Play Dead (aka Schoolgirls in Chains). 1974: Inside Amy; Freebie & the Bean. 1985: Rainy Day Friends (a/d/p/s). 1996: Flipping.

PETER KENT
(b. 1958)

This 6'5" New Jersey-born bodybuilder was recruited out of a gym to double for Arnold Schwarzenegger. He has also stood in for Hulk Hogan.

Films—1984: The Terminator; The Dungeonmaster. 1985: Re-Animator. 1986: Raw Deal. 1987: Predator; The Running Man; Dudes. 1988: Dead Heat. 1990: Total Recall; Kindergarten Cop. 1991: Terminator 2. 1992: Nemesis; Christmas in Connecticut (tv). 1993: The Last Action Hero; Mr. Nanny. 1994: True Lies; Official Denial. 1996: Eraser; Jingle All the Way. *Television*—Dangerous Curves.

HUBIE KERNS
(b. 1920)

A veteran member of the Stuntmen's Association, Kerns served as the double for Adam West on television's "Batman." He later began producing films.

Films—1949: Take Me Out to the Ball Game. 1950: Bright Leaf. 1951: Jim Thorpe, All-American; Saturday's Hero; Angels in the Outfield. 1953: The Girls of Pleasure Island; Off Limits. 1954: Them. 1955: Strategic Air Command; I Died a Thousand Times. 1956: The Ten Commandments; Four Girls in Town. 1957: Baby Face Nelson. 1958: The Young Lions; The True Story of Lynn Stuart. 1959: Don't Give Up the Ship. 1960: Spartacus. 1961: Blueprint for Robbery. 1966: Batman; Paradise Hawaiian Style. 1968: Project X; The Boston Strangler. 1969: Hello, Dolly! 1970: Brother, Cry for Me. 1972: Get to Know Your Rabbit; Conquest of the Planet of the Apes. 1973: The Long Goodbye. 1974: Mame. 1979: Stunt Seven (tv). 1980: How to Beat the High Cost of Living. 1982: The Sword & the Sorcerer. 1984: City Limits. 1985: Police Academy 2: Their First Assignment. 1986: 52 Pick-Up. 1991: Dead Men Don't Die (p). *Television*—Batman; Voyage to the Bottom of the Sea; Cimarron Strip; Mission: Impossible; The Lucy Show.

HUBIE KERNS, JR.

A member of the Stuntmen's Association, Kerns has coordinated stunts and directed second unit action.

Films—1975: Jaws. 1976: Crash. 1977: Outlaw Blues; Skateboard. 1978: The Amazing Captain Nemo; Good Guys Wear Black. 1979: Beyond the Poseidon

Adventure. **1980:** The Island. **1982:** Star Trek 2: The Wrath of Khan. **1984:** Splash. **1985:** Mischief; Moving Violations. **1987:** Wanted: Dead or Alive; Disorderlies; Million Dollar Mystery; Dragnet; The Wild Pair. **1988:** Tequila Sunrise; Rambo 3; Poltergeist 3. **1989:** Indiana Jones & the Last Crusade; Nightmare on Elm Street 5: Dream Child; CHUD 2. **1990:** Megaville. **1991:** Dead Men Don't Die; Cast a Deadly Spell. **1992:** Universal Soldier; Wayne's World; Fifty/Fifty; Dirty Work (tv). **1994:** The Naked Gun 33 1/3; Clean Slate; Pulp Fiction; Hologram Man. **1995:** Tommy Boy; American Ninja 5. **1996:** Set It Off. *Television*—Buck Rogers; Father Dowling Mysteries; Diagnosis Murder.

KAY KIMLER

A member of the United Stuntwoman's Association, this stunt coordinator/second unit director has doubled for Lindsay Wagner and Catherine Bach.

Films—**1976:** Young Pioneers' Christmas (tv). **1979:** The Lady in Red; Beyond the Poseidon Adventure. **1981:** Charlie Chan & the Curse of the Dragon Queen. **1982:** Night Warning. **1983:** Eddie Macon's Run. **1987:** Sweet Revenge. **1988:** Criminal Act. **1989:** From the Dead of Night (tv). **1990:** Masters of Menace; Night Angel; Night Visitor; The Horseplayer; Last Call. **1993:** The Soft Kill; Cyborg 2. **1994:** The River Wild; In the Army Now; Color of Night; Drop Zone; Automatic. **1995:** Demon Knight; Species; Copycat; Baja. **1996:** Lawnmower Man 2. *Television*—The Bionic Woman; The Dukes of Hazzard; The A Team; The Antagonists.

ROB KING

An independent stunt coordinator and screenwriter, King has doubled for character actor Tim Thomerson.

Films—**1983:** Metalstorm. **1985:** Trancers; Volunteers. **1987:** The Hidden; House 2. **1988:** Bulletproof; Feds. **1989:** Chopper Chicks in Zombie Town; Back to Back; Silk 2 (s). **1990:** Delta Force 2; Legal Tender. **1991:** Deadlock; Star Trek 6: Undiscovered Country; Zipperface. **1992:** Munchie. **1993:** Benefit of the Doubt; Sidekicks; Rescue Me; Cybertracker; No Escape, No Return; Firepower. **1994:** Surviving the Game; Army of One; Guardian Angel; Hologram Man; Final Mission; Bad Blood; Outside the Law. **1995:** Nature of the Beast; Frank & Jesse; Blackout; Skyscraper. **1996:** Norma Jean & Marilyn; Dark Breed; Forest Warrior. *Television*—Alien Nation.

WAYNE KING

A member of the Stuntmen's Association, King has done bit parts and utility stunts since the early seventies.

Films—**1971:** The Omega Man. **1973:** Cleopatra Jones; The Blue Knight (tv). **1974:** Black Samson. **1976:** Dr. Black, Mr. Hyde. **1977:** The Domino Principle. **1979:** H.O.T.S. **1980:** Wholly Moses. **1981:** Heartbeeps. **1983:** D.C. Cab. **1985:** The Mean Season; Remo Williams; Volunteers. **1986:** Ruthless People. **1987:** Allan Quartermain & the Lost City of Gold; Prince of Darkness; Remote Control; Death Spa. **1988:** Dead Heat; I'm Gonna Git You Sucka; Colors. **1989:** Glory. **1990:** Child's Play 2; Marked for Death; The Rookie. **1991:** Timebomb; Cast a Deadly Spell. **1994:** The Naked Gun 33 1/3. **1995:** Panther; Separate Lives.

HENRY KINGI
(b. 1943)

With his shoulder-length hair and unique black, native American features, Los Angeles-born Kingi is one of the most prolific and identifiable men in the stunt profession. A member of both Stunts Unlimited and the Professional Driver's Association, the former male model attracted media attention in the seventies when he married television's Lindsay Wagner. The comedy *Car Wash* remains one of his better acting assignments, *To Live and Die in L.A.*'s wrong-direction freeway chase a showcase for his driving skills.

Films—**1970:** Halls of Anger; R.P.M.; There Was a Crooked Man. **1971:** The Omega Man; Smoke in the Wind. **1972:** Buck & the Preacher; Conquest of the Planet of the Apes. **1973:** Cleopatra Jones; Battle for the Planet of the Apes. **1974:** Uptown Saturday Night; Truck Turner; Earthquake. **1975:** The Ultimate Warrior; Let's Do It Again; Search for the Gods (tv). **1976:** Swashbuckler; Dr. Black, Mr. Hyde; Drum; Car Wash. **1977:** A Piece of the Action; Mr. Billion; Delta Fox. **1979:** Sunnyside. **1980:** Stir Crazy. **1981:** Charlie Chan & the Curse of the Dragon Queen. **1982:** The Sword & the Sorcerer; Six Pack; Renegades (tv). **1985:** To Live & Die in L.A.; Streets of Justice (tv). **1986:** F/X; The Money Pit; Sweet Liberty. **1987:** Real Men; Predator; Night Force; Code Name Zebra; Destination America (tv). **1988:** Action Jackson; Die Hard; License to Drive; Shoot to Kill; They Live. **1989:** K-9; Johnny Handsome; Road House; She Knows Too Much (tv). **1990:** Far Out Man; Downtown; Predator 2; Marked for Death; Secret Agent 00-Soul (s/p). **1991:** Stone Cold; Grand Canyon; The Rapture; Hook; A Rage in Harlem; K-9000 (tv). **1992:** Memoirs of an Invisible Man; Deep Cover; Rapid Fire; American Me; Aces: Iron Eagle 3; Class Act; Lethal Weapon 3; Batman Returns; Nails; Patriot Games; Under Siege; Death Ring; The Bodyguard; In the Arms of a Killer (tv). **1993:** Point of No Return; Falling Down; Hot Shots Part Deux; The Last Action Hero; Demolition Man; Rising Sun;

Bound by Honor; Conflict of Interest; Sex, Love, & Cold Hard Cash (tv). **1994:** The Shadow; Double Dragon; The Client; Clear & Present Danger; The Mask; A Low Down Dirty Shame. **1995:** Just Cause; Bad Boys; Seven; Under Siege 2; Things to Do in Denver When You're Dead. **1996:** From Dusk Till Dawn; Executive Decision; Marshal Law; Barb Wire; The Rock; Spy Hard; Fled; Pure Danger; First Kid. *Television*—Daniel Boone; The Six Million Dollar Man; The Quest; The Bionic Woman; The Dukes of Hazzard; Renegades; Matt Houston; Jake & the Fatman; Werewolf; The Fifth Corner.

HENRY KINGI, JR.

Films—**1990:** Downtown. **1991:** One Good Cop; A Rage in Harlem. **1992:** Rapid Fire. **1993:** Full Eclipse; Hard Target; Demolition Man. **1994:** The Crow; Double Dragon; Clear & Present Danger; A Low Down Dirty Shame; Puppetmasters. **1995:** Bad Boys; Desperado; Assassins; Dead Presidents; Money Train. **1996:** From Dusk Til Dawn; Executive Decision; Spy Hard; Fled; Pure Danger; Ransom.

BARBARA ANN KLEIN

A former costume designer, this Florida-raised actress has doubled for Goldie Hawn.

Films—**1990:** Night Eyes; Leatherface 3; Marked for Death; Syngenor. **1991:** Out for Justice; The Hard Way; The Rapture; Dead On: Relentless 2. **1992:** Deep Cover; The Hand That Rocks the Cradle; Folks; Rapid Fire; Death Becomes Her. **1993:** Hot Shots Part Deux; Robocop 3; Weekend at Bernie's 2. **1994:** Reality Bites;

Clean Slate; The Cowboy Way; Silence of the Hams. **1995:** Batman Forever; Assassins. **1996:** Mercenary; Set It Off.

MAX KLEVEN
(b. 1934)

A Norwegian-born supporting player, stunt coordinator, and second unit director, Kleven was a competitive ski jumper prior to doubling Martin Milner on television's "Route 66." He began writing and directing his own films in the eighties.

Films—**1966:** Billy the Kid vs. Dracula; Murderer's Row; Our Man Flint. **1967:** A Covenant with Death; The Perils of Pauline; Who's Minding the Mint? **1969:** The Good Guys & the Bad Guys. **1970:** Cotton Comes to Harlem. **1972:** The Anderson Tapes; Come Back, Charleston Blue; Dealing. **1973:** Charley Varrick. **1974:** Mame; Zandy's Bride; Three Tough Guys; 99 & 44/100% Dead; Melvin Purvis, G-Man (tv). **1975:** Rollerball; Hard Times. **1976:** Silent Movie; Silver Streak; St. Ives. **1977:** The Deep; Exo-Man (tv). **1978:** Damien: Omen 2; F.I.S.T.; Crisis in Sun Valley (tv). **1979:** The Changeling. **1980:** Used Cars; Happy Birthday to Me. **1981:** Southern Comfort; The Five of Me (tv). **1982:** Ruckus (d/s). **1984:** Hot Dog: The Movie; Sheena; Conan, the Destroyer; Footloose; Protocol. **1985:** Back to the Future; My Science Project; Runaway Train; The Man with One Red Shoe. **1986:** Clan of the Cave Bear; Ruthless People; Quiet Cool; Wild Thing. **1987:** Cherry 2000; The Night Stalker (d); Wanted: Dead or Alive; Hot Pursuit. **1988:** Pass the Ammo; Vice Versa; Who Framed Roger Rabbit?; The Rescue; Border Heat (d); Bail Out (d/p/a). **1989:** Back to the Future 2; Blind Fury. **1990:** Back to the Future 3. **1991:** Sleeping with the Enemy; Robin Hood; Shattered; Paradise. **1992:** Batman Returns; Death Becomes Her. **1993:** The Fantastic Four. **1994:** The River

Wild. **1995:** Species. *Television*—Rin Tin Tin; Rescue 8; Naked City; Route 66; Combat; Star Trek; The Green Hornet; The Invaders; Mission: Impossible; Kojak; Magnum P.I.; Get Smart.

KIM ROBERT KOSCKI

Films—**1987:** The Lost Boys. **1988:** Defense Play; Miracle Mile. **1990:** Circuitry Man. **1991:** Barton Fink; Mobsters; Hook; Ricochet; Child's Play 3; Mannequin 2; Diplomatic Immunity. **1992:** Buffy, The Vampire Slayer; Hero; Dead Center (aka Crazy Joe). **1993:** Trouble Bound; The Philadelphia Experiment 2; Martial Outlaw. **1994:** The Flintstones; Color of Night; CIA 2: Target Alexa; T-Force. **1995:** Apollo 13. **1996:** Public Enemies; Mercenary; Star Trek, First Contact.

JOEL KRAMER
(b. 1958)

Top stunt coordinator got there by doubling action superstar Arnold Schwarzenegger, designing or participating in stand-out sequences in *T-2, True Lies,* and *Eraser.* A member of both Stunts Unlimited and the Professional Driver's Association, he has also stood in for Dolph Lundgren.

Films—**1979:** Mag Wheels; Star Trek, the Motion Picture. **1981:** Mausoleum. **1984:** Ninja 3: The Domination. **1985:** Commando; My Science Project; Remo Williams; Return of the Living Dead. **1986:** Invaders from Mars; Raw Deal; Never Too Young to Die. **1987:** Predator; Innerspace; The Running Man. **1988:** Action Jackson; Red Heat; They Live; Twins. **1989:** Collision Course; Ghostbusters 2. **1990:** Far Out Man; Total Recall; Another 48 HRS.; Avalon; Air America; Kindergarten Cop; Dangerous Passion (tv). **1991:** Shattered; Terminator 2. **1992:** Universal Soldier; Patriot Games; The Bodyguard; Full Eclipse. **1993:** The Last Action Hero; Cliffhanger. **1994:** Pentathalon; True Lies; Junior. **1995:** The Road Killers; Just Cause; Under Siege 2; Jade; Last Man Standing; Heat. **1996:** Eraser; Jingle All the Way.

FRED KRONE

A lifetime member of the Stuntmen's Association, this supporting player was predominantly active in Westerns. He doubled for Steven Hill on television's "Mission: Impossible."

Films — **1952:** The Steel Fist. **1953:** Last of the Pony Riders. **1956:** The Houston Story; The First Texan; Reprisal! **1957:** New Day at Sundown. **1958:** Apache Territory; The Firebrand. **1962:** Hand of Death; Young Guns of Texas. **1964:** The Quick Gun. **1965:** Arizona Raiders; Convict Stage; Fort Courageous; War Party; Young Fury. **1966:** Not with My Wife You Don't. **1969:** The Love Bug; The Undefeated; The Great Bank Robbery; Hell's Belles. **1972:** The Life & Times of Judge Roy Bean; The Limit. **1982:** Megaforce. *Television* — Zane Grey Theatre; Forest Ranger; Wyatt Earp; Maverick; The Texan; The Outer Limits; Johnny Ringo; Laredo; Lost in Space; Mission: Impossible; The Green Hornet; I Dream of Jeannie; The FBI; Mannix; High Chaparrel.

STEVE LAMBERT

A martial arts expert, stunt coordinator, and second unit director, Lambert has doubled for actor James Woods since the late eighties. He's a member of the Stuntmen's Association.

Films — **1981:** The Incredible Shrinking Woman. **1982:** The Sword & the Sorcerer. **1983:** They Call Me Bruce; Revenge of the Ninja. **1984:** Racing with the Moon; Friday the 13th: A New Beginning; Ninja 3: The Domination; Breakin 2: Electric Boogaloo; City Limits; Tuff Turf. **1985:** American Ninja; Remo Williams; My Science Project. **1986:** P.O.W. The Escape; Invaders from Mars; Raw Deal; Firewalker; Eye of the Tiger. **1987:** Aloha Summer; Best Seller; Traxx; Cop. **1988:** The Accused; Rambo 3; Two Moon Junction; Twins; Out of the Dark. **1989:** Collision Course; Indiana Jones & the Last Crusade; Always; Ghostbusters 2; Blind Fury. **1990:** Total Recall; Delta Force 2; Solar Crisis; Marked for Death. **1991:** Eve of Destruction; The Hard Way; Past Midnight; Cast a Deadly Spell; Dead On: Relentless 2. **1992:** Deep Cover; Diggstown; Hoffa; Sweet Justice. **1993:** Falling Down; Another Stakeout; Dragon; Robocop 3; Best of the Best 2; Bounty Tracker. **1994:** The Getaway; Surviving the Game; Silence of the Hams; Fear of a Black Hat; Timecop; The Specialist. **1995:** Next Door; Houseguest; The Tie That Binds; Casino. **1996:** The Quest; Don't Look Back; Escape from L.A.

SONNY LANDHAM
(b. 1941)

Popular Indian supporting player, best known as the vicious bad guy in *48HRS*. The Georgia-native played college football, spent time in the military, worked in oilfields, performed in country rock bands, preached as a self-ordained Baptist minister, and spent a number of years in prison for his proficiency at picking safes. Drifting

Actor/stuntman Sonny Landham (rear) with James Remar in 1982's *48 HRS*.

into stuntwork, Landham survived a severe car accident, then posed for a *Playgirl* centerfold and starred in nearly two dozen x-rated films. He returned to stunts for Stunt Specialists in the late seventies. His autobiography, *Total Man,* was published in 1981.

Films—**1969:** The Lost Man. **1971:** B.S. I Love You; Bananas. **1972:** Shaft's Big

Score. **1975:** Blood Bath. **1978:** King of the Gypsies. **1979:** The Warriors; Love at First Bite. **1980:** Gloria; Defiance. **1981:** Honkytonk Freeway; Southern Comfort. **1982:** Poltergeist; 48HRS. **1984:** Fleshburn. **1985:** Grace Quigley; The Dirty Dozen: The Next Mission (tv). **1986:** Firewalker. **1987:** Predator. **1988:** Action Jackson. **1989:** Lock Up. **1991:** Three Days to Kill. **1992:** Maximum Force. **1993:** Best of the Best 2; Taxi Dancers; No Goodbyes; Tribal Force. **1994:** Savage Land; Madame. **1995:** 2090, Bad Blood. **1996:** Billy Lone Bear (a/p/d). *Television*—Bonanza; Gunsmoke; The Mod Squad; The Rookies; Ryan's Hope; As the World Turns; Call to Glory; The A Team; Hardcastle & McCormick; The Fall Guy; Miami Vice.

BILL LANE

A member of the Stuntmen's Association, Lane has directed second unit, coordinated stunts, and doubled for Seymour Cassell. His sons Paul and Shawn are also in the business.

Films—**1971:** Dirty Harry. **1973:** Magnum Force. **1974:** The Front Page; Blazing Saddles; Earthquake. **1976:** Drum. **1977:** Exo-Man (tv). **1979:** Ebony, Ivory, and Jade (tv). **1981:** Escape from New York. **1983:** Blue Thunder; Smokey & the Bandit 3; Get Crazy. **1984:** Starman. **1985:** Cloak & Dagger; Teen Wolf; Commando; That Was Then, This Is Now. **1986:** Out of Bounds; Slow Burn. **1987:** Near Dark; Dragnet; The Principal; Remote Control; Planes, Trains, & Automobiles; Date With an Angel; Computer Logic (tv). **1988:** Young Guns; Midnight Run. **1989:** Collision Course; Ghostbusters 2; The Package. **1990:** Child's Play 2; The Rookie; Secret Agent 00-Soul. **1991:** Eve of Destruction. **1992:** Falling from Grace; Love Field; Out on a Limb. **1993:** Trouble Bound. *Television*—Alice.

PAUL LANE

A member of the Stuntmen's Association, Paul has coordinated stunts and doubled for character actor Lance Henriksen.

Films—**1982:** Megaforce. **1984:** Streets of Fire. **1985:** That Was Then, This Is Now; Weird Science. **1986:** Cobra; One Crazy Summer; Eye of the Tiger; Slow Burn. **1987:** The Night Stalker; Near Dark; Traxx; Remote Control; Nasty Hero. **1988:** Alien Nation; Turner & Hooch; Pumpkinhead; Two Moon Junction. **1989:** Collision Course; Indiana Jones & the Last Crusade; The January Man; Jacknife; Always; Glory. **1990:** Robocop 2; Another 48 HRS.; Shadowzone. **1991:** Stone Cold; Mobsters; The Marrying Man. **1992:** Wild Orchid 2; Buffy, The Vampire Slayer. **1993:** Hear No Evil. **1994:** Dumb & Dumber; American Yakuza. **1995:** Separate Lives; Destiny Turns on the Radio. **1996:** Broken Arrow; The Lawnmower Man 2; Down Periscope; Riot; Sunchaser.

SHAWN PATRICK LANE

Films—**1984:** Bachelor Party. **1985:** Weird Science. **1986:** Slow Burn. **1987:** The Principal; The Running Man; Remote Control. **1988:** Nightmare on Elm Street 4: Dream Master. **1989:** Indiana Jones & the Last Crusade. **1990:** Robocop 2; Secret Agent 00-Soul. **1991:** The Naked Gun 2 1/2. **1992:** Out on a Limb. **1993:** Robocop 3. **1996:** Sunchaser.

WALT LARUE

A veteran bit Western player and member of the Stuntmen's Association, LaRue has doubled for Harry Carey, Jr.

Films—1939: The New Frontier. 1943: Edge of Darkness. 1944: Tiger Woman. 1946: The Phantom Rider. 1948: Fort Apache. 1949: Ambush. 1950: Cow Town; Desert Song. 1954: Man with the Steel Whip. 1958: Cowboy; Gunman's Walk. 1963: Savage Sam. 1964: A Distant Trumpet; The Quick Gun. 1965: Major Dundee. 1967: El Dorado. 1969: Paint Your Wagon; The Good Guys & the Bad Guys. 1972: The Cowboys. 1974: Mame; Blazing Saddles. 1978: F.I.S.T. 1979: The North Avenue Irregulars. 1980: The Blues Brothers; Raging Bull. 1983: Dempsey (tv). 1985: Pale Rider; Silverado; My Science Project. 1986: The Three Amigos. 1987: Cherry 2000; The Big Easy; Walk Like a Man. 1988: Young Guns; The Dead Pool. 1989: Pink Cadillac. 1990: Back to the Future 3; The Rookie.

LANE LEAVITT

A member of the Professional Driver's Association, Leavitt is the husband of stuntwoman Debbie Evans and a prolific utility stunt player.

Films—1984: The Ice Pirates; City Limits. 1985: Commando; Explorers. 1986: Cobra; Never Too Young to Die. 1987: Death Before Dishonor; Death Wish 4; The Hidden; Timestalkers (tv). 1988: Dead Heat; Messenger of Death; The Dead Pool; Halloween 4; Bad Dreams; Nightmare on Elm Street 4: Dream Master; Critters 2. 1989: One Man Force; Kinjite; Glory. 1990: The First Power; Class of 1999; Darkman; The Exorcist 3; Puppetmaster 3; Prayer of the Rollerboys. 1991: Stone Cold; Eve of Destruction; V.I. Warshawski; Hook; Timebomb; Suburban Commando; The Perfect Weapon; Terminator 2; Shakes the Clown. 1992: Dolly Dearest; Adventures in Dinosaur City. 1993: The Last Action Hero; Cliffhanger; Rescue Me. 1994: True Lies; The Mask; Zero Tolerance; Direct Hit; CIA 2: Target Alexa; Junior. 1995: Candyman: Farewell to the Flesh; Digital Man; Blood for

Blood; The Sweeper. 1996: The Lawnmower Man 2; Barb Wire; Eraser; The Nutty Professor; Independence Day; Riot; Jingle All the Way.

DAVE LEBELL

The son of Judo Gene LeBell, Dave is a member of the Stuntmen's Association.

Films—1981: Heartbeeps. 1984: Lovelines. 1985: Fast Forward; Into the Night; The Man with One Red Shoe; Commando; Police Academy 2; Moving Violations. 1986: The Golden Child. 1987: Code Name Zebra; Night Force; The Lost Boys. 1990: Robocop 2. 1991: Mobsters; The Marrying Man. 1993: Best of the Best 2. 1995: Tyson.

GENE LEBELL
(b. 1932)

Popular red-haired supporting player was a judo and wrestling champ before entering films, having written several books on both subjects. Reputed to be one of the toughest men in Hollywood, his greatest screen moment may have come as a man with a very revealing nickname in The Jerk. A member of both the Stuntmen's Association and the Professional Driver's Association, LeBell often shows up as ring refs, another professional occupation he has excelled in. He has doubled for Darren McGavin.

Films—1968: Planet of the Apes; P.J.; The Split. 1969: Childish Things (aka Confessions of Tom Harris). 1970: There Was a Crooked Man; Beneath the Planet of the Apes; The Challenge (tv). 1972: Conquest of the Planet of the Apes; Hammer; Blacula; Melinda. **1973:** Cleopatra Jones; Walking Tall; Slaughter's Big Rip-Off; Hell Up in Harlem; Battle for the Planet of the Apes. **1974:** The Towering Inferno; Black Samson; Freebie & the Bean; Busting; Earthquake. **1975:** The Killer Elite; At Long Last Love. **1976:** No Way Back. **1977:** A Matter of Wife & Death (tv) Black Sunday; Mad Bull (tv). **1978:** The One & Only; I Wanna Hold Your hand; Almost Summer; Every Which Way But Loose; The Bad News Bears Go to Japan. **1979:** The Jerk; Goldie & the Boxer (tv); Flesh & Blood (tv); Stunt Seven (tv). **1980:** Foolin' Around; The Fifth Floor; The Big Brawl; Raging Bull. **1981:** Going Ape; Smokey Bites the Dust. **1982:** Dead Men Don't Wear Plaid. **1984:** City Heat; City Limits; Micki & Maude; P.K. & the Kid. **1985:** Remo Williams; Gotcha; Fletch. **1986:** The Golden Child; Bad Guys; Streets of Gold; Eye of the Tiger; Welcome to 18. **1987:** Number One with a Bullet; The Wild Pair; Blind Date; Million Dollar Mystery; Death Wish 4; Night Force; The Lost Boys. **1988:** Dead Heat; Mac & Me; Freeway. **1989:** No Holds Barred; Lock Up; Tango & Cash. **1990:** Darkman; Almost an Angel; Problem Child; Loose Cannons; Robocop 2; Die Hard 2; Total Recall; Death Warrant; Trancers 2. **1991:** Out for Justice; Another You; Problem Child 2; The Last Boy Scout; Another You; Shakes the Clown. **1992:** Rapid Fire; Live Wire; Mom & Dad Save the World; Batman Returns; Bloodfist 4: Die Trying. **1993:** Nowhere to Run; Conflict of Interest; Best of the Best 2; Bitter Harvest. **1994:** Eyes of an Angel; The Naked Gun 33 1/3; Surviving the Game; Blown Away; Ed Wood; Steel Frontier; CIA 2: Target Alexa. **1995:** 3 Ninjas Knuckle Up; Tyson; Money Train; Ballistic. **1996:** Jingle All the Way. ***Television***—Burke's Law; The Munsters; Voyage to the Bottom of the Sea; Honey West; The Wild Wild West; I Spy; The Green Hornet; Land of the Giants; Mission: Impossible; Cade's Country; The Night Stalker; The Man Hunter; The Six Million Dollar Man; Gemini Man; Future Cop; The Bionic Woman; Starsky & Hutch; The Man from Atlantis; The Incredible Hulk; Quincy; Taxi; The Greatest American Hero; Knight Rider; Simon & Simon; Misfits of Science; Baywatch; Superman.

RICK LE FEVOUR
(b. 1955)

Illinois-born rodeo cowboy performed in a Japanese Wild West show before returning to Chicago to form the Mid-West Stunt Association. He has doubled for Tom Cruise, Andy Garcia, Michael Keaton, and Bill Murray.

Films—**1981:** On the Right Track. **1983:** Class; Risky Business; Windy City; Through Naked Eyes (tv). **1984:** Sixteen Candles. **1985:** Code of Silence; Weird Science; Invasion USA; A Bunny's Tale (tv). **1986:** Touch & Go; Ferris Bueller's Day Off; Raw Deal; The Color of Money; No Mercy; Light of Day; One More Saturday Night. **1987:** The Untouchables; Planes, Trains, & Automobiles. **1988:** Above the Law; Child's Play; The Blob; Rent-A-Cop; Vice Versa; Biloxi Blues; Betrayed; Red Heat; A Night in the Life of Jimmy Reardon; Poltergeist 3; The Seventh Sign. **1989:** Major League; Her Alibi; The Package; Next of Kin; Tango & Cash. **1990:** Men Don't Leave; Home Alone; Internal Affairs; Flatliners; Opportunity Knocks; The Godfather Part 3. **1991:** V.I. Warshawski; Only the Lonely; Hook; Backdraft; Three Days to a Kill. **1992:** The Babe; The Applegates; Mo' Money; Folks; Shaking the Tree; Captain Ron; Hoffa; Keeper of the City. **1993:** Mad Dog & Glory; Groundhog Day; Excessive Force; Rookie of the Year; Rudy; Watch It; The Fugitive. **1994:** Blink; With Honors. **1995:** Losing Isaiah; Stuart Saves His Family; While You Were Sleeping; Sudden Death. **1996:** Primal Fear; Celtic Pride; A Family

Thing; Chain Reaction; Feeling Minnesota; Normal Life. *Television*—The Fall Guy; Chicago Story; Angel Street.

JULIUS LEFLORE

A member of the Stuntmen's Association, LeFlore coordinated stunts and helmed second unit before making his directorial debut with *Secret Agent 00-Soul,* which he also wrote, produced, and has his daughter star in. He has doubled regularly for Billy Dee Williams.

Films—**1974:** The Towering Inferno; Earthquake. **1976:** Drum; King Kong. **1982:** Night Shift; The Sword & the Sorcerer; Fast Times at Ridgemont High; Rocky 3. **1983:** Return of the Jedi. **1984:** City Heat; Firestarter; The Exterminator 2; Police Academy; Ghostbusters. **1985:** Marie; Silver Bullet. **1986:** Legal Eagles; Maximum Overdrive; Vamp; Invaders from Mars; Wisdom. **1987:** Allan Quartermain & the Lost City of Gold; Number One with a Bullet; The Big Easy; The Monster Squad; Innerspace; Traxx; Weeds; Date with an Angel; Hell Comes to Frogtown. **1988:** Action Jackson; Die Hard; Colors. **1989:** Collision Course. **1990:** House Party; The First Power; Secret Agent 00-Soul (p/d/s); Dangerous Passion (tv). **1991:** Rage in Harlem; Driving Me Crazy. **1992:** Dr. Giggles; Unlawful Entry; White Men Can't Jump; Class Act; South Central; Sneakers. **1993:** Amos & Andrew; Posse; Undercover Blues. **1994:** Clean Slate; Police Academy: Mission Moscow; Ring of the Musketeers. **1995:** Destiny Turns on the Radio; Panther; Tales from the Hood; Friday; Zooman. **1996:** Down Periscope; Mars Attacks! *Television*—Renegade.

TERRY LEONARD
(b. 1940)

A stunt legend thanks to his fantastic truck stunt for Harrison Ford in *Raiders of the Lost Ark,* Leonard was a professional football player for the British Columbia Lions, a rodeo cowboy, and twice qualified for the Olympics as a decathlete. He became one of the top stunt coordinators and second unit men in the business, staging the spectacular chopper raid in *Apocalypse Now,* the brutal sword battles in *Conan,* and the explosive train crash in *The Fugitive.* A member of the Stuntmen's Association, he made his directorial debut with the actioner *Death Before Dishonor.*

Films—**1963:** McLintock. **1967:** El Dorado. **1968:** Planet of the Apes. **1969:** Che; Hard Contract. **1970:** Beneath the Planet of the Apes; Barquero; Cover Me, Babe; A Man Called Horse; Monte Walsh; Soldier Blue. **1971:** Sometimes a Great Notion (aka Never Give an Inch). **1972:** Conquest of the Planet of the Apes; The Life & Times of Judge Roy Bean. **1973:** Cleopatra Jones; Dillinger; The Train Robbers; The Deadly Trackers; Class of '44; Battle for the Planet of the Apes. **1974:** The Towering Inferno; Black Samson; Blazing Saddles; Earthquake. **1975:** The Wind & the Lion; Night Moves; Return to Macon County. **1977:** Exo-Man (tv). **1978:** The Norseman; Big Wednesday; FM; Lord of the Rings. **1979:** Apocalypse Now; Circle of Iron; 1941; Beach Patrol (tv). **1980:** The Blues Brothers; Inside Moves; The Mountain Men; My Bodyguard; The Long Riders; Used Cars. **1981:** Legend of the Lone Ranger; Raiders of the Lost Ark. **1982:** Conan the Barbarian; Hammett; Class of 1984. **1983:** Easy Money; Christine; Blue Thunder. **1984:**

Terry Leonard (wearing coat), doubling for Richard Harris, takes a punch from actor/stuntman William Smith in 1973's *The Deadly Trackers*.

Romancing the Stone; Starman; Red Dawn; Gremlins. **1985:** Clue. **1986:** Cobra; Deadly Friend. **1987:** Death Before Dishonor (d); Dragnet; Iron Eagle 2. **1988:** Moving. **1989:** Farewell to the King; The Package. **1990:** Revenge; Downtown; The Rookie. **1991:** Flight of the Intruder; Showdown in Little Tokyo; Teenage Mutant Ninja Turtles II; Backdraft; Delirious. **1992:** Far & Away; Buffy, the Vampire Slayer; Patriot Games. **1993:** Super Mario Bros.; The Fugitive; Tombstone. **1994:** Maverick. **1995:** The Quick & the Dead; Die Hard with a Vengeance; Money Train. **1996:** Eraser. *Television*—Daniel Boone; The Wild Wild West; The Rockford Files; The Six Million Dollar Man; The Fall Guy; Voyagers; Hunter.

AL LEONG
(b. 1953)

Instantly recognizable Asian supporting player, stunt coordinator, and martial arts weapons expert seemed to be visible in the background of most major action films of the late eighties and early nineties. Best known as Mel Gibson's torturer in *Lethal Weapon* and Genghis Khan in *Bill and Ted's Excellent Adventure*. A fight opposite Brandon Lee in *Rapid Fire* also stands out on his resume. He's the father of Willie Leong.

Films—**1982:** Renegades (tv). **1983:** Twilight Zone: The Movie. **1984:** Protocol. **1985:** Big Trouble; My Science Project. **1986:** The golden Child; Big Trouble in Little China. **1987:** Lethal Weapon; Steele

Al Leong with actress Pam Grier in 1996's *Escape from L.A.*, action coordinated by Jeff Imada.

Justice. **1988:** Action Jackson; Die Hard; They Live; She's Having a Baby. **1989:** Cage; Bill & Ted's Excellent Adventure; Black Rain. **1990:** I Come in Peace; Death Warrant; Savage Beach. **1991:** Stone Cold; Showdown in Little Tokyo; The Perfect Weapon; Double Impact. **1992:** Rapid Fire; Hard Hunted. **1993:** Hot Shots Part Deux; The Last Action Hero; Martial Outlaw. **1994:** Army of One; The Shadow; Double Dragon; Deadly Target. **1996:** Escape from L.A. *Television*—Hart to Hart; Renegades; The Fall Guy; Magnum P.I.; "V" (reg.); The A Team; Riptide; The Twilight Zone; Spenser for Hire; McGyver; Renegade; Kung Fu, the Legend Continues.

WILLIE LEONG

Films—**1990:** Come See the Paradise; Kindergarten Cop; The Rookie. **1991:** Showdown in Little Tokyo; The Perfect Weapon; Hook; Double Impact; Flight of the Intruder; Leather Jackets. **1992:** Kuffs;

Rapid Fire; Dead Center (aka Crazy Joe); Martial Law 2: Undercover; Mission of Justice. **1993:** Surf Ninjas; Sidekicks; Made in America. **1994:** The Naked Gun 33 1/3; Pentathlon; Army of One; Stargate; Deadly Target; American Yakuza. **1995:** The Walking Dead; Jade; To the Limit; The Immortals; Excessive Force 2. **1996:** Executive Decision. *Television*— Walker, Texas Ranger.

ALLEN MICHAEL LERNER

The son of veteran stuntman Fred Lerner, A. Michael has stood in for *Halloween*'s "The Shape" and Robert Davi, the Bogart of B-movies.

Films—**1986:** Invaders from Mars; Convicted (tv). **1987:** Remote Control;

Hunter's Blood; Traxx; Date with an Angel. **1988:** Mississippi Burning; Twins. **1989:** Grave Secrets. **1990:** Total Recall; Legal Tender. **1991:** The Taking of Beverly Hills; Barton Fink; Late for Dinner; Dead On: Relentless 2; Mannequin 2; Diplomatic Immunity. **1992:** Stop! Or My Mom Will Shoot; Aces: Iron Eagle 3; Class Act; South Central. **1993:** Boiling Point. **1994:** The Naked Gun 33 1/3; A Low Down Dirty Shame. **1995:** Halloween: The Curse of Michael Myers. **1996:** Last Man Standing. *Television—* Beauty & the Beast.

FRED LERNER
(b. 1935)

Familiar Nevada-raised supporting player and one-time rodeo performer Lerner grew up on a cattle farm. A veteran member of the Stuntmen's Association, he has coordinated stunts and directed second unit for many television projects.

*Films—***1959:** Girls Town. **1966:** A Fine Madness. **1967:** The President's Analyst. **1968:** Planet of the Apes. **1969:** Che; Butch Cassidy & the Sundance Kid; The Sterile Cuckoo; Hello, Dolly! **1970:** Little Big Man; Flap. **1971:** Soldier Blue; Skin Game; Sometimes a Great Notion (aka Never Give an Inch); Dirty Harry. **1972:** Conquest of the Planet of the Apes; The Legend of Nigger Charley. **1973:** Battle for the Planet of the Apes. **1974:** The Towering Inferno; Foxy Brown; Earthquake. **1975:** Hard Times. **1977:** Black Oak Conspiracy; Murder in Peyton Place (tv); Killer on Board. **1978:** The New Adventures of Heidi (tv); A Real American Hero (tv). **1979:** H.O.T.S.; The Jerk; Silent Victory (tv); Samurai (tv); Stunt Seven (tv). **1980:** Witches' Brew; The Island; Seems Like Old Times; The Nude Bomb. **1981:** Escape from New York; The Four Seasons; Honkytonk Freeway; The Night the Lights Went Out in Georgia. **1982:** The Beast-

master; E.T.; The Sword & the Sorcerer; Tron; Endangered Species. **1983:** Heart Like a Wheel. **1984:** City Heat; Grandview USA; Splash; P.K. & the Kid; Celebrity (tv); Rearview Mirror (tv). **1985:** Fandango; Better Off Dead; Covenant; Badge of the Assassin (tv). **1986:** Number One with a Bullet; The Deliberate Stranger (tv); Brotherhood of the Rose (tv). **1987:** The Omega Syndrome; No Man's Land; Down Twisted; Six Against the Rock (tv). **1988:** Beetlejuice; The Seventh Sign; Die Hard; Halloween 4. **1989:** Ghostbusters 2; Blind Fury; Outside Woman (tv); Dark Holiday (tv). **1990:** Total Recall. **1991:** Switch; The Last Boy Scout; This Gun for Hire (tv). **1992:** Deep Cover; Rapid Fire; Class Act. **1993:** Boiling Point; Dazed & Confused; Posse; Coneheads. **1994:** Clean Slate; Ring of the Musketeers; A Taste for Killing (tv). **1995:** Candyman: Farewell to the Flesh; Unstrung Heroes; Halloween: The Curse of Michael Myers. **1996:** The Rock; Set It Off; Spy Hard. *Television—*Rawhide; The Man from U.N.C.L.E.; Land of the Giants; The Immortal; Kung Fu; Gunsmoke; Planet of the Apes; The Manhunter; The Six Million Dollar Man; The Rockford Files; Wonder Woman; Spiderman; Hawaii 5-0; Charlie's Angels; Vegas; The Greatest American Hero; The Powers of Matthew Star; The Fall Guy; Matt Houston; Wizards & Warriors; Sawyer & Finn; Magnum P.I.; Knight Rider; Airwolf; The A Team; The Shadow Chasers; Hunter; The Twilight Zone; The Equalizer; Beauty & the Beast; Stone Fox; Twin Peaks; The Flash; Viper; Dallas; Dynasty.

KEN LESCO

*Films—***1984:** Ninja 3: The Domination. **1985:** American Ninja. **1986:** Invaders from Mars. **1988:** Miracle Mile. **1990:** Firebirds; Peacemaker; Dark Side of the Moon; Silent Night, Deadly Night 4: The Initiation; Circuitry Man; Red Surf. **1991:** Rich Girl; Bride of RE-Animator; Silent Night, Deadly Night 5: The Toy Maker; Soldier's Fortune. **1992:** Mom & Dad

Save the World; Black Magic Woman; Reservoir Dogs. **1993:** Private Wars. **1994:** Pulp Fiction; T-Force. **1995:** White Man's Burden. *Television*—Baa Baa Black Sheep; Contact.

SCOTT LEVA

A former national gymnastics champ, Leva has worked as a stunt coordinator primarily on low-budget films.

Films—**1980:** Mother's Day. **1982:** The House on Sorority Row. **1985:** The Toxic Avenger. **1986:** Convicted (tv). **1988:** Troma's War. **1989:** The Toxic Avenger 3. **1991:** Mobsters; The Perfect Weapon. **1992:** Class Act; White Men Can't Jump; Martial Law 2: Undercover; Mission of Justice. **1993:** Private Wars; Cyborg 2. **1994:** Zero Tolerance; Deadly Target; T-Force. **1995:** Evolver; To the Limit; Last Man Standing. **1996:** Mercenary.

JAMES LEW
(b. 1952)

Popular Korean martial artist won numerous championships. After many bits, his acting career received a boost with his humorous fight scene in *Hot Shots Part Deux*. High-profile fights opposite Steven Seagal in *On Deadly Ground* and Jean-Claude Van Damme in *Timecop* solidified his reputation. A member of the Stuntmen's Association, Lew has also coordinated stunts.

Films—**1976:** The Killing of a Chinese Bookie. **1979:** When Hell Was in Session (tv); Stunt Seven (tv). **1982:** Renegades (tv). **1983:** Going Berserk; Girls of the White Orchid (tv). **1984:** Killpoint. **1986:** Big Trouble in Little China (a/p); Ninja Turf. **1988:** Action Jackson; They Live.

1989: Kinjite; Best of the Best; Black Rain; Night of the Warrior; Street Justice. **1990:** Solar Crisis; China Cry; Ninja Academy; Savage Beach; Aftershock; Guns. **1991:** Showdown in Little Tokyo; The Perfect Weapon; Double Impact; Martial Law. **1992:** Do or Die; Rapid Fire; Buffy, The Vampire Slayer; Martial Law 2: Undercover; Mission of Justice. **1993:** Hot Shots, Part Deux; Coneheads; Undercover Blues; Private Wars; Showdown. **1994:** Blue Tiger; On Deadly Ground; The Shadow; Red Sun Rising; Timecop; Cage 2; Deadly Target; The Young Dragons. **1995:** American Ninja 5; Blood for Blood; Under Siege 2; Ballistic; The Immortals; Night Hunter; Excessive Force 2; Balance of Power; Tigerman. **1996:** Escape from L.A.; Robowarriors. *Television*—Kung Fu; Renegades; Beauty & the Beast; Raven; Walker, Texas Ranger; Baywatch Nights; Deadly Games.

IRVING LEWIS

Films—**1987:** The Hidden. **1988:** The Serpent & the Rainbow; I'm Gonna Git You Sucka. **1989:** Glory; Crack House. **1990:** Marked for Death; Peacemaker; Red Surf; Backstreet Dreams. **1991:** Timebomb; Merchant of Evil; Mom. **1992:** Mom & Dad Save the World; Dead Center (aka Crazy Joe). **1993:** Streetknight; Best of the Best 2. **1995:** Tank Girl; Vampire in Brooklyn; Sudden Death; Soldier Boyz; Suspect Device. **1996:** Broken Arrow.

JIM LEWIS, JR.

Films—**1980:** Roadie. **1981:** The Cannonball Run; Sharky's Machine. **1982:** Best Friends. **1983:** Stroker Ace. **1984:** City Heat. **1988:** License to Drive. **1990:** Downtown; Young Guns 2; Problem Child; Marked for Death. **1991:** Hangfire; Mannequin 2; Flight of the Intruder; Diplomatic Immunity; The Last Boy Scout. **1992:** The Last of the Mohicans; Hero. **1993:** Striking Distance; Amos &

Andrew; Posse; Ghost in the Machine. **1994:** Bad Girls. **1995:** Die Hard with a Vengeance; Devil in a Blue Dress; One Man's Justice. **1996:** The Nutty Professor; Bulletproof; Crazy Horse.

CLAY LILLEY

A member of the Stuntmen's Association, Clint has doubled for Jimmy Smits. He's the brother of Clay Lilley and the son of horse wrangler Jack Lilley.

Films—**1980:** Used Cars. **1987:** Masters of the Universe. **1988:** Lucky Stiff; Border Heat; Bail Out. **1989:** Old Gringo. **1990:** Dollman; Syngenor. **1991:** Flight of the Intruder; Suburban Commando. **1992:** Last of the Mohicans; Buffy, the Vampire Slayer; Bram Stoker's Dracula; Rage & Honor. **1993:** Robin Hood: Men in Tights; Man's Best Friend; Ghost in the Machine; Aspen Extreme; The Last Outlaw. **1994:** City Slickers 2. **1995:** 3 Ninjas Knuckle Up; One Man's Justice. **1996:** The Phantom; Feeling Minnesota; Raven.

JACK LILLEY

Films—**1979:** Meteor. **1980:** The Mountain Men; Used Cars. **1983:** Sudden Impact; Little House: Look Back to Yesterday (tv). **1984:** Little House: Bless All the Dear Children (tv); Little House: The Last Farewell (tv). **1986:** The Three Amigos. **1988:** Bail Out. **1989:** Pink Cadillac. **1991:** City Slickers. **1992:** Hard Promises. **1993:** Man's Best Friend; The Last Outlaw. **1994:** City Slickers 2; The Gambler 4 (tv). **1995:** The Sweeper. *Television*—Little House on the Prairie.

GARY LITTLEJOHN

A custom bike designer, Littlejohn began playing supporting parts in mo-

torcycle movies and eventually broke into the stunt field. He has doubled for Gene Hackman.

Films—**1967:** Devil's Angels; Hell's Angels on Wheels. **1968:** The Savage Seven; Speedway. **1969:** Cycle Savages. **1970:** Angels Die Hard; C.C. & Company. **1971:** Angels Hard as They Come; Chrome & Hot Leather. **1972:** Bury Me an Angel; The Limit. **1973:** Badlands. **1974:** Caged Heat. **1976:** Hollywood Man; The Gumball Rally. **1979:** The Dark. **1983:** Breathless. **1986:** Howard the Duck; One Crazy Summer; Billy Galvin. **1987:** Cyclone; Near Dark; Death Spa; Nightmare on Elm Street 3: Dream Warriors; Cold Steel. **1988:** Young Guns; Bat 21. **1989:** Down the Drain; Cartel; Sundown; Pale Blood. **1990:** Joe vs. The Volcano; Peacemaker; In the Cold of the Night. **1991:** Mobsters; The Naked Gun 2 1/2; Hangfire. **1992:** Trancers 3; Sweet Justice. **1994:** The Naked Gun 33 1/3; The Mask; Color of Night; Ice; Zero Tolerance; Steel Frontier. **1995:** 3 Ninjas Knuckle Up; Vampire in Brooklyn. **1996:** Mulholland Falls; Last Man Standing.

CAREY LOFTIN
(b. 1914)

Florida-born driving legend drove in stunt shows and served in the Marine Corps before getting into films. A member of the Stuntmen's Association, he coordinated stunts or directed second unit on such classic car chase scenes as *Bullit* and *The French Connection*.

Films—**1939:** Nick Carter, Master Detective; Burn 'Em Up O'Connor; Dick Tracy's G-Men. **1940:** The Bank Dick. **1942:** Perils of Nyoka; Spy Smasher. **1943:** The Masked Marvel. **1944:** Abbott & Costello in Society; I'll Remember April; Haunted Harbor; Zorro's Black

A car jumps over a train in 1980's *Used Cars,* action coordinated by Carey Loftin.

Whip; Tuscon Raiders; Lost in a Harem; The Tiger Woman. **1945:** The Crimson Ghost; Trail to Vengeance; The Purple Monster Strikes. **1946:** The Shadow; King of the Forest Rangers. **1947:** Louisiana; Jesse James Rides Again; The Black Widow. **1948:** Raw Deal; The Adventures of Frank & Jesse James. **1949:** Sidestreet; Siren of Atlantis; Radar Patrol vs. Sky King; King of the Rocketmen; The Threat; Federal Agents vs. Underworld Inc. **1950:** The Milkman; Invisible Monster. **1951:** Radar Men from the Moon. **1952:** Don Daredevil Rides Again; Fearless Fagan. **1953:** Code Two; Army Bound; The Jalopy. **1954:** A Star Is Born; The Wild One. **1955:** Abbott & Costello Meet the Keystone Cops; Six Bridges to Cross. **1956:** The Steel Jungle. **1958:** The Perfect Furlough; Thunder Road. **1959:** On the Beach; The Big Operator. **1960:** Spartacus; Thunder in Carolina; The Rise & Fall of Legs Diamond. **1962:** Hatari. **1963:** It's a Mad, Mad, Mad, Mad World. **1964:** Viva Las Vegas; Goodbye, Charlie; The Killers. **1965:** Red Line 7000; Dr. Goldfoot & the Bikini Machine. **1966:** Grand Prix; Munster Go Home; The Silencers; Spinout. **1967:** A Guide for the Married Man. **1968:** Speedway; Bullit. **1969:** The Great Bank Robbery; The Love Bug; The Wrecking Crew. **1970:** Patton; Which Way to the Front? **1971:** The French Connection; Vanishing Point; Slaughterhouse Five; Duel (tvm). **1972:** Come Back, Charleston Blue; The Getaway; Fear Is the Key; The Hot Rock. **1973:** The Don Is Dead; Magnum Force; Walking Tall. **1974:** The Sugarland Express; Thunderbolt & Lightfoot. **1975:** Framed; Part 2: Walking Tall; White Line Fever; The Eiger Sanction. **1976:** Special Delivery. **1977:** Herbie Goes to Monte Carlo; Outlaw Blues. **1978:** The Cat from Outer Space; The Deer Hunter; Return from Witch Mountain; A Real American Hero (tv). **1979:** Sunburn; The China Syndrome; The Promise. **1980:** Foolin' Around; Resurrection; Used Cars. **1981:** Blow Out. **1983:** The Dead Zone; Sudden Impact. **1984:** Against All Odds; City Heat; Highpoint. **1985:** Black Moon Rising. **1986:** Running Scared. **1988:** License to Drive. **1990:** Desperate Hours; Days of Thunder; The Rookie. *Television*—Troubleshooters (reg.); The Fugitive; The Man from U.N.C.L.E.; Laredo; Star Trek; The Invaders; Mission: Impossible.

STACY LOGAN

The stunt partner of Rick LeFevour, Logan is a member of the Mid-West Stunt Association.

Films—**1983:** Class; Through Naked Eyes (tv). **1985:** Code of Silence; Invasion USA; Two Fathers' Justice (tv). **1986:** Raw Deal. **1987:** The Untouchables. **1988:** Above the Law; Vice Versa; Red Heat; Child's Play. **1989:** Her Alibi; The Package; Next of Kin. **1990:** Opportunity Knocks. **1991:** V.I. Warshawski; Backdraft; Three Days to a Kill. **1992:** Rapid Fire; Folks; Prelude to a Kiss; Hoffa; Keeper of the City. **1993:** The Fugitive; Excessive Force. **1994:** Blink; Richie Rich. **1995:** Losing Isaiah. **1996:** Chain Reaction; Normal Life.

KURT LOTT

Films—**1987:** The Quick & the Dead. **1989:** Rooftops; Mob Boss. **1990:** The Exorcist 3; Peacemaker; Last Call; Legal Tender. **1991:** Stone Cold; Hook; Highway to Hell. **1992:** To Sleep with a Vampire; Mission of Justice; To Protect & Serve. **1993:** No Escape, No Return; Night Eyes 3; Cybertracker; Firepower. **1994:** Scorned; Guardian Angel; Hologram Man; Fast Getaway 2; L.A. Wars; Bad Blood; Carnosaur 2. **1995:** Frank & Jesse; Avenging Angel; Number One Fan; Soldier Boyz; To the Limit; Cyber Bandits; Unknown Origin; The Immortals; Black Scorpion; Blackout; The Silencers; Best of the Best 3; Excessive Force 2; Suspect Device. **1996:** Skyscraper; Dark Breed.

JIM LOVELETT

Films—**1974:** Phantom of the Paradise. **1978:** Eyes of Laura Mars; Somebody Killed Her Husband. **1980:** The Exterminator; Times Square. **1981:** The Fan. **1982:** A Little Sex; Fighting Back. **1984:** Falling in Love. **1985:** Getting Even. **1986:** F/X. **1987:** Dirty Dancing; Wall Street; Deadly Illusion. **1988:** Kansas; Viper. **1989:** True Believer; Black Rain; True Blood. **1990:** King of New York. **1991:** Switch. **1992:** Freejack; A Stranger Among Us; The Runestone; The Double-O Kid. **1993:** Trouble Bound; Bitter Harvest; Carlito's Way. **1994:** Handgun; The Cowboy Way. **1995:** Kiss of Death.

BILLY LUCAS

A member of both the Stuntmen's Association and the Professional Driver's Association, Lucas has doubled for Arnold Schwarzenegger.

Films—**1985:** To Live & Die in L.A. **1986:** Let's Get Harry; Never Too Young to Die; Eye of the Tiger. **1987:** Kidnapped; The Wild Pair; Night Force; The Running Man. **1988:** They Live; Twins; Vampire Cop. **1989:** Ghostbusters 2; Riding the Edge. **1990:** Die Hard 2; Total Recall; Solar Crisis; Rocky 5; The Borrower; Kindergarten Cop. **1991:** Harley Davidson & the Marlboro Man; Terminator 2; Thelma & Louise; Cape Fear; Past Midnight. **1992:** Last of the Mohicans; Thunderheart; Universal Soldier; Nemesis. **1993:** The Last Action Hero; Cliffhanger; Demolition Man; Weekend at Bernie's 2. **1994:** Jimmy Hollywood; True Lies; Puppetmasters; Junior. **1995:** Village of the Damned; Waterworld; Jade; Nemesis 3. **1996:** From Dusk Till Dawn; Broken Arrow; Eraser; The Fan; Jingle All the Way.

TOM LUPO

An independent stunt coordinator, Lupo has doubled for Tom Selleck. His son Curtis has also performed stunts.

Films—**1978:** Hooper; Convoy. **1979:** Avalanche Express; Buck Rogers in the 25th Century; Tilt; Samurai (tv). **1980:** Hangar 18; Alcatraz (tv). **1981:** The Boogens. **1982:** The Border; Fighting Back; Nat'l Lampoon's Class Reunion. **1984:** Runaway. **1987:** North Shore. **1989:** Her Alibi; Lock Up. **1991:** Eve of Destruction; Bugsy. **1992:** Folks; Mr. Baseball. **1993:** Hard Target. **1994:** Surviving the Game; White Mile. **1996:** Eraser; The Phantom; Kingpin. *Television*—Star Trek; Vegas; Magnum P.I.; Jake & the Fatman.

RAY LYKINS

An independent stunt coordinator, Lykins has doubled for Michael Madsen.

Films—**1983:** Young Warriors; Lies; Fire & Ice; Deadly Force. **1984:** Savage Streets. **1985:** Trancers; Re-Animator; Nightmare on Elm Street 2: Freddy's Revenge; The Boys Next Door. **1986:** Hollywood Vice Squad. **1987:** Sweet Revenge; Survival Game; Opposing Force; Dudes. **1988:** Dead Heat; Critters 2. **1989:** Checking Out; Bill & Ted's Excellent Adventure; Night Visitor. **1990:** Blue Desert; Prayer of the Rollerboys. **1991:** Suburban Commando. **1992:** The Lawnmower Man. **1993:** Cyborg 2; Dead Connection. **1994:** The Dark Wind; Blue Tiger; The Getaway; The Mask; Automatic; American Yakuza. **1995:** 3 Ninjas Knuckle Up; Dirty Money; Species. **1996:** Primal Fear; Larger Than Life; Independence Day.

CLIFF LYONS
(b. 1901; d. 1974)

A former rodeo cowboy, Lyons was renowned as a top horseman. He performed many supporting roles and coordinated stunts on several of John Ford's classic Westerns.

Films—**1926:** West of the Law. **1928:** Flashing Hoofs; Master of the Range; The Riddle Trail; Across the Plains; Heading Westward; Manhattan Cowboy; The Old Code. **1929:** The Arizona Kid; Captain Cowboy; The Cowboy & the Outlaw; Fighters of the Saddle; The Fighting Terror; The Last Roundup; West of the Rockies; The Sheriff 's Lash; The Galloping Lover; Saddle King; Law of the Mounted; Thundering Thompson. **1930:** Code of the West; Crusaders of the West; Red Gold; Breezy Bill; Call of the Desert; Oklahoma Cyclone; Canyon Hawks; Firebrand Jordan; O'Malley Rides Alone; Oklahoma Sheriff; Western Honor; The Voice from the Sky. **1931:** Painted Desert; Red Fork Range; Night Rider; A Holy Terror. **1932:** Not Exactly Gentlemen; The Gay Caballero; The Golden West; The Rainbow Trail; Tumbling Tumbleweed; Dynamite Ranch. **1933:** Robber's Roost. **1934:** Against the Law; Call It Love; Honor of the Range; In Old Santa Fe; Love Time; Gun Justice; Stingaree; Mystery Mountain. **1935:** Outlawed Guns; The Miracle Ride; Branded a Bandit; Dante's Inferno; Rustlers of Red Dog. **1936:** Call of the Prairie; The Lawless Nineties; The Big Show. **1937:** North of the Rio Grande; Riders of the Dawn; Texas Trail. **1938:** In Early Arizona; Valley of the Giants. **1939:** Desperate Trail; Jesse James. **1940:** Dark Command; Winners of the West; Law & Order. **1941:** Cyclone on Horseback. **1943:** Wagon Tracks West; Song of Russia; The Law Rides Again. **1944:** Zorro's Black Whip; The Tiger Woman. **1945:** Dakota; Frontier Gal; Bells of Rosarita; San Antonio; The Purple Monster Strikes. **1946:** The Phantom Rider. **1948:** Three Godfathers; The Fighting Kentuckian;

An epic battle of horsemen in 1965's *Major Dundee*, action coordinated by Cliff Lyons.

Oklahoma Badlands. **1949:** She Wore a Yellow Ribbon. **1950:** Wagonmaster; Rio Grande; The Milkman; Tripoli. **1952:** Bend of the River. **1953:** Hondo; The Sun Shines Bright. **1954:** Drums Across the River. **1955:** The Prodigal. **1956:** The Searchers; Seven Men from Now. **1957:** The Abductors; Apache Warrior; Wings of Eagles. **1959:** Ben Hur; The Horse Soldiers; Branded a Bandit. **1960:** The Young Land; Spartacus; The Alamo; Sgt. Rutledge. **1961:** The Commancheros; Two Rode Together. **1962:** Taras Bulba; How the West Was Won. **1963:** McLintock; Donovan's Reef. **1964:** The Long Ships; Cheyenne Autumn. **1965:** Major Dundee; Genghis Khan; Marco the Magnificent. **1966:** Seven Women. **1967:** The War Wagon. **1968:** The Green Berets. **1969:** The Great Bank Robbery. **1970:** Chisum. **1971:** Big Jake. **1973:** The Train Robbers.

RUSTY McCLENNON

McClennon is an independent stunt coordinator and double for the comedian Sinbad. His wife Vinita also performs stunts.

Films—**1988:** I'm Gonna Git You Sucka. **1989:** Glory. **1990:** Peacemaker; Predator 2. **1992:** Deep Cover; Live Wire; Class Act; Dead Center (aka Crazy Joe). **1993:** What's Eating Gilbert Grape? **1995:** Tales from the Hood; Houseguest; Vampire in Brooklyn; Things to Do in Denver When You're Dead. **1996:** First Kid; Jingle All the Way. *Television*—Airwolf.

BUFERT McCLERKINS

Films—**1985:** To Live & Die in L.A.; Police Academy 2: Their First Assignment. **1988:** I'm Gonna Git You Sucka. **1989:** Kinjite; Second Sight; Glory. **1990:** Criminal Justice. **1991:** A Time to Die. **1992:** Maximum Force. **1993:** Private Wars. **1994:** Zero Tolerance; Direct Hit; T-Force; Witch Hunt. **1995:** The Glass Shield.

MATT McCOLM

A former male model who had doubled for David Hasselhoff on "Baywatch," McColm moved into starring roles with the film *Red Scorpion 2.*

Films—**1984:** Killpoint. **1987:** Assassination. **1988:** Shakedown; Above the Law; Maniac Cop; Elvira, Mistress of the Dark; They Live; Bail Out. **1989:** Cyborg; Under the Gun; One Man Force; Society; Pink Cadillac. **1990:** Problem Child; Hard to Kill; Marked for Death; Pacific Heights; Captain America; The Rookie; Keaton's Cop. **1991:** The Taking of Beverly Hills; Terminator 2; Highway to Hell; Diplomatic Immunity; Beastmaster 2; Knight Rider 2000 (tv). **1992:** Freejack. **1993:** Maniac Cop 3; Red Scorpion 2. **1994:** Dead Badge; Conway. **1996:** True Blue; Subterfuge. *Television*—Baywatch; Brisco County, Jr.; Knight Rider; The Fall Guy; Star Trek, the Next Generation.

LISA McCULLOUGH

A member of the Professional Driver's Association, this bit actress has doubled for Pam Anderson. She's married to stuntman Mark Dealasandro.

Films—**1987:** Cop. **1988:** Little Nikita; Bad Dreams; Nightmare on Elm Street 4: Dream Master; Criminal Act. **1990:** The Adventures of Ford Fairlane; Marked for Death. **1991:** The Rapture. **1992:** Toys. **1993:** Hot Shots Part Deux; Cliffhanger. **1994:** The Naked Gun 33 1/3; The River Wild; Wes Craven's New Nightmare; Puppetmasters. **1995:** Congo; Species; The Crossing Guard. **1996:** Barb Wire; Spy Hard; Daylight. *Television*—Baywatch; Viper.

BUCK McDANCER

A stunt coordinator and second unit director, McDancer is a member of the Stuntmen's Association. His wife Sonia has also done stunts.

Films—**1983:** D.C. Cab; Scarface. **1984:** Flashpoint; Ninja 3: The Domination. **1986:** Odd Jobs; Legal Eagles; Murphy's Law. **1987:** Witchboard; Death Wish 4; Laguna Heat. **1988:** Messenger of Death. **1989:** Kinjite; No Holds Barred; Midnight Warrior. **1990:** By Dawn's Early Light (tv). **1991:** Hell Hath No Fury (tv). **1992:** Innocent Blood; Chrome Soldiers (tv). **1993:** Hot Shots Part Deux; In the Line of Fire. **1994:** Airheads; The Expert; Zero Tolerance; Flashfire. **1995:** Tall Tale; Coldblooded; Last Man Standing; Vampire in Brooklyn; Deadly Outbreak; The Sweeper. **1996:** Larger Than Life. *Television*—Knot's Landing; Midnight Caller; Perfect Strangers; Pros & Cons.

MIKE McGAUGHEY

A stunt coordinator and horse specialist, McGaughey is a member of the Stuntmen's Association.

Films—**1978:** Hooper. **1980:** Tom Horn; The Long Riders; The Mountain Men. **1981:** Escape from New York. **1982:** The Beastmaster; Split Image. **1983:** Christine; Blue Thunder. **1984:** Racing with the Moon; Gremlins; Red Dawn. **1985:** Silverado; Pale Rider. **1986:** Gung Ho; Blue City; Cobra; The Three Amigos; Never Too Young to Die. **1987:** Number One with a Bullet; The Night Stalker; Cherry 2000; Near Dark; Made in Heaven. **1988:** Hot to Trot; Lucky Stiff; Bail Out. **1989:** Indiana Jones & the Last Crusade. **1990:**

Total Recall; Back to the Future 3; Gremlins 2; The Rookie. **1992:** Last of the Mohicans; Buffy, the Vampire Slayer; Hoffa; Trancers 3; Critters 4. **1993:** The Fugitive; Man's Best Friend; Aspen Extreme. **1994:** 8 Seconds. **1995:** Avenging Angel; Don Juan DeMarco. **1996:** Crazy Horse.

DWAYNE McGEE

The son of stuntman S.J. McGee, Dwayne has doubled for rap artist Ice-T. He's a member of the Stuntmen's Association.

Films—**1985:** Rocky 4. **1987:** Back to the Beach. **1988:** Action Jackson; Alien Nation; Colors; I'm Gonna Git You Sucka; License to Drive. **1989:** Cage; One Man Force; Crack House. **1990:** Die Hard 2. **1991:** Eve of Destruction; The Naked Gun 2 1/2; Deadlock; Beastmaster 2; Driving Me Crazy. **1992:** Unlawful Entry; Mo' Money; Sleepwalkers; Nemesis; Davinci's War. **1993:** Posse; Streetknight. **1994:** Surviving the Game; The Naked Gun 33 1/3; Gunmen; Clean Slate; Puppetmasters. **1995:** 3 Ninjas Knuckle Up; Panther; Die Hard with a Vengeance; Devil in a Blue Dress; Things to Do in Denver When You're Dead. **1996:** Original Gangstas; Escape from L.A.; Pure Danger; Riot.

BILL McINTOSH

A member of the Stuntmen's Association, McIntosh has also performed bit parts and doubled for Robert Duvall.

Films—**1974:** Blazing Saddles. **1979:** Star Trek, The Motion Picture. **1980:** Heaven's Gate. **1981:** Going Ape; Heartbeeps. **1982:** The Sword & the Sorcerer. **1984:** City Limits. **1985:** Silverado; Clue. **1986:** The Golden Child; Raw Deal; No Mercy. **1987:** Innerspace; Three O'Clock High;

Traxx; Brenda Starr. **1988:** Young Guns; Patty Hearst; Alien Nation; Criminal Act. **1989:** Collision Course; Hit List; Johnny Handsome; Nightmare on Elm Street 5: Dream Child; Glory; Nat'l Lampoon's Christmas Vacation. **1990:** Pump Up the Volume; The Gumshoe Kid. **1991:** Mobsters; The Naked Gun 2 1/2; Nothing But Trouble. **1992:** Deep Cover; Innocent Blood; Sneakers. **1993:** In the Line of Fire; Hard Target; Undercover Blues; Geronimo. **1994:** City Slickers 2. **1995:** 3 Ninjas Knuckle Up; The Stars Fell on Henrietta; Wild Bill; Heat.

COLE McKAY

A prolific stunt coordinator, director, and supporting player, McKay has worked primarily in the low-budget action and "erotic thriller" genre.

Films—**1986:** The Three Amigos. **1987:** Fatal Beauty; The Hidden. **1988:** Bulletproof; The Game (d). **1989:** Deadly Breed; Chance; East L.A. Warriors; Instant Karma; Mob Boss. **1990:** Back to Back; Cold Fire; Living to Die; Last Call; The Rookie; Legal Tender. **1991:** The Art of Dying; Killer's Edge (aka Blood Money); The Last Riders; The Killing Zone; Danger Zone 3; Star Trek: Undiscovered Country; The Perfect Weapon; Inner Sanctum; Zipperface; Evil Spirits; Double Trouble. **1992:** Article 99; Eye of the Storm; Far & Away; Seed People; Rapid Fire; To Sleep with a Vampire; Sweet Justice; To Protect & Serve; Guncrazy; Betrayal of the Dove; Sins of Desire; The Silencer. **1993:** Night Eyes 3; Forced to Kill; Super Mario Bros.; Indecent Behavior 2; Eye of the Stranger; No Escape, No Return; Cybertracker; Dangerous Touch; Firepower. **1994:** Guardian Angel; Possessed by the Night; Criminal Passion; Scorned; Victim of Desire; Steel Frontier; Hologram Man; The Force; L.A. Wars; Witch Hunt; Silk Degrees; Money to Burn. **1995:** Frank & Jesse; Top Dog; Nature of the Beast; Cybertracker 2; Cyborg

3; To the Limit; Unknown Origin; Best of the Best 3; One Man's Justice; Black Scorpion; Blackout; The Silencers; Suspect Device. **1996:** Skyscraper; Dark Breed; Rattled; One Good Turn; Piranha. *Television*—The Flash; Renegade.

PETER McKERNAN

An expert helicopter pilot and aerial coordinator, McKernan is a member of the International Stunt Association.

Films—**1986:** Riders of the Storm. **1988:** Above the Law; Die Hard. **1989:** Switching Channels; Cage; Backtrack. **1990:** Crazy People; Firebirds; The Exorcist 3; Drug Wars: The Camarena Story (tv). **1991:** Rampage; The Naked Gun 2 1/2; At

Play in the Field of the Lords; Nothing But Trouble. **1992:** Sleepwalkers; Ruby; Scent of a Woman. **1993:** So I Married an Axe Murderer. **1994:** Body Shot. **1995:** Strange Days; Casino; Sabrina; Suspect Device. **1996:** Courage Under Fire; First Kid. *Television*—Airwolf; Tour of Duty.

GARY McLARTY
(b. 1941)

A member of Stunts Unlimited, this veteran performer has coordinated stunts and directed second unit on several high-profile films, *Beverly Hills Cop* being the prime example. A big rig specialist, his wife Karen and son Cole also perform gags.

Films—**1967:** The Way West. **1968:** Ice Station Zebra; Chubasco; Bandolero; Blue; Hellfighters. **1969:** The Undefeated;

Gary McLarty jumps onto a moving train in 1969's *Run, Angel, Run!*, action coordinated by Bill Catching.

The Wild Bunch; Run, Angel, Run!; The Good Guys & the Bad Guys. **1970:** The Losers; C.C. & Company; Beneath the Planet of the Apes; Chisum. **1971:** Sometimes a Great Notion (aka Never Give an Inch); Chrome & Hot Leather. **1972:** The Thing with Two Heads. **1974:** The Front Page; The Gravy Train (aka The Dion Brothers); Policewomen. **1975:** A Boy & His Dog; Rooster Cogburn; Crazy Mama; Mitchell; Flash & the Firecat. **1976:** Mayday at 40,000 Feet (tv). **1978:** Nat'l Lampoon's Animal House; Hooper; Convoy. **1979:** The Apple Dumpling Gang Rides Again; A Time to Die. **1980:** The Blues Brothers; Coast to Coast. **1981:** All the Marbles. **1982:** Cannery Row; Blade Runner; The Beastmaster; The Entity; Yes, Giorgio. **1983:** The Man Who Loved Women; Scarface; Twilight Zone: The Movie; Stroker Ace; The Man with Two Brains. **1984:** Beverly Hills Cop; Police Academy; The Terminator; A Breed Apart. **1985:** Into the Night; Commando; To Live & Die in L.A.; Moving Violations. **1986:** Cobra; F/X; Out of Bounds; Maximum Overdrive; Never Too Young to Die; Eye of the Tiger; Big Trouble in Little China; Wisdom. **1987:** Beverly Hills Cop 2; Over the Top; Less Than Zero; Night Force; Code Name Zebra; Rolling Vengeance. **1988:** Rambo 3; The Seventh Sign; The Blob. **1989:** Lethal Weapon 2; Road House; Tango & Cash; Backtrack. **1990:** Hard to Kill; Days of Thunder; Another 48 HRS.; Ghost; Desperate Hours; Last of the Finest; Captain America. **1991:** Stone Cold; 976 Evil 2; Hook; Roots of Evil. **1992:** Memoirs of an Invisible Man; Patriot Games; Four Eyes & Six Guns. **1993:** Falling Down; Extreme Justice; The Last Action Hero; Gettysburg; Full Eclipse; Demolition Man. **1994:** Chasers; In the Army Now; A Low Down Dirty Shame; Junior; Puppetmasters; Night of the Running Man. **1995:** Destiny Turns on the Radio; The Good Old Boys. **1996:** From Dusk Till Dawn; Executive Decision; The Phantom; Ravenhawk; Sunchaser. *Television*—The Girl from U.N.C.L.E.; Kung Fu; The Bionic Woman; Airwolf; Bearcats.

CLIFF McLAUGHLIN

Films—**1979:** Prophecy. **1983:** The Gambler 2 (tv). **1987:** Teen Wolf 2. **1988:** Rambo 3. **1989:** K-9. **1990:** Impulse; Flashback; Predator 2; Dances with Wolves. **1991:** Toy Soldiers; White Fang. **1992:** Trancers 3. **1993:** Hot Shots Part Deux; Aspen Extreme; Conflict of Interest. **1995:** Tall Tale; Under Siege 2; Heat. **1996:** Marshal Law; Kingpin.

DENNIS "DANGER" MADALONE
(b. 1955)

A New Jersey-born stunt coordinator, Madalone gained some recognition for working on the updated "Star Trek" series.

Films—**1977:** Blue Sunshine. **1978:** Avalanche; Lord of the Rings. **1980:** The Island; Inside Moves. **1983:** Nightmares. **1988:** Miracle Mile; Mac & Me; I'm Gonna Git You Sucka; Nitti: The Enforcer (tv). **1989:** Kinjite; Blind Fury; Shocker; UHF; Riding the Edge; Chopper Chicks in Zombie Town. **1990:** Firebirds; Darkman; Pump Up the Volume; Trancers 2; 9 1/2 Ninjas; In the Cold of Night; Peacemaker; The Last Hour; Puppetmaster 3; Red Surf; Backstreet Dreams. **1991:** Dragonfight; Rich Girl; Mannequin 2; Prey of the Chameleon; Diplomatic Immunity; Blood & Concrete; Leather Jackets; Shakes the Clown. **1992:** Mom & Dad Save the World; Storyville; Hero; The Unnameable 2; Sweet Justice; Betrayal of the Dove; CIA: Code Name Alexa; Interceptor. **1993:** Private Wars; Cybertracker; Firepower; Rescue Me. **1994:** Pulp Fiction; Direct Hit; T-Force; Open Fire. **1995:** Digital Man; Last Man Standing; Vampire in

Brooklyn; Suspect Device. **1996:** Riot. *Television*—Wonder Woman; Quincy; The Incredible Hulk; Baa Baa Black Sheep; Kojak; Hardy Boys/Nancy Drew Mysteries; Tenspeed & Brownshoe; The Greatest American Hero; Enos; Feel the Heat; Star Trek, The Next Generation; Deep Space Nine; Star Trek, Voyager.

HARRY MADSEN

A former rodeo performer, Madsen established himself as a stunt coordinator and pyrotechnic expert for the East Coast Stuntman's Association.

Films—**1972:** Superfly. **1974:** The Taking of Pelham 1-2-3; Claudine. **1976:** God Told Me To (aka Demon). **1978:** The Eyes of Laura Mars; The Wiz. **1979:** The Warriors; Boardwalk. **1980:** Gloria; The Hitter; Atlantic City. **1981:** Four Friends; Neighbors; Prince of the City. **1982:** The Soldier; Vigilante. **1983:** Baby, It's You; Daniel; Echoes; Amityville 3-D; Trackdown (tv). **1984:** CHUD; Falling in Love; Alphabet City; The Flamingo Kid; Garbo Talks; Almost You; Old Enough; Turk 182. **1985:** After Hours; Death Wish 3; Prizzi's Honor; Sweet Dreams; Too Scared to Scream. **1986:** F/X; The Money Pit. **1987:** Angel Heart; Wall Street; Dead Aim. **1988:** Punchline; Homeboy; Kennedy (tv). **1989:** Lean on Me; See No Evil, Hear No Evil; Black Rain; True Blood. **1990:** Ghost; Q & A. **1991:** New Jack City; The Fisher King; Mannequin 2. **1993:** Wilder Napalm.

VIC MAGNOTTA
(b. 1943; d. 1987)

A college pal of Martin Scorsese, this native American taught communication arts, coached football, and scouted for the Los Angeles Rams before making stunts his full-time oc-

cupation. The founder of Stunt Specialists, Magnotta drowned in the Hudson River performing a car stunt.

Films—**1969:** Who's That Knocking at My Door? **1976:** Taxi Driver. **1978:** King of the Gypsies; Somebody Killed Her Husband. **1979:** Voices; The Warriors; The Wanderers. **1980:** Dressed to Kill; Raging Bull; Simon. **1981:** The Chosen; Endless Love; Fort Apache, The Bronx; Ragtime; Rollover; Wolfen. **1982:** A Stranger Is Watching; Fighting Back; The Soldier; Amityville 2; The World According to Garp. **1983:** Easy Money; I Am the Cheese. **1984:** Slayground; The Bounty; Beat Street; The Cotton Club; Firstborn; Moscow on the Hudson; The Muppets Take Manhattan; Splash; More Than Murder (tv). **1985:** Alamo Bay; Key Exchange; After Hours; Finnegan Begin Again (tv). **1986:** F/X; Legal Eagles; Highlander; Playing for Keeps. **1987:** Ishtar; Outrageous Fortune; The Believers; The Secret of My Success; Orphans; The Squeeze; Who's That Girl? **1988:** The In Crowd; Shakedown.

JOCK MAHONEY
(b. 1919; d. 1989)

Popular leading man of B-movies and television, best known for playing not only the best villain in a Tarzan film but perhaps the most mature screen Tarzan when he himself took over the role. Unfortunately, he contracted jungle fever while making *Tarzan's Three Challenges* and never fully recovered his once robust nature. As a top stuntman, Chicago-born Jacques O'Mahoney doubled for Errol Flynn, Gregory Peck, and *Durango Kid* star Charles Starrett. He was married to Maggie Field, making him

Legendary actor/stuntman Jock Mahoney during a more tender moment with Shawn Smith in 1957's *The Land Unknown.*

Sally Field's stepfather. The grizzled character Brian Keith portrays in *Hooper* is said to be based upon him.

Films—**1946:** The Fighting Frontiersman. **1947:** South of the Chisholm Trail; Swing the Western Way; Out West; Golden Lady. **1948:** Squareheads of the Round Table; The Adventures of Don Juan; The Stranger from Ponca City; Blazing Across the Pecos; Trail to Laredo. **1949:** Feulin' Around; Jolson Sings Again; The Doolins of Oklahoma; Horsemen of the Sierras; Bandits of El Dorado; The Blazing Trail; Renegades of the Sage; Horsemen of the Sierras; Rim of the Canyon; Strange Disappearance; Frontier Marshal. **1950:** Punchy Cowpunchers; The Nevadan; David Harding: Counterspy; Cowtown; Texas Dynamo; Pecos River; Hoedown; Lightning Guns; Frontier Outpost; Cody of the Pony Express. **1951:** Rough Riders of Durango; The Kangaroo Kid; Santa Fe;

The Texas Ranger; Roar of the Iron Horse. **1952:** The Rough Tough West; Smoky Canyon; Junction City; The Kid From Broken Gun; The Hawk of Wild River; Laramie Mountains. **1953:** Gunfighters of the Northwest. **1954:** Overland Pacific; Knutzy Knights. **1955:** A Day of Fury. **1956:** Away All Boats; Showdown at Abilene; Battle Hymn; I've Lived Before. **1957:** The Land Unknown; Joe Dakota; Slim Carter. **1958:** A Time to Live, a Time to Die; Last of the Fast Guns. **1959:** Money, Women, & Guns. **1960:** Tarzan the Magnificent; Three Blondes in Her Life. **1962:** Moro Witch Doctor; Tarzan Goes to India. **1963:** Tarzan's Three Challenges; California. **1964:** The Walls of Hell. **1965:** Marine Battleground. **1966:** Runaway Girl. **1967:** The Glory Stompers. **1968:** Bandolero. **1969:** The Love Bug. **1970:** Tarzan's Deadly Silence. **1971:** Their Only Chance. **1972:** Tom. **1976:** The Bad Bunch. **1978:** The End. **1981:** Tarzan, the Ape

Man. *Television*—The Range Rider (reg.); Loretta Young; Private Secretary; Yancy Derringer (reg.) The Millionaire; Wagon Train; Simon Lash; Rawhide; 77 Sunset Strip; Gunslinger; Laramie; Batman; Tarzan; Daniel Boone; Emergency; Banacek; Kung Fu; The Streets of San Francisco; BJ & the Bear; The Fall Guy; Simon & Simon.

ARTIE MALESCI
(b. 1951)

This Florida-based stunt coordinator was a shark wrangler before getting into films.

Films—1979: Stunt Seven (tv). 1981: For Your Eyes Only; Hardly Working; Nobody's Perfect; Eureka. 1983: Octopussy; Spring Break. 1984: Where the Boys Are '84. 1985: Cease Fire; A View to a Kill; Invasion USA; The Heavenly Kid; The New Kids; Two Fathers' Justice (tv). 1986: Band of the Hand. 1987: The Living Daylights; Revenge of the Nerds 2. 1988: The Unholy; Midnight Crossing. 1989: Cocoon: The Return; License to Kill; Parenthood. 1991: Problem Child 2. 1992: Traces of Red. 1993: Wilder Napalm; Mr. Nanny; Only the Strong; Passenger 57. 1994: China Moon; Ace Ventura, Pet Detective. 1996: The Substitute; Daylight. *Television*—Miami Vice; Superboy.

ERIC MANSKER

A member of the International Stunt Association, Mansker has performed bit acting assignments and doubled for the likes of Keith David, Ernie Hudson, and Ken Foree.

Films—1979: Prophecy. 1980: Nine to Five. 1982: The Thing. 1983: D.C. Cab. 1987: Allan Quartermain & the Lost City of Gold; Timestalkers (tv). 1988: The Ser-

pent & the Rainbow; Red Heat; I'm Gonna Git You Sucka; They Live. 1989: The Mighty Quinn; Road House; Glory; Chance; L.A. Bounty; Down the Drain. 1990: Leatherface 3; Delta Force 2; Marked for Death; Predator 2. 1991: Toy Soldiers; The People Under the Stairs; The Last Boy Scout; Driving Me Crazy. 1992: Article 99; Aces: Iron Eagle 3; Class Act. 1993: Nat'l Lampoon's Loaded Weapon. 1993: Falling Down; True Romance; Demolition Man; Best of the Best 2; Bounty Tracker; 12:01; The Naked Gun 33 1/3. 1994: Steel Frontier. 1995: 3 Ninjas Knuckle Up; The Enemy Within; Panther; Congo; Get Shorty; One Man's Justice; Hard Justice. 1996: Sgt. Bilko; Pure Danger; Mercenary.

TED MAPES
(b. 1902; d. 1984)

Nebraska-born supporting player, predominately seen in the Western genre, Mapes got his start as a grip boss but hit paydirt as the number one stunt double for both Gary Cooper and Jimmy Stewart.

Films—1929: The Taming of the Shrew. 1935: One Frightened Night; The Silent Code. 1936: End of the Trail; Legion of Terror; The Mysterious Avenger; The Law Rides; Secret Patrol; Stampede. 1937: One Man Justice. 1938: The Great Adventures of Wild Bill Hickock. 1939: Trouble in Sundown; Blue Montana Skies; In Old Caliente; Rio Grande; Three Texas Steers; Wall Street Cowboy; The Arizona Kid; Dick Tracy's G-Men; Daredevils of the Red Circle; Zorro's Fighting Legion. 1940: The Border Legion; Carson City Kid; The Ranger & the Lady; Under Texas Skies; King of the Royal Mounted. 1941: In Old Cheyenne; Riders of the Badlands; Royal Mounted Patrol; Tonto Basin Outlaws; The Gauchos of El Dorado; Red River Valley; Riders of the Badlands; Robin Hood of the Pecos; King of Dodge

City; The Adventures of Capt. Marvel. **1942:** Below the Border; Home in Wyoming; Pardon My Gun; Thunder River Feud; Yukon Patrol; The Valley of Vanishing Men; A Tornado in the Saddle; Texas Trouble Shooters; Prairie Gunsmoke; Vengeance of the West. **1943:** Calling Wild Bill Elliot; For Whom the Bell Tolls; Frontier Fury; Cowboy in the Clouds; Land of Hunted Men; The Outlaw. **1944:** Cyclone Prairie Rangers; Dead or Alive; Death Rides the Plains; Fuzzy Settles Down; Jam Session; The Last Horsemen; Black Arrow; Sundown Valley; Riding West; Law Men; Partners of the Trail. **1945:** Dakota; Incendiary Blonde; The Monster & the Ape; Blazing the Western Trail; Return of the Durango Kid; Flame of the West; Frontier Feud; Texas Panhandle. **1946:** The Phantom Rider; Roaring Rangers; Terror Trail; Conquest of Cheyenne; Drifting Along; My Pal Trigger; Under Arizona Skies. **1947:** The Fabulous Texan; The Wild Frontier; The Black Widow; Son of Zorro; Jesse James Rides Again; The Stranger from Ponca City; Riders of the Lone Star; Unconquered. **1948:** Dangers of the Canadian Mounted; Black Eagle; Desperadoes of Dodge City; Trail to Laredo; Fury at Furnace Creek; The Paleface; Winner Takes Nothing; The Strawberry Roon; Secret Service Investigator; Sundown Riders. **1949:** Desert Vigilante; El Dorado Pass; Look for the Silver Lining; Outcasts of the Trail; Samson & Delilah; Bad Men of Tombstone. **1950:** Dallas; Blondie's Hero; Cow Town; Broken Arrow; Barricade; Raiders of Tomahawk Creek; Winchester '73; Punchy Cowpunchers; The Gunfighter. **1951:** Silver City Bonanza; Distant Drums; Raton Pass; Fort Worth. **1952:** Bend of the River; High Noon; Waco; Carbine Williams; Springfield Rifle. **1953:** The Great Jesse James Raid; Vigilante Terror; The Naked Spur; Calamity Jane; Thunder Bay; Topeka. **1954:** The Boy from Oklahoma; Rear Window; Vera Cruz; Garden of Evil. **1955:** The Far Country; Strategic Air Command; The Man from Laramie. **1956:** The Man Who Knew Too Much. **1957:** Night Passage. **1958:** Bell, Book & Candle; Man of the West; Vertigo. **1959:** The Hanging Tree; The FBI Story; New Day at Sundown; They Came to Cordura. **1960:** The Mountain Road. **1961:** Two Rode Together. **1962:** The Man Who Shot Liberty Valance; How the West Was Won. **1963:** A New Kind of Love. **1964:** Cheyenne Autumn. **1965:** Dear Brigitte; Shenandoah. **1966:** The Rare Breed; The Flight of the Phoenix. **1968:** Firecreek; Bandolero. *Television*—The Cisco Kid; G.E. Theatre; Studio 57; Wagon Train; Gene Autry.

ALAN MARCUS

The stunt coordinator partner of Kane Hodder, Marcus has doubled for popular character player Brion James. His specialty is fire stunts.

Films—**1982:** Forced Vengeance; Kill Squad. **1983:** Deadly Force. **1984:** City Limits. **1985:** Volunteers; Stand Alone; Invasion USA. **1986:** Nomads; Avenging Force. **1987:** House 2; Hunk; The Hidden; Hell Comes to Frogtown. **1988:** Bulletproof; Rambo 3; The Horror Show; The Night Before. **1989:** Friday the 13th Part 8: Jason Takes Manhattan. **1990:** Peacemaker; 9 1/2 Ninjas; Backstreet Dreams. **1991:** Dragonfight; The Rapture; Star Trek 6: Undiscovered Country; Alligator 2; House 4. **1992:** Mom & Dad Save the World; Dead Center (aka Crazy Joe); Interceptor. **1993:** No Place to Hide; Jason Goes to Hell: The Final Friday. **1994:** Pumpkinhead 2; Love Is a Gun. **1995:** Four Room.

ANDERSON MARTIN

Films—**1985:** Teen Wolf; My Science Project; Moving Violations. **1986:** Out of Bounds; Back to School. **1987:** Morgan Stewart's Coming Home; Code Name Zebra. **1989:** Glory. **1990:** Mr. Destiny.

1992: Freejack. 1993: Cop & a Half; Robocop 3; The Real McCoy. 1994: Midnight Edition. 1996: Heaven's Prisoners.

SOLLY MARX

An independent stunt coordinator on low-budget material, Solomon J. Marx began his career portraying a psychotic killer in the horror film *Silent Madness*.

Films—1984: Silent Madness; Savage Dawn. 1986: Neon Maniacs. 1987: Allan Quartermain & the Lost City of Gold; Zombie High; Cyclone; Terminal Entry; Death Spa; Cold Steel; Deadly Intent; Munchies. 1988: Assault of the Killer Bimbos; Alien from L.A. 1989: Survival Quest; Lady Avenger; 976 Evil; Cartel; Down the Drain. 1990: Joe vs. The Volcano; Caged Fury. 1991: Dragonfight; Disaster in Time; Waxwork 2. 1992: Big Girls Don't Cry, They Get Even; Trancers 3. 1993: Firepower; Hidden Obsession; Martial Outlaw; Fugitive Nights (tv). 1994: The Stoned Age; Deadly Target; Hologram Man; Victim of Desire; The Disappearance of Christina (tv). 1995: Evolver; The Silencers; Suspect Device. 1996: Dark Breed.

EDDIE MATTHEWS

Films—1988: Bull Durham. 1989: Her Alibi. 1990: Prayer of the Rollerboys; Fear (tv). 1991: Highlander 2; Shakes the Clown. 1992: Trespass; The Runestone. 1993: Hot Shots Part Deux; Surf Ninjas; Hard Target; The Philadelphia Experiment 2; Brain Smasher. 1994: Airheads; The Mask; Flashfire; American Yakuza. 1995: Murder in the First; Demon Knight; Casino. 1996: Independence Day; The Crow: City of Angels.

DENVER MATTSON

A veteran member of the Stuntmen's Association, Mattson has doubled for character actor Luke Askew.

Films—1969: Flare-Up. 1970: Lost Flight. 1972: Conquest of the Planet of the Apes. 1973: Cleopatra Jones; Battle for the Planet of the Apes. 1974: The Towering Inferno; Earthquake. 1975: The Hindenburg. 1976: The House By the Lake (aka Death Weekend). 1977: The Domino Principle; Mr. Billion. 1978: Movie, Movie. 1979: The Main Event; Stunt Seven (tv). 1981: Going Ape. 1982: My Favorite Year; The Thing. 1983: Bad Boys. 1984: Police Academy. 1985: Avenging Angel. 1986: Choke Canyon; Tough Guys; Raw Deal; The Kindred; Maximum Overdrive. 1987: The Monster Squad; Cop. 1989: Cat Chaser. 1991: Mobsters. 1992: Sleepwalkers; Unlawful Entry; Universal Soldier. 1994: Army of One; Wagons East. 1995: Stuart Saves His Family. *Television*—Voyage to the Bottom of the Sea; Time Tunnel; Land of the Giants.

JOHN C. MEIER

A stunt coordinator and second unit director, Meier is a member of Stunts Unlimited. He has doubled for William Shatner.

Films—1979: Skatetown USA. 1980: Herbie Goes Bananas; The Mountain Men; Used Cars; Wholly Moses. 1981: Caveman; Ghost Story. 1982: Cannery Row; Megaforce; The Beastmaster. 1983: Second Thoughts; The Outsiders; Private School; Christine; Scarface. 1984: Ninja 3: The Domination; The Joy of Sex; Star Trek 3: The Search for Spock; 2010; Beverly Hills Cop; City Killer (tv). 1985: To Live & Die in L.A. 1986: F/X; Back to School. 1987: Aloha Summer; The Wild

Pair; World Gone Wild; The Lost Boys; Real Men; Code Name Zebra. **1988:** Above the Law; Die Hard; I'm Gonna Git You Sucka; The Blob; They Live. **1989:** Gleaming the Cube; Lethal Weapon 2; To Die For; Dead Bang; Nat'l Lampoon's Christmas Vacation; Riding the Edge. **1990:** Maniac Cop 2; Days of Thunder; Rockula; Last of the Finest; The Adventures of Ford Fairlane; The Rookie. **1991:** Lionheart; Out for Justice; Dead Again; Warlock; Point Break; Thelma & Louise; Beethoven; The Last Boy Scout. **1992:** Kuffs; Honey, I Blew Up the Kid; American Me; Rapid Fire; Lethal Weapon 3; Cool World; Patriot Games; Nemesis; Jennifer 8; Maximum Force. **1993:** Falling Down; Extreme Justice; The Last Action Hero; Gettysburg; Demolition Man; Ghost in the Machine. **1994:** Army of One; Gunmen; Maverick; The Shadow; True Lies; Terminal Velocity; Puppetmasters; A Low Down Dirty Shame. **1995:** The Road Killers; The Criminal Mind; Demon Knight; Roommates; Virtuosity; Under Siege 2; Jade; Nick of Time. **1996:** Executive Decision; Eraser; The Rock; Star Trek, First Contact; Fled; Kingpin. *Television*—Beauty & the Beast; Guns of Paradise.

TROY MELTON
(b. 1921; d. 1995)

Veteran Tennessee-born supporting player, especially active on television. Melton got into films after service in the Army Air Corps and was a co-founder of the Stuntmen's Association. He later bought into the Playboy Club and became a restaurateur.

Films—**1956:** Mohawk; Davy Crockett & the River Pirates. **1961:** The George Raft Story. **1962:** How the West Was Won; The Firebrand; The Day Mars Invaded Earth; It Happened at the World's Fair. **1963:** Young Guns of Texas. **1964:** Sex & the Single Girl. **1966:** Cyborg 2087. **1969:** The Great Bank Robbery. **1970:** Change of Habit. **1971:** Dirty Harry. **1972:** Conquest of the Planet of the Apes. **1973:** Scorpio; Magnum Force; Battle for the Planet of the Apes. **1974:** The Towering Inferno; Blazing Saddles; Earthquake; A Cry in the Wilderness (tv). **1976:** The Invisible Strangler (aka The Astral Factor). **1978:** The Deer Hunter; I Wanna Hold Your Hand; Every Which Way But Loose. **1980:** Foolin' Around. **1981:** Buddy, Buddy. **1982:** The Sword & the Sorcerer. **1988:** Dead Heat; Alien Nation. **1991:** Timebomb. *Television*—The Cisco Kid; The Lone Ranger; Roy Rogers; Davy Crockett; Rough Riders; Highway Patrol; Sea Hunt; Zane Grey Theatre; Boston Blackie; Wyatt Earp; Wild Bill Hickok; Have Gun, Will Travel; Bat Masterson; Science Fiction Theatre; Wrangler; Target; The Twilight Zone; The Rifleman; Wanted, Dead or Alive; Klondike; Cain's Hundred; The Outer Limits; Amos Burke; Gunsmoke; Bonanza; The Fugitive; The Virginian; Laredo; The Big Valley; Voyage to the Bottom of the Sea; Batman; The Green Hornet; Honey West; The Wild Wild West; The Invaders; It Takes a Thief; Mission: Impossible; The Guns of Will Sonnett; Marcus Welby M.D.; Cade's County; The Rookies; Get Christie Love; The Night Stalker; Cannon; The Six Million Dollar Man; McNaughton's Daughter; Pertocelli; Prudence & the Chief; The Fall Guy; The Dukes of Hazzard; Forever Knight.

BOB MINOR
(b. 1942)

This popular supporting player became the first black member of the Stuntmen's Association in 1972. After success as a track star and professional bodybuilder, the 6'2" actor began doubling for Fred Williamson, Jim Brown, and Sidney Poitier, but quickly became a recognizable face himself *(The Deep, Norma Rae, Action*

Jackson). As a stunt coordinator and second unit director, he's responsible for the brilliant staging of the battle scenes in *Glory*. His wife Rita and son Royce are also in the business.

Films—**1970:** Beyond the Valley of the Dolls. **1972:** Ben; The Legend of Nigger Charley; Come Back, Charleston Blue; Blacula; Black Gunn; Conquest of the Planet of the Apes. **1973:** Sweet Jesus, Preacher Man; The Soul of Nigger Charley; Sweet Suzy; Black Caesar; Scream, Blacula, Scream; Cleopatra Jones; Coffy; Detroit 9000; That Man Bolt; Battle for the Planet of the Apes. **1974:** The Towering Inferno; Black Samson; Foxy Brown; Uptown Saturday Night; Dirty Mary, Crazy Larry; The Swinging Cheerleaders; Delinquent Schoolgirls; Black Eye; Earthquake. **1975:** Hard Times; Switchblade Sisters; Rollerball; Let's Do It Again; Friendly Persuasion (tv). **1976:** Dr. Black, Mr. Hyde; J.D.'s Revenge; Drum; Swashbuckler. **1977:** A Piece of the Action; Black Sunday; MacArthur; The Deep; Mr. Billion; The Choirboys; Raid on Entebbe (tv); Billy, Portrait of a Street Kid (tv). **1978:** The Driver; Death Dimension (aka Black Eliminator; Kill Factor); FM; Dr. Scorpion (tv). **1979:** Norma Rae; Skatetown USA; Gold of the Amazon Women (tv); Samurai (tv); Flesh & Blood (tv); Stunt Seven (tv). **1980:** Smokey & the Bandit 2; Angel City (tv). **1981:** Charlie Chan & the Curse of the Dragon Queen; Escape from New York; Body & Soul; Honkytonk Freeway. **1982:** The Sword & the Sorcerer; The Beastmaster; White Dog; Rocky 3; Forced Vengeance; World War III (tv). **1983:** The Sting 2; Heart Like a Wheel; Women of San Quentin (tv). **1985:** Witness; Kids Don't Tell (tv); Commando. **1986:** Hamburger; The Morning After. **1987:** The Night Stalker; Project X; Allan Quartermain & the Lost City of Gold. **1988:** Action Jackson; Torch Song Trilogy; I'm Gonna Git You Sucka; Bail Out. **1989:** L.A. Bounty; K-9; Catch Me If You Can; Ghostbusters 2; Glory; Next of Kin; Casualties of War; Crack House.

1990: Maniac Cop 2; Downtown; Big Man on Campus; Almost an Angel; Dangerous Passion (tv). **1991:** Cool as Ice; Boyz in the Hood; 976 Evil 2; Not of This World (tv). **1992:** Love Field; Article 99; Aces: Iron Eagle 3; Unlawful Entry; Innocent Blood; The Jacksons: An American Dream (tv). **1993:** Sommersby; Amos & Andrew; Hear No Evil; Posse; Extreme Justice; Poetic Justice; CB4; Queen (tv). **1994:** Surviving the Game; Sugar Hill; Chasers; Beverly Hills Cop 3; Blown Away; Blankman; T-Force; Scarlett (tv); I Still Love L.A. (tv). **1995:** Higher Learning; Die Hard with a Vengeance; Panther; Batman Forever; The Ties That Bind; Assassins; Last Man Standing; The Sweeper; The O.J. Simpson Story (tv). **1996:** Soul of the Game; Original Gangstas; Bogus; If These Walls Could Talk; Pure Danger; Rage; Set It Off; The Cherokee Kid; Jingle All the Way; Innocent Bystander (a/p); Sunchaser. *Television*—Room 222; Search; The Six Million Dollar Man; McCloud; McCoy; Kojak; The Man from Atlantis; Baretta; Starsky & Hutch; Quincy; Wonder Woman; Spiderman; Buck Rogers; Magnum P.I.; The Greatest American Hero; The Fall Guy; The Powers of Matthew Star; Paradise; Murder She Wrote; Matlock; Jake & the Fatman; Deadly Games.

FAITH MINTON

Films—**1979:** The Wanderers; Gold of the Amazon Women (tv). **1981:** Heartbeeps. **1983:** Smokey & the Bandit 3. **1985:** Lust in the Dust. **1986:** Ruthless People; The Naked Cage; Never Too Young to Die. **1987:** Who's That Girl? **1988:** Hero & the Terror; License to Drive. **1990:** Far Out Man; Ski Patrol. **1991:** Switch. **1992:** Rage & Honor. **1994:** The Stranger. **1995:** Sudden Death. **1996:** Set If Off. *Television*—House Calls; Mike Hammer.

WILD BILL MOCK

Films—**1976:** Two Minute Warning. **1977:** Stunts. **1988:** Freeway. **1989:** Hollywood Hot Tubs 2. **1990:** Firebirds; Darkman; Trancers 2; Peacemaker; Steel & Lace; Circuitry Man; Red Surf. **1991:** Soldier's Fortune. **1993:** Pumpkinhead 2. **1994:** Zero Tolerance; Direct Hit; T-Force. **1996:** Back to Back; Yesterday's Target.

JOHN MOIO
(b. 1943)

A veteran stunt coordinator and second unit director, Moio is a member of the Stuntmen's Association.

Films—**1969:** Changes. **1972:** What's Up, Doc? **1973:** The Sting. **1975:** The Great Waldo Pepper; Night Moves. **1977:** The Car; Exo-Man (tv); Pete's Dragon. **1978:** The Manitou. **1979:** The Prisoner of Zenda; Meteor; The In-Laws. **1980:** Where the Buffalo Roam; Hero at Large; Seems Like Old Times; Borderline; Change of Seasons; Motel Hell. **1981:** Hard Country; Charlie Chan & the Curse of the Dragon Queen; The Howling; Escape from New York. **1982:** My Favorite Year; Fast Times at Ridgemont High; Night Shift; Zapped; Wacko. **1983:** Two of a Kind; Max Dugan Returns; Class; Chiefs (tv). **1984:** Bachelor Party; Friday the 13th: A New Beginning; Johnny Dangerously; Lovelines. **1985:** Into the Night; D.A.R.Y.L. **1986:** The Texas Chainsaw Massacre 2. **1987:** The Monster Squad; Planes, Trains, & Automobiles. **1988:** Midnight Run; Jack's Back; Colors; License to Drive; Earth Girls Are Easy. **1989:** Chances Are; An Innocent Man. **1990:** The First Power; I'm Dangerous Tonight (tv). **1991:** Eve of Destruction; Mobsters; Shattered; The Marrying Man. **1992:** Deep Cover; The Hand That Rocks the Cradle; Aces: Iron Eagle 3; Dr. Gig-

gles; Unlawful Entry; Live Wire; Sneakers; Chaplin. **1993:** Boiling Point; The Sandlot. **1994:** Holy Matrimony; Major League 2; The Mask. **1995:** Panther; Separate Lives; The Tie That Binds; The Crossing Guard. **1996:** Mars Attacks!; Set It Off. *Television*—The Six Million Dollar Man; Matt Helm; The Fall Guy; Matt Houston; Dynasty; The Insiders; Hollywood Beat.

JEFF MOLDOVAN

This Florida-based stunt coordinator wrote and starred in stunt ace Glenn Wilder's *Master Blaster.*

Films—**1981:** Nobody's Perfect. **1983:** Smokey & the Bandit 3; Spring Break. **1985:** Stick; Invasion USA; The New Kids; Two Fathers' Justice (tv); Knights of the City. **1986:** Vengeance (tv). **1987:** Master Blaster (a/s); Making Mr. Right. **1989:** License to Kill. **1992:** Traces of Red. **1993:** Cop & a Half; Wilder Napalm; Mr. Nanny. **1994:** The Specialist; Oblivion; Trancers 5; Thunder in Paradise (tv). **1996:** Two Much. *Television*—Miami Vice; Superboy; Thunder in Paradise.

WAYNE MONTANIO

Films—**1985:** Soldier's Revenge. **1986:** Hollywood Zap!; The Best of Times. **1987:** Extreme Prejudice. **1988:** Alien Nation; Border Heat; Bail Out. **1989:** K-9; Fright Night 2; Blind Fury; One Man Force. **1990:** Marked for Death. **1991:** Eve of Destruction; Cool as Ice. **1992:** Class Act. **1994:** Steel Frontier. **1995:** Vampire in Brooklyn. **1996:** Spy Hard; Escape from L.A.

PAULA MARIE MOODY

A member of the United Stunt-woman's Association, Moody has doubled for Linnea Quigley.

Films—**1982:** Star Trek 2: The Wrath of Khan. **1983:** Sudden Impact. **1984:** The River Rat; Sole Survivor; The River; Tuff Turf; Savage Streets. **1985:** Return of the Living Dead; The Journey of Natty Gann. **1987:** The Witches of Eastwick; Kid-napped; Down Twisted; Private Investiga-tions. **1988:** Action Jackson; Miracle Mile; Mac & Me; License to Drive; The Blob; Nightmare on Elm Street 4: Dream Master. **1989:** Spontaneous Combustion; Grave Secrets; Midnight; After Midnight. **1990:** Far Out Man; Robocop 2; Child's Play 2; Lisa; I'm Dangerous Tonight (tv). **1991:** Eve of Destruction; The People Under the Stairs; The Marrying Man; House 4; Cast a Deadly Spell.

BENNIE MOORE
(b. 1952)

A former rodeo performer, Moore is a member of Stunts Unlimited. He has doubled for Bernie Casey and acted in many small roles.

Films—**1976:** Drum. **1977:** Heroes; Smokey & the Bandit. **1978:** Hooper; Thank God, It's Friday. **1979:** The Villain. **1980:** The Blues Brothers; Smokey & the Bandit 2; Wholly Moses. **1981:** Sharky's Machine. **1982:** The Sword & the Sor-cerer. **1983:** Tough Enough; Under Fire; Stroker Ace. **1984:** The River. **1985:** Into the Night; Explorers; Moving Violations; The Mutilator. **1986:** Out of Bounds; Legal Eagles. **1987:** Critical Condition; The Wild Pair; Over the Top; Lethal Weapon; Night Force; Code Name Zebra;

Burglar; Traxx. **1988:** Action Jackson; The Presidio; I'm Gonna Git You Sucka; The Blob; They Live. **1989:** Collision Course; K-9; Loverboy; Lethal Weapon 2; Glory; Lock Up. **1990:** Die Hard 2; Total Recall; Last of the Finest; The Adventures of Ford Fairlane. **1991:** Nothing But Trouble; The Fisher King; Thelma & Louise. **1992:** Honey, I Blew Up the Kid; American Me; White Sands; Lethal Weapon 3; Class Act; Patriot Games. **1993:** Posse; Full Eclipse; The Last Action Hero; CB4; Demolition Man. **1994:** Pentathalon; A Low Down Dirty Shame; Puppetmasters. **1995:** Just Cause; Candyman: Farewell to the Flesh; Panther; Waterworld; Under Siege 2; Wild Bill; Vampire in Brooklyn; Things to Do in Denver When You're Dead. **1996:** From Dusk Till Dawn; The Arrival; Eraser; The Rock; The Cable Guy; The Nutty Profes-sor; Fled; Escape from L.A.; Mars At-tacks!; Jingle All the Way.

TOM MORGA

A member of the Stuntmen's Asso-ciation, Morga is most closely asso-ciated with being a stunt coordinator for the *Star Trek* films and series.

Films—**1976:** The Amorous Adventures of Don Quixote. **1978:** Movie, Movie. **1979:** Star Trek, the Motion Picture. **1980:** The Stunt Man; The Big Brawl; The Re-turn of Frank Cannon (tv). **1982:** Star Trek 2: The Wrath of Khan; The Sword & the Sorcerer. **1983:** Two of a Kind. **1984:** Bachelor Party; Friday the 13th: A New Beginning; Star Trek 3: The Search for Spock; City Limits. **1985:** Commando; Remo Williams. **1987:** The Night Stalker; Outrageous Fortune; Mission Kill. **1988:** Jack's Back; Heartbreak Hotel; Halloween 4; Alien Nation; Turner & Hooch; Tape-heads. **1989:** Star Trek 5: The Final Fron-tier; Kinjite; Blind Fury. **1990:** Problem Child; The First Power; Repossessed; The Exorcist 3; The Rookie. **1991:** Eve of De-struction; Child's Play 3; Star Trek 6:

Undiscovered Country; Hudson Hawk; Suburban Commando. **1992:** Deep Cover; Live Wire; Mom & Dad Save the World; Wayne's World. **1993:** Hear No Evil; Slaughter of the Innocents; The Hit List. **1994:** The Last Ride (aka F.T.W.); Clean Slate; Cops & Robberson; The Shawshank Redemption; Cobb; Silence of the Hams; Zero Tolerance. **1995:** Separate Lives; The Tie That Binds; Last Man Standing. **1996:** Independence Day. *Television*—Star Trek, the Next Generation.

BOYD "RED" MORGAN
(b. 1915; d. 1988)

A veteran horseman, the Oklahoma-born Morgan played college football for USC and played professionally for the Washington Redskins. He later served with the Navy during World War II and coached high school football before getting into stunts full-time, most notably as a double for James Arness on television's "Gunsmoke." A member of the Stuntmen's Association, Morgan and his horse Hot Rod took over a thousand falls for the camera.

Films—**1936:** Rose Bowl. **1940:** Lucky Cisco Kid. **1951:** Saturday's Hero; That's My Boy; Silver City; Snake River Desperadoes; Smoky Canyon; Desert of Lost Men; The Texas Ranger. **1952:** The Last Musketeer; Sound Off; The Rough Tough West; Thundering Caravans; Cattle Town; Laramie Mountain; Cripple Creek. **1953:** The Great Sioux Uprising; Thunder Over the Plains; The Winning of the West; The Redhead from Wyoming; Law & Order; The Woman They Almost Lynched; Column South; Gun Belt; The Nebraskan. **1954:** The Prince of Padua Hills; The Command; Riding Shotgun. **1955:** Violent

Saturday; Robber's Roost; Ten Wanted Men. **1956:** Dakota Incident; Around the World in 80 Days; D-Day, the Sixth of June; The Revolt of Mamie Stover; Between Heaven & Hell. **1957:** The Kettles on Old McDonald's Farm; Gun Duel in Durango; War Drums; The Dalton Girls; Hellbound. **1958:** The Defiant Ones; The Legend of Tom Dooley. **1959:** The Jayhawkers; Pillow Talk; A Date with Death; Ride Lonesome. **1960:** Spartacus; The Alamo; The Amazing Transparent Man; Beyond the Time Barrier; Gunfighters of Abilene; Oklahoma Territory. **1961:** Five Guns to Tombstone; The Gambler Wore a Gun. **1962:** How the West Was Won. **1964:** Robin & the Seven Hoods; The Quick Gun; A Distant Trumpet. **1965:** The Sons of Katie Elder; Requiem for a Gunfighter; Arizona Raiders; The Bounty Killer; Cat Ballou; Deadwood '76. **1966:** Waco; Nevada Smith. **1967:** Hostile Guns; Fort Utah; The War Wagon. **1968:** Five Card Stud; Where Were You When the Lights Went Out? **1969:** The Stalking Moon; True Grit; Support Your Local Sheriff. **1970:** The Cheyenne Social Club; Rio Lobo. **1971:** Wild Rovers; Dirty Harry. **1973:** The Soul of Nigger Charley; Dillinger; Santee; The Deadly Trackers; One Little Indian. **1974:** Foxy Brown; Blazing Saddles. **1975:** Little Moon & Jud McGraw (aka Gone with the West). **1976:** Captains & the Kings (tv). **1980:** Survival Run. **1984:** Last of the Great Survivors (tv). *Television*—Roy Rogers; Studio 57; Playhouse 90; G.E. Theatre; Maverick; Zane Grey Theatre; The Texan; Hotel de Paree; Wagon Train; Gunsmoke; Mission: Impossible; The Invaders; Bonanza; The Mod Squad; Here's Lucy; Kung Fu; The Rookies; Cimarron Strip.

GARY MORGAN
(b. 1950)

The son of acrobats Barney Morgan and Dottie May, Morgan became a tumbler/gymnast himself. He's a member of the Stuntmen's Association.

Films—**1960:** The Alamo. **1967:** Wait Until Dark. **1969:** Popi; Skullduggery. **1970:** The Psychiatrist (tv). **1971:** The Peace Killers; Sarge (tv). **1972:** Fuzz. **1973:** The Student Teachers; Linda (tv). **1974:** Jonathan Livingston Seagull; The California Kid (tv). **1975:** The Night God Screamed; The Missing Are Deadly (tv); Medical Story (tv). **1976:** The Treasure of Matecumbe; Logan's Run; Pinocchio (tv). **1977:** Summer School Teachers; Pete's Dragon. **1978:** Matilda. **1979:** The North Avenue Irregulars. **1980:** The Final Countdown. **1981:** Going Ape; The Devil & Max Devlin. **1983:** Cujo. **1984:** 2010; Lovelines. **1981:** The Seduction of Gina. **1985:** Explorers. **1986:** Band of the Hand; The Golden Child; Eye of the Tiger. **1987:** Outrageous Fortune. **1988:** Alien Nation; The Great Outdoors; Two Moon Junction. **1989:** Back to the Future 2; The Burbs; Troop Beverly Hills. **1990:** Back to the Future 3; Streets. **1991:** Hook; Ricochet; Freddy's Dead. **1992:** Honey, I Blew Up the Kids; Under Siege. **1993:** The Beverly Hillbillies. **1995:** Silence of the Hams; Batman Forever. *Television*—Bonanza; Adam-12; CHiPs; Alien Nation.

EDGARD MOURINO

Films—**1981:** Arthur; Wolfen. **1982:** The Soldier; The World According to Garp. **1984:** Splash; The Brother from Another Planet; The Exterminator 2; Rappin'. **1985:** Preppies. **1986:** Legal Eagles; Maximum Overdrive. **1987:** The Believers; Raising Arizona. **1987:** Deadly Illusion; My Demon Lover. **1988:** Shakedown. **1989:** See No Evil, Hear No Evil. **1990:** Tales from the Darkside; Street Hunter; The Ambulance. **1991:** Sgt. Kubikiman, NYPD. **1995:** The Basketball Diaries.

JOE MURPHY

Nicknamed Broadway Joe, this Jersey-born stunt coordinator has doubled for Bill Paxton and Lorenzo Lamas. He holds the world record for a van jump.

Films—**1986:** Psychos in Love. **1988:** The Wrong Guys; It's Alive 3; L.A. Heat; Emperor of the Bronx. **1989:** Midnight Warrior; L.A. Vice. **1990:** Delta Force 2. **1991:** A Time to Die. **1992:** CIA: Code Name Alexa; Alien Intruder; Maximum Force. **1993:** Street Crimes; Private Wars; Hellraiser 3; Monolith; Fist of Honor; Passenger 57. **1994:** Ice; Zero Tolerance; Direct Hit; Steel Frontier; CIA 2: Target Alexa; T-Force. **1995:** Top Dog; Digital Man; To the Limit; The Crossing Guard. *Television*—Star Trek, the Next Generation; Land's End.

HAL NEEDHAM
(b. 1931)

A stunt legend, the Tennessee-born Needham was an Army paratrooper, wingwalker, and a billboard model for Viceroy Cigarettes before getting into films as a stuntman for Richard Boone, Clint Walker, Christopher George, and his pal Burt Reynolds. Needham formed Stunts Unlimited and became a top stunt coordinator and second unit director, staging and performing such memorable gags as the horse transfer in *Little Big Man* and a car jump onto a moving barge in *White Lightning*. Reynolds gave him the chance to direct *Smokey and the Bandit,* and Needham subsequently directed several car crash pictures.

Films—**1957:** The Spirit of St. Louis.

Top: **Action from Hal Needham's 1978 film** *Hooper.* *Bottom:* **An action scene from 1980's** *Smokey and the Bandit 2*, **directed by stunt ace Hal Needham.**

1958: The Big Country. **1959:** Porkchop Hill. **1961:** A Thunder of Drums. **1962:** How the West Was Won. **1963:** McLintock; Four for Texas. **1964:** Advance to the Rear. **1965:** Major Dundee; The Great Race; Shenandoah; The War Lord. **1966:** The Rare Breed; Beau Geste; Alvarez Kelly; Our Man Flint. **1967:** The War Wagon; The Way West; Tobruk; Camelot; Hell's Angels on Wheels. **1968:** The Ballad of Josie; Bandolero; The Devil's Brigade; Hellfighters. **1969:** The Bridge at Remagen; The Great Bank Robbery; The Undefeated; Che; 100 Rifles. **1970:** Little Big Man; Cover Me, Babe; Dirty Dingus Magee. **1971:** One More Train to

Rob; Sometimes a Great Notion (aka Never Give an Inch); The Organization; Something Big; Chrome & Hot Leather; Man on a Swing (tv); Escape (tv); Hardcase (tv). **1972:** The Culpepper Cattle Company; The Life & Times of Judge Roy Bean; The Night Stalker (tv); The Bounty Man (tv); The Heist (tv); Goodnight, My Love (tv). **1973:** The Man Who Loved Cat Dancing; White Lightning; Call to Danger (tv). **1974:** Chinatown; The Longest Yard; Blazing Saddles; Busting; Three the Hard Way; McQ. **1975:** W.W. & the Dixie Dancekings; The French Connection 2; Peeper; Take a Hard Ride; Lucky Lady. **1976:** Jackson County Jail; Gable & Lombard; Gator; A Star Is Born; Nickelodeon. **1977:** Semi-tough; Smokey & the Bandit (d). **1978:** Foul Play; The End; Hooper (d). **1979:** The Villain (d); Death Car on the Freeway (d) (tv). **1980:** Smokey & the Bandit 2 (d); Stunts Unlimited (d) (tv). **1981:** The Cannonball Run (d). **1982:** Megaforce (d). **1983:** Stroker Ace (d). **1984:** The Cannonball Run 2 (d). **1986:** RAD (d). **1987:** Body Slam (d). **1994:** Beauty & the Bandit (tv). **1996:** Sunchaser. *Television*—Have Gun, Will Travel; The Restless Gun; Riverboat; Tales of Wells Fargo; The Rebel; Rawhide; Gunsmoke; Stoney Burke; Laramie; Wagon Train; The Virginian; The Richard Boone Show; Laredo; Cimarron Strip; Custer; Star Trek; Mission: Impossible; The Immortal; Dan August; The Night Stalker; Egan; Kodiak; Harry O; Charlie's Angels; The Stockers (d); Sledge Hammer; B.L. Stryker (d).

PHIL NEILSON

This East Coast stunt coordinator has worked extensively with directors Oliver Stone and Abel Ferrara. His wife Cynthia also does stunts.

Films—**1984:** Scream for Help. **1985:** Remo Williams. **1986:** F/X; The Money Pit; Sweet Liberty; Legal Eagles; Raw Deal; The Boy in Blue; Popeye Doyle (tv).

1987: Outrageous Fortune; Mannequin; China Girl; Deadly Illusion. **1988:** Shakedown; Last Rites; Masquerade; Miles from Home; Homeboy; Crossing Delancey. **1989:** See No Evil, Hear No Evil; Slaves of New York; Ghostbusters 2; Lock Up; True Blood. **1990:** Quick Change; Two Evil Eyes; Jacob's Ladder; King of New York; Night of the Living Dead; GoodFellas; Street Hunter; Basket Case 2. **1991:** Bonfire of the Vanities; Mortal Thoughts. **1992:** Mississippi Masala; The Bad Lieutenant. **1993:** The Dark Half; Dangerous Game; Heaven & Earth; Daybreak. **1994:** Body Snatchers; The Cowboy Way; Natural Born Killers. **1995:** Boys on the Side; Kiss of Death; New Jersey Drive; Amateur; 12 Monkeys. **1996:** The Addiction; The Juror; Striptease; The Funeral; Boys; Rough Magic.

LARRY NICHOLAS

A child double, Nicholas has stood in for Charlie Korsmo and Elijah Wood.

Films—**1987:** The Lost Boys. **1988:** Return of the Living Dead Part 2. **1989:** Her Alibi. **1990:** Satan's Princess; Dick Tracy; Desperate Hours; Flatliners; Child's Play 2; The Rookie. **1991:** Hook. **1992:** Radio Flyer. **1993:** Ghost in the Machine. **1994:** North. **1995:** 3 Ninjas Knuckle Up; Demon Knight. **1996:** Spy Hard.

JIM NICKERSON
(b. 1949)

This Pennsylvania-born stunt coordinator/fight choreographer was a former rodeo cowboy and amateur boxer before getting into films. A member of Stunts Unlimited, he doubled for James Caan in the seventies.

Jim Nickerson battles Charles Bronson in one of *Hard Times'* early fight scenes. The fights were coordinated by Max Kleven.

Films—1970: M.A.S.H. 1972: Kansas City Bomber. 1973: Slither; Freebie & the Bean. 1974: The Gambler; Earthquake. 1975: Hard Times; Rollerball; The Hindenburg. 1976: Rocky; Harry & Walter Go to New York. 1977: The Deep; MacArthur. 1978: Movie, Movie; I Wanna Hold Your Hand; Ice Castles; Paradise Alley. 1979: Rocky 2. 1980: The Long Riders; Raging Bull. 1981: Caveman; The Cannonball Run. 1983: Tough Enough; Dempsey (tv). 1985: Into the Night; To Live & Die in L.A. 1986: 8 Million Ways to Die; Streets of Gold; Big Trouble in Little China; Out of Bounds. 1987: Real Men; Lethal Weapon; Night Force; Code Name Zebra. 1988: Split Decisions; They Live; Fistfighter. 1989: Her Alibi. 1991:

Kickboxer 2. 1992: Diggstown. 1993: The Last Action Hero. 1994: True Lies; Terminal Velocity; In the Army Now; Puppetmasters. 1995: Village of the Damned; Tyson; Nine Months; Under Siege 2; Jade. 1996: Executive Decision; Mulholland Falls; My Fellow Americans. *Television*— Lancer; Matt Houston; Mike Hammer; Crime Story; Guns of Paradise.

CAROL NIELSEN

Films—1986: Ratboy; Ruthless People. 1987: Outrageous Fortune; Mannequin; Hot Pursuit; Walk Like a Man; Laguna Heat; Brenda Starr; Dead Man Walking. 1988: Freeway; Hero & the Terror; Colors;

Martial arts star Chuck Norris (left) with his brother, director/stuntman Aaron Norris.

Angel 3; The Dead Pool; Earth Girls Are Easy; Dangerous Love; Border Heat. **1989:** Transylvania Twist; The Karate Kid 3. **1990:** Bad Influence; Streets; Disturbed; Pump Up the Volume; Basket Case 2; Syngenor. **1991:** The Servants of Twilight; Deadlock. **1992:** Star Time; Adventures in Dinosaur City. **1994:** Speed; Color of Night; Silence of the Hams. **1995:** Sudden Death.

CHRIS NIELSEN

Films—**1990:** Almost an Angel; Liberty & Bash; Disturbed; Martians Go Home. **1992:** The Runestone; The Double-0 Kid. **1993:** Robocop 3; Trouble Bound; Bitter Harvest; The Philadelphia Experiment 2; Attack of the 50 Foot Woman. **1994:** Tollbooth. **1995:** Excessive Force 2; Crosscut.

AARON NORRIS

A martial arts champion like his more famous brother Chuck, Aaron began coordinating stunts for his brother and eventually moved into directing his films. His own starring vehicle, *Overkill,* was directed by stunt pal Dean Ferradini. He's the one who actually executed the famous kick through the car windshield in *Good Guys Wear Black.*

Films—**1978:** Good Guys Wear Black; Go Tell the Spartans. **1979:** A Force of One; Elvis (tv). **1981:** An Eye for an Eye. **1982:** I, the Jury; Forced Vengeance; Silent Rage. **1983:** Lone Wolf McQuade; Chained Heat; Lies. **1984:** Missing in Action. **1985:** Missing in Action 2; Code of Silence; Invasion USA. **1986:** The Naked Cage; Dangerously Close; Firewalker. **1987:** Survival Game. **1988:** Braddock: Missing in Action 3 (d); Platoon Leader (d). **1990:** Delta Force 2 (d). **1991:** The Hitman (d). **1993:** Sidekicks (d); Hellbound (d). **1994:** Ripper Man (p). **1995:** Top Dog (d). **1996:** Forest Warrior (d); Overkill.

ERIC NORRIS

The stunt coordinator son of karate star Chuck Norris, Eric is a member of the Stuntmen's Association.

Films—1985: Invasion USA. **1986:** The Delta Force. **1988:** Hero & the Terror. **1990:** Delta Force 2; Peacemaker. **1991:** The Naked Gun 2 1/2; Beastmaster 2; Star Trek 6: Undiscovered Country. **1992:** Universal Soldier; Dead Center (aka Crazy Joe). **1993:** Rescue Me; Sidekicks; Best of the Best 2; Hellbound. **1994:** Army of One. **1995:** Top Dog. *Television*—Walker, Texas Ranger.

RICHARD NORTON

A popular Australian-born martial arts champ, Norton began working as a stuntman/fight choreographer on Chuck Norris films, eventually starring in several of his own low-budget action films. Highly regarded in Hong Kong as a top villain, he has starred opposite Cynthia Rothrock several times.

Films—1980: The Octagon. **1981:** An Eye for an Eye; Force: Five. **1982:** Forced Vengeance. **1985:** Gymkata; Shanghai Express. **1986:** Equalizer 2000; Future Hunters. **1987:** Crossfire; The Magic Crystal. **1988:** Twinkle, Twinkle, Lucky Stars; Eye of the Dragon; Screwball Hotel; China O'Brien. **1989:** China O'Brien 2. **1990:** The Kickfighter; Fight to Win; The Deadliest Art. **1991:** Karate Cops; Revenge of the Kickfighter; Iron Heart; Lady Dragon. **1992:** City Hunter; Blood Streets; Rage & Honor; Raiders of the Sun; Rage & Honor 2: Hostile Takeover. **1993:** Deathfight; Cyberseeker. **1994:** Guardian Angel; Direct Hit; Tough & Deadly. **1995:** Under the Gun. **1996:** Fugitive X. *Television*—Walker, Texas Ranger.

JOHN NOWAK

Trained by Paul Stader, Nowak achieved some cult recognition doubling for Patrick Stewart on "Star Trek, the Next Generation" and Robert Picardo on its sister series "Star Trek, Voyager."

Films—1974: The Towering Inferno. **1975:** Lucky Lady. **1978:** The Swarm. **1979:** Boulevard Nights. **1980:** The Fifth Floor; Any Which Way You Can. **1982:** The Sword & the Sorcerer. **1983:** Sudden Impact. **1984:** City Limits. **1986:** Critters. **1988:** The Horror Show. **1992:** Mom & Dad Save the World. **1993:** Army of Darkness. **1994:** Star Trek, Generations. *Television*—Harry O; The Man from Atlantis; Buck Rogers; Star Trek, the Next Generation; Star Trek, Voyager.

PAUL NUCKLES

A stunt coordinator and second unit director specializing in motorcycles, Nuckles is most closely associated with the muscular films of low-budget seventies director Jack Starrett. A memorable car roll from *Race with the Devil* was seen weekly on the opening of television's "The Fall Guy."

Films—1968: Chubasco; Bullit. **1969:** The Undefeated. **1970:** The Losers; C.C. & Co.; There Was a Crooked Man; Which Way to the Front? **1972:** Slaughter; The Thing with Two Heads. **1973:** Camper John; Cleopatra Jones. **1974:** The Gravy Train; Policewomen; Tigercage; The Front Page; Earthquake; The Taking of Pelham One Two Three. **1975:** Mitchell; Race with the Devil. **1976:** A Small Town in Texas; Scorchy; Hollywood Man; Dixie Dynamite; Futureworld. **1977:** Final Chapter: Walking Tall; Speedtrap; Saturday Night Fever; Stunts; Nowhere to Hide (tv). **1978:** Big Bob Johnson & His Fantastic Speed Circus (tv). **1979:** C.H.O.M.P.S.; When You Comin' Back Red Ryder? **1980:** Phobia. **1981:** Butterfly. **1984:** Places in the Heart. **1987:** Making Mr. Right. *Television*—Gunsmoke; The Immortal; Mission: Impossible; Emergency; The Rookies; CHiPs; Miami Vice; Cutter to Houston.

BETH NUFER

A bit actress, Nufer doubled for Lynda Carter on television's "Wonder Woman."

Films—**1976:** King Kong; Logan's Run. **1981:** Forbidden Zone; Going Ape; Under the Rainbow. **1982:** The Cat People; Blade Runner; Poltergeist; Star Trek 2: The Wrath of Khan. **1983:** Fire & Ice; Spacehunter; Two of a Kind. **1984:** Country. **1985:** Into the Night; Iron Eagle. **1986:** Invaders from Mars; Poltergeist 2; King Kong Lives; Big Trouble in Little China. **1987:** The Monster Squad; Code Name Zebra. **1988:** Illegally Yours; Beetlejuice; Patty Hearst. **1989:** Backtrack. **1991:** The People Under the Stairs; The Marrying Man. *Television*—Wonder Woman.

DANNY O'HACO

Films—**1986:** The Three Amigos. **1988:** Bulletproof; World Gone Wild; Who Framed Roger Rabbit?; Kansas; Earth Girls Are Easy; Bail Out. **1989:** Back to Back. **1990:** Back to the Future 3. **1991:** Shattered; Beastmaster 2. **1992:** Rapid Fire; Live Wire. **1993:** Geronimo. **1994:** Bad Girls; Blind Justice; Desperate Trail. **1995:** Frank & Jesse; Heat. **1996:** Crazy Horse. *Television*—The Young Riders.

JEFF O'HACO

The brother of Danny O'Haco, Jeff has doubled for Sylvester Stallone.

Films—**1985:** Back to the Future; Commando. **1986:** The Three Amigos; Killer in the Mirror (tv). **1987:** Bloody Wednesday;

No Man's Land; Extreme Prejudice. **1988:** Bulletproof; Rambo 3; Earth Girls Are Easy; Bail Out. **1989:** Indiana Jones & the Last Crusade; Lock Up; Tango & Cash. **1990:** Back to the Future 3. **1991:** Flight of the Intruder; Toy Soldiers. **1992:** The Gun in Betty Lou's Handbag. **1993:** Cliffhanger. **1994:** Blind Justice; Desperate Trail. **1996:** Crazy Horse. *Television*—Renegade; The Young Riders; Dr. Quinn.

ALAN OLINEY

A member of Stunts Unlimited, this veteran stunt coordinator and second unit director has doubled for Richard Pryor, Eddie Murphy, and Denzel Washington.

Films—**1969:** Che; Justine. **1974:** Policewomen; Hang Up (aka Super Dude). **1975:** Mandingo. **1976:** Drum. **1977:** Which Way Is Up?; Firesale; Delta Fox; Exo-Man (tv). **1978:** Gray Lady Down; Hooper; Convoy; California Suite; Blackjack. **1979:** The Black Hole; Buck Rogers in the 25th Century. **1980:** The Blues Brothers; Seems Like Old Times. **1981:** Crazy Time (tv). **1982:** Fast Times at Ridgemont High; Renegades (tv). **1983:** D.C. Cab; The Star Chamber; The Osterman Weekend; Scarface; Get Crazy; Missing Pieces (tv). **1984:** Beverly Hills Cop; The Karate Kid; Buckaroo Banzai; Star Trek 3: The Search for Spock; Purple Rain; Off Sides (tv). **1985:** Police Academy 2: Their First Assignment; Death Wish 3; Gus Brown & Midnight Brewster (tv). **1986:** Odd Jobs; Police Academy 3: Back in Training; Legal Eagles; Murphy's Law; The Golden Child; Out of Bounds; 52 Pick-Up. **1987:** The Wild Pair; Over the Top; Critical Condition; Leonard Part 6; Beverly Hills Cop 2; Private Investigations. **1988:** Moving; Die Hard; The Presidio; I'm Gonna Git You Sucka. **1989:** The Abyss; Kinjite; Harlem Nights; Blind Fury; Crack House. **1990:** Peacemaker; Ghost Dad; Last of the Finest; Predator 2;

In the Cold of the Night. **1991:** Rich Girl; Ricochet; The Last Boy Scout. **1992:** Deep Cover; Memoirs of an Invisible Man; Sister Act; Mom & Dad Save the World; Nails; Class Act; Patriot Games; The Distinguished Gentleman. **1993:** Nat'l Lampoon's Loaded Weapon; Hot Shots Part Deux; Full Eclipse; The Last Action Hero; Demolition Man; Rising Sun. **1994:** The Crow; Airheads. **1995:** Village of the Damned; Crimson Tide; Showgirls; Seven; A Vampire in Brooklyn. **1996:** Executive Decision; Sgt. Bilko; Eraser; Spy Hard; Courage Under Fire; First Kid; Ravenhawk. *Television*—The Immortal; The Rookies; Gemini Man; The Fall Guy.

RON OLINEY

The brother of Alan Oliney, Ron also doubled for Richard Pryor.

Films—**1979:** The Black Hole. **1981:** Bustin' Loose; Pennies from Heaven. **1982:** The Sword & the Sorcerer; Penitentiary 2; Renegades (tv). **1983:** D.C. Cab; Bad Boys; Scarface; Get Crazy. **1984:** Purple Rain. **1986:** Jo Jo Dancer, Your Life Is Calling; 52 Pick-Up. **1987:** Critical Condition; Police Academy 4: Citizens on Patrol. **1988:** Moving.

KITTY O'NEIL

A former AAU diving champion, O'Neil garnered some media attention and a television bio-pic in the late seventies due to the fact that she was deaf. She married stuntman Duffy Hamilton.

Films—**1976:** Two Minute Warning. **1977:** Airport '77. **1978:** Foul Play; Damien: Omen 2. **1979:** Silent Victory: The Kitty O'Neil Story (tv). **1980:** The Blues Brothers; Smokey & the Bandit 2. *Television*—Baretta; Gemini Man; The

Bionic Woman; The San Pedro Bums; Quincy.

JANET LEE ORCUTT

A member of the United Stuntwoman's Association, Orcutt has doubled for Traci Lords.

Films—**1985:** Lust in the Dust; Vendetta. **1987:** Cold Steel; Munchies. **1988:** Night of the Demons; Criminal Act; Critters 2. **1990:** The Guardian; Circuitry Man; The Adventures of Ford Fairlane; Red Surf. **1991:** Bill & Ted's Bogus Journey; Beastmaster 2; The Rocketeer; Merchant of Evil; House 4; A Time to Die. **1992:** Basic Instinct; Nemesis; Toys; CIA, Code Name Alexa. **1993:** Boiling Point.

MICK O'ROURKE

Films—**1982:** Barbarosa. **1986:** Quicksilver; Quiet Cool. **1987:** Brenda Starr. **1988:** Shakedown; Running on Empty. **1989:** Ghostbusters 2. **1990:** Quick Change; Two Evil Eyes; Night of the Living Dead; King of New York; Basket Case 2; The Kill-Off. **1992:** Malcolm X. **1993:** The Pelican Brief; Daybreak. **1994:** Body Snatchers; The Cowboy Way. **1995:** Kiss of Death; Hackers. **1996:** Sleepers; Ransom; Daylight; Bullet.

BOB ORRISON

A member of the Stuntmen's Association, Orrison is the brother of George Orrison and father of Mark and Brad.

Films—**1968:** Bandolero; Five Card Stud. **1969:** The Wild Bunch; Che; The Great Bank Robbery; The Undefeated. **1970:** Chisum. **1972:** The Culpepper Cattle Company. **1973:** Class of 43. **1974:** Three the Hard Way. **1975:** A Boy & His Dog; Mitchell. **1977:** Smokey & the Bandit. **1978:** Hooper; Convoy. **1979:** Sunburn. **1980:** Tom Horn; In God We Trust. **1988:** Action Jackson; Rambo 3; The Seventh Sign. **1989:** Road House; Tango & Cash. **1990:** Far Out Man; Die Hard 2; Days of Thunder. **1991:** Stone Cold. **1992:** Universal Soldier; Hoffa. **1994:** Speed; Stargate. **1995:** Avenging Angel; Bigfoot. *Television*—Star Trek; The Immortal; Vegas.

BRAD ORRISON

The son of Bob Orrison, Brad is a member of the International Stunt Association.

Films—**1980:** The Blues Brothers; Smokey & the Bandit 2. **1982:** Megaforce; Fighting Back. **1983:** Lone Wolf McQuade; Scarface. **1984:** Purple Rain; Savage Streets. **1985:** Girls Just Want to Have Fun. **1986:** Invasion USA; Legal Eagles; Never Too Young to Die. **1987:** Allan Quartermain & the Lost City of Gold. **1988:** Bulletproof; Hero & the Terror. **1990:** Delta Force 2; Satan's Princess. **1991:** Highway to Hell; Deadlock; Servants of Twilight; Beastmaster 2; Soldier's Fortune. **1992:** Article 99; Innocent Blood. **1993:** Private Wars. **1995:** 3 Ninjas Knuckle Up; Things to Do in Denver When You're Dead; One Man's Justice. **1996:** Thinner. *Television*—Alien Nation.

GEORGE ORRISON

Best known as the chief double for Clint Eastwood, Orrison has performed

bits in his pal's films and occasionally coordinated stunts.

Films—**1964:** Taggart. **1968:** The Pink Jungle. **1973:** High Plains Drifter. **1974:** Thunderbolt & Lightfoot. **1975:** The Eiger Sanction. **1976:** The Outlaw Josey Wales; The Enforcer. **1977:** The Gauntlet. **1978:** Every Which Way but Loose. **1979:** Escape from Alcatraz. **1980:** Bronco Billy; Heaven's Gate; Any Which Way You Can. **1982:** Firefox; Honkytonk Man. **1983:** Sudden Impact. **1984:** City Heat; Tightrope. **1985:** Pale Rider. **1986:** Ratboy. **1988:** The Dead Pool; Bird. **1989:** Pink Cadillac. **1990:** White Hunter, Black Heart; The Rookie. **1992:** The Unforgiven. **1993:** In the Line of Fire; A Perfect World. **1995:** The Bridges of Madison County. *Television*—Laramie; Laredo; Emergency; The Tall Men.

MARK ORRISON
(b. 1955)

Like his brother Brad, Mark is a member of the International Stunt Association.

Films—**1980:** The Blues Brothers; Smokey & the Bandit 2. **1984:** Girls Just Want to Have Fun; The River. **1985:** Invasion USA. **1986:** Legal Eagles; Radioactive Dreams. **1987:** Allan Quartermain & the Lost City of Gold; Back to the Beach; The Hidden. **1988:** Bulletproof; Crocodile Dundee 2; The Dead Pool; The Serpent & the Rainbow. **1990:** Delta Force 2. **1991:** Beastmaster 2. **1992:** The Lawnmower Man; Innocent Blood. **1995:** 3 Ninjas Knuckle Up. **1996:** The Glimmer Man.

ERNIE ORSATTI
(b. 1939)

The son of singer Inez Gorman and agent Ernest Orsatti, Ernie played several supporting roles in the early seventies, taking a memorable and spectacular fall into glass in *The Poseidon Adventure*. A member of the Professional Driver's Association, he moved into coordinating stunts and directing second unit for Charles Bronson movies. He went by the humorous pseudonym Brick Wahl early in his career.

Films—**1968:** The Green Berets; The Acid Eaters. **1971:** Star Spangled Girl. **1972:** The Poseidon Adventure; The Mechanic. **1973:** The Last American Hero; The Stone Killer; The Towering Inferno. **1975:** Night Moves. **1976:** Sky Riders. **1977:** Viva Knievel; The Car. **1978:** The Swarm. **1980:** Schizoid; Defiance; Underground Aces. **1982:** Dead Men Don't Wear Plaid; Death Wish 2; The Entity. **1983:** 10 to Midnight; D.C. Cab; The Winds of War (tv). **1984:** The Evil That Men Do. **1985:** Death Wish 3; Mischief; Alice in Wonderland (tv). **1986:** Hoosiers; Murphy's Law. **1987:** Winners Take All; Death Wish 4; Like Father, Like Son; Murder by the Book (tv). **1988:** Fresh Horses; Messenger of Death; I'm Gonna Git You Sucka. **1989:** Kinjite; Blind Fury. **1990:** The Gumshoe Kid; Almost an Angel; Opportunity Knocks; Welcome Home, Roxy Carmichael. **1991:** The Taking of Beverly Hills; Hot Shots; Another You. **1992:** Into the Sun. **1993:** Hot Shots Part Deux; Surf Ninjas; Sister Act 2; Grumpy Old Men; Excessive Force. **1994:** The Favor; Andre; Airheads; Bitter Vengeance; Flashfire; Black Cat Run (d). **1995:** Tall Tale; Coldblooded; Unstrung Heroes; Tremors 2. **1996:** Primal Fear; Ed; The Truth About Cats & Dogs; Sgt. Bilko; Don't Look Back; Larger Than Life. *Television*—Wonder Woman; The Incredible Hulk; The Greatest American Hero; Hill Street Blues; St. Elsewhere; Remington Steele; Beverly Hills Buntz; Private Eye; L.A. Law; Matlock; Hooperman; Cop Rock; Civil Wars; Loose Cannon; Capital News; Picket Fences; Live Shot.

FRANK ORSATTI
(b. 1942)

The brother of Ernie Orsatti, Frank was once a centerfielder in the St. Louis Cardinals organization. He has directed episodic television, handled second unit, and coordinated stunts.

Films—**1968:** Planet of the Apes; Bullit; Rosemary's Baby. **1969:** Paint Your Wagon; Che; Viva Max; The Arrangement. **1971:** Star Spangled Girl; B.S. I Love You; The Jesus Trip; Once Upon a Dead Man (tv). **1972:** The Poseidon Adventure; Fuzz; The Mechanic. **1973:** The Stone Killer. **1974:** The Towering Inferno; Black Samson; Freebie & the Bean; The Midnight Man; Lenny; The Longest Yard. **1975:** Rancho Deluxe; Flash & Firecat; Street People; Cleopatra Jones & the Casino of Gold. **1976:** Marathon Man. **1978:** Blue Collar; Three on a Date (tv). **1980:** The Great American Traffic Jam (tv). **1981:** Ryan's Four (tv). **1982:** The Beastmaster; First Blood; Johnny Belinda (tv). **1983:** The Star Chamber; Girls of the White Orchid (tv). **1984:** The Terminator. **1985:** Into the Night; Stark (tv). **1988:** The Presidio. **1989:** Who's Harry Crumb?; Kinjite; The Burbs; Road House; Lethal Weapon 2; Star Trek 5: The Final Frontier; Lock Up. **1990:** The Adventures of Ford Fairlane. **1991:** The Perfect Weapon; Point Break; Highlander 2; The Last Boy Scout. **1992:** Ruby; Rapid Fire; Lethal Weapon 3; Mom & Dad Save the World. **1993:** Cop & a Half; Hard Target; Nowhere to Run; Rescue Me; No Place to Hide. **1994:** Maverick; Me & the Kid; Roadracers; Strays (tv). **1995:** Nine Months. **1996:** Heaven's Prisoners. *Television*—Mission: Impossible; The Immortal; The FBI; Dan August; McMillan & Wife; Cannon; The Streets of San Francisco; Barnaby Jones; The Magician; Man Hunter; Planet of the Apes; The New People; The Barbary Coast; Serpico; Starsky & Hutch; Happy Days; The Incredible Hulk (d); Matt Houston; Renegades; Hill Street Blues; Outlaws (d).

NOON ORSATTI

The son of Ernie Orsatti, Noon is a member of the Professional Driver's Association. He has coordinated stunts and doubled for Johnny Depp and C. Thomas Howell.

Films—**1983:** Amityville 3-D. **1985:** Mischief. **1986:** Legal Eagles; The Golden Child; Hoosiers; Back to School; Welcome to 18. **1987:** Winners Take All; Death Wish 4; Less Than Zero; Like Father, Like Son; Back to the Beach; Dudes; Private Investigations. **1988:** Above the Law; Dead Heat; Shakedown; Messenger of Death; Fresh Horses; Critters 2; Bad Dreams; Beetlejuice; Nightmare on Elm Street 4: Dream Master. **1989:** Cage; Kinjite; To Die For; Bill & Ted's Excellent Adventure; Nat'l Lampoon's Christmas Vacation; One Man Force; CHUD 2. **1990:** Almost an Angel; Opportunity Knocks; Welcome Home, Roxy Carmichael; Prayer of the Rollerboys; Angel Town. **1991:** Highway to Hell; Another You; Harley Davidson & the Marlboro Man; Ricochet; Cool as Ice; Star Trek 6: Undiscovered Country. **1992:** Into the Sun; Sleepwalkers; A River Runs Through It; The Double-0 Kid. **1993:** Rescue Me; Hot Shots Part Deux; King of the Hill; True Romance; Benny & Joon; The Beverly Hillbillies; Jailbait. **1994:** Blue Tiger; Airheads; Eyes of an Angel; Past Tense; Payback; Flashfire. **1995:** The Road Killers; Tall Tale; Coldblooded; The Sweeper; Tremors 2. **1996:** Primal Fear; Marshal Law; Sgt. Bilko; Don't Look Back; A Very Brady Sequel; Riot; Ed; Larger Than Life. *Television*—The Costigans; Alien Nation; Baywatch.

JIMMY ORTEGA

A member of the Stuntmen's Association, Ortega is a familiar bit player of Spanish origin.

Films—**1985:** Moving Violations. **1987:** Extreme Prejudice; Night Force; Death Wish 4. **1988:** Bulletproof; The Seventh Sign. **1989:** Cage; K-9. **1990:** Satan's Princess; Internal Affairs; Delta Force 2; Taking Care of Business; The Rookie; Predator 2; Prayer of the Rollerboys; Angel Town; Drug Wars: The Camarena Story (tv). **1991:** Toy Soldiers; Ricochet; Guilty as Charged; Night Eyes 2. **1992:** Freejack; Deep Cover; American Me; Nemesis; Bram Stoker's Dracula. **1993:** Hot Shots Part Deux; Tombstone; Blindside; Dead Connection; Jailbait; Fugitive Nights (tv). **1994:** Beverly Hills Cop 3; A Low Down Dirty Shame; Silence of the Hams. **1995:** 3 Ninjas Knuckle Up; The Brady Bunch Movie; Blood for Blood. **1996:** Escape from L.A.; Last Man Standing; Mars Attacks!; Forest Warrior. *Television*—CHiPs; Beauty & the Beast; Star Trek, The Next Generation; Renegade.

CONRAD PALMISANO

A former Marine in Vietnam, Palmisano was working as a carpet layer when he began to appear as a film extra. He moved into stunts and emerged as a top coordinator, second unit director, and helmer of low-budget action films. He's a member of the Stuntmen's Association.

Films—**1976:** Moving Violation. **1977:** Grand Theft Auto. **1978:** Almost Summer; Piranha. **1979:** The Amityville Horror; The Black Hole; Breaking Away; Concorde, Airport '79; Meteor; The Electric Horseman; The Jerk; The Lady in Red. **1980:** Airplane; Alligator; Fade to Black; A Change of Season; Roadie; Seems Like Old Times; Smokey & the Bandit 2; OHMS (tv). **1981:** Heartbeeps; The Night the Lights Went Out in Georgia; Pennies from Heaven; Southern Comfort; Hard

Country; Whose Life Is It Anyway?; Madame X (tv). **1982:** Endangered Species; Fast Walking; First Blood; One from the Heart; Split Image. **1983:** Heart Like a Wheel; Cujo; Christine; Uncommon Valor. **1984:** Bachelor Party; Surf 2; Grandview USA. **1985:** Space Rage (d); Certain Fury; Gotcha. **1986:** Busted Up (d); Tough Guys. **1987:** Stakeout; It's Alive 3; Beverly Hills Cowgirl Blues (tv). **1988:** Alien Nation; License to Drive; Little Nikita; She's Having a Baby; The Naked Gun; Turner & Hooch; War & Remembrance (tv). **1989:** Weekend at Bernie's; See No Evil, Hear No Evil; Troop Beverly Hills. **1990:** Short Time; Robocop 2; Marked for Death. **1991:** Out for Justice. **1992:** Deep Cover; Folks; Straight Talk; Unlawful Entry; Under Siege. **1993:** Sleepless in Seattle; Robocop 3; Another Stakeout; Weekend at Bernie's 2. **1994:** On Deadly Ground; The Cowboy Way; No Escape. **1995:** Freewilly 2; Batman Forever; Assassins. **1996:** Carpool; Set It Off. *Television*—Simon & Simon; Spenser for Hire; Alien Nation; McCloud.

CHRIS PALOMINO

The wife of stuntman Freddie Hice, Palomino is a member of the United Stuntwoman's Association. She has doubled for Rebecca DeMornay.

Films—**1987:** Programmed to Kill. **1988:** License to Drive; Miracle Mile; Critters 2; Beetlejuice. **1989:** Her Alibi; Chopper Chicks in Zombie Town. **1990:** The First Power; Tremors; The Guardian; Maniac Cop 2; Repossessed; Boris & Natasha; I'm Dangerous Tonight (tv). **1991:** The Taking of Beverly Hills; Shattered; Driving Me Crazy. **1992:** Memoirs of an Invisible Man; The Hand That Rocks the Cradle; Nemesis. **1993:** Maniac Cop 3; Dennis the Menace; Dead Connection;

Excessive Force; Quick. **1994:** Blue Tiger; Automatic. **1996:** Spy Hard; Independence Day; Escape from L.A.

REG PARTON
(b. 1912)

A veteran supporting player and stunt driver, Parton doubled early in his career for both Gary Cooper and Tyrone Power. A member of the Stuntmen's Association, he has also coordinated stunts and directed second unit.

Films—**1951:** Texas Carnival; Rawhide. **1952:** High Noon; Pony Soldier. **1954:** Four Guns to Dodge; Four Guns to the Border. **1955:** Chief Crazy Horse; The Man from Bitter Ridge; This Island Earth. **1956:** Backlash; A Day of Fury; The Price of Fear; The Last Frontier; The Mole People. **1957:** Battle Hymn; The Sixth Man; The Hired Gun; The Incredible Shrinking Man. **1958:** Man Afraid; High School Confidential; Apache Territory. **1959:** Never Steal Anything Small. **1960:** Spartacus. **1961:** The Outsider. **1964:** Law of the Lawless. **1965:** Young Fury; Black Spurs. **1966:** Johnny Reno; Waco; Apache Uprising. **1967:** Fort Utah; Hostile Guns; Red Tomahawk. **1968:** Arizona Bushwhackers; Planet of the Apes; Rogue's Gallery; The Split; Sol Madrid. **1969:** The Love Bug. **1970:** The Molly Maguires. **1971:** The Skin Game. **1972:** Conquest of the Planet of the Apes. **1973:** Slaughter's Big Rip-Off; Battle for the Planet of the Apes. **1974:** The Towering Inferno; Freebie & the Bean; Blazing Saddles; Earthquake. **1975:** The Ultimate Warrior. **1976:** The Amazing Dobermans. **1977:** Herbie Goes to Monte Carlo. **1978:** Hooper. **1979:** Butch & Sundance: The Early Days. **1980:** The Stunt Man. **1981:** Heartbeeps. **1982:** The Sword & the Sorcerer. **1985:** Avenging Angel. **1987:** The Monster Squad; Remote Control. **1988:** Alien Nation; Freeway. *Television*—G.E. Theatre; Wyatt Earp; The Texan; Rawhide; Johnny

Guitar; Branded; The Green Hornet; Cimarron Strip; The Rockford Files; The Barbary Coast; The Rifleman.

REGINA PARTON
(b. 1945)

The daughter of Reg Parton, Regina was working as a dental assistant when she decided to pursue stuntwork. She became the president of the Stuntwoman's Association and later doubled for Jaclyn Smith.

Films—**1969:** The Love Bug; The Reivers; The Lonely Profession (tv). **1971:** Dirty Harry. **1972:** Conquest of the Planet of the Apes. **1973:** Battle for the Planet of the Apes; The Night Strangler (tvm). **1974:** The Trial of Billy Jack; The Towering Inferno; Freebie & the Bean; Blazing Saddles; Earthquake. **1975:** The Hindenburg; Crazy Mama. **1976:** Logan's Run. **1978:** The Cat from Outer Space; Hooper; Convoy. **1979:** The Black Hole; The Villain; 1941; Stunt Seven (tv). **1980:** Midnight Madness; Rough Cut. **1981:** The Cannonball Run. **1982:** The Sword & the Sorcerer. **1986:** Legal Eagles. *Television*—T.H.E. Cat; Star Trek; The FBI; The Mod Squad; Adam-12; Emergency; Search; The Night Stalker; The Rockford Files; Charlie's Angels; Hart to Hart.

VICTOR PAUL

A former Olympic sabre champion, Paul doubled for Burt Ward on the television series "Batman." He later moved into stunt coordinating and second unit work, specializing in films showcasing fencing weapons. He's a member of the Stuntmen's Association.

Films—**1948:** The Adventures of Don Juan. **1949:** Scene of the Crime. **1950:** Gambling House. **1952:** Against All Flags. **1956:** Guys & Dolls. **1958:** The Party Crashers. **1960:** Spartacus. **1966:** Batman. **1968:** The Boston Strangler. **1969:** Che; The Big Bounce; Hello, Dolly! **1970:** WUSA; Move. **1971:** The Skin Game; Dirty Harry; Star Spangled Girl. **1972:** What's Up, Doc?; Conquest of the Planet of the Apes. **1973:** The Don Is Dead; Cleopatra Jones; Magnum Force; Battle for the Planet of the Apes. **1974:** The Towering Inferno. **1975:** Night Moves; The Master Gunfighter. **1976:** Swashbuckler. **1977:** Opening Night. **1978:** Straight Time. **1979:** The Prisoner of Zenda; The Jazz Singer. **1980:** The Baltimore Bullet; The Blues Brothers; The Island; Borderline; Wholly Moses. **1981:** Going Ape; Zorro, the Gay Blade. **1981:** History of the World, Part One. **1982:** Homework; My Favorite Year. **1983:** Flashdance; The Man Who Loved Women; Mr. Mom. **1984:** Bachelor Party; Racing with the Moon; The Wild Life. **1985:** Cloak & Dagger; Police Academy 2: Their First Assignment; Moving Violations; North & South (tv). **1986:** Sweet Liberty; 8 Million Ways to Die; Blind Justice (tv). **1987:** Project X; Brenda Starr; Prison for Children (tv). **1988:** Die Hard; License to Drive. **1989:** Lethal Weapon 2; Bert Rigby, You're a Fool. **1990:** Die Hard 2; The Adventures of Ford Fairlane. **1991:** Mobsters; Ricochet; The Rocketeer; The Last Boy Scout. **1992:** Stay Tuned. **1993:** Nat'l Lampoon's Loaded Weapon; Robin Hood: Men in Tights. **1994:** The Chase; Back to the Streets of San Francisco (tv). **1995:** Don Juan DeMarco; Stuart Saves His Family; The Jessica McClure Story (tv). **1996:** Mars Attacks! *Television*—Batman; Cimarron Strip; Mission: Impossible; Banyon; Fame; The Untouchables.

GIL PERKINS
(b. 1907)

A lifetime member of the Stuntmen's Association, this Australian supporting player and former swim champion estimated that he worked on some 1500 films during a 50 year career. He doubled for William "Hopalong Cassidy" Boyd, Bruce Cabot, Red Skelton, and the movie monsters Frankenstein, the Wolf Man, and Mr. Hyde.

Films—**1929:** The Delightful Rogue. **1930:** Moby Dick; Journey's End. **1931:** The Sea Wolf; An American Tragedy. **1932:** Cavalcade; Sky Hawk; The Big Gamble; The Most Dangerous Game. **1933:** The Invisible Man; King Kong; Lucky Devils. **1935:** She; A Feather in Her Hat. **1936:** Suicide Fleet. **1937:** Captains Courageous; Fight for Your Lady; God's Country and the Woman. **1938:** Mutiny on the Bounty; The Adventures of Robin Hood. **1939:** Blackmail; Dodge City. **1940:** Virginia City; Seven Sinners; Wildcat Bus. **1941:** Dr. Jekyl and Mr. Hyde; They Died with Their Boots On; Riders of Death Valley; Hellzapoppin; A Yank in the RAF; The Timber Beast. **1942:** Spy Smashers; Journey for Margaret; Mrs. Miniver; Random Harvest; They Got Me Covered. **1943:** Frankenstein Meets the Wolf Man; The Man from Down Under; Slightly Dangerous; G-Men vs. The Black Dragon; Captain America. **1944:** Heavenly Days; I'll Remember April. **1945:** Son of Lassie. **1946:** Cloak & Dagger; The Killers; Fatal Witness. **1947:** The Black Widow; G-Men Never Forget; Desire Me; Twilight on the Rio Grande; Jesse James Rides Again; Son of Zorro. **1948:** A Southern Yankee; The Three Musketeers; Fort Apache; The Fuller Brush Man. **1949:** Bride of Vengeance; Take Me Out to the Ballgame; Neptune's Daughter; The Lost Tribe. **1950:** The Yellow Cab Man; Father of the Bride; The Admiral Was a Lady; Watch the Birdie. **1951:** Texas Carnival; Double Dynamite. **1952:** Hans Christian Anderson; The Steel Fist; Fearless Fagan; Kansas City Confidential; Lovely to Look At; Brave Warrior; The Member of the Wedding; Scandal Sheet. **1953:** Half a Hero; Abbott & Costello Meet Jekyll & Hyde; The Clown; Private Eyes; Code

Two; City of Bad Men. **1954:** Demetrius & the Gladiators; The Big Chase. **1955:** The Phoenix City Story; I Died a Thousand Times; The Sea Chase. **1956:** Around the World in 80 Days; Bundle of Joy; The Outlanders. **1957:** Calypso Heat Wave; Baby Face Nelson; House of Numbers; Shotout at Medicine Bend; Public Pigeon #1; Teenage Monster (a/p). **1958:** The Buccaneer; Teenage Thunder; The Brain from Planet Arous; High School Confidential; Joyride; Violent Road. **1959:** Gunmen from Laredo; The Beat Generation. **1960:** Spartacus; The Alamo. **1961:** Portrait of a Mobster; Valley of the Dragons. **1962:** Confessions of an Opium Eater; Experiment in Terror; How the West Was Won. **1963:** Twilight of Honor; Black Gold. **1964:** A Distant Trumpet. **1966:** Batman; Blindfold; The Silencers; The Sand Pebbles. **1969:** The Wrecking Crew; The Undefeated. **1970:** Lost Flight; The Molly Maguires; Flap. **1972:** The Poseidon Adventure. **1973:** Walking Tall. **1975:** Framed. **1978:** FM. **1979:** The Prisoner of Zenda. **1980:** Raging Bull. *Television*—Telephone Time; Zane Grey Theatre; Dupont Theatre; Gateway to the Mind; Black Saddle; Colt .45; Richard Diamond, Private Detective; The Californians; The Millionaire; The Virginian; Laredo; The Man from U.N.C.L.E.; Voyage to the Bottom of the Sea; Star Trek; Land of the Giants; Mission: Impossible; Batman; Cimarron Strip; Shaft; Wagon Train; Bonanza; Its a Man's World; The Beverly Hillbillies.

DAVE PERNA
(b. 1935)

Films—**1967:** Hour of the Gun; The St. Valentine's Day Massacre. **1969:** A Man Called Gannon; Che. **1973:** The Don Is Dead. **1977:** Delta Fox. **1980:** The Blues Brothers. **1984:** Grandview USA. **1986:** Raw Deal; Houston: The Legend of Texas (tv). **1988:** Above the Law; Twins. **1989:** Her Alibi. **1990:** Almost an Angel; Rockula; The Rookie. **1991:** K-9000 (tv). *Television*—The Restless Gun; Have Gun,

Will Travel; Riverboat; Laramie; The Virginian; Laredo; The Green Hornet; Mission: Impossible; The Heat.

HARVEY G. PERRY

(b. 1900; d. 1985)

San Francisco-raised stunt legend was a national high dive champ and professional boxer before getting into stunts as a double for Harold Lloyd, James Cagney, and Humphrey Bogart. He continued to perform gags well into his eighties.

Films—1923: Safety Last. 1932: Winner Take All. 1933: Hoop-La; King Kong. 1934: Love Time; 365 Nights in Hollywood; Men of the Night; Three on a Honeymoon. 1935: The Irish in Us; Call of the Wild; Silk Hat Kid; This Is the Life. 1936: After the Thin Man; The Crime of Dr. Forbes; Earthworm Tractors; Every Saturday Night; High Tension; Song & Dance Man. 1937: Alcatraz Island; Mountain Music; A Star Is Born; Heidi. 1938: Happy Landing; The Mad Miss Manton; Mysterious Mr. Moto; One Wild Night; Mr. Moto's Gamble; Suez. 1939: Dodge City. 1940: Sailor's Lady; They Drive By Night. 1942: Casablanca. 1943: Action in the North Atlantic. 1948: Treasure of the Sierra Madre; Whiplash; Trouble Preferred. 1949: Miss Mink of 1949. 1952: Silver City; Hurricane Smith. 1953: Devil's Canyon. 1954: Superman Flies Again. 1955: Conquest of Space; Francis in the Navy. 1956: Santiago. 1958: The Last Hurrah. 1959: The Gazebo; On the Beach; The Flying Fontaines; Never Steal Anything Small. 1960: Spartacus. 1962: How the West Was Won. 1964: Viva Las Vegas. 1966: An American Dream; A Fine Madness; Harper. 1967: The St. Valentine's Day Massacre; Bonnie & Clyde. 1969: Paint Your Wagon. 1973: Oklahoma Crude. 1974: Blazing Saddles. 1976: Drum. 1978: Movie, Movie. 1979: The Main Event. 1980: Raging Bull. 1981: Escape from New York. 1983: To Be or Not to Be. 1986: A Fine Mess. *Television*—Superman; Dupont Theatre; F-Troop (reg.); Laredo; The Green Hornet; Baretta; Vegas; Fantasy Island; CHiPs.

MANNY PERRY

Massachusetts-born bodybuilder was a Mr. California before doubling for Lou Ferrigno on television's "The Incredible Hulk." His greatest notoriety stems from his humorous bit as Big Jim Slade in the spoof *Kentucky Fried Movie*. A member of Stunts Unlimited, he has also doubled for Tiny "Zeus" Lister.

Films—1977: The Kentucky Fried Movie. 1985: To Live & Die in L.A. 1986: Blue City; Back to School; Convicted (tv). 1987: Number One with a Bullet; Night Force; Death Wish 4. 1988: License to Drive; The Great Outdoors. 1989: Collision Course; Who's Harry Crumb?; No Holds Barred; Uncle Buck; Glory; Lock Up; Tango & Cash. 1990: Heart Condition; Marked for Death; Predator 2. 1991: The Naked Gun 2 1/2 ; V.I. Warshawski; Out for Justice; Hook; The Last Boy Scout. 1992: Basic Instinct; Kuffs; Stop! Or My Mom Will Shoot; American Me; Rapid Fire; Nemesis; The Mighty Ducks. 1993: Point of No Return; Nat'l Lampoon's Loaded Weapon; Falling Down; The Last Action Hero; Best of the Best 2; Nowhere to Run. 1994: Blankman; Drop Zone; Steel Frontier. 1995: Men of War; Bad Boys; Panther; Under Siege 2; Money Train; Sudden Death. 1996: From Dusk Till Dawn; Heaven's Prisoners; Eraser; The Rock; Spy Hard; Fled; Escape from L.A.; Bulletproof; Jingle All the Way; Sunchaser. *Television*—The Incredible Hulk; Outlaws; The Flash.

MARY K. PETERS

A member of the Stuntwoman's Association, Peters has doubled for Sigourney Weaver.

Films—**1975:** At Long Last Love. **1978:** Hooper; American Hot Wax. **1979:** The Lady in Red; The Electric Horseman; Gold of the Amazon Women (tv); Topper (tv). **1981:** Going Ape; The Nashville Grab (tv). **1982:** The Sword & the Sorcerer; Star Trek 2: The Wrath of Khan. **1985:** Command 5 (tv). **1986:** Dangerously Close. **1987:** Lethal Weapon; Baby Boom; Morgan Stewart's Coming Home. **1988:** Feds; Beetlejuice. **1989:** Midnight. **1990:** The Adventures of Ford Fairlane. **1991:** The Naked Gun 2 1/2; The Addams Family; Beastmaster 2; Thelma & Louise; Prey of the Chameleon; The Bride of Re-Animator. **1992:** Deep Cover; Dolly Dearest; Sweet Justice; Sins of Desire; Mission of Justice. **1993:** Extreme Justice; Boiling Point. **1994:** The Naked Gun 33 1/3; Midnight Ride. **1995:** Copycat; Suspect Device; Bodycount. **1996:** Independence Day.

PATRICIA PETERS

A former gymnast, Trish Peters has doubled for the likes of Michelle Pfeiffer, Kathleen Turner, and Drew Barrymore. She's a member of the Stuntwoman's Association.

Films—**1987:** Dragnet. **1988:** Halloween 4; Big Top Pee Wee. **1989:** War of the Roses; CHUD 2. **1991:** Hook; Double Trouble. **1992:** Poison Ivy; Batman Returns. **1993:** Hot Shots Part Deux; The Beverly Hillbillies; Cyborg 2. **1994:** Wolf; Double Dragon; Silence of the Hams; Flashfire. **1995:** Mad Love; Batman Forever; Showgirls; Assassins; Strange Days; The Crossing Guard. **1996:** Barb Wire; Norma Jean & Marilyn; Last Man Standing; Mars Attacks!

DIANE PETERSON
(b. 1958)

A New-Jersey born actress and former Playboy Bunny, Peterson has doubled for the likes of Rebecca DeMornay, Darlanne Fluegel, Sharon Stone, Faye Dunaway, and Jessica Lange. She's a member of the Stuntwoman's Association.

Films—**1975:** The Stepford Wives; Seven Alone. **1976:** King Kong. **1977:** Annie Hall; Grand Theft Auto. **1978:** The Hi-Riders. **1979:** The Lady in Red. **1981:** Heartbeeps. **1983:** The Man with Two Brains; Loose Joints (aka Flicks). **1984:** Bachelor Party. **1985:** Just One of the Guys. **1986:** Let's Get Harry; Tough Guys. **1987:** Allan Quartermain & the Lost City of Gold; Death Wish 4; Million Dollar Mystery; Barfly; Tough Guys Don't Dance; Return to Horror High; Remote Control; Cold Steel; The Hidden. **1988:** Bulletproof; Action Jackson; Feds; Colors; Permanent Record; Freeway; Midnight Cabaret; Criminal Act. **1989:** River of Death. **1990:** Robocop 2. **1991:** The Hard Way; Suburban Commando. **1992:** Universal Soldier. **1993:** The Last Action Hero; Robocop 3; Blindside. **1994:** Blue Sky. *Television*—Kojak; Charlie's Angels; Taxi; Magnum P.I.; Cagney & Lacey; Alfred Hitchcock Presents; Matlock; Father Dowling Mysteries; Doogie Howser; Tales from the Crypt; Walker, Texas Ranger.

CHARLES PICERNI

(b. 1937)

A veteran member of Stunts Unlimited, Picerni has distinguished himself as a supporting player, stunt coordinator, second unit man, and episodic television director. The brother of character actor Paul Picerni, he worked such odd jobs as setting up carnivals and knocking down houses prior to his entrance into the movie business. His sons are also stuntmen.

Films—**1968:** The Boston Strangler. **1969:** Che. **1970:** Which Way to the Front?; Flap. **1971:** Star Spangled Girl. **1972:** Fuzz. **1973:** Shamus; The Don Is Dead; The Letters (tv). **1974:** Black Samson; Newman's Law; Earthquake. **1975:** The Barbary Coast. **1976:** A Matter of Wife & Death (tv). **1977:** Kill Me If You Can (tv). **1979:** Seven; The Prizefighter. **1980:** The Baltimore Bullet; The Blues Brothers; Borderline; The Private Eyes; Stunts Unlimited (tv); Rivkin, Bounty Hunter (tv). **1981:** Margin for Murder (tv); Sizzle (tv). **1982:** My Favorite Year; Tron; Dead Men Don't Wear Plaid. **1984:** Against All Odds. **1985:** Into the Night. **1986:** F/X; The Money Pit; Bad Guys; Playing for Keeps. **1987:** Kidnapped; The Wild Pair; Code Name Zebra. **1988:** Die Hard. **1989:** Road House; Lethal Weapon 2; Nat'l Lampoon's Christmas Vacation. **1990:** Die Hard 2; Ghost; Captain America; The Adventures of Ford Fairlane. **1991:** Hudson Hawk; Ricochet; The Last Boy Scout. **1992:** Basic Instinct; Lethal Weapon 3; Rapid Fire; The Fifth Corner (tv). **1993:** Nat'l Lampoon's Loaded Weapon; True Romance; Demolition Man; Fatherhood; Best of the Best 2. **1994:** True Lies; I Love Trouble; Streetfighter; A Low Down Dirty Shame. **1995:** The Babysitter; Fair Game; Vampire in Brooklyn; To the Limit. **1996:** Don't Be a Menace...; 2 Days in the Valley; Maximum Risk. *Television*—The Untouchables; Voyage to the Bottom of the Sea; Daniel Boone; Batman; Mission: Impossible; Mannix; The Magician; Toma; Kojak; The Rockford Files; Police Woman; SWAT; Charlie's Angels; Starsky & Hutch; Vegas (d); The Incredible Hulk (d); Matt Houston (d); Gavilan (d); Strike Force (d); T.J. Hooker (d); Blue Thunder (d); Hardcastle & McCormick (d); Finder of Lost Loves (d); MacGruder & Loud (d); Hollywood Beat (d); Hunter (d); Stingray (d); Spenser for Hire (d); J.J. Starbuck (d); Beauty & the Beast; The Fifth Corner; Tales from the Crypt.

CHARLES PICERNI, JR.

A member of Stunts Unlimited, Picerni has followed in his father's footsteps as a stunt coordinator.

Films—**1979:** Seven. **1982:** The Beastmaster. **1983:** Scarface. **1984:** Star Trek 3: The Search for Spock; Racing with the Moon. **1985:** Cloak & Dagger; Into the Night. **1986:** F/X; The Money Pit; Sweet Liberty; Out of Bounds; Back to School. **1987:** The Wild Pair; The Lost Boys; Night Force. **1988:** Off Limits; Die Hard; The Presidio; They Live. **1989:** Lethal Weapon 2; Best of the Best; Road House. **1990:** The Hunt for Red October; Die Hard 2; Vital Signs; Last of the Finest; The Adventures of Ford Fairlane; Predator 2. **1991:** Mobsters; Out for Justice; V.I. Warshawski; Hook; Hudson Hawk; Ricochet; The Last Boy Scout; Martial Law. **1992:** Memoirs of an Invisible Man; American Me; Lethal Weapon 3; Rapid Fire; Patriot Games; Beyond the Law. **1993:** Nat'l Lampoon's Loaded Weapon; True Romance; The Last Action Hero; Demolition Man; Excessive Force; Robin Hood: Men in Tights; Fatherhood; Best of the Best 2. **1994:** The Naked Gun 33 1/3; True Lies; The Shadow; In the Army Now;

Clear & Present Danger; A Low Down Dirty Shame; Night of the Demons 2. **1995:** Just Cause; Village of the Damned; The Brady Bunch Movie; 3 Ninjas Knuckle Up; Bad Boys; Congo; Under Siege 2; Copycat; Seven; Fair Game; They; The Claiming. **1996:** The Lawnmower Man 2; Marshal Law; Barb Wire; Eraser; The Fan; 2 Days in the Valley; An Occasional Hell. *Television*—Occhio-Pinocchio; Beauty & the Beast; Hard Time on Planet Earth; Jake & the Fatman; Tales from the Crypt.

STEVE PICERNI

A member of Stunts Unlimited, the youngest Picerni has worked as a stunt coordinator for the mega-producing team of Donald Simpson and Jerry Bruckheimer.

Films—**1986:** Back to School. **1987:** Teen Wolf 2; Brenda Starr; Night Force. **1988:** Die Hard; The Presidio. **1989:** Wired; Lethal Weapon 2; Best of the Best; Road House; Nat'l Lampoon's Christmas Vacation. **1990:** The Hunt for Red October; Die Hard 2; Total Recall; Maniac Cop 2; Last of the Finest; The Adventures of Ford Fairlane; Predator 2. **1991:** Mobsters; Out for Justice; Hook; 29th Street; Hudson Hawk; Ricochet; The Last Boy Scout; Shakes the Clown. **1992:** Ruby; American Me; Lethal Weapon 3; Rapid Fire; Patriot Games; Live Wire; Doppelganger. **1993:** Nat'l Lampoons' Loaded Weapon; Hot Shots Part Deux; True Romance; Full Eclipse; The Last Action Hero; Hard Target; Demolition Man; Robin Hood: Men in Tights; Fatherhood; Best of the Best 2; Bounty Tracker. **1994:** The Chase; Clean Slate; True Lies; The Shadow; Clear & Present Danger; A Low Down Dirty Shame; Blankman; Puppetmasters; Deadly Target. **1995:** Just Cause; Candyman: Farewell to the Flesh; Bad Boys; Crimson Tide; Clueless; The Criminal Mind; Under Siege 2; Jade; Seven; Fair Game. **1996:** Executive Decision; Marshal Law; Mulholland Falls; Don't Be a Menace ..; Barb Wire; Eraser; The Rock; The Fan; Courage Under Fire; 2 Days in the Valley; Maximum Risk; Jingle All the Way. *Television*—Matt Houston; Baywatch.

RICHARD "PEE WEE" PIEMONDTE

Films—**1987:** My Demon Lover. **1990:** Street Hunter. **1991:** The Naked Gun 2 1/2; Out for Justice; The Hard Way. **1992:** American Me; Rapid Fire; Universal Soldier; Under Siege; Hoffa; Martial Law 2: Undercover; Dr. Mordrid. **1993:** Weekend at Bernie's 2; Conflict of Interest; Martial Outlaw. **1994:** Army of One; The Naked Gun 33 1/3; The Mask; American Yakuza. **1995:** Under Siege 2; Money Train; The Immortals; Excessive Force 2. **1996:** Executive Decision; The Great White Hype; Spy Hard; Pure Danger; Back to Back.

DENNY PIERCE

A member of the International Stunt Association, Pierce has doubled for Eric Stoltz.

Films—**1985:** Nightmare on Elm Street 2: Freddy's Revenge. **1986:** Trick or Treat; Never Too Young to Die. **1987:** Terminal Entry; Dudes. **1988:** Sunset; Two Moon Junction; Waxwork. **1989:** The Abyss; Cartel. **1990:** The Rookie; Prayer of the Rollerboys; The Ambulance. **1991:** 976 Evil 2; The Rapture; Mobsters; Terminator 2; Ambition. **1992:** The Lawnmower Man; 3 Ninjas; Sneakers; Davinci's War; Dead Center (aka Crazy Joe). **1993:** Hot Shots Part Deux; Streetknight; Poetic Justice; Rising Sun; Maniac Cop 3; Brain Smasher; Best of the Best 2. **1994:** Woman with a Past; Airheads; Class of 1999 2; Blankman. **1995:** Village of the Damned;

Frank & Jesse; 3 Ninjas Knuckle Up; Last Man Standing; Best of the Best 3; One Man's Justice; The Sweeper. **1996:** Bio-Dome; Primal Fear; Don't Look Back; Pure Danger; Fast Money; Riot; Mercenary; Raven; Beautiful Girls.

bustion. **1990:** Delta Force 2. **1991:** Lionheart; Star Trek 6: Undiscovered Country; Soldier's Fortune. **1992:** Seed People; Dolly Dearest; Death Ring; Guncrazy. **1993:** Rescue Me; Sidekicks; Firepower. **1994:** Blue Sky; Final Mission; Bad Blood. **1995:** Frank & Jesse; Painted Hero. *Television*—Walker, Texas Ranger.

REX PIERSON

Films—**1979:** A Time to Die. **1983:** The Sting 2. **1984:** Beverly Hills Cop. **1985:** Stick; My Science Project. **1987:** Over the Top; Brenda Starr; Code Name Zebra. **1988:** Tapeheads. **1989:** Cohen & Tate; Night Game; Road House; Lock Up; Return of the Swamp Thing. **1990:** Satan's Princess; Darkman; Another 48 HRS. **1991:** Nothing But Trouble; The Perfect Weapon; Deadlock; Beastmaster 2. **1991:** Alligator 2. **1992:** Mom & Dad Save the World; Davinci's War. **1993:** Fist of Honor; Excessive Force; Rescue Me. **1994:** Surviving the Game; Wagons East. **1995:** 3 Ninjas Knuckle Up; Tall Tale; One Man's Justice. **1996:** The Lawnmower Man 2; Riot; Somebody to Love; Back to Back.

GARY PIKE

Films—**1983:** Lone Wolf McQuade; Chained Heat. **1985:** Stand Alone; Code of Silence; Invasion USA. **1986:** The Delta Force; Nomads; Firewalker; Born American. **1987:** Allan Quartermain & the Lost City of Gold. **1987:** Back to the Beach; Overboard; The Hidden. **1988:** Bulletproof; Feds; Permanent Record; The Night Before. **1989:** River of Death; Halloween 5. **1991:** The Perfect Weapon; Star Trek 6: Undiscovered Country. **1992:** Seed People; Interceptor; The Unnameable 2; To Protect & Serve; Death Ring; Guncrazy. **1993:** Rescue Me; Firepower; Sidekicks. **1994:** Bad Blood. **1995:** Frank & Jesse; Painted Hero; The Silencers.

DON PIKE

Long associated as a stunt coordinator for Chuck Norris films, Don's brother Gary has often worked alongside him.

Films—**1968:** Faces. **1978:** Go Tell the Spartans. **1978:** Good Guys Wear Black; A Force of One. **1979:** Flatbed Annie & Sweetie Pie (tv). **1981:** An Eye for an Eye. **1982:** I, the Jury; Silent Rage. **1983:** Deadly Force; Lone Wolf McQuade; Chained Heat; Lies. **1984:** A Nightmare on Elm Street. **1985:** Stand Alone; Code of Silence; Invasion USA. **1986:** The Delta Force; Wisdom. **1987:** Allan Quartermain & the Lost City of Gold; The Hidden; Tough Guys Don't Dance. **1988:** Bulletproof; Feds; Permanent Record; The Night Before. **1989:** Spontaneous Com-

ALLEN PINSON

A lifetime member of the Stuntmen's Association, Pinson doubled for Clayton Moore on television's "Lone Ranger" and performed many bits.

Films—**1937:** A Million to One. **1944:** Practically Yours; Frenchman's Creek. **1945:** Masquerade in Mexico; Wonder Man. **1948:** Joan of Arc. **1950:** In a Lonely Place. **1951:** Lorna Doone; The Texas Rangers. **1952:** Singin' in the Rain; The Marrying Kind. **1953:** From Here to Eternity; The Bandits of Corsica; Thunder Bay. **1955:** Lady Godiva. **1956:** Around the World in 80 Days; The Last Frontier; The Burning Hills. **1957:** Hell on Devil's Island. **1958:** Gunman's Walk. **1959:** The

Crimson Kimono; Timbuktu. **1964:** Advance to the Rear. **1965:** Once Before I Die; McHale's Navy Joins the Air Force. **1968:** Coogan's Bluff. **1969:** The Great Bank Robbery; The Wrecking Crew; The Mad Room; The Pigeon (tv); The Over the Hill Gang (tv). **1971:** Desperate Mission (tv). **1972:** Conquest of the Planet of the Apes; Melinda. **1973:** Battle for the Planet of the Apes; Deliver Us from Evil (tv). **1974:** Mr. Majestyk. *Television*—The Lone Ranger; Zane Grey Theatre; Ozzie & Harriet; The Outer Limits; I Spy; Mission: Impossible; The Mod Squad.

JON POCHRAN

Films—**1982:** Megaforce; The Beastmaster. **1983:** Get Crazy. **1984:** Lovelines. **1985:** To Live & Die in L.A.; Moving Violations. **1986:** Let's Get Harry. **1987:** Survival Game. **1988:** License to Drive; Assault of the Killer Bimbos; Night of the Demons. **1989:** The Fabulous Baker Boys; Hollywood Hot Tubs 2. **1990:** Joe vs. The Volcano; Peacemaker; Puppetmaster 3; 9 1/2 Ninjas. **1991:** Alligator 2. **1992:** Universal Soldier; Leather Jackets; Interceptor; Stepfather 3; Death Ring; Guncrazy. **1993:** Firepower. **1994:** Bad Blood.

BERNIE POCK

A stunt coordinator and member of the International Stunt Association, Pock has doubled regularly for Emilio Estevez and Mike Myers. He had a leading role in the action flick *24 Hours to Midnight.*

Films—**1984:** Streets of Fire. **1985:** Back to the Future; Mischief; Remo Williams; Police Academy 2: Their First Assignment. **1986:** Invaders from Mars; Maximum Overdrive; Wisdom; Eye of the Tiger; Dangerous Love. **1987:** The Omega Syndrome; No Man's Land; The Lost Boys; Cold Steel. **1988:** Maniac Cop; Die

Hard; Two Moon Junction; License to Drive; Plainclothes. **1989:** Hit List; Always; Casualties of War; Far from Home; One Man Force. **1990:** Young Guns 2; Wild at Heart; Maniac Cop 2; The Adventures of Ford Fairlane; Men at Work. **1991:** Deadlock; Fast Getaway. **1992:** Freejack; Last of the Mohicans; Thunderheart; Sneakers; Wayne's World; 24 Hours to Midnight; Adventures in Dinosaur City; Rage & Honor. **1993:** Nat'l Lampoon's Loaded Weapon; Hear No Evil; Another Stakeout; The Temp; So I Married an Axe Murderer; Judgment Night; Wayne's World 2; Maniac Cop 3. **1994:** Star Trek Generations; Class of 1999 2. **1995:** Dangerous Minds; Last Man Standing; The Sweeper. **1996:** A Very Brady Sequel; Riot. *Television*—Beauty & the Beast.

BOBBY PORTER
(b. 1952)

Standing only five feet tall, this stunt coordinator has doubled young actors such as Henry Thomas, Edward Furlong, and Elijah Wood. He's a member of both the Stuntmen's Association and the Professional Driver's Association.

Films—**1973:** Battle for the Planet of the Apes. **1977:** Day of the Animals. **1978:** Every Which Way but Loose; Return from Witch Mountain. **1980:** Human Experiments; First Family; The Nude Bomb; Oh, God Book II; Herbie Goes Bananas; The Last Flight of Noah's Ark; Resurrection; Any Which Way You Can. **1981:** Under the Rainbow; On Golden Pond. **1982:** Annie; Blade Runner; E.T.; The Toy. **1983:** Something Wicked This Way Comes; Angel of H.E.A.T. **1984:** Night of the Comet; Places in the Heart; The River Rat. **1985:** Cloak & Dagger. **1986:** Odd Jobs; Radioactive Dreams. **1987:** Over the Top; Summer Camp Nightmare; Project X. **1988:** Above the Law; Mac & Me; The Blob; Freeway; Purple People Eater. **1989:** Immediate

Family; Prancer; Nightmare on Elm Street 5: Dream Child; Riding the Edge. **1990:** Flatliners; Problem Child. **1991:** Highway to Hell; Suburban Commando; Terminator 2; Not of This World (tv). **1992:** Pet Sematary 2; Live Wire; Radio Flyer; The Bodyguard; Adventures in Dinosaur City. **1993:** Slaughter of the Innocents; Jack the Bear; Man's Best Friend. **1994:** Camp Nowhere; In the Army Now. **1995:** Jumanji. *Television*—Planet of the Apes; Fantastic Journey; Quark (reg.); Voyagers; Wizards & Warriors.

DEBBIE PORTER

Films—**1981:** Honkytonk Freeway; Heartbeeps. **1982:** The Sender; Split Image. **1983:** Get Crazy; Sudden Impact; Twilight Zone: The Movie. **1984:** City Heat. **1985:** Moving Violations. **1987:** Nightmare on Elm Street 3: Dream Warriors; Private Investigations; Return to Horror High; Laguna Heat. **1988:** The Blob; Nightmare on Elm Street 4: Dream Master. **1990:** Robocop 2; Pacific Heights. **1992:** Love Field.

GARY PRICE

Films—**1988:** I'm Gonna Git You Sucka. **1990:** Bad Influence; The Guardian; Peacemaker; Edward Scissorhands. **1991:** The Perfect Weapon; Slacker. **1992:** Sister Act; The Distinguished Gentleman; Wayne's World. **1993:** Full Eclipse; Wayne's World 2. **1994:** Clean Slate; Payback. **1995:** Crimson Tide; Seven; Vampire in Brooklyn. **1996:** First Kid.

KAREN PRICE

Films—**1985:** Invasion USA. **1986:** Murphy's Law; The Wraith. **1987:** The Running Man; Hot Pursuit; Laguna Heat. **1988:** Above the Law. **1989:** Old Gringo; One Man Force; Cutting Class; Night Life. **1990:** The Gumshoe Kid. **1992:** Rage & Honor. **1993:** Cyborg 2; Maniac Cop 3.

DON PULFORD

A supporting player and member of the International Stunt Association, Pulford has doubled regularly for both William Shatner and Nick Nolte. His wife Lee has also done stunts.

Films—**1976:** Vigilante Force. **1978:** Thank God, It's Friday. **1979:** The Black Hole; From Here to Eternity (tv). **1980:** The Stunt Man. **1981:** Hard Country. **1983:** Nat'l Lampoons' Vacation; Scarface; The Star Chamber. **1985:** Invasion USA; Black Moon Rising. **1986:** Manhunter; King Kong Lives. **1987:** Code Name Zebra; Kidnapped. **1988:** Maniac Cop. **1989:** Star Trek 5: The Final Frontier. **1990:** Everybody Wins; Another 48 HRS.; Last of the Finest. **1991:** Shattered; Nothing But Trouble; The Perfect Weapon; Star Trek 6: Undiscovered Country; Point Break; Deadlock; Cape Fear; The Last Boy Scout. **1992:** Thunderheart; Forever Young; Innocent Blood. **1994:** The Getaway; The Naked Gun 33 1/3; Clean Slate; I Love Trouble; Body Shot; The Shadow; Clear & Present Danger; Star Trek Generations. **1995:** Tommy Boy; 3 Ninjas Knuckle Up; Under Siege 2; Jade. **1996:** Executive Decision; Mulholland Falls; The Glimmer Man. *Television*—The Streets of San Francisco; The Six Million Dollar Man; The Greatest American Hero.

VICTOR QUINTERO

A member of the Stuntmen's Association, Quintero has coordinated stunts and performed bits in a number of Chuck Norris films.

Films—**1984:** Missing in Action. **1985:** Invasion USA. **1986:** Born American. **1987:** Back to the Beach. **1988:** Bulletproof; Hero & the Terror; Feds. **1990:**

Hard to Kill. **1992:** Maximum Force; Stepfather 3; Dead Center (aka Crazy Joe); Sunset Grill; Death Ring. **1993:** Sidekicks; Hellbound. **1994:** Army of One. **1995:** Top Dog. *Television*—Walker, Texas Ranger.

CHERIE RAE (BRYSON)

A member of the United Stuntwoman's Association, Rae has doubled for Colleen Camp.

Films—**1978:** Katie, Portrait of a Centerfold (tv). **1979:** Gold of the Amazon Women (tv). **1981:** Legend of the Lone Ranger. **1983:** Nat'l Lampoon's Vacation; Scarface; Spacehunter. **1984:** Oh, God! You Devil. **1985:** Perfect; Hellhole; Clue; Fright Night; Command 5 (tv). **1986:** Dangerously Close; Eye of the Tiger. **1987:** Creepshow 2. **1988:** Illegally Yours; Alien Nation; My Stepmother Is an Alien. **1990:** Total Recall. **1991:** Highway to Hell; Diplomatic Immunity. **1992:** Love Field; Hero. **1992:** Hoffa. **1994:** The Naked Gun 33 1/3; Wes Craven's New Nightmare; Stargate. **1996:** Eye for and Eye; The Nutty Professor.

J. SUZANNE RAMPE (FISH)

A stunt coordinator and double for Linda Blair, Rampe is a member of the Stuntwoman's Association.

Films—**1982:** Ruckus. **1983:** Chained Heat. **1984:** Footloose; Lovelines; City Limits; The Terminator; Savage Street. **1988:** Bad Dreams. **1990:** Joe vs. the Volcano; The Adventures of Ford Fairlane; Shadowzone; Repossessed; Keaton's Cop. **1991:** The Rocketeer; Deadlock. **1992:**

Sweet Justice. **1993:** Cliffhanger; Kalifornia. **1994:** Red Sun Rising; Drop Zone; Scorned; Relentless 4. **1995:** Showgirls; Money Train; Last Man Standing; Black Scorpion; **1996:** Out There.

JEFF RAMSEY

A member of the Stuntmen's Association, Ramsey has performed an occasional bit role.

Films—**1973:** Electra Glide in Blue. **1979:** The Villain. **1980:** Tom Horn; Herbie Goes Bananas. **1981:** Ghost Story; The Legend of the Lone Ranger. **1984:** Firestarter; Romancing the Stone; Red Dawn; Starman. **1985:** Clue; Commando; The Journey of Natty Gann; Silverado. **1986:** Blue City; Raw Deal; No Mercy; Slow Burn. **1987:** The Night Stalker; Fatal Beauty; Best Seller; Dragnet; The Bedroom Window; Innerspace; Laguna Heat. **1988:** Sunset; Alien Nation; Out of the Dark; Dangerous Love; Criminal Act. **1989:** The 'burbs; The Package; Glory; Nightmare on Elm Street 5: Dream Child. **1990:** Downtown; The Rookie. **1991:** Toy Soldiers; Showdown in Little Tokyo; Nothing but Trouble. **1992:** Deep Cover; Thunderheart; Far & Away; Sleepwalkers; The Double O-Kid. **1993:** The Fugitive; Nowhere to Run. **1994:** Hologram Man. **1995:** Die Hard with a Vengeance; Top Dog.

CHAD RANDALL

The stunt coordinator son of Glenn Randall, Chad is a member of Stunts Unlimited.

Films—**1985:** To Live & Die in L.A.; Moving Violations. **1987:** Lethal Weapon; Night Force; World Gone Wild. **1988:** Off Limits; Die Hard; Rambo 3; The Presidio; Tequila Sunrise. **1989:** Who's Harry

Crumb?; Gleaming the Cube; Lethal Weapon 2; Casualties of War; Nat'l Lampoon's Christmas Vacation. **1990:** Days of Thunder; Pacific Heights; The Godfather 3. **1991:** One Good Cop; Hook; Point Break; Beethoven; Dead Again; The Last Boy Scout. **1992:** Kuffs; Memoirs of an Invisible Man; Lethal Weapon 3; Patriot Games; Beyond the Law. **1993:** Carlito's Way. **1994:** Gunmen; Pentathalon; Double Dragon; Puppetmasters. **1995:** The Road Killers; Men of War; Waterworld. **1996:** From Dusk Till Dawn; Mulholland Falls; The Long Kiss Goodnight.

GLEN RANDALL, JR.
(B. 1941)

This top-level stunt coordinator and second unit director started as a horse trainer and premier high-fall specialist, but an injury forced him out of stuntwork for nearly five years during the mid-seventies. A member of the Stuntmen's Association, he's best known for staging the rousing action in the *Indiana Jones* films.

Films—**1959:** Ben Hur. **1965:** Harum Scarum. **1966:** The Ugly Daschund; Munster, Go Home; Duel at Diablo. **1968:** Planet of the Apes. **1969:** The Good Guys & the Bad Guys; The Great Bank Robbery; Che. **1970:** Flap; Little Big Man; Soldier Blue. **1971:** The Omega Man; The Skin Game. **1972:** The Great Northfield Minnesota Raid; Conquest of the Planet of the Apes; The Cowboys; What's Up, Doc? **1973:** The Don Is Dead; Battle for the Planet of the Apes. **1974:** The Towering Inferno; Mame; Blazing Saddles; Earthquake. **1979:** The Black Stallion. **1981:** Lion of the Desert; Ghost Story; Honkytonk Freeway; Raiders of the Lost Ark. **1982:** E.T.; Poltergeist; Fast Times at Ridgemont High. **1983:** Never Say Never Again; Return of the Jedi. **1984:** Mrs. Soffel; Firestarter; Indiana Jones & the Temple of Doom; Red Dawn. **1985:** Cat's Eye; Remo Williams; Jewel of the Nile. **1986:** Raw Deal; Maximum Overdrive; Eye of the Tiger; No Mercy. **1987:** Best Seller; Traxx; Innerspace. **1988:** Midnight Run. **1989:** Collision Course. **1990:** Loose Cannons. **1991:** V.I. Warshawski; If Looks Could Kill; Beethoven. **1992:** Used People; Out on a Limb; Sneakers. **1993:** Amos & Andrew; The Fugitive; Undercover Blues. **1994:** On Deadly Ground; The Scout; Timecop. **1995:** Separate Lives; Panther; Species; The Tie That Binds; Chameleon. **1996:** The Substitute; Down Periscope. *Television*—Gunsmoke; Cimarron Strip; Hondo.

LARRY RANDLES

A member of the Stuntmen's Association, Randles is a horsefall specialist.

Films—**1968:** Chubasco. **1972:** The Cowboys; Ulzana's Raid. **1979:** The Villain. **1980:** The Mountain Men; Used Cars; Heaven's Gate. **1981:** The Legend of the Lone Ranger. **1982:** The Sword & the Sorcerer; The Beastmaster; Conan the Barbarian. **1983:** Blue Thunder. **1984:** Red Dawn. **1985:** Pale Rider; Commando; Silverado. **1986:** F/X; The Three Amigos. **1987:** The Monster Squad. **1988:** Rambo 3; Two Moon Junction. **1989:** The Package. *Television*—Gunsmoke.

SPIRO RAZATOS

This stunt coordinator is the man responsible for several incredible action scenes in otherwise marginal low-budget features *(Hit List, Maniac Cop 2, Last Man Standing)*. He drew attention initially for being pulled behind a car in the film *Rainy Day Friends,* a wild variation on the traditional "horse drag." A member of the Professional Driver's Association, he has moved from second unit into full-fledged directing assignments.

Films—**1984:** Streets of Fire. **1985:** Back to the Future; Commando; Rainy Day Friends (aka L.A. Bad). **1986:** The Golden Child; Invaders from Mars. **1987:** The Omega Syndrome; Private Investigations; Code Name Zebra; Night Force; Silent Night, Deadly Night 2. **1988:** Maniac Cop; Midnight Run; Colors; Full Moon in Blue Water; 976 Evil; My Best Friend Is a Vampire; Tripwire (s). **1989:** Hit List; Cameron's Closet; Cage; One Man Force; Relentless; Crackhouse; Blind Fury; Night Life. **1990:** The Gumshoe Kid; Spaced Invaders; Double Revenge; Last of the Finest; Maniac Cop 2; The Ambulance. **1991:** Waxwork 2; 976 Evil; Hook; Too Much Sun; Fast Getaway (d); Past Midnight; Driving Me Crazy; Shakes the Clown. **1992:** Encino Man; Adventures in Dinosaur City; Lake Consequence; Innocent Blood; Rage & Honor. **1993:** Extreme Justice; Maniac Cop 3; Sliver; Martial Outlaw. **1994:** Airheads; Class of 1999 2 (d); T-Force. **1995:** 3 Ninjas Knuckle Up; Panther; Last Man Standing; Money Train; The Sweeper; Tremors 2. **1996:** Lawnmower Man 2; Riot; Pure Danger; Uncle Sam. *Television*—Sledge Hammer.

ROSS REYNOLDS

A lifetime member of the Stuntmen's Association, Reynolds is an ace helicopter pilot.

Films—**1977:** Maniac. **1979:** Escape from Alcatraz; Concorde, Airport '79; Stunt Seven (tv). **1980:** The Stunt Man; Bor-

derline; The Nude Bomb; Where the Buffalo Roam. **1981:** Heartbeeps. **1982:** The Border; Tron. **1983:** Blue Thunder; Uncommon Valor. **1984:** Red Dawn; Ghost Warrior (aka Swordkill). **1985:** Fandango; Rainy Day Friends (aka L.A. Bad). **1986:** 52 Pick-Up. **1987:** Over the Top. **1988:** Midnight Run. **1991:** Eve of Destruction; V.I. Warshawski; Flight of the Intruder. *Television*—The Rockford Files.

SIMON RHEE

The fight choreographer brother of martial arts actor/producer Phillip Rhee, Simon has shown up prominently in the *Best of the Best* films. He had the lead in the obscure *Furious.*

Films—**1977:** The Kentucky Fried Movie. **1983:** Furious. **1986:** Ninja Turf. **1988:** Silent Assassins. **1989:** Best of the Best. **1991:** Showdown in Little Tokyo; Double Impact. **1992:** Universal Soldier. **1993:** Best of the Best 2. **1994:** Hologram Man. **1995:** Bad Blood; To the Limit; Blackout; The Silencers; Best of the Best 3. **1996:** Skyscraper; Escape from L.A.

SANDY RICHMAN

This Los Angeles-born stunt coordinator has made her career in New York, doubling for Kim Basinger, Sharon Gless, and Joanna Cassidy.

Films—**1981:** Blow Out. **1982:** The Soldier. **1984:** The Exterminator 2; Ghostbusters; Broadway Danny Rose. **1986:** Sweet Liberty; F/X; 9 1/2 Weeks. **1987:** Deadly Illusion. **1988:** Last Rites; Masquerade; Homeboy. **1989:** See No Evil, Hear No Evil; Black Rain. **1990:** The

Lemon Sisters; King of New York. *Television*—All My Children; As the World Turns.

BRANSCOMBE RICHMOND

(b. 1955)

Instantly recognizable supporting player of Hawaiian/native American ancestry, best known as the co-star of the popular television show "Renegade." The son of stuntman Leo Richmond, Branscombe made his first film at the age of six and hasn't let up. He would take tremendous screen beatings at the hands of Steven Seagal in *Hard to Kill* and Chuck Norris in *Hero and the Terror* before moving into more cerebral character assignments. A member of both the International Stunt Association and the Professional Driver's Association, the 6'3" star has coordinated stunts and directed second unit, but is in much more demand now as an actor.

Films—1961: The Devil at Four O'Clock. 1962: Mutiny on the Bounty. 1963: Donovan's Reef; The Ugly American. 1974: The Castaway Cowboy. 1976: Two Minute Warning. 1977: The Chicken Chronicles; The Kentucky Fried Movie. 1978: Death Moon (tv); Three on a Date (tv); Ishi: Last of His Tribe (tv). 1979: The Fish That Saved Pittsburgh; Hurricane. 1980: Waikiki (tv); Damien: Leper Priest (tv). 1982: The Legend of Walks Far Woman; Rocky 3. 1984: Mystic Warrior (tv); The Cannonball Run 2; The River; Star Trek 3: The Search for Spock; Thief of Hearts. 1985: Commando; Kids Don't Tell (tv). 1986: Cobra; Never Too Young to Die; Firewalker; Sunday Drive (tv); Bloodsport (tv). 1987: Best Seller; The Running Man; No Safe Haven; Night Force; The Hidden; The Highwayman (tv). 1988: Action Jackson; Bulletproof; The New Adventures of Pippi Longstocking; Hero & the Terror; They Live. 1989: Cage; License to Kill; Road House; L.A. Bounty; Parent Trap Hawaiian Honeymoon (tv). 1990: Hard to Kill; Far Out Man; Kindergarten Cop; Death Warrant. 1991: Harley Davidson & the Marlboro Man; Curly Sue; The Taking of Beverly Hills; Grand Canyon; Showdown in Little Tokyo; The Perfect Weapon; Driving Me Crazy; Beastmaster 2; The Hit Man (tv). 1992: Deep Cover; Article 99; American Me; Aces: Iron Eagle 3; Batman Returns; Christopher Columbus: the Discovery; Inside Edge; Innocent Blood; Sweet Justice; Davinci's Way; Nemesis; Sunset Grill; Death Ring. 1993: No Escape, No Return; Jericho Fever (tv). 1994: 3 Ninjas Knuckle Up; CIA 2: Target Alexa; Hard Vice; Ring of the Musketeers; The Corpse Had a Familiar Face (tv); Lakota Woman (tv). 1995: To the Limit (a/p). *Television*—Adventures in Paradise; The Six Million Dollar Man; Young Dan'l Boone; Police Story; The Bionic Woman; Battlestar Galactica; The Rockford Files; Buck Rogers; Vegas; Charlie's Angels; Magnum P.I.; Tales of the Gold Monkey; Simon & Simon; Cagney & Lacey; The Fall Guy; Hawaiian Heat (reg.); Automan; Knight Rider; Matt Houston; Cover Up; Mike Hammer; The A Team; Riptide; Misfits of Science; MacGyver; Airwolf; Heart of the City (reg.); Hunter; Falcon Crest; Houston Knights; Doctor's Wilde; Paradise; Jake & the Fatman; Baywatch; Island Son; Life Goes On; Snoops; Alien Nation; L.A. Law; Pros & Cons; Raven; Renegade (reg.); Vanishing Son.

CHUCK ROBERSON

(b. 1919; d. 1988)

Legendary Texas-born supporting player, best known as John Wayne's

Stuntman/supporting actor Branscombe Richmond.

friend and double for over 20 years. A former stable boy, ranch hand, cop, and WWII vet, the 6'4" actor also doubled for Clark Gable and Robert Mitchum. Among many notable as-signments stands out his riding a horse through a saloon window in *Chisum*. Roberson's autobiography is entitled *The Fall Guy*.

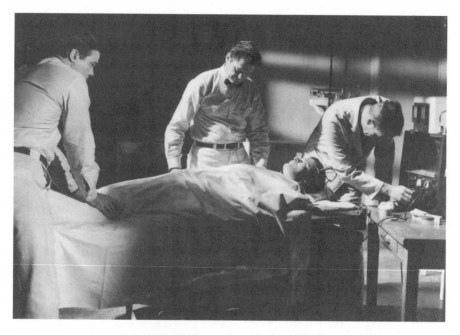

Chuck Roberson (center) in 1963's *Shock Corridor.*

Films—**1944:** Calendar Girl. **1946:** Renegades; In Old Wyoming; The Plainsman & the Lady. **1947:** Angel & the Badman; Jesse James Rides Again; Song of Scheherazade. **1948:** The Fighting Kentuckian; Wake of the Red Witch; The Three Musketeers. **1949:** Haunted Trails; I Shot Jesse James; Stampede; Ghost of Zorro. **1950:** Rio Grande; Bandit Queen; Cowtown; Frontier Outpost; Lightning Guns; The Outcast of Black Mesa; Frenchie; Trail of the Rustlers; The James Brothers of Missouri; Western Renegades; The Eagle & the Hawk; The Baron of Arizona; Tripoli; Winchester '73; The Hills of Oklahoma. **1951:** Cattle Drive; Barbed Wire; Ridin' the Outlaw Trail; Fort Dodge Stampede; The Last Outpost; Across the Wide Missouri; War Cry. **1952:** Lone Star; The Lusty Men; The Blazing Forest; Blackbeard the Pirate. **1953:** Gun Belt; Hondo; The Naked Spur; Cow Country; Calamity Jane. **1954:** Sign of the Pagan; The Lone Gun. **1955:** The Prodigal; The Far Country; The Tall Men; Timberjack; The Man from Laramie. **1956:** The Conqueror; The

Rawhide Years; The Hired Gun; Red Sundown; Backlash; The Searchers; Seven Men from Now. **1957:** Forty Guns; The Hired Hand; Night Passage; Run of the Arrow; The Wings of Eagles. **1958:** The Big Country; Man of the West; The Barbarian & the Geisha. **1959:** The Horse Soldiers; The Wonderful Country; Texas John Slaughter. **1960:** Spartacus; The Alamo; Sgt. Rutledge. **1961:** The Misfits; Two Rode Together; The Commancheros. **1962:** The Man Who Shot Liberty Valance; How the West Was Won; Merrill's Marauders. **1963:** McLintock; Donovan's Reef; Shock Corridor; Four for Texas. **1964:** Rio Conchos; Mail Order Bride; Advance to the Rear; Cheyenne Autumn. **1965:** The Rounders; Black Spurs; The Sons of Katie Elder; Shenandoah; The War Lord; Cat Ballou. **1966:** Smoky; Nevada Smith. **1967:** Welcome to Hard Times; The War Wagon; El Dorado. **1968:** The Green Berets; The Scalphunters; Hellfighters. **1969:** Hard Contract; 100 Rifles; The Undefeated. **1970:** Beneath the Planet of the Apes; The Hawaiians; Chisum; A Man

Called Horse; Rio Lobo. **1971:** Shootout; Big Jake. **1972:** The Cowboys. **1973:** The Train Robbers; Cahil, U.S. Marshal. **1974:** 99 & 44/100% Dead; McQ. **1975:** Doc Savage, The Man of Bronze; Rooster Cogburn. **1976:** The Shootist. **1983:** Blue Thunder. **1986:** Cobra. **1988:** Miracle Mile. *Television*—Forest Ranger; Roy Rogers; Swamp Fox; Zane Grey; G.E. Theatre; Texas John Slaughter; Have Gun, Will Travel; Panic; Rawhide; Laramie; Kraft Suspense; Laredo; Gunsmoke; Lost in Space; Lancer; The Mod Squad; Quincy; Gene Autry; Wells Fargo; Lucy; Wagon Train; Daniel Boone; Death Valley Days.

DENISE LYNN ROBERTS

A national high school basketball star, Roberts has doubled for actresses such as Goldie Hawn, Ellen Barkin, Meg Ryan, and Meryl Streep.

Films—**1991:** Switch. **1992:** Death Becomes Her; Stepmonster; Sweet Justice; Mission of Justice. **1993:** Boiling Point; In the Line of Fire. **1994:** The Naked Gun 33 1/3; Bad Girls; Forest Gump; The River Wild; Steel Frontier. **1995:** Don Juan DeMarco; Species; Strange Days; Nemesis 3. **1996:** Courage Under Fire; 2 Days in the Valley. *Television*—Santa Barbara (reg.); Renegade.

JIMMY N. ROBERTS

A motorcycle specialist and veteran bit player, J.N. Roberts is an original member of Stunts Unlimited.

Films—**1969:** The Undefeated. **1970:** Angel Unchained; Little Big Man. **1971:**

Sometimes a Great Notion (aka Never Give an Inch). **1972:** The Mechanic. **1973:** Electra Glide in Glue; The Stone Killer. **1974:** Three the Hard Way. **1976:** A Small Town in Texas. **1977:** Smokey & the Bandit. **1978:** Hooper; Ski Lift to Death (tv). **1980:** The Blues Brothers; Foolin' Around. **1981:** Honkytonk Freeway. **1982:** Megaforce. **1983:** Nat'l Lampoon's Vacation; Scarface. **1985:** Black Moon Rising; Invasion USA. **1987:** Over the Top; The Untouchables; Morgan Stewart's Coming Home; Less Than Zero. **1988:** The Seventh Sign. **1989:** Tango & Cash. **1990:** Days of Thunder. **1991:** Hook; The Rocketeer. **1992:** White Sands; Hoffa. **1994:** The Last Ride (aka F.T.W.); The Naked Gun 33 1/3; Speed; True Lies; Double Dragon; Junior. **1995:** Demon Knight; The Sweeper. **1996:** Broken Arrow; Eraser; Escape from L.A.; Bulletproof; 2 Days in the Valley; Ravenhawk; Sunchaser.

MARIO ROBERTS

A member of the Stuntmen's Association, Roberts has doubled for Michael Ontkean and performed a number of bit parts.

Films—**1982:** Fighting Back; Nat'l Lampoon's Class Reunion; The Sword & the Sorcerer. **1983:** Scarface. **1984:** The River; The Cannonball Run 2. **1985:** Gotcha; Commando; Vendetta. **1986:** Legal Eagles; 8 Million Ways to Die; Hollywood Vice Squad; Radioactive Dreams. **1987:** No Man's Land; Prince of Darkness; Wanted: Dead or Alive; Remote Control. **1988:** Freeway; Dead Heat; Midnight Run. **1989:** Glory; Nightmare on Elm Street 5: Dream Child; Next of Kin; Street Justice. **1990:** Lisa; Solar Crisis; Robocop 2; Marked for Death; Kindergarten Cop; The Rookie; Payback; Drug Wars: The Camarena Story (tv). **1991:** Eve of Destruction; Out for Justice; The Perfect

Weapon; Soldier's Fortune; Not of This World (tv). **1992:** Freejack; Last of the Mohicans; Trespass; Aces: Iron Eagle 3. **1993:** Excessive Force; Streetknight; By the Sword. **1994:** City Slickers 2; Blankman; The Specialist; Automatic. **1995:** 3 Ninjas Knuckle Up; Panther; Under Siege 2; Casino; Heat; The Crossing Guard; Ballistic. **1996:** Broken Arrow; Fled; Multiplicity; The Crow: City of Angels; Escape from L.A.; The Glimmer Man. *Television*—MacGyver; Renegade.

DAR ROBINSON
(b. 1947; d. 1986)

Ambitious high-fall specialist and former gymnast set numerous world stunt records and made many appearances on such shows as "That's Incredible," making him somewhat of a public celebrity. He was moving into supporting parts, as evidenced by his memorable turn as an albino killer in *Stick,* when he died in a motorcycle wreck during the filming of *Million Dollar Mystery.* Among his greatest stunts were a cliff dive for *Papillon,* being shot out of a high-rise window in *Sharky's Machine,* a mammoth fall off of Toronto's CNN tower for *Highpoint,* his backfall from an apartment balcony while firing a gun and staying in character in *Stick,* and a then frightening bungee jump from a bridge for *To Live and Die in L.A.* The California-born Robinson was a member of the Stuntmen's Association.

Films—**1968:** Star. **1969:** Paint Your Wagon. **1972:** Conquest of the Planet of the Apes. **1973:** Magnum Force; Papillon; Battle for the Planet of the Apes. **1974:** The Towering Inferno; Smile, Jenny, You're Dead (tv). **1975:** Doc Savage, The Man of Bronze; Rollerball; Breakout; They Only

Come Out at Night (tv). **1976:** St. Ives; Kiss Me, Kill Me (tv). **1977:** Stunts; Airport '77. **1978:** F.I.S.T.; The Manitou; Hooper; Paradise Alley. **1979:** Concorde, Airport '79; H.O.T.S.; Stunt Seven (tv). **1981:** Nighthawks; Sharky's Machine. **1982:** Ruckus. **1983:** Starflight (tv). **1984:** Iceman; Bachelor Party; Highpoint; Firstborn; Police Academy. **1985:** Stick; Turk 182; To Live & Die in L.A.; Police Academy 2: Their First Assignment. **1986:** King Kong Lives; Vamp; Scorpion. **1987:** Cyclone; Lethal Weapon; Million Dollar Mystery. *Television*—Harry O; That's Incredible; The World's Greatest Stuntman.

ROBBY ROBINSON

Films—**1988:** Colors; I'm Gonna Git You Sucka; L.A. Heat. **1990:** Last of the Finest; Marked for Death; Peacemaker; Backstreet Dreams. **1991:** One Good Cop; Martial Law. **1992:** American Me; Martial Law 2: Undercover; Mission of Justice. **1993:** Streetknight; True Romance; The Sandlot; Percy & Thunder (tv). **1994:** The Expert; Pentathalon; Drop Zone. **1995:** 3 Ninjas Knuckle Up; Outbreak; The Walking Dead. **1996:** Courage Under Fire; Larger Than Life.

WALT ROBLES
(b. 1938)

This familiar supporting player broke into the business as a stunt coordinator on biker films. A member of the Stuntmen's Association, he has doubled for such beefy blond actors as Clancy Brown and Charles Napier.

Films—**1967:** Hell's Angels on Wheels; Born Losers; The Glory Stompers. **1968:** The Savage Seven; Psych-Out. **1969:** Cycle Savages; 2000 Years Later. **1970:** Imago; Sinner's Blood (a/p). **1973:** The

Stunt legend Dar Robinson (with contact lens) in 1985's *Stick.*

Clones. **1974:** The Towering Inferno. **1975:** Crazy Mama; The Apple Dumpling Gang. **1976:** Two-Minute Warning; Logan's Run. **1977:** The Great Gundown; Airport '77; MacArthur; Delta Fox. **1978:** The Cat from Outer Space; Capricorn One; Lord of the Rings. **1979:** Butch & Sundance: The Early Days; Concorde, Airport '79; Stunt Seven (tv). **1980:** The Stunt Man; The Big Brawl; Melvin & Howard; Heaven's Gate; Die Laughing; Any Which Way You Can. **1981:** Charlie Chan & the Curse of the Dragon Queen. **1982:** Vice Squad; The Sword & the Sorcerer. **1983:** Two of a Kind; Bad Boys; Fire & Ice; Yellowbeard. **1984:** City Heat. **1985:** Remo Williams; Avenging Angel; Rainy Day Friends; Fandango. **1986:** Choke Canyon; The Golden Child; Slow Burn; A Winner Never Quits (tv). **1987:** Fatal Beauty; The Monster Squad; Masters of the Universe; Russkies. **1988:** Colors; Twins. **1989:** One Man Force. **1990:** Total Recall; The Gumshoe Kid; Secret Agent 00-Soul. **1991:** Mobsters; Silence of the Lambs. **1992:** Universal Soldier; Hoffa; Rage & Honor. **1993:** Boiling Point; Coneheads; Geronimo. **1994:** Army of One; Color of Night. **1995:** Stuart Saves His Family.

1996: Set It Off; Flipping. *Television—* The Six Million Dollar Man; Herndon; Happy Days.

GEORGE ROBOTHAM
(b. 1921)

A member of the Stuntmen's Association, this 6'2" supporting actor, stunt coordinator, and second unit director was a football player and UCLA business administration graduate before getting into films as a double for Clark Gable, John Wayne, and Rock Hudson. A fight specialist, he also did a great deal of underwater work.

*Films—***1944:** Destination Tokyo. **1948:** Joan of Arc. **1949:** Bride of Vengeance. **1950:** Chain Gang; Atom Man vs. Superman. **1951:** Captain Video. **1952:** Invitation; Lone Star. **1953:** The Robe; Savage Mutiny. **1954:** Seven Brides for Seven Brothers. **1955:** The Prodigal; Many Rivers to Cross. **1956:** The Ten Commandments; The Great Locomotive Chase. **1957:** The Deerslayer; The Way to the Gold; The Garment Jungle. **1958:** Twilight for the Gods. **1959:** Warlock. **1960:** Spartacus; North to Alaska. **1961:** The Last Sunset. **1962:** Confessions of an Opium Eater; The Spiral Road; The Mermaids of Tiburron. **1963:** The Ugly American. **1965:** Strange Bedfellows; Aqua Sex. **1966:** Blindfold; Seconds. **1967:** Tobruk. **1968:** The Split; Five Card Stud. **1969:** The Undefeated. **1970:** Darling Lili; I Love My Wife. **1972:** What's Up, Doc? **1973:** Showdown; The Don Is Dead; Magnum Force; Charley Varrick; Cleopatra Jones. **1974:** The Towering Inferno. **1975:** Rooster Cogburn. **1977:** Oh, God; The Amazing Captain Nemo; Spectre (tv). **1978:** The Manitou. **1979:** Meteor; The Prisoner of Zenda. **1980:** The Island; The Last Flight of Noah's Ark. **1982:** Fast-Walking; The Sword & the Sorcerer. **1983:** The Man Who Loved Women; Something Wicked This Way Comes; Flashdance. **1984:** Bachelor Party. **1985:** The Goonies. **1987:** Brenda Starr. **1988:** Alien Nation; Mississippi Burning. **1991:** Mobsters. **1996:** Mars Attacks! *Television*—Zane Grey Theatre; Studio '57; G.E. Theatre; The Outer Limits; Voyage to the Bottom of the Sea; Laredo; Daniel Boone; Land of the Giants; The Invaders; Time Tunnel; Batman; The Green Hornet; It Takes a Thief; McMillan & Wife; Farraday & Company; Planet of the Apes; The Rockford Files; Wonder Woman; Half-Nelson; Bonanza; Alias Smith & Jones.

JOHN ROBOTHAM

The son of George Robotham, John has worked most often as a stunt coordinator for director Jonathan Demme. A member of the Stuntmen's Association, he has doubled for Chevy Chase and Jeff Daniels.

Films—**1977:** Exo-Man (tv). **1978:** Big Wednesday. **1980:** The Island. **1982:** Star Trek 2: The Wrath of Khan. **1983:** Flashdance; The Man with Two Brains. **1984:** Bachelor Party. **1985:** The Goonies. **1986:** Something Wild. **1987:** Brenda Starr. **1988:** Mississippi Burning; Married to the Mob. **1989:** Ghostbusters 2; Pet Sematary; Fletch Lives; Nat'l Lampoon's Christmas Vacation. **1990:** Come See the Paradise; Pump Up the Volume; Arachonophobia. **1991:** Nothing But Trouble; Billy Bathgate; Silence of the Lambs; Cast a Deadly Spell. **1992:** Ruby; Deep Cover; Memoirs of an Invisible Man; Aces: Iron Eagle 3; Pet Sematary 2; A River Runs Through It. **1993:** Amos & Andrew; In the Line of Fire; A Perfect World. **1994:** Cops & Robbersons; Clean Slate; The Road to Wellville. **1995:** Candyman: Farewell to the Flesh; Man of the House; Apollo 13. **1996:** Sgt. Bilko; A Very Brady Sequel.

MIC RODGERS
(b. 1953)

Best known as Mel Gibson's regular stunt double, Rodgers is also a noted stunt coordinator and second unit director, having guided the epic battle scenes in *Braveheart*. He's a member of Stunts Unlimited.

Films—**1977:** The Amazing Captain Nemo. **1978:** Movie, Movie; Lord of the Rings. **1979:** A Time to Die. **1980:** Survival Run; In God We Trust; Resurrection. **1982:** Megaforce; Wrong Is Right; Yes, Giorgio. **1983:** The Sting 2; D.C. Cab; Stroker Ace. **1984:** 2010; Beverly Hills Cop; City Heat; Reckless; Buckaroo Banzai; Birdy. **1985:** Into the Night; Iron Eagle. **1986:** Legal Eagles; Let's Get Harry; Out of Bounds. **1987:** Lethal Weapon; World Gone Wild; Night Force; Kidnapped; Down Twisted. **1988:** Bulletproof; Off Limits; Rambo 3; Tequila Sunrise; Scrooged. **1989:** K-9; Dead Bang; Lethal Weapon 2; Road House; Riding the

Edge. **1990:** Bird on a Wire; Rockula; Dollman. **1991:** For the Boys. **1992:** Year of the Comet; Lethal Weapon 3; Radio Flyer; Forever Young. **1993:** Point of No Return; Heart & Souls; Gettysburg. **1994:** Intersection; Chasers; Maverick; Drop Zone; Puppetmasters. **1995:** The Road Killers; Village of the Damned; Braveheart; Virtuosity; Under Siege 2. **1996:** Twister; The Rock; Fled; Ransom. *Television*—Airwolf; Cover Up; Misfits of Science; Shannon's Deal.

DANNY ROGERS

A member of Stunts Unlimited, the prolific Rogers has performed an occasional bit part but is most often used for versatile utility work.

Films—**1975:** Crazy Mama. **1983:** Revenge of the Ninja. **1984:** Star Trek 3: The Search for Spock; Beverly Hills Cop; Flashpoint; Scorned & Swindled (tv). **1985:** To Live & Die in L.A.; Invasion USA. **1986:** The Hitcher; Firewalker. **1987:** Talking Walls; The Wild Pair; Burglar; The Untouchables; Code Name Zebra. **1988:** The Seventh Sign; The Presidio; The Blob; My Stepmother Is an Alien; They Live. **1989:** Who's Harry Crumb?; Lethal Weapon 2; Road House; Dead Bang. **1990:** Impulse; Die Hard 2; Days of Thunder; Predator 2; Angel Town. **1991:** V.I. Warshawski; Star Trek 6: Undiscovered Country; Hook; The Addams Family; The Rapture. **1992:** American Me; Lethal Weapon 3; Beyond the Law. **1993:** Full Eclipse; The Last Action Hero; The Ballad of Little Jo. **1994:** Maverick; In the Army Now; Drop Zone; Puppetmasters. **1995:** Bad Boys; Waterworld. **1996:** From Dusk Till Dawn; Executive Decision; Eraser; The Rock; Courage Under Fire.

J.P. ROMANO

A member of the Stuntmen's Association, Jean-Pierre Romano has co-ordinated stunts and doubled regularly for Charles Bronson.

Films—**1982:** The Beastmaster. **1985:** Remo Williams. **1987:** The Wild Pair; Blind Date; Death Wish 4; Night Force; Brenda Starr. **1988:** Jack's Back; Messenger of Death; Freeway; License to Drive. **1989:** Cage. **1990:** Repossessed; Child's Play 2; Megaville; The Rookie; Predator 2. **1991:** Mobsters; Out for Justice; Intimate Stranger. **1992:** Aces: Iron Eagle 3; Live Wire; Rapid Fire; Far & Away; Martial Law 2. **1993:** By the Sword; Bounty Tracker. **1994:** The Naked Gun 33 1/3; Blown Away; Silence of the Hams; Steel Frontier. **1995:** Ballistic; Under Siege 2; Halloween: The Curse of Michael Myers; Casino; Hard Justice. **1996:** Spy Hard.

PAT ROMANO

A motorcycle specialist and independent stunt coordinator, the prolific Romano has doubled for Keanu Reeves and Andrew McCarthy.

Films—**1983:** Something Wicked This Way Comes. **1984:** Lovelines; The Karate Kid. **1985:** Mischief; Silver Bullet; To Live & Die in L.A.; Moving Violations; The Man with One Red Shoe. **1986:** Ruthless People; Welcome to 18. **1987:** Morgan Stewart's Coming Home; The Wild Pair; Night Force; Code Name Zebra; Over the Top; Who's That Girl?; Mannequin; The Lost Boys. **1988:** Colors; The Blob; License to Drive. **1989:** Riding the Edge; The Abyss; Back to the Future 2; After Midnight; To Die For; Tango & Cash. **1990:** Bad Influence; Leatherface 3; Captain America; The Guardian; Last of the Finest; The Godfather 3; Predator 2; Drug Wars: The Camarena Story (tv); By Dawn's Early Light (tv). **1991:** FX-2; Bill & Ted's Bogus Journey; Hook; The Rocketeer; Beastmaster 2; Deadlock; Intimate Stranger. **1992:** Trancers 3; 3 Ninjas; Nails. **1993:** Falling Down; Full Eclipse;

Knights; Prophet of Evil (tv). **1994:** Body Shot; Past Tense; Blank Check; Speed; The Flintstones; Pentathalon; Clear & Present Danger; Double Dragon. **1995:** Tall Tale; 3 Ninjas Knuckle Up; The Brady Bunch Movie; Clueless; The Babysitter's Club; Under Siege 2; Jade; Seven; Blackout. **1996:** The Lawnmower Man 2; Executive Decision; Marshal Law; Barb Wire; Mulholland Falls; Sgt. Bilko; Fled; Dark Breed; The Glimmer Man; Pure Danger.

PHIL ROMANO

Films—**1982:** The Beastmaster. **1984:** Racing with the Moon. **1985:** Cloak & Dagger. **1987:** Who's That Girl?; Brenda Starr. **1989:** Nat'l Lampoon's Christmas Vacation. **1990:** The Hunt for Red October; The Adventures of Ford Fairlane; I'm Dangerous Tonight (tv). **1991:** Mobsters. **1992:** Stay Tuned. **1993:** Robin Hood: Men in Tights. **1995:** Don Juan DeMarco; Seven. **1996:** The Rock.

ERIK RONDELL

Films—**1983:** Private School. **1990:** Last of the Finest; Dances with Wolves; Prayer of the Rollerboys. **1991:** Hook. **1992:** Kuffs; American Me; Captain Ron; Nemesis. **1993:** Full Eclipse; Beethoven's 2nd; Body of Evidence; Knights. **1994:** The Crow; Pentathalon; Baby's Day Out; Double Dragon; Puppetmasters; The Last Word. **1995:** Waterworld. **1996:** The Cable Guy; Bulletproof; My Fellow Americans. *Television*—Baywatch.

R.A. RONDELL

The oldest son of Ronnie Rondell, Jr., R.A. has worked as a stunt coordinator and second unit director. He's a member of both Stunts Unlimited and the Professional Driver's Association.

Films—**1976:** Bound for Glory; Dogs. **1977:** 9/30/55. **1978:** American Hot Wax; Nat'l Lampoon's Animal House; Hooper. **1979:** Fast Charlie, The Moonbeam Rider. **1980:** The Blues Brothers; Loving Couples. **1981:** Caveman. **1982:** The Legend of Walks Far Woman; The Beastmaster. **1983:** Heart Like a Wheel; Star Trek 3: The Search for Spock. **1985:** To Live & Die in L.A. **1986:** Top Gun; Star Trek 4: The Voyage Home. **1987:** Someone to Watch Over Me; Mannequin. **1988:** Die Hard; Twins; The Diamond Trap (tv). **1989:** Her Alibi; Lethal Weapon 2; Star Trek 5: The Final Frontier; Road House; Night Life. **1990:** The Hunt for Red October; Almost an Angel; Days of Thunder; Last of the Finest; Misery. **1991:** Hook; The Doctor. **1992:** Kuffs; Buffy, the Vampire Slayer; Cool World. **1993:** Point of No Return; Nat'l Lampoon's Loaded Weapon; Warlock 2; Wilder Napalm; Made in America. **1994:** Iron Will; North; Clear & Present Danger; Milk Money; Midnight Ride. **1995:** Waterworld; Virtuosity; Jade. **1996:** Mulholland Falls; Matilda. *Television*—Sam; T.J. Hooker.

REID RONDELL

(b.1963; d. 1985)

The late son of Ronnie Rondell, Jr., Reid was standing in for Jan-Michael Vincent when he died in a helicopter crash on television's "Airwolf." He had also doubled for Tom Cruise.

Films—**1978:** Skateboard; Hooper. **1980:** Foxes; The Burning. **1982:** Cannery Row; Megaforce. **1983:** Heart Like a Wheel; All the Right Moves; Class; Risky Business; The Outsiders; Private School; Murder One, Dancer Zero (tv). **1984:** Windy City; Birdy; No Small Affair. **1985:** Fandango; Into the Night; St. Elmo's Fire; D.A.R.Y.L.

1986: Modern Girls. *Television*—Airwolf.

RONNIE RONDELL, JR.
(b. 1937)

Once the double for Robert Blake, this second generation stuntman has coordinated stunts, directed second unit, and performed many bit parts. An underwater specialist responsible for the wild action in *Waterworld,* he's a member of both Stunts Unlimited and the Professional Driver's Association. His sons R.A., Reid, and nephew Erik have all followed in his footsteps.

Films—**1957:** The Enemy Below. **1958:** Monster on the Campus; The Naked & the Dead; The Deep Six. **1960:** Spartacus. **1963:** Kings of the Sun. **1964:** Ensign Pulver; Pajama Party. **1965:** Dr. Goldfoot & the Bikini Machine; Shenandoah; The War Lord. **1967:** Tobruk; The Young Runaways; The King's Pirate; First to Fight. **1968:** Ice Station Zebra; The Mini-Skirt Mob; Hellfighters. **1969:** The Love Bug; Che. **1972:** The Night Stalker (tv). **1973:** The Outfit; Electra Glide in Blue. **1974:** Policewomen; The Front Page; Busting; McQ. **1975:** Night Moves. **1977:** Delta Fox. **1978:** Hooper. **1981:** The Pride of Jesse Hallam (tv). **1983:** All the Right Moves. **1984:** Against All Odds. **1985:** To Live & Die in L.A.; Commando. **1986:** Legal Eagles. **1987:** Over the Top; Lethal Weapon; La Bamba; Mannequin; Someone to Watch Over Me; No Safe Haven (d); Down Twisted. **1988:** Maniac Cop; The Seventh Sign; The Presidio; They Live; My Best Friend is a Vampire. **1989:** Her Alibi; Tango & Cash; Relentless; Crack House. **1990:** The Hunt for Red October; Almost an Angel; Days of Thunder; Maniac Cop 2; Death Warrant; The Rookie; Predator 2; Courage Mountain;

The Ambulance. **1991:** Shattered; Thelma & Louise; K9000 (tv). **1992:** Captain Ron; Nemesis; The Mighty Ducks. **1993:** Point of No Return; Falling Down; Sliver; the Last Action Hero; Demolition Man; Beethoven's 2nd; Rising Sun; Brain Smasher. **1994:** Army of One; The Crow; Speed; Midnight Ride; One Woman's Courage (tv). **1995:** Waterworld; Vampire in Brooklyn. **1996:** Twister; Star Trek, First Contact. *Television*—The Virginian; Laredo; Mission: Impossible; Dragnet; Adam-12: The Young Rebels; The Immortal; The Mod Squad; The Night Stalker; Baretta; Charlie's Angels; Fantasy Island; Hart to Hart; MacGruder & Loud; Baywatch; Thunder in Paradise; Wagon Train.

GILBERT ROSALES

Films—**1990:** Angel Town; Drug Wars: The Canarena Story (tv). **1992:** Nails; American Me; Trespass; Class Act; Mission of Justice. **1993:** Falling Down; Sliver. **1994:** The Crow; A Low Down Dirty Shame. **1995:** Cold Blooded; Desperado. **1996:** Escape from L.A.; Last Man Standing.

THOMAS ROSALES, JR.
(B. 1953)

Instantly recognizable Hispanic supporting player has probably whipped out more switchblades than anyone else in the history of film. A member of the Stuntmen's Association, this stunt coordinator has doubled for comedian Paul Rodriguez. He is the father of Gilbert Rosales.

Films—**1973:** Battle for the Planet of the Apes. **1974:** The Towering Inferno. **1975:**

Lucky Lady; Aloha Bobby & Rose. **1976:** Two Minute Warning; Scott Free (tv). **1977:** Airport '77; Billy, Portrait of a Street Kid (tv). **1978:** Big Wednesday; The Norseman; FM. **1979:** Sunnyside; Boulevard Nights; Concorde, Airport '79; Walk Proud. **1980:** Borderline; Die Laughing; The Island; The Hunter; Detour to Terror (tv). **1981:** Nighthawks; Charlie Chan & the Curse of the Dragon Queen. **1982:** The Sword & the Sorcerer. **1983:** Blue Thunder; They Call Me Bruce; Max Dugan Returns; Scarface; The Lost Empire. **1984:** Oh, God! You Devil!; Red Dawn; Breakin' 2; Sweet Revenge (tv). **1985:** Fright Night; Commando; Stick; Stand Alone; Space Rage; Rainy Day Friends (aka L.A. Bad). **1986:** The Three Amigos; Raw Deal; 8 Million Ways to Die; Eye of the Tiger; Out of Bounds; No Mercy. **1987:** Cherry 2000; The Omega Syndrome; The Wild Pair; Extreme Prejudice; The Running Man; *batteries not included; The Bedroom Window; Date with an Angel; Traxx; Remote Control; Weeds. **1988:** Alien Nation; Midnight Run; Two Moon Junction; They Live; License to Drive; Border Heat; Bail Out; Made in the USA. **1989:** Weekend at Bernie's; K-9; One Man Force; Crack House. **1990:** Impulse; Downtown; Robocop 2; Death Warrant; The Rookie; Predator 2; Drug Wars: The Camarena Story (tv). **1991:** One Good Cop; Rush; Harley Davidson & the Marlboro Man; The Perfect Weapon; Ricochet; Alligator 2; Not of This World (tv). **1992:** Deep Cover; Memoirs of an Invisible Man; Aces: Iron Eagle 3; American Me; Class Act; Universal Soldier; Honeymoon in Vegas; Bram Stoker's Dracula. **1993:** Falling Down; Streetknight; Extreme Justice; Amos & Andrew; Bound by Honor; Demolition Man; Nowhere to Run; Man's Best Friend; No Escape, No Return. **1994:** The Naked Gun 33 1/3; Jimmy Hollywood; Beverly Hills Cop 3; The Crow; Speed; In the Army Now; A Low Down Dirty Shame; Stargate; Silence of the Hams; The Hard Truth; Hologram Man; Bad Blood. **1995:** 3 Ninjas Knuckle Up. **1995:** My Family; The Tie That Binds; Vampire in Brooklyn; Heat; Blackout;

Tremors 2. **1996:** The Crow: City of Angels; Rough Magic; Escape from L.A.; Last Man Standing; Mars Attacks!; Sunchaser. *Television*—The Six Million Dollar Man; Emergency; Swiss Family Robinson; Joe Forrester; The Rookies; Police Story; Police Woman; The Rockford Files; Baa Baa Black Sheep; Barnaby Jones; Young Dan'l Boone; The Fall Guy; Airwolf; Jake & the Fatman; Beauty & the Beast; The Owl; Renegade; Babylon 5.

WALLY ROSE

A veteran bit player, animal trainer, and boxing referee, Rose is a member of the Stuntmen's Association.

Films—**1938:** Hawk of the Wilderness. **1941:** Dick Tracy vs. Crime Inc. **1944:** Together Again. **1945:** Alias Mr. Twilight. **1946:** The Killers; Night Editor; Life with Blondie; The Return of Rusty; Boston Blackie & the Law; One Life Too Many. **1947:** Brute Force; It's Great to Be Young; The Thirteenth Hour; It Had to Be You; Bulldog Drummond at Bay; For the Love of Rusty. **1948:** Street with No Name; Whiplash. **1949:** Undercover Man; Mr. Soft Touch; Let's Fall in Love; Bodyhold. **1950:** The Milkman. **1953:** The Neandrathal Man. **1956:** The Harder They Fall; The World in My Corner; Calling Homicide; Back from Eternity. **1959:** The Flying Fontaines. **1960:** Spartacus; Ma Barker's Killer Brood; The Rise & Fall of Legs Diamond. **1961:** The George Raft Story; Twist Around the Clock; Pirates of Tortuga. **1965:** Young Dillinger. **1966:** Batman; Not with My Wife You Don't. **1967:** 52 Miles to Terror. **1969:** The Wrecking Crew; The Undefeated. **1970:** Flap. **1972:** Conquest of the Planet of the Apes; What's Up, Doc? **1973:** The Don Is Dead; Cleopatra Jones; Battle for the Planet of the Apes. **1974:** The Towering Inferno; The Front Page; Mame; Blazing Saddles. **1975:** Day of the Locust. **1977:** Exo-Man (tv). **1978:** Movie, Movie. **1979:** The Champ. **1980:** The Blues Brothers; The

Man with Bogart's Face; Where the Buffalo Roam; In God We Trust. **1981:** Honkytonk Freeway. **1983:** Carpool (tv); Dempsey (tv). **1985:** Runaway Train; Gotcha. **1987:** The Night Stalker; Throw Momma from the Train. **1988:** Action Jackson; Alien Nation. **1989:** The Burbs; Kill Me Again. **1990:** Wild at Heart; Peacemaker; Boris & Natasha; 9 1/2 Ninjas. **1991:** Rich Girl. **1992:** Unlawful Entry. **1993:** Private Wars; Sidekicks; Trouble Bound; Bitter Harvest. **1994:** Army of One; Blown Away; Zero Tolerance; Direct Hit. **1995:** Murder in the First. **1996:** Spy Hard. *Television*—Voyage to the Bottom of the Sea; Future Cop; Battlestar Galactica; Beauty & the Beast.

DEBBY LYNN ROSS

(b. 1953)

An Oregon-born stunt coordinator, Ross is one of the most in-demand talents in the industry. She has doubled for actresses such as Goldie Hawn, Virginia Madsen, Lori Singer, and Sarah Jessica Parker.

Films—**1984:** Friday the 13th: A New Beginning; Night of the Comet; Girls Just Want to Have Fun. **1985:** Certain Fury; To Live & Die in L.A. **1986:** Quicksilver; The Naked Cage; Fire with Fire; Murphy's Law; Crimes of the Heart. **1987:** The Wild Pair; Barfly; Million Dollar Mystery; Death Wish 4; My Demon Lover; Laguna Heat; House of the Rising Sun. **1988:** Child's Play; Vibes; Bad Dreams; The Serpent & the Rainbow; Everybody's All American; Two Moon Junction; Out of the Dark; Tapeheads; Nightmare on Elm Street 4: Dream Master; They Live. **1989:** The Karate Kid 3; Spontaneous Combustion; After Midnight; Nightmare on Elm Street 5: Dream Child; Kill Me Again; Midnight Warrior; Witchcraft 2: The Temptress; The Revenge of Al Capone

(tv). **1990:** Big Man on Campus; Robocop 2; Satan's Princess; Slumber Party Massacre 3; The Guardian; Rainbow Drive. **1991:** Showdown in Little Tokyo; Harley Davidson & the Marlboro Man; Nothing But Trouble; The Hard Way; Intimate Stranger. **1992:** Deep Cover; Last of the Mohicans; Candyman; Death Becomes Her; Honeymoon in Vegas; Trancers 2. **1993:** Striking Distance; Robocop 3; Boiling Point; Another Stakeout; Man's Best Friend; Indecent Behavior 2. **1994:** Blue Tiger; The Naked Gun 33 1/3; Bad Girls; Silence of the Hams; The Last Ride (aka F.T.W.); American Yakuza; The Stranger; Dead Badge. **1995:** Demon Knight; The Tie That Binds; The Prophecy; Halloween: The Curse of Michael Myers. **1996:** Eye for an Eye; Spy Hard; Escape from L.A.; First Kid. *Television*—Amazing Stories; Shadow Chasers; Hunter.

LORI LYNN ROSS

The sister of Debby Lynn Ross, Lori is a member of the United Stuntwoman's Association.

Films—**1987:** Cold Steel; Death Spa. **1989:** Bill & Ted's Excellent Adventure; Nightmare on Elm Street 5: Dream Child. **1990:** Edward Scissorhands. **1991:** V.I. Warshawski; The People Under the Stairs; Iron Maze; The Rocketeer. **1993:** Jack the Bear; Trouble Bound. **1994:** The Crow; True Lies; The Client; Double Dragon. **1995:** 3 Ninjas Knuckle Up; Waterworld; Houseguest. **1996:** Independence Day; Escape from L.A.; Jingle All the Way.

RONNIE C. ROSS

Films—**1968:** The Green Berets. **1970:** The Losers. **1972:** Slaughter. **1973:** Cleopatra Jones. **1974:** Earthquake. **1975:** Death Race 2000. **1977:** Joyride to Nowhere (a/p). **1980:** Battle Beyond the Stars; Smokey & the Bandit 2. **1982:** Baby Dolls. **1983:** Metalstorm. **1985:** The Boys Next Door; Moving Violations. **1986:** Stewardess School; Wired to Kill; KGB: The Secret War. **1987:** Dracula's Widow. **1988:** Weekend at Bernie's. **1994:** Blue Tiger. **1995:** Bad Boys.

KERRY ROSSALL

A former Navy aviator and downhill skiing instructor, the California-born Rossall was one of the men in *Apocalyspe Now*'s famous exploding chopper. A member of the Stuntmen's Association, he has directed second unit and worked as a stunt coordinator.

Films—**1975:** The Wind & the Lion. **1979:** Apocalypse Now; 1941. **1980:** In God We Trust. **1983:** Blue Thunder; Christine. **1984:** Starman; Red Dawn. **1986:** Never Too Young to Die; Cobra. **1987:** Death Before Dishonor; Dragnet; Dudes. **1988:** Shakedown; Rambo 3; They Live. **1989:** The Abyss. **1990:** Downtown; The Rookie; Genuine Risk. **1991:** Flight of the Intruder; Delta Force 3. **1992:** The Lawnmower Man. **1994:** The Hard Truth; Automatic. **1995:** Die Hard with a Vengeance. **1996:** The Crow: City of Angels. *Television*—Babylon 5.

TIM ROSSOVICH
(b. 1947)

The older brother of actor Rick Rossovich and a recognizable supporting player in his own right, the 6'4" California-born Rossovich was a former professional football player

Stuntman/supporting player Tim Rossovich hoists Burt Reynolds in 1978's *Hooper*.

with the Philadelphia Eagles and the San Diego Chargers before breaking into films as a stuntman. He's best known as the assassin in *Looker.*

Films—**1977:** Semi-Tough. **1978:** Smokey & the Bandit; Hooper. **1979:** The Main Event; Goldie & the Boxer (tv). **1980:** The Ninth Configuration; The Long Riders. **1981:** Looker; Cheech & Chong's Nice Dreams; The Cannonball Run. **1982:** Night Shift; Trick or Treats. **1983:** The Sting 2; Smokey & the Bandit 3. **1985:** Stick; Cloak & Dagger; Avenging Angel. **1987:** Johnny B. Good. **1989:** Fists of Steel. **1990:** Secret Agent 00-Soul. *Television*—Charlie's Angels; Soap; When the Whistle Blows (reg.); Fantasy Island ; The Love Boat; Trapper John, M.D.; Hart to Hart; Magnum P.I.;' Voyagers; The Fall Guy; The A Team; Matt Houston; Simon & Simon; Knight Rider; We Got It Made; Cover Up; Mike Hammer; Automan; Remington Steele; Dallas; Hunter; Ace Crawford; Double Dare; Perfect Strangers; Highwayman; Alf; Jake & the Fatman.

DAVE ROWDEN

Films—**1988:** Border Heat. **1989:** Curfew. **1990:** The Rookie. **1991:** Flight of the Intruder; Teenage Mutant Ninja Turtles 2; Leather Jackets. **1992:** Buffy, the Vampire Slayer. **1993:** Judgment Night; Forced to Kill; Blindside. **1994:** Cabin Boy; Bad Girls. **1995:** Tank Girl; One Man's Justice. **1996:** Sgt. Bilko; Chain Reaction; Last Man Standing; Fast Money.

GLYNN RUBIN

A veteran bit actress, Rubin doubled regularly for Goldie Hawn during the late seventies and early eighties.

Films—**1976:** Cannonball. **1978:** Foul Play. **1979:** Nightwing. **1980:** Steel; When

Time Ran Out; Private Benjamin; The Nude Bomb; Seems Like Old Times. **1981:** Cutter's Way; Halloween 2; Sharky's Machine. **1983:** Independence Day; The Sting 2. **1989:** Blaze. **1990:** Robocop 2. **1991:** This Gun for Hire. **1993:** Hard Target. **1994:** The Chase.

DON RUFFIN

Films—**1981:** The Night the Lights Went Out in Georgia. **1983:** Get Crazy. **1985:** Invasion USA; The Annihilators. **1986:** One Crazy Summer; Something Special. **1987:** Allan Quartermain & the Lost City of Gold; The Principal. **1988:** Bulletproof; Bat 21. **1989:** No Holds Barred; Bill & Ted's Excellent Adventure. **1990:** Impulse. **1991:** Star Trek 6: Undiscovered Country. **1992:** Freejack. **1993:** Red Rock West. **1994:** American Yakuza. *Television*—Campus Cops.

GEORGE MARSHALL RUGE

A stunt coordinator and fencing expert, Ruge is a member of the Stuntmen's Association. He has doubled for Ray Liotta.

Films—**1981:** Going Ape. **1984:** Bachelor Party. **1985:** My Wicked, Wicked Ways (tv). **1986:** Sweet Liberty; Something Wild. **1987:** Brenda Starr; Barfly. **1991:** The Naked Gun 2 1/2; Mobsters; The Doors; The Marrying Man. **1992:** Aces: Iron Eagle 3; Rapid Fire; Stay Tuned; Chaplin. **1993:** Robin Hood: Men in Tights; Malcolm X; Attack of the 50 Foot Woman. **1995:** The Enemy Within; Separate Lives; The Tie That Binds; Chameleon. **1996:** Mars Attacks!; Mercenary. *Television*—Wizards & Warriors; Tour of Duty.

MICHAEL RUNYARD

A motorcycle expert, Runyard has also directed second unit and coordinated stunts. He's a member of Stunts Unlimited and the regular double for Michael Douglas.

Films—**1982:** The Border; Megaforce; Grease 2. **1983:** The Sting 2; Scarface; The Star Chamber; Stroker Ace; Never Say Never Again. **1984:** The River Rat; Birdy; Buckaroo Banzai. **1985:** Into the Night; Iron Eagle; To Live & Die in L.A.; A View to a Kill; Covenant (tv). **1986:** Modern Girls; My Man Adam; Cobra; Out of Bounds; Back to School. **1987:** The Omega Syndrome; Code Name Zebra; Kidnapped. **1988:** The Seventh Sign; They Live. **1989:** War of the Roses; Dead Calm; Black Rain; Tango & Cash. **1990:** The Gumshoe Kid; Almost an Angel; Desperate Hours; V.I. Warshawski; Death Warrant. **1991:** Hook; The Rocketeer. **1992:** Basic Instinct; Lethal Weapon 3; Toys; Nemesis. **1993:** Point of No Return; Falling Down; The Last Action Hero; Gettysburg. **1994:** Drop Zone; Steel Frontier. **1995:** Demon Knight; Men of War; Waterworld; Virtuosity. **1996:** Executive Decision; Twister; Eraser; Jack; Bulletproof. *Television*—Spenser for Hire.

TANYA RUSSELL

A member of the United Stuntwoman's Association, Russell has doubled for Karen Valentine.

Films—**1978:** Skateboard. **1979:** Concorde, Airport '79; The Last Embrace; Amateur Night at the Dixie Bar and Grill (tvm). **1980:** The Blues Brothers; Borderline; Bronco Billy. **1982:** The Soldier; A Stranger Is Watching; Muggable Mary, Street Cop (tv). **1983:** Under Fire. **1984:**

A Nightmare on Elm Street; Savage Streets. **1985:** Hellhole. **1986:** Dangerously Close; Legal Eagles; The Golden Child. **1987:** Number One with a Bullet. **1991:** The Perfect Weapon.

MIKE RUSSO

A prolific New York based stunt coordinator and supporting player, Russo has doubled for Robert De Niro.

Films—**1984:** Streetwalkin'. **1985:** Death Wish 3; The Toxic Avenger. **1986:** F/X; The Money Pit; Quiet Cool. **1987:** The Hanoi Hilton; Death Wish 4; China Girl; Deadly Illusion; Dead Aim. **1988:** Shakedown; Last Rites; Homeboy; Nitti: The Enforcer (tv). **1989:** Ghostbusters 2; See No Evil, Hear No Evil; Jacknife; True Blood. **1990:** Two Evil Eyes; Maniac Cop 2; Night of the Living Dead; King of New York; GoodFellas; Street Hunter; The Ambulance; Backstreet Dreams. **1991:** The Serpent of Death; Mortal Thoughts; 29th Street; Billy Bathgate. **1992:** The Runestone; Malcolm X; Demonic Toys. **1993:** The Dark Half. **1994:** Body Snatches; Sugar Hill; Angie; North; The Cowboy Way; The Scout; The Professional. **1995:** Kiss of Death; Die Hard with a Vengeance. **1996:** City Hall; Barb Wire; Independence Day; Pure Danger; Bullet; Sleepers; My Fellow Americans. *Television*—Tour of Duty; Columbo; P.S. I Love You.

BILL RYUSAKI
(b. 1937)

A martial arts instructor and highly regarded referee, Ryusaki has done occasional bits. His daughter Kim also does stunts.

Films—**1967:** The President's Analyst. **1969:** The Wrecking Crew; Marooned.

1974: Golden Needles. **1982:** Some Kind of a Hero; The Sword & the Sorcerer. **1983:** Fire & Ice; Blue Thunder. **1985:** Rambo 2; Police Academy 2: Their First Assignment. **1986:** Big Trouble in Little China; Police Academy 3: Back in Training. **1987:** Number One with a Bullet; Laguna Heat. **1988:** Above the Law; Alien Nation. **1989:** Kinjite; No Holds Barred; Cage; Black Rain; Tango & Cash. **1990:** Robocop 2; Come See the Paradise. **1991:** Showdown in Little Tokyo; Double Impact; Iron Maze; Leather Jackets. **1992:** Rapid Fire; Universal Soldier; Davinci's War. **1993:** Robocop 3; Rising Sun. **1994:** Blue Tiger; Deadly Target. **1995:** To the Limit. **1996:** Warrior of Justice. *Television*—Combat; Kung Fu; Hawaii Five-0.

BILL SAITO
(b. 1936)

Veteran Oklahoma-born bit player of Asian descent, often playing as soldiers or henchmen.

Films—**1957:** Sayanara. **1958:** Hong Kong Confidential. **1959:** Green Mansions; Blood & Steel. **1962:** A Girl Named Tamiko. **1966:** The Sand Pebbles; Walk, Don't Run. **1967:** The President's Analyst. **1968:** Hawaii 5-0 (tv). **1969:** The Wrecking Crew. **1970:** Too Late the Hero. **1974:** Airport '75. **1975:** The Yakuza. **1976:** Midway. **1977:** Rollercoaster; Sidewinder One. **1979:** When Hell Was in Session (tv). **1981:** The Devil & Max Devlin. **1983:** Girls of the White Orchid (tv); Special Bulletin (tv). **1984:** All of Me. **1985:** My Science Project. **1986:** The Golden Child; Big Trouble in Little China. **1989:** Collision Course. **1991:** Showdown in Little Tokyo; The Perfect Weapon. **1992:** Memoirs of an Invisible Man; Rapid fire. **1994:** Blue Tiger. *Television*—Mission: Impossible; Get Smart; Kung Fu; The Six Million Dollar Man; Iron Horse; WKRP; Knot's Landing; Knight Rider; Paradise.

LYNN SALVATORE

An actress and stunt coordinator, Salvatore is a member of both the International Stunt Association and the Professional Driver's Association. She has doubled for Heather Langenkamp and Lisa Eilbacher.

Films—**1987:** Deadly Intent. **1988:** Night of the Demons; Assault of the Killer Bimbos. **1989:** 976 Evil; Nightmare on Elm Street 5: Dream Child; Chopper Chicks in Zombie Town. **1990:** Joe vs. The Volcano; The Adventures of Ford Fairlane; In the Cold of the Night. **1991:** Grand Canyon; Servants of Twilight; The People Under the Stairs; Cast a Deadly Spell; Deadlock; Pure Luck; Lonely Hearts. **1992:** The Hand That Rocks the Cradle; Live Wire; Honey, I Blew Up the Kid; Cool World; Stepfather 3. **1993:** Streetknight; The Beverly Hillbillies; Caroline at Midnight. **1994:** Even Cowgirls Get the Blues; Airheads; Steel Frontier. **1995:** Frank & Jesse; 3 Ninjas Knuckle Up; Across the Moon; Indian in the Cupboard; Wes Craven's New Nightmare; Halloween: The Curse of Michael Myers. **1996:** Mars Attacks!; Ravenhawk; Larger Than Life; Thinner.

STEVE SANTOSUSSO

Films—**1985:** Into the Night. **1986:** Big Trouble in Little China. **1987:** Teen Wolf 2; Night Force; Code Name Zebra. **1989:** Best of the Best. **1991:** Out for Justice; Point Break. **1992:** Rapid Fire. **1993:** Best of the Best 2. **1994:** Chasers; Pentathalon; Automatic; Terminal Velocity; In the Army Now; T-Force. **1995:** 12 Monkeys. **1996:** The Juror; Mulholland Falls; Maximum Risk.

BOBBY SARGENT
(b. 1952)

Texas-born gymnastic and trampoline champ once performed high dives for the circus and won the famed Acapulco Cliff Diving competition. He has doubled for Burt Reynolds, coordinated stunts, and directed second unit.

Films—**1977**: Smokey & the Bandit; Outlaw Blues. **1978**: Piranha. **1979**: The Black Hole; The Villain. **1980**: Alligator; Roadie; Smokey & the Bandit 2. **1981**: The Night the Lights Went Out in Georgia; Sharky's Machine. **1982**: Cannery Row; Split Image; Endangered Species; Fast Times at Ridgemont High; First Blood. **1983**: Heart Like a Wheel; Private School. **1984**: Surf 2. **1985**: Stick; Avenging Angel. **1988**: Alien Nation; Heartbreak Hotel; License to Drive. **1989**: Weekend at Bernie's; Valentino Returns. **1990**: Masters of Menace; Texasville. **1991**: Knight Rider 2000 (tv). **1992**: Hard Promises. **1993**: Slaughter of the Innocents. **1995**: The Underneath.

MICHAEL JOHN SARNA
(b. 1965)

A member of the Stuntmen's Association, Sarna has coordinated stunts and doubled for low-budget action star Wings Hauser.

Films—**1989**: Deadly Breed; East L.A. Warriors; Chance; Angels of the City. **1990**: Repo Jake; Dead Women in Lingerie; Last Call; Coldfire; Syngenor. **1991**: Beastmaster 2; The Rocketeer; Shakes the Clown; Killers' Edge; Night of the Wild-ing. **1992**: To Sleep with a Vampire; Innocent Blood; To Protect & Serve. **1993**: Firepower. **1994**: Steel Frontier. **1995**: Hard Justice; Black Scorpion; One Man's Justice; The Sweeper. **1996**: Public Enemies; Power 98; Set It Off; Forest Warrior; Mercenary.

RUSS SAUNDERS

A former Olympic gymnast and football player, Saunders doubled for the likes of Alan Ladd, Richard Widmark, Mickey Rooney, and Red Buttons. A member of the Stuntmen's Association, he eventually moved into directing second unit. His brother Ray sometimes performed acrobatic stunts with him.

Films—**1931**: Maybe It's Love; Touchdown. **1932**: The All-American; That's My Boy. **1933**: The House on 56th Street; King Kong. **1934**: Gentlemen Are Born; Kansas City Princess. **1935**: Black Fury; Dangerous; A Midsummer's Night Dream; We're in the Money. **1936**: The Golden Arrow; Love Begins at Twenty; Polo Joe; The Walking Dead. **1937**: Blazing Sixes; The Go Getter; Guns of the Pecos; The Life of Emile Zola. **1938**: Broadway Musketeers; Comet Over Broadway; When Were You Born?; The Adventures of Jane Arden. **1939**: City in Terror; Nancy Drew, Reporter; On Dress Parade; Pride of Blue Grass; They Made Me a Criminal; Torchy Runs for Mayor; Nancy Drew & the Hidden Staircase. **1940**: Brother Rat & a Baby; Sails Again; A Fugitive from Justice. **1941**: They Died with Their Boots On. **1947**: Variety Girl. **1948**: Joan of Arc; The Night Has a Thousand Eyes; Master of Lassie. **1950**: West Point Story; The Rogues of Sherwood Forest. **1951**: Appointment with Danger. **1952**: The Greatest Show on Earth; Singin' in the Rain. **1953**: Here Come the Girls; A Slight Case of Larceny; The Veils of Bagdad; Botany Bay. **1954**: Seven Brides for Seven Brothers; Saskatchewan; Broken Lance. **1955:** Battle Cry. **1956:** Around the World in 80 Days. **1959:** The Trap. **1960:** Spartacus; Guns of the Timberland. **1961:** The Sins of Rachel Cade. **1962:** Hatari; House of Women. **1963:** PT 109. **1964:** A Distant Trumpet; Cheyenne Autumn. **1965:** King Rat; Mickey One. **1966:** The Chase; Walk Don't Run; Birds Do It. **1967:** Bonnie & Clyde; Thoroughly Modern Millie; The Happening; Double Trouble. **1968:** Star. **1969:** The Stalking Moon; The Comic; The Extraordinary Seaman. **1970:** Which Way to the Front?; The Liberation of L.B. Jones. **1972:** The Poseidon Adventure; The New Centurions. **1973:** The Way We Were. **1974:** The Towering Inferno; The Longest Yard. **1975:** The Hindenburg. **1976:** Logan's Run; The Shootist; Drum. **1978:** The Driver.

TOM SAVINI

A make-up and special effects technician with a fervent cult following, the Pennsylvania-born Savini has also done stuntwork in several films. Given his flashiest role in *From Dusk Till Dawn,* he directed the remake of George Romero's *Night of the Living Dead.*

*Films—***1972:** Deathdream. **1974:** Deranged. **1978:** Martin; Dawn of the Dead. **1980:** Friday the 13th; Maniac; Effects. **1981:** Eyes of a Stranger; The Burning; Knightriders; The Prowler; Midnight; Nightmares in a Deranged Brain. **1982:** Creepshow; Alone in the Dark; Til Death Do Us Scare. **1984:** Friday the 13th, The Final Chapter. **1985:** Day of the Dead; Invasion USA. **1986:** The Texas Chainsaw Massacre 2; The Ripper. **1987:** Creepshow 2. **1988:** Monkey Shines. **1989:** Red Scorpion; Heartstopper; Document of the Dead. **1990:** Two Evil Eyes; Bloodsucking Pharos from Pittsburgh; Night of the Living Dead (d). **1992:** Innocent Blood. **1993:** Trauma; Necronomicon. **1994:** Killing Zoe; The Stand (tv). **1995:** Mr. Stitch. **1996:** From Dusk Till Dawn. *Television—* Tales from the Darkside (a/d).

GEORGE SAWAYA

A veteran supporting player and lifetime member of the Stuntmen's Association, Sawaya has doubled for Ernest Borgnine. He's the father of Rick Sawaya.

*Films—***1949:** We Were Strangers. **1952:** Narrow Margin; With a Song in My Heart; One Minute to Zero. **1953:** Salome; Desert Legion; The Desert Song. **1954:** Dragnet. **1955:** The Prodigal. **1956:** The Black Sleep; Hot Cars; Emergency Hospital. **1957:** Bop Girl Goes Calypso. **1960:** Walking Target; Police Dog Story. **1961:** Everything's Ducky. **1962:** Hands of a Stranger; Diary of a Madman; Escape from Zahrain; Five Weeks in a Balloon. **1963:** Drums of Africa; Come Blow Your Horn. **1965:** Convict Stage; Fort Courageous; The Lollipop Cover. **1966:** Batman; The Money Trap. **1967:** The Young Warriors; Bonnie & Clyde. **1968:** Panic in the City; The Boston Strangler; The Green Berets; Sol Madrid. **1969:** Che; Justine; Hello, Dolly! **1970:** Cover Me, Babe; Beneath the Planet of the Apes. **1971:** Dirty Harry. **1972:** The Poseidon Adventure; Private Duty Nurses; Moon of the Wolf (tv). **1973:** Magnum Force; The Don Is Dead. **1974:** Blazing Saddles; The Red Badge of Courage (tv). **1975:** The Devil's Rain. **1976:** St. Ives; The Invisible Strangler (aka The Astral Factor). **1977:** The Domino Principle. **1978:** FM; I Wanna Hold Your Hand. **1979:** Concorde, Airport '79; Beggarman Thief (tv). **1980:** Cheech & Chong's Next Movie. **1981:** Bustin" Loose; Escape from New York. **1982:** Blade Runner; Dead Men Don't Wear Plaid; Six Pack. **1984:** Repo Man. *Television—*Perry Mason; The Aquanauts; The

Virginian; Combat; Voyage to the Bottom of the Sea; Branded; The Man from U.N.C.L.E.; I Spy; Mission: Impossible; Batman; Get Smart; Star Trek; Dragnet; Emergency; The FBI; Columbo; Banyon; The Rookies; The Streets of San Francisco; Cannon; Barnaby Jones; Joe Forrester; Future Cop; The Powers of Matthew Star; Voyagers; The Rebel; Laredo.

RICK SAWAYA

A member of the Stuntmen's Association, Sawaya has doubled for Billy Crystal.

Films—1973: The Don Is Dead. 1978: I Wanna Hold Your Hand. 1979: Concorde, Airport '79; Boulevard Nights; Walk Proud; The In-Laws. 1980: Cheech & Chong's Next Movie. 1981: Bustin' Loose. 1982: The Sword & the Sorcerer. 1983: Joysticks. 1985: Commando. 1986: Running Scared. 1987: Allan Quartermain & the Lost City of Gold; Throw Momma from the Train; The Bedroom Window. 1988: Alien Nation; Criminal Act. 1989: The Burbs; Kill Me Again. 1990: Robocop 2. 1991: Cast a Deadly Spell. 1994: City Slickers 2; The Mask. 1995: Casino 1996: Back to Back. *Television*—Future Cop.

CARL SAXE

A veteran bit player and double for Van Heflin, Van Johnson, and Brian Donlevy, Saxe is a long-time member of the Stuntmen's Association.

Films—1934: Cleopatra. 1937: All-American Sweetheart. 1939: They All Came Back. 1942: Forest Rangers. 1943: Pilot No. 5; Thousands Cheer. 1946: O.S.S. 1947: Desperate; High Barbaree; Johnny O'Clock; Where There's Life; To Kiss & to Keep; Killer McCoy; The Beginning or the End. 1948: Force of Evil; Race Street; A Southern Yankee; The Three Musketeers. 1949: The Stratton Story; Easy Living; The Threat; Neptune's Daughter; Samson & Delilah; The Window; The Numbers Racket; East Side, West Side; Battleground. 1950: Where Danger Lives; The Violent Hour; Walk Softly, Stranger; Undercover Girl; Armored Car Robbery. 1951: Jim Thorpe, All-American; Rhubarb; Sailor Beware; The Strip; Weekend with Father. 1952: Against All Flags; Scarlett Angel. 1953: Off Limits; Jalopy; Private Eyes; Young Bess. 1954: Executive Suite; Rose Marie; Superman's Peril. 1956: The Ten Commandments. 1957: The Kettles on Old McDonald's Farm; Omar Khayyem; Hear Me Good. 1958: The Buccaneer; The Party Crashers. 1959: Night of the Quarter Moon; Career; The Young Philadelphians; Last Train from Gun Hill. 1961: All in a Night's Work. 1963: Hud. 1968: The Split. 1969: The Great Bank Robbery. 1970: Lost Flight; The Molly Maguires; There Was a Crooked Man; Which Way to the Front? 1972: What's Up, Doc? *Television*—Superman; Land of the Giants; Star Trek.

SHARON SCHAFFER

Films—1980: The Blues Brothers; Motel Hell. 1981: Bustin' Loose. 1982: Fighting Back. 1983: D.C. Cab; Scarface; The Star Chamber. 1984: City Heat; Places in the Heart; City Limits. 1985: Certain Fury; Weird Science. 1986: The Naked Cage; Jumpin' Jack Flash. 1987: Burglar; Down Twisted. 1988: Colors; Alien Nation; I'm Gonna Git You Sucka; Captive Rage. 1989: Under the Gun; Pink Cadillac. 1990: Peacemaker; Kindergarten Cop; Backstreet Dreams. 1991: Timebomb; Driving Me Crazy. 1992: Article 99; American Me; Buffy, the Vampire Slayer. 1993: Another Stakeout; In the Line of Fire. 1994: The Naked Gun 33 1/3. 1995: Showgirls; Vampire in Brooklyn.

FRED SCHIEWILLER

A burly member of the Stuntmen's Association, Schiewiller performed bit parts primarily during the sixties and seventies.

Films—**1959:** Night of the Quarter Moon. **1961:** The Fiercest Heart. **1963:** The Prize. **1964:** The Seven Faces of Dr. Lao. **1966:** The Money Trap. **1969:** The Good Guys & the Bad Guys; The Great Bank Robbery. **1970:** Flap. **1972:** Conquest of the Planet of the Apes; What's Up, Doc? **1973:** Charley Varrick; Magnum Force; Battle for the Planet of the Apes. **1974:** Black Samson; The Towering Inferno; Mame; Blazing Saddles; Earthquake; The Swinging Cheerleaders. **1975:** Day of the Locust. **1977:** Black Sunday. **1978:** Movie, Movie; Hooper. **1980:** Die Laughing. **1981:** Honkytonk Freeway; Heartbeeps. **1982:** The Sword & the Sorcerer. **1983:** The Lost Empire. **1984:** Repo Man. **1987:** Computer Logic (tv). **1988:** Action Jackson; Bail Out. **1992:** Passed Away. **1994:** The Hard Truth; Dead Badge. **1995:** The Tie That Binds. *Television*—Laredo; The Mod Squad; Harry O; Blue Thunder.

ANTHONY G. SCHMIDT

Films—**1985:** Ewoks: The Battle for Endor (tv). **1987:** Dead Man Walking. **1988:** Rambo 3; Beetlejuice; License to Drive. **1989:** Honey, I Shrunk the Kids; Nightmare on Elm Street 5: Dream Child; One Man Force. **1990:** Downtown; Quick Change; The Guardian; Martians Go Home. **1991:** Delirious; Bill & Ted's Bogus Journey. **1992:** Wayne's World. **1993:** Geronimo. **1994:** Stargate. **1995:** Painted Hero; The Crossing Guard. **1996:** The Nutty Professor; Spy Hard; Kingpin.

ART SCHOLL
(b. 1933; d. 1985)

A top aerialist and acrobatic flying champ of fixed-wing aircraft and helicopters. Scholl died in a plane crash while filming shots for the film *Top Gun.*

Films—**1975:** The Great Waldo Pepper. **1978:** Capricorn One. **1980:** Cloud Dancer; Where the Buffalo Roam; Herbie Goes Bananas. **1981:** The Pursuit of D.B. Cooper. **1983:** Blue Thunder; To Be or Not to Be; The Right Stuff; Shooting Stars (tv). **1984:** Flashpoint. **1985:** The Man with One Red Shoe; Explorers; Iron Eagle; Prime Risk; The Blue Yonder (tv). **1986:** Top Gun.

JAN-MICHAEL SCHULTZ

Films—**1980:** The Blues Brothers. **1986:** Legal Eagles; Odd Jobs. **1987:** Allan Quartermain & the Lost City of Gold; Blind Date. **1988:** Braddock: Missing in Action 3; Critters 2; License to Drive; They Live; Platoon Leader. **1989:** L.A. Bounty; True Believer. **1990:** Child's Play 2; Delta Force 2. **1992:** CIA: Code Name Alexa; Alien Intruder; Maximum Force; Sunset Grill; Fifty/Fifty. **1993:** Private Wars; Street Crimes; Fist of Honor; Sidekicks. **1995:** 3 Ninjas Knuckle Up; Blood for Blood; Top Dog. *Television*—Off Duty; Walker, Texas Ranger.

BEN SCOTT

A stunt coordinator and member of the Stuntmen's Association, Ben is the son of Walter Scott.

Films—**1982:** Ruckus; Conan the Barbarian; Fast Times at Ridgemont High.

1983: Christine; Spacehunter; Cowboy (tv). 1984: Red Dawn; Starman. 1985: Silverado; Commando; Rambo 2. 1986: Cobra; Jumpin' Jack Flash; The Three Amigos; Ruthless People. 1987: The Night Stalker; Cherry 2000; Wanted: Dead or Alive; Blind Date; Dragnet; Masters of the Universe. 1988: The Great Outdoors; Poltergeist 3; They Live; My Stepmother Is an Alien; Earth Girls Are Easy; Bail Out. 1989: Pet Sematary; Nightmare on Elm Street 5: Dream Child; Second Sight; Glory; Next of Kin; Tango & Cash. 1990: Back to the Future 3; Pump Up the Volume; Lisa; The Rookie. 1991: Delirious; Suburban Commando. 1992: Far & Away; Live Wire; Buffy, the Vampire Slayer. 1993: The Adventures of Huck Finn; Tombstone. 1994: The Last Ride (aka F.T.W.); Cabin Boy; Bad Girls; Corrina, Corrina; Wagons East; Blankman; The Shawshank Redemption; Every Breath. 1995: Tall Tale; Tank Girl; Houseguest; The Set Up. 1996: Chain Reaction; Raven; Fast Money; Ruby Jean & Joe. *Television*—Guns of Paradise.

DENNIS SCOTT

An occasional bit player and stunt coordinator, Scott is a member of the International Stunt Association.

Films—1982: Megaforce. 1984: Against All Odds. 1985: To Live & Die in L.A.; Black Moon Rising. 1986: F/X; King Kong Lives; Manhunter; Big Trouble in Little China; Wisdom. 1987: The Wild Pair; The Lost Boys; Kidnapped; Code Name Zebra. 1988: Midnight Run; Child's Play; The Blob; In Dangerous Company. 1989: Shocker; After Midnight. 1990: Chattahoochee; Navy Seals; Desperate Hours; Dick Tracy; The Adventures of Ford Fairlane; Predator 2. 1991: FX-2; The Servants of Twilight; Harley Davidson & the Marlboro Man; The Doors; Deadlock; What About Bob?; Suburban Commando; Bugsy; Soldier's Fortune. 1993: The Temp; Free Willy; Conflict of Interest;

Prophet of Evil (tv). 1994: A Low Down Dirty Shame; Payback. 1995: Indian in the Cupboard; Things to Do in Denver When You're Dead; The Set Up; Chameleon. 1996: Spy Hard; The Phantom; Mars Attacks! *Television*—Automan.

JOHN-CLAY SCOTT

The stunt coordinator brother of Ben Scott, John-Clay is a member of the Stuntmen's Association.

Films—1980: Happy Birthday to Me. 1981: Eureka. 1982: Ruckus; Conan the Barbarian; Fast Times at Ridgemont High. 1983: Christine; Spacehunter. 1984: Footloose; Red Dawn; Starman. 1985: Certain Fury; Back to the Future; The Man with One Red Shoe; Silverado; Rambo 2; Clue; Runaway Train. 1986: Band of the Hand; Ruthless People; Busted Up; Jumpin' Jack Flash; The Boy Who Could Fly. 1987: Cherry 2000; Wanted: Dead or Alive; Dragnet; Masters of the Universe; Dead Man Walking. 1988: Off Limits; Vice Versa; Poltergeist 3; The Great Outdoors; They Live; Border Heat. 1989: The Burbs; Second Sight; Back to the Future 2; Dead Bang; Glory; We're No Angels; From the Dead of Night (tv). 1990: The Rookie. 1991: Eve of Destruction; Shattered; Flight of the Intruder; Pink Lightning (tv). 1992: Far & Away; Live Wire; Buffy, the Vampire Slayer; Class Act; Nemesis; Sunset Grill. 1993: The Fugitive; Judgment Night. 1994: Legends of the Fall; Blown Away; Vanishing Son (tv). 1995: Tall Tale; Die Hard with a Vengeance; Tank Girl; Devil in a Blue Dress. 1996: Chain Reaction; First Kid; Feeling Minnesota.

WALTER SCOTT
(b. 1940)

A veteran supporting player, second unit director, and stunt coordina-

The land rush in 1992's *Far & Away*, action coordinated by Walter Scott.

tor, Scott is a former rodeo cowboy and father of stuntmen Ben Scott and John-Clay Scott. A member of the Stuntmen's Association, he has doubled for James Caan and coordinated the sweeping land rush in *Far and Away*.

Films—**1961:** Wild in the Country. **1965:** The Glory Guys. **1968:** Panic in the City; The Boston Strangler. **1969:** The Good Guys & the Bad Guys. **1970:** Beneath the Planet of the Apes; Cotton Comes to Harlem. **1971:** Summer of '42; Dirty Harry. **1972:** The Great Northfield Minnesota Raid; Joe Kidd; Ulzana's Raid; The Culpepper Cattle Company; Buck & the Preacher; The Cowboys; Come Back, Charleston Blue. **1973:** Pat Garrett & Billy the Kid. **1974:** Three Tough Guys; Mame; 99 & 44/100% Dead. **1975:** Bite the Bullet; Hard Times; Mr. Sycamore; Night Moves; Rollerball; Friendly Persuasion (tv). **1976:** The Missouri Breaks; The Duchess & the Dirtwater Fox; The

Outlaw Josey Wales; The November Plan. **1977:** Another Man, Another Chance; Mr. Billion. **1978:** Comes a Horseman. **1979:** Over the Edge. **1980:** Heaven's Gate; Tom Horn; Ruckus; Used Cars; The Mountain Men; Hide in Plain Sight. **1981:** Going Ape; On Golden Pond; Thief. **1982:** Ruckus; Conan the Barbarian; Tron; 48HRS. **1983:** Spacehunter. **1984:** Thief of Hearts; P.K. & the Kid; Calamity Jane (tv). **1985:** Commando; Silverado; Back to the Future. **1986:** Jumpin' Jack Flash; Ruthless People; Short Circuit. **1987:** Wanted: Dead or Alive; Fatal Beauty; Masters of the Universe. **1988:** Off Limits; The Great Outdoors; They Live. **1989:** Back to the Future 2; Second Sight; Next of Kin. **1990:** Back to the Future 3. **1991:** Shattered; Sleeping with the Enemy; Backdraft; Career Opportunities. **1992:** Far & Away; Candyman; Death Becomes Her; The Bodyguard. **1993:** Indecent Proposal; Judgment Night; The Last Outlaw; Sexual Response. **1994:** Bad Girls; Blankman. **1995:** Die Hard with a Vengeance; Tank Girl. **1996:** Chain Reaction; Ruby Jean & Joe. *Television*—Gunsmoke; Cimarron

Strip; Star Trek; Archer; Starsky & Hutch; Vegas; When the Whistle Blows.

RICK SEAMAN

A member of the Stuntmen's Association, Seaman once crashed cars at county fairs. He's now the head of Rick's Stunt Cars.

Films—**1974:** The Taking of Pelham 1-2-3. **1977:** Grand Theft Auto; Maniac. **1979:** The Amityville Horror; The Electric Horseman; The Lady in Red. **1980:** Seems Like Old Times; Roadie; Alligator. **1981:** The Nashville Grab (tv). **1982:** Parasite; Eating Raoul; Endangered Species. **1983:** Heart Like a Wheel; Get Crazy; Smokey & the Bandit 3; The Lost Empire. **1984:** Repo Man. **1985:** Death Wish 3; Space Rage. **1987:** Million Dollar Mystery. **1988:** Off Limits; Illegally Yours; Alien Nation; Messenger of Death; License to Drive; Made in the USA. **1989:** Under the Gun; Weekend at Bernie's; Hit List; Second Sight; See No Evil, Hear No Evil. **1990:** Short Time; Marked for Death; Robocop 2. **1991:** Out for Justice; Mortal Thoughts; The Hard Way; Deadlock. **1992:** Deep Cover; Sneakers. **1993:** Robocop 3; Another Stakeout; Weekend at Bernie's 2; Trouble Bound. **1994:** The Chase; The Cowboy Way. **1995:** Assassins. **1996:** Carpool; Set It Off.

BILLY SHANNON
(b. 1935; d. 1981)

Shannon was a former rodeo cowboy and bit player who specialized in Western work, doubling for Mel Brooks and Joey Bishop. He died from a heart attack after a bout of pneumonia.

Films—**1957:** Young & Dangerous. **1960:** Spartacus. **1962:** Rome Adventure. **1964:** Mail Order Bride. **1965:** The War Lord. **1966:** Texas Across the River; Harper. **1967:** Chuka. **1968:** The Green Berets; Blue. **1969:** The Wild Bunch. **1970:** Little Big Man. **1972:** Buck & the Preacher. **1973:** Magnum Force. **1974:** Mame; Blazing Saddles; Freebie & the Bean; Sidekicks (tv). **1978:** F.I.S.T. *Television*— Honey West; The High Chaparral; Silent Force; Cade's County.

ALEX SHARPE

A lifetime member of the Stuntmen's Association, Sharpe was the chief double for James Arness during "Gunsmoke's" extended television run.

Films—**1948:** Harpoon. **1949:** Easy Living. **1950:** Rocky Mountain. **1951:** Little Egypt; Jim Thorpe, All-American; Apache Drums. **1952:** The Winning Team; A Girl in Every Port; Horizons West; Androcles & the Lion; One Minute to Zero; Yankee Buccaneer. **1953:** The Mississippi Gambler; Seminole. **1955:** Wichita. **1956:** Red Sundown; Please Murder Me; Showdown at Abilene. **1957:** The Night Runner. **1962:** Young Guns of Texas. **1964:** Law of the Lawless. **1968:** Planet of the Apes; Bullit. **1969:** The Great Bank Robbery. **1970:** Flap; Catch-22. **1971:** Dirty Harry. **1972:** Conquest of the Planet of the Apes; What's Up, Doc? **1973:** Battle for the Planet of the Apes. **1976:** Harry & Walter Go to New York. **1977:** Telefon. **1979:** Sunburn. **1982:** The Sword & the Sorcerer. **1985:** Pee Wee's Big Adventure. **1990:** The Rookie. **1993:** In the Line of Fire. *Television*—Gunsmoke; Cheyenne; The Californians; The Virginian; Branded; Batman; Mission: Impossible; Little House on the Prairie.

DAVE SHARPE
(b. 1910; d. 1980)

Missouri-born stunt ace won the AAU Tumbling Title twice and performed in the circus before getting into films and serials as a bit player and occasional leading man. Sharpe doubled for such athletic swashbucklers as Douglas Fairbanks, Jr., Douglas Fairbanks, Sr., and Tony Curtis, pausing only to serve in the Army Air Corps during WWII. He died of Parkinson's disease.

Films—**1924:** The Thief of Bagdad. **1929:** Masked Emotions. **1935:** Adventurous Knights; Roaring Roads; Social Error. **1936:** Desert Justice; Galloping Dynamite; Ghost Town; Gun Grit; Idaho Kid; Mind Your Own Business; Mr. Cinderella; Our Relations; Pigskin Parade. **1937:** Two Minutes to Play; Doomed at Sundown; Drums of Destiny; The Law Commands; Melody of the Plains; Santa Fe Rider; Where Trails Divide; Young Dynamite. **1938:** The Devil's Partner; Man's Country; Shine on Harvest Moon. **1939:** Gunga Din; Cowboys from Texas; The Night Rider; The Law Comes to Texas; Lone Star Pioneers; Roarin' Tumbleweeds; Three Texas Steers; Daredevils of the Red Circle; Wyoming Outlaw. **1940:** Riders of Pasco Basin; The Thief of Bagdad; Covered Wagon Trails; The Adventures of Red Ryder; Danger Ahead; Seven Sinners. **1941:** Silver Stallion; Along the Rio Grande; The Mysterious Dr. Satan; Thunder Over the Prairie; King of the Texas Rangers; The Adventures of Capt. Marvel; The Corsican Brothers. **1942:** Yukon Patrol; King of the Mounties; Pirates of the Prairie; The Arabian Nights; Texas to Bataan; Trail Riders. **1943:** The Haunted Ranch; Daredevils of the West; Sagebrush Law; The Avenging Rider; Red River Robin Hood; Two Fisted Justice. **1946:** King of the Forest Rangers; Colorado Serenade; The Falcon's Adventure; Crime of

the Century. **1947:** Bells of San Angelo; G-Men Never Forget; The Exile; Sinbad the Sailor; The Wistful Widow of Indian Gap. **1948:** The Adventures of Frank & Jesse James; The Valiant Hombre; Dangers of the Canadian Mounted; The Three Musketeers; Sleep, My Love; The Fuller Brush Man; A Southern Yankee; You Gotta Stay Happy. **1949:** Susanna Pass; The Fighting O'Flynn; Federal Agents vs. Underworld Inc. **1950:** The James Brothers of Missouri; The Girl from San Lorenzo; Invisible Monster; The Good Humor Man. **1951:** Don Daredevil Rides Again; Tomahawk; The Wild Blue Yonder; Little Egypt. **1952:** The Cimarron Kid; Montana Belle; Singin' in the Rain; Blackhawk. **1953:** The Man from the Alamo; Forbidden; Canadian Mounties vs. The Atomic Invaders; War of the Worlds; The Redhead from Wyoming; Desert Legion; Prince Valiant; The Black Shield of Falworth. **1955:** The Purple Mask. **1956:** Champions of Justice. **1962:** The Spiral Road. **1965:** The Third Day; The Great Race; Fluffy. **1966:** Not with My Wife You Don't. **1968:** In Enemy Country; Day of the Evil Gun. **1969:** Paint Your Wagon. **1972:** The Poseidon Adventure; The Life & Times of Judge Roy Bean; Conquest of the Planet of the Apes. **1974:** Blazing Saddles; Blazing Stewardesses. **1978:** Heaven Can Wait. *Television*—The Lone Ranger; The Cisco Kid; Zorro; Wild Bill Hickok; The FBI.

JIM SHEPPARD
(b. 1937; d. 1977)

A former rodeo cowboy and double for both Audie Murphy and Marty Feldman, the Oregon-born Sheppard died doing a horsefall for Jason Robards on the set of the film *Comes a Horseman.*

Films—**1959:** The Wild & the Innocent. **1960:** Seven Ways from Sundown. **1961:** Posse from Hell. **1962:** Six Black Horses.

1963: The Birds; Showdown. 1964: Bullet for a Badman; Apache Rifles. 1965: Major Dundee; Arizona Raiders; The War Lord. 1966: Gunpoint; 40 Guns to Apache Pass. 1967: Hour of the Gun. 1968: Planet of the Apes. 1969: The Wild Bunch. 1971: A Time for Dying. 1976: Silent Movie; Silver Streak. 1977: The Last Remake of Beau Geste. 1978: Comes a Horseman. *Television*—Rawhide; Gunsmoke; Iron Horse; Cade's County; McCloud; Police Story; The Rockford Files.

JOHN SHERROD

This Mississippi-raised stunt coordinator/second unit director was a professor of urban studies before getting into films. His son Paul also performs stunts.

Films—1974: Mame. 1976: Drum. 1979: Penitentiary. 1980: The Fifth Floor; Smokey & the Bandit 2. 1981: Penitentiary 2. 1982: White Dog; Fighting Back; Fast Walking; The Sword & the Sorcerer; Friday the 13th Part 3. 1983: The Big Score; Fire & Ice; The Man Who Wasn't There. 1984: Friday the 13th: The Final Chapter; Meatballs 2. 1985: Friday the 13th: A New Beginning; Commando. 1986: Murphy's Law; The Golden Child; Out of Bounds. 1987: Penitentiary 3; Critical Condition; My Demon Lover; Dudes. 1988: The Night Before; Coming to America; Die Hard; The Seventh Sign; Red Heat; Colors; Big Top Pee Wee; Nightmare on Elm Street 4: Dream Master; Critters 2. 1989: The Mighty Quinn; Johnny Handsome; Next of Kin; Glory; After Midnight; Crack House. 1990: Downtown; Child's Play 2; Death Warrant. 1991: Prayer of the Rollerboys.

PAUL SHORT

Films—1986: Armed Response; Wired to Kill. 1987: Cyclone; Cold Steel; Deadly Intent; Death Spa; Zombie High;

Munchies; Hell Comes to Frogtown. 1988: Nightmare at Noon; Terminal Entry; Night of the Demons; Waxwork; The Horror Show; Rollerblade Warriors; Take Two. 1989: Survival Quest; Sundown; Mob Boss. 1990: Leatherface 3; Joe vs. The Volcano; Keaton's Cop. 1991: Grand Canyon; Neon City. 1992: Big Girls Don't Cry, They Get Even; Afterburn; Hoffa. 1994: The Naked Gun 33 1/3; Blown Away; Ice; Steel Frontier; Army of One; Final Mission; Bad Blood. 1995: Strange Days; Suspect Device. 1996: Yesterday's Target.

SPIKE SILVER

A member of the International Stunt Association, this Texas-born stunt coordinator has doubled for Martin Short, Dana Carvey, and Robert Downey, Jr.

Films—1982: The Border. 1983: Scarface. 1984: The River. 1985: The Protector. 1986: Legal Eagles; Back to School; Radioactive Dreams; Thunder Run. 1987: Down Twisted; The Witches of Eastwick; Big Shots; Assassination; Less Than Zero. 1988: Bulletproof; Above the Law; Shakedown; The Dead Pool; Crocodile Dundee 2. 1989: Three Fugitives; Chances Are; L.A. Bounty; Pink Cadillac. 1990: Almost an Angel; Opportunity Knocks; The Rookie. 1991: The Taking of Beverly Hills; Star Trek 6: Undiscovered Country; Highway to Hell. 1993: In the Line of Fire; Striking Distance; A Perfect World. 1994: Foreign Student; Midnight Ride. 1995: American Ninja 5; Copycat. 1996: Sgt. Bilko; Kingpin; Wildside.

LINCOLN SIMONDS

A former acrobat, Simonds is a member of the Stuntmen's Association.

Films—**1983:** Get Crazy. **1985:** Invasion USA; Moving Violations. **1986:** Invaders from Mars; Blue City. **1987:** Date with an Angel; The Bedroom Window. **1988:** Miracle Mile; In Dangerous Company; Nitti: The Enforcer (tv). **1989:** Glory; Midnight. **1990:** Arachnophobia; Marked for Death; Fear (tv). **1991:** Femme Fatale; Rich Girl; Mannequin 2; Liquid Dreams. **1992:** Buffy, the Vampire Slayer; Out on a Limb. **1993:** Amos & Andrew. **1994:** Airheads; Past Tense. **1995:** Ballistic. **1996:** Mars Attacks!; Raven.

MONTY L. SIMONS

Films—**1982:** The Beastmaster. **1988:** Two Moon Junction. **1993:** Rio Diablo (tv). **1994:** Zero Tolerance; Airheads; Automatic; T-Force; Relentless 4. **1995:** Soldier Boyz; The Tie That Binds; Digital Man; The Sweeper. **1996:** Don't Be a Menace ..; Eraser; The Nutty Professor; Independence Day; Riot; Back to Back.

JOHN SISTRUNK

Films—**1969:** The Great Bank Robbery. **1970:** There Was a Crooked Man. **1979:** Van Nuys Blvd. **1980:** Don't Answer the Phone; The Blues Brothers; Motel Hell; Galaxina. **1982:** My Tutor. **1984:** Weekend Pass; Beverly Hills Cop. **1987:** Steele Justice; Over the Top. **1988:** The Horror Show. **1989:** Case of the Hillside Strangler (tv). **1990:** Trancers 2; Peacemaker; Delta Force 2; Backstreet Dreams. **1993:** Rescue Me; Love, Cheat, & Steal. **1994:** Zero Tolerance; Direct Hit; T-Force. **1995:** Top Dog. *Television*—It Takes a Thief.

WILLIAM "CHARLIE" SKEEN

An independent stunt coordinator, Skeen has doubled for B-movie vet Ross Hagen.

Films—**1981:** An Eye for an Eye. **1983:** Lone Wolf McQuade. **1985:** Invasion USA. **1986:** Avenging Force. **1987:** Allan Quartermain & the Lost City of Gold; Back to the Beach; Assassination; The Hidden. **1988:** Bulletproof; Feds; Hero & the Terror; The Night Before. **1989:** Shocker. **1990:** Delta Force 2; Peacemaker. **1991:** Timebomb. **1992:** Click: the Calendar Girl Killer; Death Ring. **1993:** Best of the Best 2. **1994:** Dead Center; T-Force. **1996:** Ravenhawk. *Television*—Alien Nation.

BRIAN SMIRZ

Brother of the late stuntman Brett Smirz, this stunt coordinator began his career on the East Coast but moved West in the late eighties.

Films—**1981:** They All Laughed. **1984:** The Exterminator 2. **1985:** The Protector. **1986:** F/X; Quiet Cool; Ruthless People. **1987:** Dead Man Walking; Masters of the Universe. **1988:** Messenger of Death; Who Framed Roger Rabbit?; The Dead Pool; Border Heat; Perfect Victims; Bail Out. **1989:** Cage; Transylvania Twist; Time Trackers; Second Sight. **1990:** Back to the Future 3; Sorority Girls & the Creature from Hell; Streets; Delta Force 2; Syngenor. **1991:** Teenage Mutant Ninja Turtles 2; Beastmaster 2; Ultraviolet. **1992:** Poison Ivy; Batman Returns. **1993:** A Perfect World; Cyborg 2. **1994:** True Lies; The Flintstones; Color of Night. **1995:** 3 Ninjas Knuckle Up; The Stars Fell on Henrietta; Demon Knight; Tank Girl;

Congo; Get Shorty; Sudden Death. **1996:** Broken Arrow; Barb Wire.

GREG SMIRZ

The youngest member of the Smirz brothers, Greg has doubled for James Spader. He's a member of Stunt Specialists.

Films—**1986:** F/X; Quiet Cool. **1987:** Masters of the Universe. **1988:** Dead Man Walking; Who Framed Roger Rabbit?; Border Heat; Angel 3. **1989:** Cage; Street Asylum; Ministry of Vengeance; Back to Back. **1990:** Night of the Living Dead; Maniac Cop 2; Syngenor. **1991:** New Jack City; Mannequin 2; December. **1993:** Whispers in the Dark. **1992:** Malcolm X; Innocent Blood. **1993:** The Dark Half; Gettysburg. **1994:** Body Snatchers; Sugar Hill; The Professional; Stargate. **1995:** Tank Girl; Waterworld.

DEAN SMITH
(b. 1932)

A Texas rodeo champion and Olympic gold medalist in the sprint relay at Helsinke in 1952, Smith briefly played pro football for the Los Angeles Rams before getting into films as a supporting player and Western specialist. A member of the Stuntmen's Association, he doubled regularly for both Paul Newman and Robert Redford.

Films—**1958:** Cat on a Hot Tin Roof; Auntie Mame. **1959:** Born Reckless; They Came to Cordura. **1960:** The Alamo; Seven Ways from Sundown. **1961:** Two Rode Together; The Comancheros. **1962:** How the West Was Won. **1963:** Kings of the Sun; McLintock; PT 109. **1964:** Cheyenne Autumn; A Distant Trumpet;

Blood on the Arrow; Rio Conchos. **1965:** The Great Race. **1966:** Stagecoach. **1967:** The War Wagon; What Did You Do in the War Daddy?; El Dorado; Hurry Sundown. **1969:** The Stalking Moon; True Grit; Butch Cassidy & the Sundance Kid. **1970:** Airport; The Cheyenne Social Club; Rio Lobo. **1971:** Big Jake; Sometimes a Great Notion (aka Never Give an Inch). **1972:** Riding Tall; The Gatling Gun; The Life & Times of Judge Roy Bean; Jeremiah Johnson; Ulzana's Raid; Hickey & Boggs; Evel Knievel; The Legend of Nigger Charley. **1973:** The Sting; Westworld. **1974:** The Towering Inferno; The Sugarland Express; Earthquake; Airport '75; Mrs. Sundance (tv); Season of the Wolf (tv); Melvin Purvis, G-Man (tv). **1975:** The Great Waldo Pepper; MacKintosh & T.J.; Seven Alone; Three Days of the Condor; The Drowning Pool; The Kansas City Massacre (tv). **1976:** The Invisible Strangler. **1977:** Black Sunday; Fraternity Row. **1978:** FM. **1979:** Concorde, Airport '79; The Last Ride of the Dalton Gang (tv); Legend of the Golden Gun (tv). **1983:** Christine. **1984:** Rhinestone; The Lonely Guy. **1985:** Cloak & Dagger. **1986:** Raw Deal. **1987:** Creepshow 2; Timestalkers (tv). **1988:** Hot to Trot. **1989:** Three Fugitives. **1991:** Son of Darkness: To Die For 2. **1994:** Maverick. **1995:** The Quick & the Dead. *Television*—The Outer Limits; The Bold Ones; The Six Million Dollar Man; Bret Maverick; The Fall Guy; Simon & Simon; Guns of Paradise; Have Gun Will Travel; Wells Fargo; Jesse James; Cimarron Strip.

EDDIE SMITH
(b. 1938)

This stunt coordinator, best known for smashing a speedboat into a wedding cake in *Live and Let Die,* founded the now defunct Black Stuntman's Association in the late sixties.

Films—**1970:** Halls of Anger; Beneath the Planet of the Apes; M*A*S*H. **1971:**

Dirty Harry. **1972:** Unholy Rollers; Across 110th Street; Conquest of the Planet of the Apes. **1973:** Live & Let Die; Cleopatra Jones; Battle for the Planet of the Apes. **1974:** Black Belt Jones; Blazing Saddles; Cockfighter; Truck Turner; Dirty Mary, Crazy Larry; Earthquake. **1976:** Dr. Black, Mr. Hyde; Drum. **1977:** Which Way is Up?; New York, New York. **1978:** Youngblood; Death Drug. **1980:** The Dogs of War. **1982:** White Dog; The Sword & the Sorcerer. **1983:** D.C. Cab; Scarface; Under Fire. **1989:** Harlem Nights. **1990:** House Party; Predator 2; Secret Agent 00-Soul. **1995:** Panther. **1996:** The Nutty Professor.

EDDIE "BO" SMITH, JR.

A Chicago-based supporting player, Smith and his shaven-pate have proven memorable in films for director Andrew Davis.

Films—**1989:** The Package; Do the Right Thing. **1990:** Opportunity Knocks. **1992:** Folks; Mo' Money; Under Siege. **1993:** Mad Dog & Glory; The Fugitive. **1994:** Jason's Lyric; Richie Rich. **1995:** Losing Isaiah; Steal Big, Steal Little. **1996:** Original Gangstas; Chain Reaction.

LONNIE SMITH

An independent stunt coordinator, Smith is based out of Atlanta, Georgia.

Films—**1981:** The Night the Lights Went Out in Georgia. **1982:** Six Pack. **1984:** Mutant (aka Night Shadows). **1985:** Invasion USA; The Annihilators. **1987:** Funland; Dead Aim. **1988:** Stars & Bars; In a Shallow Grave. **1989:** No Holds Barred; Sleepaway Camp 3. **1990:** Mr. Destiny;

Blood Salvage. **1991:** Livin' Large. **1992:** Freejack; Consenting Adults; Love Crimes; Love Potion #9. **1993:** Robocop 3; The Real McCoy; Boxing Helena; Queen (tv); A Kiss to Die For (tv). **1994:** The Yearling. **1995:** Getting Out. **1996:** Fled.

WILLIAM SMITH
(b. 1933)

Legendary low-budget action star, best known to wider audiences as the evil Falconetti on television's "Rich Man, Poor Man." He had worked on some 50 films as a child and reportedly doubled for former screen Tarzan Lex Barker before devoting his life to becoming a true renaissance man. After time as an Air Force weightlifting champ, Cold War spy, CIA interpreter, linguistic instructor at UCLA, and two-time arm-wrestling champion of the world, the Missouri-born Smith broke into films full-time as a stuntman and MGM contract player. At 6'2" and 210 lbs., he quickly gained popularity as a well-muscled Texas Ranger on the television western "Laredo," later doing many of his own motorcycle stunts in a slew of drive-in favorites that earned him the title "King of the Motorcycle Movies." One of the best fight-men in the business, Smith had many memorable screen battles, most notably opposite David Carradine on television's "Kung Fu," Nick Nolte in *Rich Man,* Clint Eastwood in *Any Which Way You Can,* and Rod Taylor in the incredibly brutal *Darker Than Amber,* for which both men were made honorary members of the Stuntmen's Association.

Top: Actor William Smith often performed his own motorcycle stunts, here in 1973's *Camper John* (aka *Gentle Savage*). *Bottom:* Legendary stuntman/actor William Smith battles Clint Eastwood in 1980's *Any Which Way You Can*, directed by stuntman Buddy Van Horn.

Films—**1951:** Saturday's Hero. **1959:** The Mating Game; Ask Any Girl; Never So Few; The Gazebo; Girls Town. **1960:** The Subterraneans; Cimarron. **1961:** Go Naked in the World; Atlantis, The Lost Continent; The Lawbreakers. **1964:** Mail Order Bride. **1968:** Three Guns for Texas; The Banditos; The Man Hunter (tv). **1969:** Backtrack!; Run, Angel, Run!; The Over the Hill Gang (tv). **1970:** Darker Than Amber; The Losers; Angels Die Hard!; C.C. & Company; Darker Than Amber; Crowhaven Farm (tv). **1971:** Summertree; Chrome & Hot Leather; The Runaway (aka Runaway, Runaway). **1972:** Piranha; Grave of the Vampire; Hammer; The Thing with Two Heads. **1973:** Camper John (aka Gentle Savage) (a/p); A Taste of Hell; The Deadly Trackers; The Last American Hero; Sweet Jesus, Preacher Man; Cleopatra Jones; Invasion of the Bee Girls. **1974:** Black Samson; Policewomen; Tigercage; The Sex Symbol (tv); The Rockford Files (tv). **1975:** Win, Place, or Steal; Boss Nigger; Dr. Minx; Death Among Friends; The Ultimate Warrior; The Swinging Barmaids (aka Eager Beavers). **1976:** Hollywood Man (aka Death Threat) (a/s/p); Rich Man, Poor Man (tv); Scorchy. **1977:** Twilight's Last Gleaming. **1978:** Blood & Guts; Fast Company; Blackjack. **1979:** Seven; The Frisco Kid; The Rebels (tv). **1980:** Any Which Way You Can; Wild Times (tv). **1982:** Conan the Barbarian. **1983:** The Outsiders; Rumble Fish. **1984:** Red Dawn; Toronto Alley; The Jerk, Too (tv). **1985:** The Mean Season; Fever Pitch. **1986:** Eye of the Tiger. **1987:** Red Nights; Commando Squad; Moon in Scorpio; Hell Comes to Frogtown. **1988:** Bulletproof; Hell on the Battleground; Maniac Cop; Evil Altar; Platoon Leader; The Kill Machine (a/d); Emperor of the Bronx. **1989:** Action U.S.A.; Last of the Warriors (aka Empire of Ash 3); Memorial Valley Massacre; B.O.R.N.; Terror in Beverly Hills; Jungle Assault; Forgotten Heroes (aka Covert Action); Spirit of the Eagle; The Badd One; Deadly Breed; Slow Burn; L.A. Vice; East L.A. Warriors; Chance; The Last Battle (tv). **1990:** Instant Karma; Kiss & Be Killed; The Final Sanction; Cartel;

Merchant of Evil. **1991:** Cybernator; Highway Warrior; The Last Riders. **1992:** American Me; Legend of the Roller Blade Seven; Shadow of the Dragon. **1993:** Surf Samuraiis from Atlantis; Hard Time Romance (aka Vaya Con Dios); The Feast; Sunday. **1994:** Maverick; Taken Alive. **1995:** Trailers from the Crypt; Road to Revenge; Big Sister 2000; Raw Energy. **1996:** Neon Signs; Billy Frankenstein; Space Explorers; Judee Strange; Uncle Sam. *Television*—The Ed Wynn Show; The Thin Man; Peter Gunn; Mr. Lucky; The Asphalt Jungle (reg.); Zero One (reg.); Stoney Burke; The Virginian; Combat; The Farmer's Daughter; Kraft Suspense Theatre; Wagon Train; 90 Bristol Court; Broadside; The Alfred Hitchcock Hour; Laredo (reg.); The Guns of Will Sonnett; Legend of Custer; Daniel Boone; The Second Hundred Years; Batman; I Dream of Jeannie; Lassie; Here Come the Brides; Felony Squad; Death Valley Days; Ironside; The Mod Squad; The Most Deadly Game; Mission: Impossible; Julia; Dan August; Longstreet; Bearcats; Columbo; Alias Smith & Jones; Gunsmoke; Search; The Fuzz Brothers; Kung Fu; The Streets of San Francisco; The Six Million Dollar Man; Mannix; The Rockford Files; Planet of the Apes; The Night Stalker; SWAT; Bronk; Movin' On; Barnaby Jones: The Blue Knight; City of Angels; Bert D'Angelo, Superstar; Police Woman; Rich Man, Poor Man Book II (reg.); Logan's Run; Fantasy Island; The Eddie Capra Mysteries; Vegas; Hawaii 5-0 (reg.); CHiPs; Trapper John M.D.; Buck Rogers; Hagen; BJ & the Bear; The Dukes of Hazzard; The Fall Guy; Tales of the Apple Dumpling Gang; Code Red; Matt Houston; Seven Brides for Seven Brothers; The A Team; Knight Rider; Simon & Simon; Benson; Emerald Point N.A.S. (reg.); Masquerade; Riptide; The Master; Scarecrow & Mrs. King; The Yellow Rose; T.J. Hooker; Wildside (reg.); Hunter; Airwolf; The Twilight Zone; Murder She Wrote; Downtown; Houston Knights; O'Hara; Supercarrier; Paradise; Danger Bay; Shades of L.A.; The Young Riders; Vinnie & Bobby; Due South; Walker, Texas Ranger.

JEFF SMOLEK

A member of the Stuntmen's Association, this stunt coordinator and martial arts expert has doubled for Leif Garrett.

Films—**1982:** Megaforce. **1984:** Streets of Fire; City Limits. **1985:** Sunset Strip. **1986:** Blue City. **1987:** Suspect; The Bedroom Window; Dirty Laundry. **1988:** Two Moon Junction; Criminal Act; Party Line. **1989:** Glory; The Burbs; Kill Me Again; The Banker. **1990:** Arachnophobia; Wild at Heart. **1991:** Eve of Destruction; Mobsters; Late for Dinner; Martial Law; The Perfect Bride (tv). **1992:** Memoirs of an Invisible Man; Final Analysis; Twin Peaks: Fire Walk With Me; Sneakers. **1993:** Matinee; Cop & a Half; Rescue Me; Martial Outlaw. **1994:** Monkey Trouble; Silence of the Hams; Cobb; Steel Frontier. **1995:** The Quick & the Dead; Batman Forever; Leaving Las Vegas. *Television*—The Fall Guy.

TONY SNEGOFF

Films—**1985:** Commando. **1987:** Nightmare on Elm Street 3: Dream Warriors. **1988:** Dr. Hackenstein. **1989:** The Karate Kid 3; Time Trackers. **1990:** Secret Agent 00-Soul; The Rain Killer. **1991:** Out for Justice. **1993:** Robocop 3; Martial Outlaw; Cyborg 2. **1994:** Silence of the Hams; Red Sun Rising; Zero Tolerance. **1995:** Batman Forever. **1996:** Skyscraper.

RUSSELL SOLBERG

A member of the Stuntmen's Association, this second unit director and car crash specialist moved into producing and directing.

Films—**1983:** Eddie Macon's Run. **1985:** Runaway Train. **1986:** Never Too Young to Die; Quiet Cool. **1987:** The Night Stalker; Death Before Dishonor; Death Wish 4; Dragnet; Walk Like a Man; Private Road: No Trespassing; Three on a Match (tv); Confessions of a Married Man (tv). **1988:** Die Hard; They Live. **1990:** The Rookie. **1991:** Sleeping with the Enemy; Showdown in Little Tokyo; Payback (d/p). **1992:** Rapid Fire; Far & Away. **1993:** Tombstone; Forced to Kill (d/p); Firepower. **1995:** Separate Lives; Bigfoot. **1996:** Fast Money (p); Raven (d). *Television*—Hunter; Renegade; Silk Stalkings.

JERRY SPICER

An independent stunt coordinator and supporting player, Spicer has doubled regularly for James Spader. His brother Jeff also does stunts.

Films—**1987:** Less Than Zero; Survival Game. **1988:** Jack's Back; License to Drive; Earth Girls Are Easy; Dangerous Love; The Wizard of Speed & Time. **1989:** Under the Gun; Cold Feet. **1990:** Bad Influence; White Palace; Pump Up the Volume; Peacemaker. **1991:** Mobsters; True Colors; Rich Girl; Alligator 2; Liquid Dreams. **1992:** Sunset Grill; Live Wire; Storyville; Betrayal of the Dove; To Protect & Serve; The Double-0 Kid; Guncrazy. **1993:** No Escape, No Return; Eye of the Stranger; Night Eyes 3; Firepower. **1994:** Witchcraft 6; The Naked Gun 33 1/3; Dream Lover; Money to Burn; L.A. Wars. **1995:** Bad Blood; Bigfoot; One Man's Justice; Suspect Device; Blackout. *Television*—Star Trek, Voyager.

ERIK STABENAU

A member of the International Stunt Association, Stabenau has doubled for Johnny Depp.

Films—**1990:** Men at Work; Prayer of the Rollerboys; Hangfire. **1991:** The Taking of Beverly Hills; Mobsters; Hook; Star Trek 6: Undiscovered Country; The Perfect Weapon; Beastmaster 2; Child's Play 3. **1992:** The Lawnmower Man; Article 99; 3 Ninjas. **1993:** Rescue Me; Streetknight; Judgment Night. **1994:** Past Tense; Class of 1999 2; The Crow; Forest Gump; Wagons East; Blown Away; Star Trek Generations; Killing Zoe; Sioux City. **1995:** 3 Ninjas Knuckle Up; Across the Moon; The Indian in the Cupboard; The Prophecy; Things to Do in Denver When You're Dead; Best of the Best **1996:** Dead Man; Phenomenon; Kingpin; Escape from L.A.; The Trigger Effect; Riot; Mercenary; Mars Attacks!; Back to Back; Thinner.

PAUL STADER
(b. 1911; d. 1991)

A former lifeguard and high-diver, Stader doubled for Johnny Weissmuller, John Wayne, Cary Grant, and Gregory Peck. Specializing in water-based stunts, he performed many bits and graduated to coordinating stunts and directing second unit for producer Irwin Allen's large-scale disaster films. He was a member of the Stuntmen's Association.

Films—**1937:** The Hurricane. **1939:** Tarzan Finds a Son. **1941:** Tarzan's Secret Treasure; Gentleman Jim. **1942:** Reap the Wild Wind; Tarzan's New York Adventure. **1943:** Tarzan Triumphs; Tarzan's Desert Mystery. **1945:** Tarzan & the Amazons; Adventure. **1946:** Nocturne; Tarzan & the Leopard Woman; Swamp Fire; Till the End of Time. **1947:** Tarzan & the Huntress. **1948:** Tarzan & the Mermaids; Superman; Abbott & Costello Meet Frankenstein; Wake of the Red Witch. **1949:** Counterpunch. **1950:** Atom Man vs. Superman; Surrender. **1952:** Montana Belle. **1954:** Demetrius & the Gladiators; Jubilee Trail; Creature from the Black Lagoon; The Outlaw's Daughter. **1955:** Hell's Outpost; Prince of Players. **1956:** Moby Dick; Giant; 54 Washington Street; The Boss; One Mask Too Many. **1957:** Ghost Diver; The Monster That Challenged the World; Spoilers of the Forest. **1958:** Revolt in the Big House; Enchanted Island; Satan's Satellites. **1960:** Swiss Family Robinson; Dinosaurus! **1961:** Pirates of Tortuga; Voyage to the Bottom of the Sea. **1962:** Confessions of an Opium Eater. **1963:** Charade. **1965:** Dr. Goldfoot & the Bikini Machine. **1966:** Blindfold; Our Man Flint. **1967:** Tobruk. **1969:** Alfred the Great; Flare-Up. **1970:** Lost Flight. **1971:** The Andromeda Strain; The Seven Minutes. **1972:** The Poseidon Adventure; What's Up, Doc? **1973:** Battle for the Planet of the Apes. **1974:** The Towering Inferno; 99 & 44/100% Dead; Blazing Saddles. **1975:** The Great Waldo Pepper; Lucky Lady. **1976:** Rocky. **1978:** The Swarm; The Amazing Captain Nemo. **1979:** Beyond the Poseidon Adventure. **1982:** The Sword & the Sorcerer. **1983:** The Survivors. **1985:** Doin' Time. **1987:** Million Dollar Mystery. **1988:** Split Decisions; It's Alive 3. **1989:** The Wicked Stepmother. **1990:** Repossessed; Coup De Ville. **1991:** Eve of Destruction. *Television*—Panic; The Lone Ranger; Zane Grey Theatre; Sea Hunt; Wagon Train; The Outer Limits; Voyage to the Bottom of the Sea; Daniel Boone; Lost in Space; Star Trek; Time Tunnel; Planet of the Apes; The Man from Atlantis; Sword of Justice.

PETER STADER

The son of Paul Stader, Peter is a member of both Drivers, Inc. and the Stuntmen's Association.

Films—**1972:** The Poseidon Adventure. **1974:** The Towering Inferno. **1975:** Lucky Lady. **1978:** Movie, Movie. **1979:** Beyond the Poseidon Adventure; Concorde, Airport '79. **1980:** Alligator; The Blues Brothers. **1981:** Bustin' Loose; Goliath

Awaits (tv). **1982:** Megaforce; The Sword & the Sorcerer; Zapped. **1983:** Scarface. **1984:** Firestarter; The Vindicator. **1985:** Avenging Angel; D.A.R.Y.L. **1986:** Raw Deal; Invaders from Mars; No Mercy. **1987:** The Night Stalker; Traxx; Best Seller; Blind Date; Date with an Angel; The Bedroom Window; Surrender. **1988:** Mississippi Burning. **1989:** Pet Sematary; CHUD 2. **1990:** Loose Cannons; Almost an Angel; Come See the Paradise; Megaville. **1992:** Deep Cover; Martial Law 2: Undercover. **1994:** Midnight Ride; Zero Tolerance. **1995:** Separate Lives; A Walk in the Clouds. **1996:** A Very Brady Sequel. *Television*—Magnum P.I.

ELLEN STATHAM

Films—**1990:** Streets. **1991:** Dance with Death; Ultraviolet; The Unborn. **1992:** Betrayal of the Dove; The Terror Within 2; Stepmonster; To Sleep with a Vampire. **1993:** Sexual Response; Dangerous Touch; Carnosaur; No Escape, No Return; Acting on Impulse. **1994:** Guardian Angel; Red Sun Rising; Steel Frontier; Carnosaur 2. **1995:** Excessive Force 2; Unknown Origin; Suspect Device; Black Scorpion.

PATRICK STATHAM

This stunt coordinator works primarily for Roger Corman's low-budget outfit Concorde Films, often with his wife Ellen.

Films—**1987:** Hour of the Assassin; Steele Justice; Killer Workout; Summer Camp Nightmare. **1988:** Border Heat; Angel 3; Not of this Earth; Vibes; Nightfall; The Drifter. **1989:** Masque of the Red Death; Brain Dead; The Terror Within;

Ministry of Vengeance; Stripped to Kill. **1990:** Demonstone; Watchers 2; Trancers 2; Hollywood Boulevard 2; Streets; Naked Obsession; The Rain Killer; Slumber Party Massacre 3; Syngenor. **1991:** Ultraviolet; The Unborn; Dance with Death; Guilty as Charged; Double Trouble; Dead Space; Poison Ivy. **1992:** Betrayal of the Dove; The Terror Within 2; Stepmonster; Night Eyes 2; To Sleep with a Vampire; The Unnameable; Sins of Desire; Munchie; Final Judgment. **1993:** No Escape, No Return; Carnosaur; Cybertracker; Fire Power; Cyborg 2; Martial Outlaw; Acting on Impulse. **1994:** Bloodfist 5: Human Target; Guardian Angel; Outside the Law; The Force; Steel Frontier; Red Sun Rising; Hologram Man; Deadly Target; New Crime City; Scanners: The Showdown; Witch Hunt; The Fighter (aka Savate); Bad Blood; Bloodfist 6: Ground Zero; Carnosaur 2; Ripper Man. **1995:** Frank & Jesse; The Spy Within; Soldier Boyz; To the Limit; Unknown Origin; Cyber Bandits; Outside the Law; One Night Stand; Dillinger & Capone; The Immortals; One Man's Justice; Suspect Device; Black Scorpion; Blackout; The Silencers; The Sweeper. **1996:** Skyscraper; Piranha; Dark Breed; The Trigger Effect; Fast Money; Forest Warrior; Carnosaur 3.

TOM STEELE
(b. 1909; d. 1990)

Veteran Scotland-born supporting player and versatile stunt legend, best known for being *The Masked Marvel* in thirties serials. Steele also doubled such stars as Rod Cameron and Clayton Moore.

Films—**1932:** The Red Rider. **1935:** Captain Blood. **1936:** Charge of the Light Brigade; Flash Gordon; Spaceship to the Unknown; The Glory Trail; Nobody's Fool. **1937:** Riders of the Whistling Skull; Westbound Limited. **1938:** Call the Mesquiteers; Nurse from Brooklyn; Renegade

Ranger; Flash Gordon's Trip to Mars; The Deadly Ray from Mars; Red Barry. **1939:** Gunga Din; I Stole a Million; In Old Monterey; Missing Daughters. **1939:** Destination Saturn. **1940:** Flash Gordon Conquers the Universe; Purple Death from Outer Space; Santa Fe Trail. **1941:** Citizen Kane; South of Tahiti; King of the Texas Rangers; Cyclone on Horseback; The Mysterious Dr. Satan. **1942:** Outlaws of Pine Ridge; Raiders of the Range; The Perils of Nyoka; Texas to Bataan. **1943:** Lone Star Trail; Captain America; Carson City Cyclone; Daredevils of the West; Beyond the Last Frontier; Overland Mail Robbery; Wagon Tracks West; King of the Mounties. **1944:** Cheyenne Wildcat; Song of Nevada; Firebrands of Arizona; Wyoming Hurricane; Code of the Prairie; Hidden Valley Outlaws; Marshal of Reno; Mojave Firebrand; San Antonio Kid; Beneath Western Skies; The Tiger Woman; Silver City Kid; Tuscon Raiders; Zorro's Black Whip. **1945:** God Is My Co-Pilot; Lone Texas Ranger; Trail of Kit Carson; Phantom of the Plains; Federal Operator 99; Manhunt of Mystery Island; The Purple Monster Strikes. **1946:** The Phantom Rider; Stagecoach to Denver; King of the Forest Rangers; The Crimson Ghost; Alias Billy the Kid. **1947:** Son of Zorro; Brute Force; Vigilantes of Boom Town; Jesse James Rides Again. **1948:** The Adventures of Frank & Jesse James; The Denver Kid. **1949:** Outcasts of the Trail; King of the Rocket Men; Federal Agents vs. Underworld Inc.; Ghost of Zorro. **1950:** The James Brothers of Missouri; The Milkman; Desperadoes of the West; Gunmen of Abilene; Trigger, Jr.; Salt Lake Raiders; Invisible Monster. **1951:** Government Agents vs. the Phantom Legion; Lost Planet Airmen; Don Daredevil Rides Again; The Thing; Secrets of Monte Carlo; Silver City Bonanza; Flying Disc Men from Mars. **1952:** Rose of Cimarron; Montana Belle; Jungle Drums of Africa; Radar Men from the Moon. **1953:** Six Gun Decision; Robin Hood of Darkest Africa; Trader Tom of the China Seas. **1954:** Man with the Steel Whip; Cattle Queen of Montana. **1955:** The Prodigal; King of the

Carnival. **1956:** Tension at Table Rock; Showdown at Abilene; Kelly and Me; The Search; Justice of the West. **1957:** The Restless Breed. **1958:** Satan's Satellites. **1959:** These Thousand Hills. **1960:** Spartacus. **1961:** The Great Impostor. **1962:** The Spiral Road. **1963:** McLintock. **1964:** Taggart. **1965:** Cat Ballou; The Great Race. **1966:** Harper; The Silencers. **1967:** Welcome to Hard Times; The Gnomemobile. **1968:** Bullit. **1969:** The Love Bug. **1971:** Slaughterhouse Five; Diamonds Are Forever. **1974:** Freebie & the Bean; The Towering Inferno; The Front Page; Blazing Saddles; Earthquake. **1980:** The Blues Brothers. **1983:** Scarface. **1984:** Lovelines; Last of the Great Survivors (tv). **1986:** Tough Guys. *Television*—The Lone Ranger; Have Gun, Will Travel; The Westerner; Laramie; Iron Horse; Mission: Impossible.

MARK STEFANICH

This Independent stunt coordinator has doubled regularly for Jean-Claude Van Damme.

Films—**1990:** Navy Seals. **1991:** The Taking of Beverly Hills; Nothing But Trouble; Double Impact; Alligator 2. **1992:** Universal Soldier; Under Siege; Hoffa; Dead Center (aka Crazy Joe). **1993:** Hard Target; Calendar Girl; The Good Son. **1994:** Timecop. **1996:** The Quest; Maximum Risk; Mars Attacks!

RON STEIN

A member of Stunts Unlimited, Stein has worked as a stunt coordinator, second unit director, and boxing choreographer.

Films—**1970:** There Was a Crooked Man; M*A*S*H. **1974:** Hang Up (aka Super

Dude). **1976:** Nickelodeon; Charlie's Angels (tv). **1977:** The Hills Have Eyes. **1981:** Body Heat; Caveman; Cheech & Chong's Nice Dreams; True Confessions. **1982:** Lookin' to Get Out; Rocky 3. **1983:** The Sting 2; D.C. Cab; Scarface. **1984:** Star Trek 3: The Search for Spock; The Jerk, Too (tv). **1986:** Power. **1987:** The Wild Pair. **1988:** Action Jackson. **1989:** Wired; Road House; Dead Bang. **1990:** Heart Condition; Predator 2. **1992:** Death Becomes Her. **1993:** The Last Action Hero. **1994:** The Shadow; True Lies; Puppetmasters. **1996:** Executive Decision; Courage Under Fire. *Television*—Voyage to the Bottom of the Sea; The FBI; Night Gallery; The Night Stalker; Planet of the Apes; SWAT; Charlie's Angels; Airwolf (d); Jake & the Fatman (d); Downtown (d); Crime Story.

GAR STEPHEN

A Florida-based stunt player, Stephen is married to stuntwoman Amy Wilder.

Films—**1983:** Halloween 3. **1990:** Narrow Margin; Edward Scissorhands. **1991:** Point Break; Cape Fear; Problem Child 2. **1993:** Wilder Napalm; Cop & a Half; Passenger 57. **1994:** The Getaway; The Specialist. **1995:** Bad Boys; Fair Game. **1996:** Heaven's Prisoners; The Substitute. *Television*—Quantum Leap.

JIM STEPHEN

Stephen is a member of both the Stuntmen's Association and the Professional Driver's Association.

Films—**1987:** The Monster Squad. **1988:** Colors. **1991:** Eve of Destruction; Stone Cold; Hook; Timebomb; Driving Me Crazy; Shakes the Clown. **1992:** Adventures in Dinosaur City; The Double-0 Kid; CIA: Code Name Alexa; Alien Intruder.

1993: Boiling Point; The Last Action Hero; Kalifornia. **1994:** Surviving the Game; The Mask; Deadly Target; Relentless 4. **1995:** Demon Knight; Mighty Morphin Power Rangers; Digital Man; Excessive Force **1996:** The Great White Hype; Skyscraper; The Crow: City of Angels; Mars Attacks!

ALEX STEVENS
(b. 1936)

A supporting player best known for participating in *The French Connection*'s famous chase scene, Stevens is a member of the East Coast Stuntman's Association.

Films—**1968:** A Lovely Way to Die; Lady in Cement. **1969:** The Groove Tube. **1970:** House of Dark Shadows. **1971:** The Projectionist; The French Connection; Night of Dark Shadows. **1972:** Lady Liberty; Shaft's Big Score. **1973:** Silent Night, Bloody Night; Shamus. **1974:** Claudine; The Gravy Train (aka Dion Brothers). **1975:** Aaron Loves Angela. **1976:** Demon (aka God Told Me To). **1978:** The Eyes of Laura Mars; Superman. **1980:** Gloria. **1981:** Times Square. **1982:** Vigilante; I, the Jury; A Little Sex. **1984:** Alphabet City; The Exterminator 2; The Pope of Greenwich Village; Splash. **1985:** Grace Quigley; Code of Silence; Invasion USA. **1987:** Allan Quartermain & the Lost City of Gold; *batteries not included; The Hidden; China Girl. **1989:** Black Rain; True Blood. **1990:** King of New York; Good Fellas; Street Hunter. **1995:** Kiss of Death. *Television*—Dark Shadows.

WARREN STEVENS
(b. 1948)

A Brooklyn-born stunt coordinator and low-budget film director, Stevens was a former rodeo performer and U.S. Marine. He has doubled for Robert Duvall.

Films—1974: The Towering Inferno. 1979: Beyond the Poseidon Adventure. 1982: Death Valley. 1983: Stroker Ace. 1988: Mr. North. 1989: Second Sight; Fat Man & Little Boy. 1990: Lambada; Blood Games; Twisted Justice; Dragonfight (d); Highway Warrior (d). 1991: Alligator 2. 1992: Mom & Dad Save the World. 1993: Cybertracker; Firepower; No Escape, No Return. 1994: Ice; Leprechaun 2; Guardian Angel; Steel Frontier; The Fighter (aka Savate). 1995: Frank & Jesse; Bad Blood; The Scarlett Letter. *Television*—The Six Million Dollar Man; St. Elsewhere; Spenser for Hire.

JOHN STEWART

This stunt coordinator and director has worked primarily on low-budget fare, often staging elaborate car crashes for director Fred Olen Ray.

Films—1984: Surf 2; Savage Dawn. 1985: The Tomb; Star Slammer. 1986: Armed Response; Billy Galvin; Wired to Kill; Neon Maniacs. 1987: Cyclone; Cold Steel; Deadly Intent; Zombie High; Commando Squad; Deep Space; Open House; Stripped to Kill; Death Spa; Munchies; Creepozoids; The Hidden. 1988: Terminal Entry; Slaughterhouse Rock; Nightmare at Noon; Outlaw Force; Assault of the Killer Bimbos; Take Two; The Invisible Kid; Night of the Demons. 1989: Survival Quest; Lady Avenger; Warlords; Girlfriend from Hell; 976 Evil; Down the Drain; Action USA; Cartel (d); B.O.R.N.; Ghettoblaster. 1990: Thunder & Lightning (d). 1991: Prime Target. 1992: Click: The Calendar Girl Killer (d). 1993: Hidden Obsession (d); Time Wars. 1994: The Stoned Age; Merlin; Blindfold; Deadly Target. 1995: Evolver.

MIKE STONE
(b. 1943)

Hawaiian martial arts champ remains infamously known as the man that Priscilla Presley left Elvis for. Stone doubled Dean Martin in his first assignment and has worked sporadically in Hollywood circles as a fight coordinator ever since. He had a bonified starring role in *Tiger Shark*.

Films—1969: The Wrecking Crew. 1973: That Man Bolt. 1981: Enter the Ninja. 1982: Raw Force. 1986: American Ninja. 1987: Tiger Shark; American Ninja 2; Kick or Die. 1988: White Ghost. 1991: Highlander 2; Suburban Commando. 1992: Martial Law 2: Undercover. 1993: No Place to Hide; No Escape, No Return. 1996: Eraser.

FRED STROMSOE

A veteran supporting player and stunt performer, predominantly active during the fifties and sixties, Stromsoe is best known as Officer Woods on television's "Adam-12."

Films—1955: The McConnell Story; The Sea Chase. 1956: The Mole People; The Girl He Left Behind; Miracle in the Rain. 1958: No Time for Sergeants; The Perfect Furlough; The Deep Six. 1959: Westbound; The Young Philadelphians. 1965: Dr. Goldfoot & the Bikini Machine. 1967: The Karate Killers. 1969: The Love Bug; The Wrecking Crew; The Good Guys & the Bad Guys; The Pigeon (tv). 1971: Dirty Harry. 1972: What's Up, Doc? 1973: The Don Is Dead; Cleopatra Jones; Charley Varrick. 1974: The Last of Shelia; The Thief Who Came to Dinner; Blazing Saddles. 1975: Blood Voyage. 1978:

Pearl (tv). **1979:** Crisis in Mid-Air (tv). *Television*—The Outer Limits; Voyage to the Bottom of the Sea; The Fugitive; The Man from U.N.C.L.E.; The Wild Wild West; Gunsmoke; Adam-12 (reg.); Dallas (reg.).

JERRY SUMMERS
(b. 1931)

A lifetime member of the Stuntmen's Association, Summers has worked as a supporting actor and second unit director. At one time, he held the record for performing the highest-paid stunt in film history for the film *Darling Lili*. A vehicular expert, he was behind the wheel during the classic car chases in both *The French Connection* and *The Seven-Ups*.

Films—**1957:** The Young Rebels; The Brothers Rico. **1959:** Lone Texan. **1960:** Spartacus. **1961:** The Little Shepard of Kingdom Come; The Purple Hills; Love in a Goldfish Bowl. **1962:** The Firebrand. **1963:** The Young Swingers; Your Cheatin' Heat. **1964:** Law of the Lawless. **1965:** Surf Party; Young Fury; Dr. Goldfoot & the Bikini Machine. **1966:** Harper; Scalplock. **1967:** First to Fight; The Karate Killers. **1968:** The Green Berets; Coogan's Bluff. **1969:** Che; The Great Bank Robbery. **1970:** Darling Lili; The Phynx; Flap. **1971:** The French Connection. **1972:** The Great Northfield Minnesota Raid; Hickey & Boggs; What's Up, Doc? **1973:** Dillinger; The Seven-Ups; Magnum Force; Cleopatra Jones; Charley Varrick. **1974:** The Front Page; The Thief Who Came to Dinner; 99 & 44/100% Dead; Blazing Saddles; Dirty Mary, Crazy Larry; Airport '75. **1975:** Rooster Cogburn. **1978:** Avalanche. **1979:** The Lady in Red. **1980:** The Man with Bogart's Face; In God We Trust. **1981:** Charlie Chan & the Curse of

the Dragon Queen. **1982:** Night Warning; Six Pack; Knight Rider (tv). **1983:** Eddie Macon's Run; Heart Like a Wheel. **1985:** D.A.R.Y.L. **1987:** The Monster Squad; Throw Momma from the Train. **1988:** Midnight Run; Alien Nation; Colors; License to Drive. **1989:** Hit List; Relentless; Chances Are; Backtrack; One Man Force. **1990:** The Gumshoe Kid. **1991:** Mobsters. **1992:** Out on a Limb. **1993:** Forced to Kill. **1995:** Separate Lives. *Television*—Have Gun, Will Travel; The Tales of Wells Fargo; The Beachcomber (reg.); Laramie; The Virginian; Gunsmoke; The Man from U.N.C.L.E.; Star Trek; Mission: Impossible; I Spy; It Takes a Thief; The Wild Wild West; The High Chaparral; The FBI; The Mod Squad; Silent Force; Night Gallery; Roll Out (reg.); Barnaby Jones; Emergency; The Manhunter; The Rockford Files; Police Woman; The Dukes of Hazzard; Knight Rider.

NEIL SUMMERS

Lean Arizona-raised supporting player, predominantly active in the Western genre. A member of the Stuntmen's Association, he was featured as one of the comic book characters in *Dick Tracy*.

Films—**1965:** Arizona Raiders. **1966:** Duel at Diablo. **1971:** A Time for Dying. **1972:** The Life & Times of Judge Roy Bean. **1973:** My Name Is Nobody; Guns of a Stranger. **1975:** Adios Amigo; White Line Fever. **1976:** Hawmps. **1977:** Mr. Billion. **1978:** Good Time Outlaws. **1980:** The Gambler (tv). **1981:** Going Ape. **1982:** Zapped; Rascals & Robbers (tv). **1983:** Get Crazy. **1984:** Lovelines. **1986:** Raw Deal; Eye of the Tiger. **1987:** Wanted: Dead or Alive; The Monster Squad; Blind Date; Robocop. **1988:** Jack's Back; Sunset; Midnight Run; Young Guns; License to Drive; Dangerous Love; The Tracker. **1989:** Under the Gun; Glory. **1990:** Dick Tracy; Peacemaker; Wild at Heart. **1991:**

Eve of Destruction; Mobsters; The Naked Gun 2 1/2. **1992:** Out on a Limb; Live Wire; Chaplin. **1993:** Posse; CB4. **1994:** The Naked Gun 33 1/3; Bad Girls; The Shawshank Redemption. **1995:** Bigfoot. **1996:** Mars Attacks! *Television*—Gunsmoke; Petrocelli; The Fall Guy; "V."

GARY TACON

Originating on the East Coast, Tacon is now the regular stunt double for Alec Baldwin.

Films—**1984:** Alphabet City; The Muppets Take Manhattan. **1985:** Remo Williams. **1986:** Legal Eagles; Popeye Doyle (tv). **1987:** Who's That Girl?; My Demon Lover; China Girl; Morgan Stewart's Coming Home. **1988:** Shakedown. **1989:** Heart of Dixie; See No Evil, Hear No Evil. **1990:** Loose Cannons; Blue Steel; Miller's Crossing; Awakenings; Street Hunter. **1991:** Toy Soldiers; McBain. **1993:** Bound by Honor. **1994:** The Getaway; The Shadow. **1996:** The Juror; Heaven's Prisoners; Striptease.

PATRICIA TALLMAN

(b. 1957)

This Illinois-born actress, who once sang with the Pittsburgh Civic Light Opera, made her film debut in George Romero's *Knightriders* and got into stunts while working as a soap actress in New York. Moving to the West Coast, she landed the role of Red Sonja on the Universal Studio Tour before Romero cast her as the lead in his remake of *Night of the Living Dead.* Regular work on sci-fi television shows and prominent exposure

doubling for Laura Dern in *Jurassic Park* helped solidify her cult rep.

Films—**1981:** Knightriders. **1983:** Stuck on You. **1988:** Creepshow 2; Monkey Shines; Last Rites; Shakedown. **1989:** Road House; Shocker; After Midnight. **1990:** Peacemaker; Another 48 HRS.; Night of the Living Dead. **1991:** Deadlock. **1992:** Sweet Justice; The Runestone; Me & Veronica; Lake Consequence. **1993:** Benefit of the Doubt; Attack of the 50 Foot Woman; The Naked Gun 33 1/3. **1994:** Speed; The Flintstones; Ice; Ring of the Musketeers; Criminal Passion; Star Trek Generations; Cobb; CIA 2: Target Alexa; Direct Hit. **1996:** Larger Than Life. *Television*—The Guiding Light (reg.); One Life to Live (reg.); Generations (reg.); Tales from the Darkside; Hard Time on Planet Earth; Star Trek, the Next Generation; The Flash; Red Shoe Diaries; Deep Space Nine; Babylon 5 (reg.); Brisco County, Jr.

CHUCK TAMBURRO

Though he has done bits and general stunt work, Tamburro has emerged as one of the premiere helicopter pilots working in film. He's a member of Stunts Unlimited.

Films—**1975:** Mitchell. **1976:** Gator; Two Minute Warning; Nickelodeon. **1977:** Foes; Stunts; New York, New York. **1978:** Gray Lady Down; Convoy; Avalanche; Hooper. **1979:** The Ultimate Impostor (tv); Beach Patrol (tv). **1980:** Steel; Smokey & the Bandit 2; Stunts Unlimited (tv). **1981:** King of the Mountain; Cheech & Chong's Nice Dreams; Margin for Murder (tv). **1982:** Blade Runner; First Blood; Masserati & the Brain (tv). **1983:** Something Wicked This Way Comes; Scarface. **1984:** Birdie. **1985:** A View to a Kill. **1986:** Police Academy 3: Back in Training. **1987:** Code Name Zebra. **1988:** Ac-

Actress/stuntwoman Patricia Tallman starred in the 1990 remake of *Night of the Living Dead*, action coordinated by Phil Neilson.

tion Jackson; Die Hard. **1989:** Riding the Edge; Cage; Backtrack. **1990:** The Guardian; The Adventures of Ford Fairlane; Predator 2. **1991:** Stone Cold; Ricochet; Terminator 2; The Chase (tv). **1992:** White Sands; Man Trouble. **1993:** Hot Shots Part Deux; The Last Action Hero; Father Hood. **1994:** Gunmen; The Chase; True Lies. **1995:** Just Cause; Outbreak; Seven; Heat. **1996:** Sgt. Bilko; The Arrival; The Rock; Spy Hard; The Long Kiss Goodnight. *Television*—Vegas; Airwolf.

MIKE TAMBURRO
(b. 1965; d. 1996)

The son of Chuck Tamburro, Mike worked primarily as a helicopter pilot, often in tandem with his dad. He died in a chopper crash while shooting a television commercial.

Films—**1988:** Action Jackson; Die Hard. **1989:** Road House; Backtrack. **1990:** Pump Up the Volume; Die Hard 2; The Adventures of Ford Fairlane. **1991:** Stone Cold; The Last Boy Scout; Timebomb. **1992:** Rampage; Man Trouble. **1993:** Hot Shots Part Deux; Fearless. **1994:** Body Snatchers; Speed. **1995:** Outbreak; Virtuosity; The Immortals. **1996:** Sgt. Bilko; Barb Wire; The Rock; Dark Breed; The Glimmer Man.

CHERIE TASH

Films—**1985:** Rainy Day Friends (aka L.A. Bad). **1987:** Shy People; Death Spa; Hell Comes to Frogtown. **1988:** Colors; Tapeheads; Out of the Dark; Viper; In Dangerous Company. **1989:** Honey, I Shrunk the Kids; Nightmare on Elm Street 5: Dream Child; Blind Fury; Kill Me Again. **1990:** Total Recall; Problem Child; Blood Games; In the Cold of the Night. **1991:** Bride of Re-Animator. **1993:** The Beverly Hillbillies; Dead Connection. **1994:** City Slickers 2; Killing Zoe.

KEITH TELLEZ

This independent stunt coordinator has doubled for both Dustin Hoffman and Harvey Keitel.

Films—**1983:** Scarface. **1985:** To Live & Die in L.A.; Iron Eagle. **1987:** Lethal Weapon; World Gone Wild; Ernest Goes to Camp. **1988:** Bulletproof. **1989:** Dead Bang; After Midnight. **1990:** The Hunt for Red October; The Borrower; Another 48 HRS.; The Adventures of Ford Fairlane; Dollman. **1991:** Lionheart; Barton Fink; Hook; Diplomatic Immunity. **1992:** Article 99; Hero. **1993:** Point of No Return; Blindside. **1994:** Blue Tiger; I Love Trouble; Dropzone; Stargate; Dead Badge. **1995:** Demon Knight; Outbreak; Money Train. **1996:** The Crow: City of Angels; Escape from L.A. *Television*—Hard Time on Planet Earth; Weird Science.

BOB TERHUNE

A member of the Stuntmen's Association, Terhune has worked as a supporting player, horse wrangler, and double for George Kennedy. He's the son of thirties Western star Max Terhune.

Films—**1959:** Rio Bravo. **1960:** Seven Ways from Sundown. **1966:** Smoky. **1967:** The King's Pirate; Welcome to Hard Times. **1968:** The Pink Jungle. **1969:** The Good Guys & the Bad Guys. **1972:** Conquest of the Planet of the Apes. **1973:** High Plains Drifter; Cahil, U.S. Marshal; Battle for the Planet of the Apes. **1974:** The Towering Inferno; Earthquake. **1976:** St. Ives; Moving Violations. **1977:** Which Way Is Up? **1978:** FM; F.I.S.T. **1979:** The Villain; The Frisco Kid; The Prophecy; Concorde, Airport '79. **1980:** Melvin & Howard; The Blues Brothers; Oh, God! Book II; Wholly Moses; The Mountain Men. **1981:** Going Ape. **1982:** Conan the Barbarian; My Favorite Year; The Beastmaster; Six Pack. **1983:** Loose Joints; Get Crazy; The Gambler 2 (tv). **1984:** The River Rat; City Heat; Dreamscape. **1985:** Silverado; Runaway Train; Avenging Angel. **1986:** Odd Jobs. **1987:** Near Dark. **1988:** Rambo 3; Demonwarp; Two Moon Junction; Red River (tv). **1989:** Old Gringo. **1990:** Pump Up the Volume; Peacemaker; Downtown; Grim Prairie Tales; Love at Large; Wild at Heart. **1991:** Delirious; Suburban Commando. **1992:** Hoffa; Four Eyes & Six Guns. **1994:** Dumb & Dumber. **1996:** Ravenhawk. *Television*—The Texan; Search; The Six Million Dollar Man; Vegas; The Fall Guy; Daniel Boone.

ROBERT TESSIER

(b 1934; d. 1990)

Immensely popular supporting player, best known as the grinning, shaven-pated convict with all the tattoos in *The Longest Yard*. A Massachusetts-born Algonquin Indian, Tessier won a Purple Heart and a Silver Star as a paratrooper in the Korean War, later studying law enforcement and opening a gym. Having dabbled as a stunt cyclist in the circus, Tessier began working on biker films as a stunt coordinator and second unit director. A founding member of Stunts Unlimited, he had great fight scenes in both *Hard Times* and *The Deep*. Tessier died of cancer.

Films—**1967:** Born Losers; The Glory Stompers; The Girl from Thunder Strip. **1969:** Run, Angel, Run!; The Babysitter; Five the Hard Way (aka The Sidehackers). **1970:** Little Big Man; Cry Blood, Apache; Outlaw Riders. **1971:** The Hard Ride; The Velvet Vampire; The Jesus Trip. **1973:** How Come Nobody's on Our Side?;

Stuntman/character actor Robert Tessier (right) battles Charles Bronson in 1975's
Hard Times, **action coordinated by Max Kleven.**

Camper John (aka Gentle Savage). **1974:** The Longest Yard. **1975:** Doc Savage, The Man of Bronze; Hard Times. **1976:** Breakheart Pass. **1977:** Another Man, Another Chance; the Deep; Last of the Mohicans (tv). **1978:** Hooper; Desperate Women (tv). **1977:** Centennial (tv). **1979:** Starcrash; The Villain; The Billion Dollar Threat (tv). **1980:** Steel. **1981:** The Cannonball Run. **1982:** The Sword & the Sorcerer; Double Exposure. **1983:** The Lost Empire. **1984:** The Fix. **1985:** Avenging Angel. **1987:** No Safe Haven. **1989:** Fists of Steel; One Man Force; Triangle of Terror; Nightwish; Future Force; Beverly Hills Brats; The Blower. *Television*—Cannon; Kung Fu; Little House on the Prairie; Charlie's Angels; Starsky & Hutch; Buck Rogers; Hart to Hart; The Dukes of Hazzard; The Incredible Hulk; Vegas; The Stockers; Fantasy Island; The Fall Guy; CHiPs; Silver Spoons; The A Team; Sawyer & Finn; Manimal; The Rousters; The Master; The Yellow Rose; Magnum P.I.; Spenser for Hire; Amazing Stories; Sledgehammer; B.L. Stryker.

SVEN OLE THORSEN

Bearded, instantly recognizable supporting player has been displayed prominently in virtually all of his pal Arnold Schwarzenegger's action films. Thorsen was a former powerlifter and karate champ in his native Denmark.

Films—1982: Conan the Barbarian. 1984: Conan the Destroyer. 1986: Raw Deal. 1987: The Running Man; Lethal Weapon. 1988: Red Heat; Twins. 1989: Pink Cadillac; Ghostbusters 2. 1990: The Hunt for Red October. 1991: Harley Davidson & the Marlboro Man; Relentless 2: Dead On; Abraxas. 1992: Lethal Weapon 3; Nemesis; Bram Stoker's Dracula. 1993: Cyborg 2; Dragon; The Last Action Hero; Hard Target; Nowhere to Run. 1994: On Deadly Ground; A Low Down Dirty Shame. 1995: The Quick & the Dead; The Dangerous; Mallrats. 1996: Eraser; Bulletproof; Jingle All the Way. *Television*—Captain Power (reg.); The Flash.

SAMMY THURMAN

One-time president of the Girls Rodeo Association, Thurman was a world champion barrel racer before

Sven Ole Thorsen (right) battles Arnold Schwarzenegger in 1982's *Conan the Barbarian*, action coordinated by Terry Leonard.

entering films, most notably as a victim in the classic *In Cold Blood.* A member of the United Stuntwoman's Association, she has doubled for Jane Fonda, Kathy Bates, and Rosie O'Donnell.

Films—**1967:** In Cold Blood. **1978:** Comes a Horseman; Hooper; The Blues Brothers; Dudes. **1988:** Critters 2. **1989:** Nat'l Lampoon's Christmas Vacation. **1990:** Peacemaker; Young Guns 2; Misery. **1991:** K-9000 (tv). **1993:** Another Stakeout. **1995:** Dolores Claiborne. **1996:** Diabolique.

MIKE TILLMAN

Films—**1974:** The Front Page. **1975:** Shell Game (tv). **1979:** H.O.T.S. **1980:** Seems Like Old Times; Any Which Way You Can. **1981:** Hard Country. **1982:** Megaforce; Cat People; Pink Motel; The Sword & the Sorcerer; Wacko. **1983:** Max Dugan Returns; Joysticks; Hysterical. **1984:** Bachelor Party; Ninja 3: The Domination. **1985:** D.A.R.Y.L. **1986:** Blue City; Cobra; Jumpin' Jack Flash. **1987:** Death Wish 4; Assassination; Throw Momma from the Train; Like Father, Like Son; Remote Control; Planes, Trains, & Automobiles; Laguna Heat. **1988:** Colors; Freeway; License to Drive. **1989:** Hit List; One Man Force; Night Life; Crack House. **1990:** The Gumshoe Kid; The First Power; Almost an Angel. **1991:** Eve of Destruction; The Taking of Beverly Hills.

R.L. TOLBERT

A lean supporting player, second unit director, and member of the Stuntmen's Association, Tolbert is an expert horseman and Western specialist. He has doubled regularly for Sam Elliot.

Films—**1979:** Buck Rogers in the 25th Century; Legend of the Golden Gun (tv); The Sacketts (tv). **1980:** Heaven's Gate; Wild Times (tv). **1981:** The Legend of the Lone Ranger. **1985:** Silverado; Pale Rider. **1986:** The Three Amigos. **1987:** Fatal Beauty; Angel Heart; The Quick & the Dead. **1988:** Lucky Stiff; Bail Out. **1989:** Bonanza: The Next Generation (tv); Three Fugitives; Road House; Back to the Future 2; Glory; Next of Kin. **1990:** Back to the Future 3; Eternity; The Rookie. **1991:** Conagher (tv). **1992:** Far & Away. **1993:** Amos & Andrew; Posse; Gettysburg; Judgment Night. **1995:** Dracula, Dead & Loving It. **1996:** Chain Reaction; Fast Money.

JOSEPH ANTHONY TORNATORE
(b. 1936)

Familiar seventies character player, most often seen in mafioso fare, Tornatore got his start as a stuntman and coordinator. He later turned to writing, producing and directing low-budget action films.

Films—**1967:** The Venetian Affair. **1968:** Planet of the Apes. **1969:** The Gay Deceivers. **1970:** Machismo: 40 Graves for 40 Guns. **1971:** The Scavengers; Sweet Sweetback's Badass Song. **1972:** Top of the Heap. **1973:** The Stone Killers; Cleopatra Jones; Sweet Jesus, Preacher Man; The Sting. **1974:** Black Samson; McQ; The Gravy Train (aka The Dion Brothers). **1975:** Trained to Kill, USA; The Fortune. **1976:** Trackdown; The Gumball Rally. **1977:** Zebra Force (d/s/p). **1978:** F.I.S.T. **1979:** The Champ; Marciano (tv). **1980:** Angel on My Shoulder (tv). **1981:** The Gangster Chronicles (tv). **1984:** Chattanooga Choo Choo. **1985:** Into the Night. **1986:** Free Ride; Hollywood Vice Squad; Big Trouble in Little China. **1987:** Code

Name Zebra (d/s/p); Night Force (p). **1988:** Bulletproof; Grotesque (a/d/s/p); Bail Out; Screwball Hotel (e). **1989:** Curse of the Crystal Eye (d/p); Man Against the Mob: The Chinatown Murders (tv). **1993:** Demon Keeper (d/p/e). **1996:** The Third Force (d). *Television*—The FBI; Mission: Impossible; The Mod Squad; Ironside; Planet of the Apes; The Rockford Files; Cannon; M*A*S*H; Hill Street Blues; The Fall Guy.

RUSSELL TOWERY

A Texas-based stunt coordinator and double for Peter Weller, Towery has the distinction of doing stunts for the title character in all three of the *Robocop* films. His wife Diane also performs stunts.

Films—**1983:** Tender Mercies. **1987:** Robocop. **1988:** Johnny Be Goode. **1989:** Cohen & Tate; Pow Wow Highway. **1990:** Flashback; Robocop 2; Marked for Death; Rainbow Drive. **1992:** Ruby; Delta Heat. **1993:** Robocop 3; Hexed; Trouble Bound. **1994:** Love and a .45; The Chase. **1995:** Curse of the Starving Class; The Stars Fell on Henrietta; Leaving Las Vegas. **1996:** Bottle Rocket; Public Enemies; Foxfire; The Evening Star.

TIM TRELLA

An independent stunt coordinator, Trella has doubled regularly for Woody Harrelson.

Films—**1988:** Bad Dreams. **1989:** Transylvania Twist; Shocker ; Night Life; One Man Force; Relentless; From the Dead of Night (tv). **1990:** Peacemaker; Trancers 2; Darkman; Maniac Cop 2; Syngenor; Doll-man; Demon Wind; The Last Hour; The Ambulance; Puppetmaster 3; The Rain Killer. **1991:** Eve of Destruction; V.I. Warshawski; 976 Evil 2; Alligator 2; Mom; The Guyver; Blood & Concrete; Shakes the Clown. **1992:** Last of the Mohicans; Lethal Weapon 3; The Runestone; Mom & Dad Save the World; Poison Ivy; Adventures in Dinosaur City. **1993:** Maniac Cop 3. **1994:** The Cowboy Way; Natural Born Killers; Steel Frontier. **1995:** Under Siege 2; Money Train. **1996:** From Dusk Till Dawn; Eraser; Fled; Kingpin; Riot; The Long Kiss Goodnight; Sunchaser; Dead Weekend; The People vs. Larry Flynt.

TIERRE TURNER
(b. 1962)

A former child actor, the Michigan-born Turner re-entered films in the late eighties after time as a baseball player and rodeo performer. He has coordinated stunts and doubled for both Mario Van Peebles and Cuba Gooding, Jr.

Films—**1974:** Devil Times Five (aka People Toys). **1975:** Cornbread, Earl, & Me; Bucktown; Friday Foster; The Runaways (tv). **1989:** Glory. **1990:** Die Hard 2; Last of the Finest; Marked for Death; Predator 2. **1991:** Out for Justice; One Good Cop; Harley Davidson & the Marlboro Man; Hudson Hawk; Ricochet; Driving Me Crazy; The Last Boy Scout. **1992:** American Me; Rapid Fire; Trespass; One False Move. **1993:** Posse; Daybreak. **1994:** Gunmen; Lightning Jack; The Crow; Double Dragon; Junior; Mantis (tv). **1995:** 3 Ninjas Knuckle Up. **1996:** The Rock; Donor Unknown; The Fan; Escape from L.A.; First Kid. *Television*—The Cop & the Kid (reg.); Emergency; McCloud; The Six Million Dollar Man; James at 16; M*A*S*H; Out of This World; Alien Nation; Earth 2 (reg.)

EDWARD J. ULRICH

Films—**1985:** Turk 182; Real Genius. **1987:** The Omega Syndrome; Three for the Road. **1988:** Dead Heat; Elvira, Mistress of the Dark; Fright Night 2; The Boost; Plainclothes. **1989:** Cage; L.A. Bounty; The Banker; The Revenge of Al Capone (tv). **1990:** Satan's Princess; Rainbow Drive. **1991:** FX-2. **1992:** Single White Female; Of Mice & Men. *Television*—Sledge Hammer.

WAYNE (BUDDY) VAN HORN
(b. 1929)

A lifetime member of the Stuntmen's Association, the 6'2" Holly-wood-born Van Horn entered films as an extra and livestock wrangler after service in the Army. The brother of the late actor/horseman James Van Horn, he began working as a stunt coordinator and double for Clint Eastwood, who eventually gave him the chance to direct several of his films. His son Casey has also done stunts.

Films—**1951:** Silver City; Cave of Outlaws. **1952:** Son of Paleface. **1953:** Gunsmoke. **1954:** Taza, Son of Cochise. **1955:** Escape to Burma; Lady Godiva. **1956:** Around the World in 80 Days; 54 Washington Street. **1960:** Spartacus; The Sign of Zorro. **1965:** Major Dundee; The War Lord. **1966:** The Rare Breed; Chamber of Horrors. **1968:** Bandolero; Coogan's Bluff. **1969:** The Stalking Moon; Paint Your Wagon. **1970:** Two Mules for Sister Sara. **1971:** Dirty Harry; The Beguiled. **1972:** Prime Cut; Joe Kidd; The Cowboys. **1973:** High Plains Drifter; Magnum Force.

Stuntman/director Buddy Van Horn (left) with Clint Eastwood on the set of 1980's *Any Which Way You Can.*

1974: The Towering Inferno; Thunderbolt & Lightfoot. **1975:** The Great Waldo Pepper; Bite the Bullet; The Eiger Sanction. **1976:** Swashbuckler; The Enforcer. **1977:** The Last Remake of Beau Geste; The Gauntlet. **1978:** The Deer Hunter; FM; Every Which Way But Loose. **1979:** Stunt Seven (tv). **1980:** Heaven's Gate; Any Which Way You Can (d). **1981:** Return of the Beverly Hillbillies (tv). **1982:** The Beastmaster; The Sword & the Sorcerer. **1983:** Yellowbeard; Sudden Impact. **1984:** City Heat; Tightrope. **1985:** Year of the Dragon; Pale Rider. **1986:** Ratboy; Legal Eagles; Heartbreak Ridge. **1987:** The Night Stalker; Nadine; The Big Easy; Three O'Clock High. **1988:** Off Limits; Shakedown; Crocodile Dundee 2; The Dead Pool (d). **1989:** Pink Cadillac (d). **1990:** The Rookie. **1991:** Diplomatic Immunity. **1992:** The Unforgiven. **1993:** In the Line of Fire; A Perfect World. **1995:** The Stars Fell on Henrietta; Outbreak; The Net. *Television*—Zorro; Rawhide; Voyage to the Bottom of the Sea; Laredo; Bret Maverick; Magnum P.I.; Wildside.

DALE VAN SICKEL
(b. 1907; d. 1977)

Stunt legend Van Sickel was an all-American football star for the University of Florida and later played professionally before getting into stunts in Republic serials and the Commander Cody series. Doubling for Robert Taylor, Dana Andrews, and Clark Gable, he was a founding member of the Stuntmen's Association.

Films—**1933:** Duck Soup; Haunted Harbour; After Office Hours. **1934:** The Richest Girl in the World; Student Tour. **1935:** Roberta. **1936:** Mr. Deeds Goes to Town; Dodsworth. **1937:** This Is My Affair; King of the News Boys. **1938:** Rocket Busters.

1939: Second Fiddle; Sgt. Madden; You Can't Cheat an Honest Man. **1940:** The Return of Frank James; King of the Royal Mounted. **1941:** Law of the Tropics; Hellzapoppin. **1942:** They All Kissed the Bride; It Happened in Flatbush; The Spirit of Stamford; Saboteur; Reap the Wild Wind; Yukon Patrol; Destroyer. **1943:** The Masked Marvel; G-Men vs. The Black Dragon; Captain America. **1944:** Kismet; The Cobra Woman; Girl Rush; The Tiger Woman; Destiny; Zorro's Black Whip. **1945:** The Purple Monster Strikes; Manhunt on Mystery Island; God Is My Co-Pilot; Lone Texas Ranger. **1946:** The Crimson Ghost; A Stolen Life; The Well Groomed Bride; The Phantom Rider; The Daughter of Don Q; King of the Forest Rangers. **1947:** The Black Widow; The Last Round-Up; Bells of San Angelo; The Trespasser; Jesse James Rides Again; Son of Zorro. **1948:** Oklahoma Badlands; Lightning in the Forest; Carson City Raiders; The Adventures of Frank & Jesse James; Dangers of the Canadian Mounted; Desperadoes of Dodge City; Renegades of Sonora; Lightning in the Forest. **1949:** Bruce Gentry, Daredevil of the Skies; The Golden Stallion; The Ghost of Zorro; Duke of Chicago; the Threat; Mighty Joe Young; King of the Rocket Men; Radar Patrol vs. Spy King. **1950:** Flying Disc Men from Mars; The Invisible Monster; Sideshow; Desperadoes of the West; The James Brothers of Missouri; The Desert Hawk; Storm Warning; The Vanishing Westerner; Rough Riders of Durango; Trigger, Jr.; Gunfire; Ranger of Cherokee Strip. **1951:** Jim Thorpe, All American; He Ran All the Way; Radar Men from the Moon; Govt. Agents vs. Phantom Legion; Thunder in God's Country; Don Daredevil Rides Again. **1952:** The Greatest Show on Earth; Scarlet Angel; Zombies of the Stratosphere; Dead Man's Trail; The Brigand; Thundering Caravans; Arctic Flight. **1953:** Thunder Bay; The Veils of Baghdad; Topeka; Northern Patrol; Abbott & Costello Go to Mars; Commander Cody; War of the Worlds; Canadian Mounties vs. Atomic Invaders; Mississippi Gambler; Arena; Here Come the Girls. **1954:** Man with the Steel Whip; A Star Is Born; Trader Tom of the China Seas; Rogue Cop. **1955:** Love Me or Leave Me. **1956:** Earth vs. the Flying Saucers; He Laughed Last; The Searchers; Tea & Sympathy; Behind the High Wall; Around the World in 80 Days; Rock, Pretty Baby; The Burning Hills. **1957:** 20 Million Miles to Earth; The Garment Jungle; Omar Khayyam; Rock Pretty Baby; Shootout at Medicine Bend; The Night Runner; The Girl in the Kremlin; Gunsight Ridge; Night Riders of Montana. **1958:** Satan's Satellites; Behind the High Wall; Onionhead; Missile Monsters; Enchanted Island. **1959:** North By Northwest; On the Beach; Cast a Long Shadow. **1960:** Spartacus; Seven Ways from Sundown. **1962:** Six Black Horses. **1963:** It's a Mad, Mad, Mad, Mad World; Showdown. **1964:** Viva Las Vegas; Iron Collar. **1965:** Requiem for a Gunfighter; Town Tamer; That Funny Feeling. **1966:** Johnny Reno; Cyborg 2087; An American Dream; Murderer's Row. **1967:** The St. Valentine's Day Massacre; The Gnome-Mobile; A Guide for the Married Man; The Flim Flam Man; Bonnie & Clyde. **1968:** Bullit. **1969:** The Love Bug; The Wrecking Crew. **1971:** Slaughterhouse Five; Duel (tv). **1974:** The Sugarland Expres **1976:** No Deposit, No Return. *Television* — Superman; Roy Rogers; Sgt. Preston; Zane Grey Theatre; Peter Gunn; Harbour Command; G.E. Theatre; Colgate Theatre; Wanted, Dead or Alive; The Wild Wild West; Mission: Impossible; Markham; Perry Mason.

STEVE VANDEMAN

Films — **1979:** Tilt. **1980:** Herbie Goes Bananas; In God We Trust. **1982:** The Beastmaster; Friday the 13th Part 3. **1985:** Invasion USA. **1987:** The Hidden. **1988:** Action Jackson; Die Hard; Dead Heat; Hero & the Terror. **1989:** K-9; Shocker; Tango & Cash. **1990:** Far Out Man. **1991:** Stone Cold; The Perfect Weapon; Dead-

lock; Soldier's Fortune. **1992:** Universal Soldier; Hoffa. **1993:** Forced to Kill. **1995:** 3 Ninjas Knuckle Up. *Television* — The Fall Guy; Alien Nation.

VICTORIA VANDERKLOOT
(b. 1957)

This East Coast stunt coordinator broke into the stunt business by performing the required action on soap operas. The wife of director William Vanderkloot, she has doubled for Madeline Stowe, Deborah Van Valkenburgh, and Lucie Arnez.

Films — **1979:** The Warriors; Concorde, Airport '79. **1980:** Times Square. **1981:** Nighthawks; The Fan; Cold River; Four Friends; Wolfen. **1982:** Wrong Is Right; A Little Sex; The Mating Season. **1983:** Amityville 3-D; Echoes; The Lost Empire. **1984:** Firestarter; Mrs. Soffel; Oh, God! You Devil! **1987:** Planes, Trains, & Automobiles; Dead Aim. **1988:** Miracle Mile. **1990:** Love at Large; Secret Agent 00-Soul. **1991:** Nothing But Trouble. **1992:** Aces: Iron Eagle 3; Unlawful Entry. **1995:** The Tie That Binds. *Television* — Ryan's Hope; Love of Life; Search for Tomorrow.

MIKE VENDRELL

The husband of stuntwoman Ceci Vendrell, this supporting player and sometime stunt coordinator was a professional cage fighter before joining the Stuntmen's Association. He has doubled for Sean Connery.

Films—**1979:** Circle of Iron; Fast Charlie, The Moonbeam Rider; Buck Rogers in the 25th Century. **1981:** Bustin' Loose; Goliath Awaits (tv). **1982:** The Sword & the Sorcerer; Fast Times at Ridgemont High. **1983:** They Call Me Bruce; Heart Like a Wheel; Under Fire. **1984:** Grandview U.S.A.; Ninja 3: The Domination. **1985:** Commando; Remo Williams; Fandango. **1987:** The Omega Syndrome. **1988:** Colors; They Live; Twins. **1989:** Ghostbusters 2; Brotherhood of the Rose (tv). **1990:** Death Warrant. **1991:** The Taking of Beverly Hills. **1992:** Newsies; Universal Soldier; Hoffa; Adventures in Dinosaur City; The Harvest. **1995:** Bad Boys; Last Man Standing; Hour Glass; The Sweeper. **1996:** The Lawnmower Man 2; The Rock; Pure Danger; Jingle All the Way. *Television*— Matt Houston; Tag Team; Twin Peaks.

JACK VERBOIS

An archery expert, Verbois is a member of the Stuntmen's Association. He has doubled for Robert De Niro.

Films—**1969:** The Great Bank Robbery. **1970:** The Phynx. **1972:** Conquest of the Planet of the Apes; What's Up, Doc? **1973:** Battle for the Planet of the Apes. **1974:** The Towering Inferno; Black Samson; Earthquake. **1975:** The Hindenburg. **1976:** Swashbuckler; Nickelodeon; Futureworld. **1978:** The Cat from Outer Space; The Deer Hunter; Lord of the Rings. **1979:** Stunt Seven (tv). **1980:** Melvin & Howard. **1981:** Charlie Chan & the Curse of the Dragon Queen; Escape from New York; Halloween 2; True Confessions. **1983:** Scarface. **1984:** Angel. **1987:** Predator. **1989:** Best of the Best. **1990:** I Come in Peace; Far Out Man. **1992:** Unlawful Entry; Live Wire. **1993:** Robin Hood: Men in Tights; Geronimo. **1994:** The Chase. **1995:** Avenging Angel; Don Juan DeMarco; Casino. **1996:** Down Periscope. *Television*—Kung Fu; Airwolf.

GREG WALKER

A stunt coordinator, second unit director, and one-time stunt double for David Carradine and Kris Kristofferson, Walker has worked often on the quirky films of director Alan Rudolph. A member of the Stuntmen's Association, his son Grady also performs stunts.

Films—**1970:** M*A*S*H. **1972:** Conquest of the Planet of the Apes; Gargoyles (tv). **1973:** Battle for the Planet of the Apes. **1974:** The Towering Inferno. **1975:** Death Race 2000. **1976:** Cannonball. **1978:** Deathsport; F.I.S.T.; Lord of the Rings. **1979:** Freedom Road (tv). **1980:** A Change of Season; The Long Riders; Heaven's Gate. **1981:** Americana; The Legend of the Lone Ranger; Heartbeeps. **1982:** The Sword & the Sorcerer. **1983:** Heart Like a Wheel; Triumphs of a Man Called Horse; The Dead Zone; Spacehunter. **1984:** Choose Me. **1985:** Certain Fury; Commando; American Flyers; Trouble in Mind. **1986:** Quicksilver; Raw Deal; Made in Heaven. **1987:** Innerspace; Nadine; The Big Easy; Undercover. **1988:** Illegally Yours; The Moderns; Alien Nation; Patty Hearst; Turner & Hooch. **1989:** The January Man; Weekend at Bernie's. **1990:** Robocop 2; Love at Large. **1991:** Out for Justice; Mortal Thoughts. **1992:** Final Analysis; The Player; Singles. **1993:** Equinox; Robocop 3; Short Cuts; Weekend at Bernie's 2; Geronimo. **1995:** Chameleon. *Television*—Kung Fu.

ROCK WALKER

The stunt coordinator brother of Greg Walker, Rock is a member of the Stuntmen's Association.

Films—**1968:** Will Penny; Chubasco; Bandolero; Hellfighters. **1970:** M*A*S*H. **1972:** Conquest of the Planet of the Apes;

Gargoyles (tv). **1973:** Electra Glide in Blue; Battle for the Planet of the Apes. **1974:** The Towering Inferno; Earthquake. **1977:** The Car; Black Oak Conspiracy. **1978:** Thank God, It's Friday; F.I.S.T. **1979:** The Electric Horseman; Charleston (tv). **1980:** Heaven's Gate. **1981:** Going Ape; Southern Comfort. **1982:** Endangered Species; The Sword & the Sorcerer; The Thing; 48 HRS. **1983:** Heart Like a Wheel. **1984:** Streets of Fire; Ghost Warrior (aka Swordkill); City Limits. **1985:** Commando; Silverado; Weird Science; Avenging Angel; Trouble in Mind. **1986:** Blue City; The Three Amigos; Eye of the Tiger. **1987:** Innerspace; Nadine; The Big Easy; Traxx. **1988:** Illegally Yours; Freeway; Midnight Run; Alien Nation; Blood Red. **1989:** Weekend at Bernie's; Glory. **1990:** Robocop 2; Marked for Death. **1991:** Beastmaster 2. **1992:** Deep Cover; Far & Away. **1993:** Weekend at Bernie's 2. *Television*—Kung Fu.

MARVIN WALTERS

An independent stunt coordinator, Walters has doubled for Roger E. Mosley.

Films—**1972:** Shaft's Big Score; What's Up, Doc?; Across 110th Street. **1973:** Sweet Jesus, Preacher Man. **1974:** Black Samson; The Front Page; Blazing Saddles; Freebie & the Bean; Earthquake. **1976:** Dr. Black, Mr. Hyde; The River Niger. **1979:** Buck Rogers in the 25th Century. **1980:** The Dogs of War; Smokey & the Bandit 2. **1982:** White Dog; The Sword & the Sorcerer. **1987:** Traxx. **1988:** The Serpent & the Rainbow; Mac & Me; Alien from L.A.; Return of Desperado (tv). **1989:** Glory. **1990:** Robocop 2; Keaton's Cop. **1993:** Queen (tv). **1995:** Panther. *Television*—Star Trek; Magnum P.I.

JEFF WARD

A member of Stunt Specialists, this stunt coordinator has served regularly as the double for Wesley Snipes.

Films—**1985:** The Last Dragon. **1987:** Angel Heart. **1988:** Shakedown; Spike of Bensonhurst. **1989:** Lock Up; Hell High; Penn & Teller Get Killed; True Blood. **1990:** Quick Change; Mo' Better Blues; State of Grace; Blue Steel; Ghost; King of New York; Streethunter. **1991:** New Jack City. **1992:** Juice; Malcolm X. **1993:** Who's the Man?; Passenger 57; Meteor Man; Demolition Man; The Saint of Fort Washington. **1994:** Sugar Hill; The Paper; Above the Rim; Crooklyn; Fresh. **1995:** Die Hard with a Vengeance; Clockers; Money Train; Dead President **1996:** Ransom; High School High; Girl 6; Daylight.

DICK WARLOCK
(b. 1940)

An Ohio-born roller derby skater, Warlock worked at a stunt show for Ray "Crash" Corrigan in the early sixties, eventually becoming a stunt coordinator for Walt Disney studios and a double for their young star Kurt Russell. He later achieved cult infamy for portraying both Michael in the *Halloween* films and Jason in the *Friday the 13th* series. He's a member of both the Stuntmen's Association and the Professional Driver's Association.

Films—**1963:** Ballad of a Gunfighter. **1968:** Ice Station Zebra; The Green Berets; Chubasco; Blackbeard's Ghost. **1969:** The Love Bug. **1971:** The Computer Wore Tennis Shoes; The Barefoot Executive. **1972:** Conquest of the Planet of the Apes; Now You See Him, Now You Don't. **1973:** Battle for the Planet of the Apes. **1974:** The Towering Inferno; Superdad;

Blazing Saddles; Herbie Rides Again; Earthquake. **1975:** The Strongest Man in the World; The Hindenburg; Jaws; Rollerball. **1977:** Freaky Friday; Herbie Goes to Monte Carlo. **1978:** The Cat from Outer Space. **1979:** 1941; H.O.T.S.; Stunt Seven (tv). **1980:** The Stunt Man; Used Cars. **1981:** Ghost Story; Escape from New York; Honkytonk Freeway; Halloween 2. **1982:** The Thing. **1983:** Christine; The Dead Zone; Halloween 3: Season of the Witch. **1984:** Angel; Body Double; Firestarter; Friday the 13th: A New Beginning. **1985:** The Mean Season; Commando. **1986:** Big Trouble in Little China; Convicted (tv). **1987:** Spaceballs; Remote Control; Innerspace; The Omega Syndrome; The Running Man. **1988:** Child's Play; Tequila Sunrise; Midnight Run; The Dead Pool; Pumpkinhead; Angel 3. **1989:** Spontaneous Combustion; The Abyss. **1990:** Delta Force 2; Child's Play 2. **1991:** The Perfect Weapon; Beastmaster 2; Child's Play 3; Guilty as Charged; The Rocketeer; Ambition; Driving Me Crazy. **1992:** Unlawful Entry; Live Wire; Guncrazy. **1993:** Robin Hood: Men in Tights; Rising Sun. **1995:** Casino. **1996:** Ravenhawk. *Television*—The Rockford Files; Police Story; McNaughton's Daughter; The Bionic Woman; Renegade.

BILLY WASHINGTON

This independent stunt coordinator has doubled for Keenan Ivory Wayans, Damon Wayons, Tony Todd, Samuel L. Jackson, and Lawrence Fishbourne.

Films—**1990:** Marked for Death. **1991:** Showdown in Little Tokyo; Another You; Intimate Stranger. **1992:** Candyman; White Sands; Class Act; Sneakers; Sunset Heat; The Bodyguard; Rage & Honor; To Protect & Serve. **1993:** Nat'l Lampoon's Loaded Weapon; Amos & Andrew; Street-

knight; Posse; CB4; Cliffhanger; What's Love Got to Do with It; No Escape, No Return. **1994:** Blankman; A Low Down Dirty Shame; Hologram Man. **1995:** 3 Ninjas Knuckle Up; Die Hard with a Vengeance; Bad Blood; Candyman: Farewell to the Flesh; Ballistic; Suspect Device; One Man's Justice. **1996:** Don't Be a Menace; The Rock; Fled; The Crow: City of Angels; Pure Danger.

KIM WASHINGTON
(b. 1960)

A member of the Stuntwoman's Association, Washington has served as Whoppi Goldberg's stunt double since the mid-eighties.

Films—**1981:** Charlie Chan & the Curse of the Dragon Queen; Bustin' Loose. **1982:** Star Trek 2: The Wrath of Khan; The Sword & the Sorcerer. **1985:** Explorers; Fright Night. **1986:** The Naked Cage. **1987:** Fatal Beauty; Walk Like a Man; Remote Control. **1988:** Colors; Mississippi Burning; I'm Gonna Git You Sucka. **1989:** Ghostbusters 2. **1990:** Ghost; Night Angel; The Guardian; The Adventures of Ford Fairlane. **1991:** Cool as Ice; Timebomb. **1992:** Sister Act; Class Act; One False Move. **1993:** Made in America; What's Love Got to Do with It; Sister Act 2. **1994:** Corrina, Corrina. **1995:** Die Hard with a Vengeance; Boys on the Side; Vampire in Brooklyn. **1996:** Eddie; Bogus; First Kid.

RICHARD WASHINGTON

Father of Kim Washington, this stunt coordinator once served as the double for Richard Roundtree.

Films—**1971**: Dirty Harry. **1972**: What's Up, Doc?; Conquest of the Planet of the Apes. **1973**: Scream, Blacula, Scream; Battle for the Planet of the Apes. **1974**: The Towering Inferno; The Front Page; Earthquake. **1975**: Sheba, Baby. **1976**: Swashbuckler; Dr. Black, Mr. Hyde; Drum. **1977**: The Deep. **1979**: Charleston (tv); Stunt Seven (tv). **1980**: The Nude Bomb; Seems Like Old Times. **1981**: Bustin' Loose; Charlie Chan & the Curse of the Dragon Queen. **1982**: Some Kind of a Hero; The Sword & the Sorcerer. **1985**: Gotcha; Avenging Angel. **1986**: Blue City; Invaders form Mars; Eye of the Tiger. **1987**: Million Dollar Mystery; Innerspace. **1988**: Mississippi Burning. **1989**: The Abyss; Lock Up; Glory. **1993**: Weekend at Bernie's 2. **1994**: Blown Away. **1995**: Panther; Die Hard with a Vengeance. **1996**: First Kid. *Television*—The Fall Guy; Murder She Wrote.

MIKE WASHLAKE

A former gymnast, Washlake's most infamous moment was doubling for actress Daryl Hannah in *Blade Runner.*

Films—**1981**: Raggedy Man. **1982**: Blade Runner; Star Trek 2: The Wrath of Khan. **1984**: Bachelor Party. **1985**: Explorers; Fright Night. **1986**: Nomads; Big Trouble in Little China. **1987**: Walk Like a Man. **1988**: Sunset; License to Drive. **1991**: Hook. **1993**: Surf Ninjas. **1994**: The Naked Gun 33 1/3; Past Tense. **1995**: Dracula, Dead & Loving It. **1996**: The Lawnmower Man 2.

CHUCK WATERS

A veteran stunt coordinator and second unit director, this former plumber has served as a double for actor Jim Varney in the *Ernest* films, as well as for Bruce Dern. He is the father of Jim Waters.

Films—**1966**: The Russians Are Coming, The Russians Are Coming. **1968**: The Sweet Ride. **1969**: Che. **1970**: The Molly Maguires; There Was a Crooked Man. **1972**: Conquest of the Planet of the Apes. **1973**: High Plains Drifter; The Exorcist; Magnum Force; Battle for the Planet of the Apes. **1974**: The Towering Inferno; The Parallax View. **1975**: The Hindenburg. **1976**: Swashbuckler. **1978**: The Boys in Company C; The Manitou; The Deer Hunter; I Wanna Hold Your Hand; Every Which Way But Loose. **1979**: Apocalypse Now; The In-Laws; Stunt Seven (tv). **1980**: Bronco Billy; Foolin' Around; The Hollywood Knights; Melvin & Howard; Inside Moves; Heaven's Gate. **1981**: Honkytonk Freeway; Raiders of the Lost Ark. **1982**: E.T.; Poltergeist; The Sword & the Sorcerer; Night Shift. **1983**: Bad Boys; Hysterical; Sudden Impact; Yellowbeard. **1984**: Body Double; American Dreamer; City Heat; Indiana Jones & the Temple of Doom; Mrs. Soffel; Tuff Turf. **1985**: Fandango; Mischief; Lady Blue (tv). **1986**: At Close Range; The Golden Child; American Anthem; Eye of the Tiger; No Mercy. **1987**: Russkies. **1988**: Colors; The Couch Trip; The Dead Pool; Ernest Saves Christmas. **1989**: Collision Course; Indiana Jones & the Last Crusade; Fletch Lives; Distant Thunder; Renegades. **1990**: Ernest Goes to jail; Arachnophobia; Secret Agent 00-Soul. **1991**: Eve of Destruction; Ernest Scared Stupid; Toy Soldiers. **1992**: Freejack; Diggstown. **1993**: Boiling Point; Fire in the Sky; Demolition Man; Malice. **1994**: Cops & Robbersons; The Scout. **1994**: T-Force. **1995**: Separate Lives; Last of the Dogmen; The Crossing Guard. **1996**: Down Periscope; Mercenary; Back to Back. *Television*—The Night Stalker; Cannon; Dalton; Nasty Boys.

JIM WATERS

Films—**1990:** Arachnophobia. **1991:** Toy Soldiers. **1992:** Freejack; Hoffa. **1993:** Boiling Point; Fire in the Sky. **1994:** Cops & Robbersons; Ice; Zero Tolerance; Direct Hit; T-Force. **1995:** The Crossing Guard. **1996:** Mercenary; Back to Back.

JENNIFER WATSON (JOHNSON)

Films—**1986:** The Three Amigos. **1988:** Lucky Stiff; Nightmare on Elm Street 4: Dream Master. **1990:** Back to the Future 3; Leatherface 3. **1991:** The Rapture. **1992:** Far & Away; Stay Tuned. **1993:** Hexed; Sliver; Jailbait. **1994:** Gunmen; Bad Girls; Drop Zone; CIA 2: Target Alexa. **1995:** Avenging Angel; Showgirls. **1996:** Lawnmower Man 2; Fast Money; Raven.

MIKE WATSON

A stunt coordinator, Watson is a member of the Stuntmen's Association. He had a lead in the horror film *Subspecies.*

Films—**1986:** The Three Amigos; Ruthless People. **1987:** Teen Wolf 2. **1988:** Fear; Rambo 3; Blood Red; Plainclothes; Bail Out. **1989:** Back to the Future 2. **1990:** Back to the Future 3; Eternity; The Rookie. **1991:** Subspecies; Bugsy. **1992:** Far & Away; Buffy, the Vampire Slayer; Bram Stoker's Dracula. **1993:** In the Line of Fire; The Adventures of Huck Finn; Geronimo; Jailbait. **1995:** Blood for Blood; Painted Hero. **1996:** Riders of the Purple Sage; Raven.

FRED WAUGH

A member of the Stuntmen's Association, this former trapeze artist has coordinated stunts and directed second unit, specializing in high work and aerial cinematography. He's best known for doubling on the television series "Spiderman."

Films—**1964:** Circus World. **1965:** Inside Daisy Clover. **1969:** Paint Your Wagon; The Undefeated. **1970:** Monte Walsh; Little Big Man. **1971:** Sometimes a Great Notion (aka Never Give an Inch). **1972:** Conquest of the Planet of the Apes; Buck & the Preacher. **1973:** Battle for the Planet of the Apes. **1974:** The Towering Inferno; The Front Page; McQ. **1975:** Night Moves. **1977:** The Amazing Spiderman (tv). **1978:** Our Winning Season. **1979:** Buck Rogers in the 25th Century. **1981:** Looker. **1982:** Rocky 3. **1983:** D.C. Cab; The Osterman Weekend. **1984:** Splash; Dreamscape. **1985:** Porky's Revenge; Vendetta. **1986:** Fire with Fire. **1987:** The Omega Syndrome; Heat; Number One with a Bullet; The Wild Pair; Code Name Zebra; Kidnapped; Six Against the Rock (tv). **1988:** Beetlejuice; Shoot to Kill. **1989:** Speed Zone; Backtrack; To Die For; Third Degree Burn (tv). **1990:** Ghost Dad. **1992:** Medicine Man; Raising Cain. **1993:** The Last Action Hero; Blindsided (tv). **1994:** White Fang 2. **1995:** Don Juan DeMarco; Sudden Death. **1996:** Spy Hard; Exit. *Television*—The Man from U.N.C.L.E.; The Girl from U.N.C.L.E.; The Invaders; Kodiak; Gemini Man; Spiderman; Vegas.

RIC WAUGH

The son of Fred Waugh, Ric has quickly graduated from performing and coordinating stunts into directing films.

Films—**1987:** The Wild Pair; Teen Wolf 2. **1988:** The Blob; They Live. **1989:** Road

House. **1990:** Days of Thunder; Dollman; Total Recall; Coup de Ville. **1991:** Hook; Shakes the Clown. **1992:** Kuffs; Last of the Mohicans; Rapid Fire; Universal Soldier; Forever Young. **1993:** Striking Distance; The Last Action Hero; True Romance; Hard Target; Body of Evidence. **1994:** The Crow; Double Dragon; Arcade. **1995:** Sudden Death. **1996:** Exit (d). *Television*—Nasty Boys; Viper; F/X (reg.)

BIG DADDY WAYNE

Films—**1992:** South Central. **1993:** CB4; True Romance. **1994:** The Naked Gun 33 1/3. **1995:** Panther; Crimson Tide; Devil in a Blue Dress; Get Shorty; Things to Do in Denver When You're Dead. **1996:** The Great White Hype; Don't Be a Menace; Independence Day; The Crow: City of Angels; Pure Danger; Set It Off.

JESSE WAYNE

Standing only 5'3", Wayne has doubled for such small performers as Wally Cox, Mickey Rooney, Frankie Avalon, and even Barbara Stanwyck. He's a lifetime member of the Stuntmen's Association.

Films—**1965:** Young Fury. **1969:** The Love Bug. **1970:** Darker Than Amber; There Was a Crooked Man. **1972:** Chandler; Conquest of the Planet of the Apes. **1973:** Oklahoma Crude; Battle for the Planet of the Apes. **1974:** The Towering Inferno; The Front Page; Earthquake. **1975:** The Master Gunfighter; Return to Macon County. **1977:** Herbie Goes to Monte Carlo; The House By the Lake; Black Oak Conspiracy. **1978:** The Manitou. **1979:** The Lady in Red; Meteor; H.O.T.S. **1980:** Hopscotch. **1981:** Halloween 2. **1982:** Having It All; The Sword

& the Sorcerer. **1983:** Testament; Loose Joints (aka Flicks); Get Crazy. **1984:** Splash. **1985:** Explorers; Avenging Angel. *Television*—Nichols; Emergency.

GARY WAYTON

A member of the Stuntmen's Association, this stunt coordinator's wife Paula has also performed stunts.

Films—**1985:** Sky High. **1987:** Terminal Entry. **1988:** Midnight Run. **1989:** Collision Course; The Banker. **1990:** Total Recall; The Lords of Magic. **1993:** The Fugitive; Cybertracker; The Hit List. **1994:** Color of Night; Bad Blood. **1995:** Girl in the Cadillac; The Fear; Strange Days; Chameleon; Crosscut. **1996:** The Great White Hype; Mercenary.

J. DAVID WEBSTER

Films—**1986:** Let's Get Harry. **1989:** Ghostbusters 2; Black Rain. **1990:** Total Recall; King of New York. **1991:** Out for Justice; Thelma & Louise; Terminator 2. **1992:** Last of the Mohicans; Under Siege; The Bodyguard. **1993:** The Last Action Hero. **1994:** True Lies. **1995:** Waterworld. **1996:** Fled.

DANNY WESELLIS

Films—**1983:** Scarface. **1987:** No Safe Haven; Down Twisted. **1988:** Shakedown; The Dead Pool; They Live. **1989:** The Abyss; Pink Cadillac; One Man Force. **1990:** Night Angel; Die Hard 2; Total Recall; Last of the Finest. **1991:** Highlander 2; K-9000 (tv). **1992:** One False Move; Captain Ron. **1993:** Excessive Force.

1996: Escape from L.A. *Television* –Matt Houston; Baywatch.

CHERYL WHEELER-DIXON
(b. 1960)

A former kickboxing champion, wife of stuntman Shane Dixon, and regular double for Kathleen Turner, Ellen Barkin, and Rene Russo, Wheeler is a member of both the United Stuntwoman's Association and the Professional Driver's Association.

Films—**1987:** The Night Stalker; No Safe Haven; Fatal Beauty; Outrageous Fortune; Night Force; Brenda Starr. **1988:** Sunset; Police Academy 5: Assignment Miami Beach; They Live; Scrooged; Something Is Out There (tv). **1989:** Back to the Future 2; Johnny Handsome; Lethal Weapon 2; L.A. Bounty; Relentless; Night Life; Dead Bang; Nat'l Lampoon's Christmas Vacation; Crack House. **1990:** Bird on a Wire; Maniac Cop 2; Night Angel; Die Hard 2; Another 48 HRS.; Run; Last of the Finest; The Adventures of Ford Fairlane; Kindergarten Cop; Angel Town. **1991:** Stone Cold; Terminator 2; V.I. Warshawski; Billy Bathgate; The Rocketeer; Fast Getaway; 976 Evil 2; Past Midnight. **1992:** Memoirs of an Invisible Man; Lethal Weapon 3; Honey, I Blew up the Kid; A River Runs Through It; Man Trouble; Sweet Justice; Rage & Honor; Men Don't Tell (tv). **1993:** Point of No Return; The Last Action Hero; Sliver; Demolition Man; Undercover Blues; The Temp; House of Cards; Malice. **1994:** Body Shot; Serial Mom; The Mask; Ring of Steel. **1996:** Ransom. *Television* –The Fall Guy; Baywatch; The Antagonists; Civil Wars.

WEBSTER WHINERY
(b. 1954)

An Oklahoma-born stunt coordinator and long-time double for Mickey Rourke, Whinery got his start on the East Coast. He's now a member of the Stuntmen's Association and standing in for Nicolas Cage.

Films—**1980:** The Exterminator; Friday the 13th Part 2. **1981:** So Fine. **1982:** Alone in the Dark. **1983:** Scarface. **1984:** Alphabet City; Maria's Lovers; Bolero. **1985:** Scream for Help; Remo Williams. **1986:** 9 1/2 Weeks; The Money Pit; Sweet Liberty; Raw Deal. **1987:** Angel Heart; Number One with a Bullet; Barfly; The Oracle; Teen Wolf; Innerspace. **1988:** Masquerade; Bull Durham; The Dead Pool. **1989:** Homeboy; Johnny Handsome; Hell High. **1990:** Desperate Hours; Wild Orchid. **1991:** Mobsters; Hudson Hawk; The Doors; JFK. **1992:** Wild Orchid 2; Thunderheart; Wayne's World; Sneakers. **1993:** Fire in the Sky; Hear No Evil; In the Line of Fire; Geronimo; The Last Outlaw. **1994:** Conflict of Interest; The Last Ride (aka F.T.W.); On Deadly Ground; A Simple Twist of Fate. **1995:** The Stars Fell on Henrietta; Fall Time; Mad Love; Destiny Turns on the Radio; The Net; Wild Bill; Sudden Death; Chameleon. **1996:** The Rock; Last Man Standing; The Chamber. *Television* –The Guiding Light.

TED WHITE

This 6'4" Texas-born stunt coordinator and supporting player was a star football player for the University of Oklahoma, later standing in for both Lee Marvin and Jason in the *Friday the 13th* series. White is a lifetime member of the Stuntmen's Association.

Films—**1958:** The Naked & the Dead; The Perfect Furlough. **1959:** Born Reckless; These Thousand Hills; Rio Bravo; And Ride a Tiger. **1960:** The Alamo. **1962:** Escape from Zahrain. **1965:** Cat Ballou. **1966:** Smoky. **1967:** Point Blank. **1968:** Planet of the Apes. **1972:** Prime Cut; Conquest of the Planet of the Apes. **1973:** The Don Is Dead; Battle for the Planet of the Apes; Jarrett (tv). **1974:** The Towering Inferno; The Comeback Trail. **1977:** Black Oak Conspiracy. **1978:** The Manitou; Comes a Horseman. **1979:** Battlestar Galactica; Flesh & Blood (tv). **1980:** Used Cars; Oh, God! Book II; Up the Academy; Power (tv). **1981:** Going Ape; Legend of the Lone Ranger; Cutter's Way; Escape from New York (tv). **1982:** Wrong Is Right; Tron. **1983:** A Killer in the Family (tv). **1984:** Against All Odds; Romancing the Stone; Starman; The Wild Life; Friday the 13th: The Final Chapter. **1985:** Cloak & Dagger; Silverado. **1986:** Fire in the Night; One Crazy Summer; Quiet Cool; Ruthless People. **1987:** Friday the 13th Part 7: The New Blood; Wanted: Dead or Alive; Hot Pursuit; Death Wish 4; The Hidden. **1988:** Shakedown; Sunset; Border Heat. **1989:** 84 Charlie Mopic; Road House. **1990:** Downtown. **1991:** Conagher (tv). **1994:** City Slickers 2. *Television*—Maverick; Daniel Boone; Mission: Impossible; Kung Fu; Kojak; Battlestar Galactica; CHiPs; The Fall Guy; Matt Houston; Hunter; Perry Mason.

GEORGE P. WILBUR

(b. 1942)

This Connecticut-born stunt coordinator served in the Navy and spent time on the rodeo circuit before finding work on an Arizona dude ranch. Local Westerns got him into stuntwork and he eventually became the double for Peter Graves on television's "Mission: Impossible." A Member of the Stuntmen's Association, Wilbur achieved cult status for portraying Michael in the *Halloween* films.

Films—**1967:** El Dorado; Hombre. **1972:** Blacula; Hammer; The Poseidon Adventure; Conquest of the Planet of the Apes. **1973:** High Plains Drifter; Cleopatra Jones; Battle for the Planet of the Apes; Call to Danger (tv). **1974:** The Towering Inferno; Blazing Saddles. **1975:** The Hindenburg; Lepke; Dead Man on the Run (tv); Sky Heist (tv). **1976:** Drum. **1977:** Black Oak Conspiracy. **1978:** Every Which Way But Loose; Movie, Movie; The Clonus Horror. **1979:** Pearl (tv); Stunt Seven (tv). **1980:** The Mountain Men; Coast to Coast; Virus. **1981:** Pennies from Heaven; Escape from New York; Goldie & the Boxer Go to Hollywood (tv). **1982:** White Dog; The Beastmaster; Poltergeist; Star Trek 2: The Wrath of Khan; The Sword & the Sorcerer. **1983:** The Sting 2; Hysterical; The Osterman Weekend; Yellowbeard; Max Dugan Returns; The Fighter (tv); City Heat. **1984:** Firestarter; City Limits. **1985:** The Mean Season; Re-Animator; Murphy's Romance; Ewoks: The Battle for Endor (tv). **1986:** Poltergeist 2; Raw Deal. **1987:** The Monster Squad; The Running Man; Extreme Prejudice; Brenda Starr; Remote Control. **1988:** Dead Heat; Die Hard; Colors; Two Moon Junction; Halloween 4. **1989:** Collision Course; The Burbs; Nightmare on Elm Street 5: Dream Child; Lock Up; Halloween 5; Ghostbusters 2. **1990:** Loose Cannons; Total Recall; Repossessed; Come See the Paradise; Pump Up the Volume; The Exorcist 3; Secret Agent 00-Soul. **1991:** Eve of Destruction; Silence of the Lambs; Flight of the Intruder; Suburban Commando; Defenseless; The Marrying Man; Cast a Deadly Spell; Bright Angel; The Last Boy Scout; Leather Jackets; Not of This World (tv). **1992:** Dr. Giggles; Unlawful Entry. **1993:** Hot Shots Part Deux; Boiling Point; Excessive Force; Undercover Blues. **1994:** Cops & Robbersons; Cobb; Bad Blood. **1995:** Panther; Halloween: The Curse of Michael Myers; Casino. **1996:** Broken Arrow; Jingle All the Way; Mars Attacks! *Television* –The Monroes; Mission: Impossible; The Six Million Dollar Man; Hardcase; Best of Friends; Renegade.

AMY WILDER

The daughter of Glenn Wilder, this stunt coordinator is married to Florida stuntman Gar Stephen.

Films—**1988:** The Presidio. **1989:** Wired. **1990:** Narrow Margin; Problem Child; Psycho 4: The Beginning (tv). **1992:** Folks. **1993:** Matinee; Cop & a Half. **1994:** The Getaway. **1995:** Bad Boys; Nine Months. **1996:** Heaven's Prisoners.

GLENN R. WILDER
(b. 1934)

A USC business administration graduate and former football player for the Los Angeles Chargers, Wilder worked as both a stockbroker and private detective before his modeling sideline moved him into films as a stunt double for Troy Donahue, David Janssen, and Richard Crenna. Once the roommate of Burt Reynolds, Wilder was a founding member of Stunts Unlimited and has since been a top stunt coordinator and second unit director. He relocated to Florida in the late eighties.

Films—**1963:** Palm Spring Weekend. **1964:** Roustabout; The Carpetbaggers; John Goldfarb, Please Come Home. **1966:** The Sand Pebbles; Our Man Flint. **1967:** Wait Until Dark. **1968:** The Boston Stran-

gler. **1969:** The Love Bug; The Good Guys & the Bad Guys; The Arrangement. **1970:** Darling Lili. **1972:** Fuzz; The Bounty Man (tv). **1973:** Cleopatra Jones; The Friend of Eddie Coyle; Shamus; White Lightning. **1974:** Three the Hard Way; Lenny. **1975:** Night Moves. **1976:** Logan's Run; Mother, Jugs, & Speed; Two Minute Warning; Street People; Revenge for a Rape (tv). **1977:** March or Die; Moonshine County Express; Zebra Force. **1978:** King of the Gypsies; Blue Collar; Hooper; Convoy. **1979:** Buck Rogers in the 25th Century; The Fish That Saved Pittsburgh; A Time to Die; Goldie & the Boxer (tv). **1980:** The Last Flight of Noah's Ark. **1981:** Caveman; Sharky's Machine; Shogun (tv); Margin for Murder (tv). **1982:** Cannery Row; Tron; I'm Dancing as Fast as I Can. **1983:** The Star Chamber; The Osterman Weekend; Nat'l Lampoon's Vacation; Scarface. **1984:** Against All Odds; Firstborn; Hard to Hold; City Heat; The Last Starfighter; The Outlaws (tv). **1985:** Moving Violations; Stick; My Science Project; Witness; Rainy Day Friends (aka L.A. Bad). **1987:** The Wild Pair; Burglar; Morgan Stewart's Coming Home; Outrageous Fortune; Lethal Weapon; Revenge of the Nerds 2; Someone to Watch Over Me; Real Men; Masterblaster (d); Code Name Zebra. **1988:** Action Jackson; Die Hard; And God Created Woman; The Presidio. **1989:** K-9; Star Trek 5: The Final Frontier; Lock Up; The Neon Empire; Road House; Wired; Backtrack. **1990:** Far Out Man; Days of Thunder; Edward Scissorhands; Narrow Margin; Mr. Destiny; Psycho 4: The Beginning (tv). **1991:** Bill & Ted's Bogus Journey; Hook; Point Break; The Perfect Weapon; Terminator 2; The Last Boy Scout. **1992:** Freejack; American Me; Folks. **1993:** Wilder Napalm; Hocus Pocus; The Last Action Hero; Passenger 57; Striking Distance; Cop & a Half. **1994:** The Getaway; True Lies; Exit to Eden; Trapped in Paradise. **1995:** Bad Boys; Nine Months; Fair Game. **1996:** Fled; Set It Off. *Television*—Ozzie & Harriet; The Fugitive; The Green Hornet; Mission: Impossible; Mannix; The Mod Squad; Ghost Story; Cannon; Planet of the Apes; SWAT; Dynasty; The Six Million Dollar Man; Vegas; CHiPs; Cabot Connection; The Greatest American Hero; T.J. Hooker; Swamp Thing; Seaquest DSV.

SCOTT WILDER

The son of Glenn Wilder, this stunt coordinator is a member of Stunts Unlimited. He has doubled for Rob Lowe and Keanu Reeves.

Films—**1981:** Archer (tv). **1982:** Cannery Row; Megaforce; Grease 2. **1983:** Amityville 3-D; The Osterman Weekend; The Outsiders; Scarface; The Star Chamber. **1984:** Firstborn; Lovelines; Tuff Turf. **1985:** Into the Night; Mischief; Fast Forward; To Live & Die in L.A.; Moving Violations. **1986:** The Money Pit; Out of Bounds; Back to School. **1987:** The Wild Pair; Mannequin; Masterblaster; Night Force; Police Academy 4: Citizens on Patrol; Morgan Stewart's Coming Home; The Lost Boys. **1988:** Off Limits; Illegally Yours; The Presidio; They Live. **1989:** Wired; K-9; Lethal Weapon 2; Riding the Edge. **1990:** Bad Influence; Die Hard 2; Days of Thunder; Edward Scissorhands. **1991:** Out for Justice; V.I. Warshawski; Bill & Ted's Bogus Journey; Hook; Point Break. **1992:** Cool World. **1993:** Full Eclipse; The Last Action Hero; Demolition Man; Wilder Napalm. **1994:** Speed; Clear & Present Danger; Double Dragon; A Low Down Dirty Shame; Puppetmasters; Payback. **1995:** Nine Months; Waterworld; Jade; Seven; Nick of Time; Body Language. **1996:** From Dusk Till Dawn; Executive Decision; Eraser; Bordello of Blood. *Television*—T.J. Hooker.

BOB WILKE
(b. 1915; d. 1989)

Burly Ohio-born supporting player, Wilke was predominantly active in the Western genre. A former lifeguard, high-diver, and World War II veteran, Wilke was best known as one of Gary Cooper's antagonists in *High Noon* and as the thug James Coburn knifes in *The Magnificent Seven.*

Films—**1936:** San Francisco. **1938:** Come on Rangers; Under Western Stars. **1939:** Rough Riders Roundup; In Old Monterey. **1940:** The Adventures of Red Ryder; King of the Royal Mounted. **1943:** California Joe; The San Antonio Kid. **1944:** Call of the Rockies; Sheriff of Las Vegas; Beneath Western Skies; Hidden Valley Outlaws; The Cowboy & the Senorita; Yellow Rose of Texas; Stagecoach to Monterey; Marshal of Reno; Code of the Prairie; Firebrands of Arizona; The Big Bonanza; Bordertown Trail; Cheyenne Wildcat; Vigilantes of Dodge City; Sheriff of Sundown. **1945:** Sunset in El Dorado; Trail of Kit Carson; The Topeka Terror; Sheriff of Cimarron; Lone Texas Ranger; Santa Fe Saddlemates; Rough Riders of Cheyenne; Corpus Christi Bandits; Trail of the Badlands; The Man from Oklahoma. **1946:** Roaring Rangers; The Michigan Kid; The Phantom Rider; The El Paso Kid; King of the Forest Rangers; Out California Way; White Tie & Tails. **1947:** West of Dodge City; Law of the Canyon; The Vigilantes Return; Last Days at Boot Hill. **1948:** River Lady; Carson City Raiders; Desperadoes of Dodge City; Six Gun Law; West of Sonora; Trail to Laredo. **1949:** The Wyoming Bandit; Laramie; Gunplay; Hot Lead; Overland Telegraph. **1950:** Outcast of Black Mesa; Mule Train; Beyond the Purple Hills; Across the Badlands; Frontier Outpost; The James Brothers of Missouri; Twilight in the Sierras; Tales of the West. **1951:** Saddle Legion; Best of the Badmen; Cyclone Fury; Pistol Harvest; Fargo. **1952:** High Noon; Las Vegas Story; The Maverick; Road Agent; Cattle Town; Hellgate; Laramie Mountains; Wyoming Roundup. **1953:** Powder River; Arrowhead; Cow Country; From Here to Eternity; War Paint. **1954:** The Lone Gun; 20,000 Leagues Under the Sea; The Lone

Ranger; Two Guns & a Badge; Shotgun; Wichita; Canyon River. **1955:** The Far Country; Strange Lady in Town; Smoke Signal. **1956:** Raw Edge; The Rawhide Years; Backlash; Written on the Wind; Gun the Man Down; Hot Summer Night. **1957:** Night Passage; The Tarnished Angels. **1958:** Man of the West; Return to Warbow; Mountain Fortress. **1959:** Never Steal Anything Small. **1960:** Spartacus; The Magnificent Seven; Blueprint for Robbery. **1961:** The Long Rope. **1963:** Gun Hawk. **1964:** Fate Is the Hunter; Shock Treatment. **1965:** The Hallelujah Trail; Morituri. **1966:** Smoky. **1967:** Tony Rome. **1969:** Desperate Mission (tv). **1970:** The Cheyenne Social Club. **1971:** A Gunfight; The Resurrection of Zachary Wheeler; They Call it Murder (tv). **1972:** The Rookies (tv). **1973:** The Boy Who Cried Werewolf; Santee. **1978:** Days of Heaven; Wild & Wooly (tv). **1979:** The Sweet Creek County War; The Great Monkey Rip-Off. **1981:** Stripes. *Television*—Superman; Roy Rogers; Cheyenne; Jim Bowie; Tombstone Territory; Zorro; Colt .45; Gunsmoke; Lawman; Bat Masterson; The Texan; The Deputy; Wanted, Dead or Alive; The Rifleman; Have Gun, Will Travel; Law of the Plainsman; Bonanza; The Tall Man; Laramie; Tales of Wells Fargo; Frontier Circus; Texas John Slaughter; Bourbon Street Beat; The Americans; Rawhide; Maverick; Andy Bennett; The Boston Terrier; The Slowest Gun in the West; The Virginian; Jesse James (reg.); Daniel Boone; Tarzan; Cimarron Strip; The Guns of Will Sonnett; The Wild Wild West; The Monroes; Lancer; The Quest; Starsky & Hutch; How the West Was Won; The Texas Rangers; Death Valley Days; Perry Mason; Lucy; Dallas.

Eye of the Tiger; Gladiator (tv). **1987:** Number One with a Bullet; Over the Top; Near Dark; Throw Momma from the Train; Cop. **1988:** Midnight Run; Alien Nation; Messenger of Death; The Milagro Beanfield War; Two Moon Junction; Freeway. **1989:** The Package; Blind Fury. **1990:** Dick Tracy; Robocop 2; The Handmaid's Tale; The Rookie. **1991:** Out for Justice; Mobsters. **1992:** Deep Cover; Class Act; Love Field; Sleepwalkers; Chaplin; Betrayal of the Dove. **1993:** The Fugitive; Undercover Blues; Streetknight; Trouble Bound. **1994:** The Naked Gun 33 1/3; Clean Slate; The Hard Truth; Ring of the Musketeers; Payback; Bad Blood. **1995:** Murder in the First; Top Dog; Die Hard with a Vengeance; Casino. **1996:** Fled; Last Man Standing; Ravenhawk.

BRIAN J. WILLIAMS

Films—**1984:** Bachelor Party; Lovelines. **1987:** Number One with a Bullet; Weeds. **1988:** Sunset; Alien Nation; License to Drive; Turner & Hooch. **1989:** The Burbs; An Innocent Man; Glory. **1990:** Robocop 2; Repossessed; Taking Care of Business; Dangerous Passion (tv). **1991:** Mobsters; Out for Justice; Toy Soldiers; Mom. **1992:** Final Analysis; Under Siege; Wayne's World; Chaplin. **1993:** Robocop 3; CB4. **1994:** The Naked Gun 33 1/3; Silence of the Hams; Steel Frontier. **1996:** Multiplicity; Mars Attacks!; Star Trek, First Contact. *Television*—Star Trek, The Next Generation; Deep Space Nine.

JIM WILKEY

A member of the Stuntmen's Association, Wilkey's specialty is driving big rigs.

Films—**1983:** Christine. **1986:** Cobra; The Golden Child; Never Too Young to Die;

GERARD WILLIAMS

Films—**1987:** *batteries not included. **1988:** Action Jackson; I'm Gonna Git You Sucka. **1989:** Johnny Handsome; Glory. **1990:** The Last Hour; House Party; Marked for Death; Predator 2. **1991:** Terminator 2; Boyz N the Hood; Driving Me Crazy. **1992:** American Me; Class Act; Love Field; Trespass; Universal Soldier. **1993:** Posse; CB4. **1994:** The Naked Gun 33 1/3; Silence of the Hams. **1995:** Panther; Die Hard with a Vengeance. **1996:** Heaven's Prisoners; Original Gangstas; Chain Reaction; Fled; Set It Off.

JACK WILLIAMS
(b. 1920)

This veteran bit actor was the son of stuntman Paris Williams and a champion bronco rider. A graduate of USC, he's a member of the Stuntmen's Association.

Films—**1940:** Rollin' Home to Texas. **1943:** Change of heart (aka Hit Parade of 1943). **1946:** It's Great to Be Young. **1950:** Tripoli. **1951:** I'll See You in My Dreams; The Last Outpost. **1952:** The Lion & the Horse; Talk About a Stranger. **1953:** Hondo. **1955:** The Far Country; Strange Lady in Town. **1956:** Backlash; The Burning Hills. **1957:** Night Passage; Band of Angels. **1958:** Man of the West. **1959:** Westbound; Rio Bravo. **1960:** Spartacus; The Alamo. **1961:** El Cid; Gold of the Seven Saints. **1962:** Hatari; Merril's Marauders; The Spiral Road; The Man Who Shot Liberty Valance; How the West Was Won. **1964:** Cheyenne Autumn; Fall of the Roman Empire. **1965:** The Sons of Katie Elder; The War Lord. **1966:** Billy the Kid vs. Dracula; Smoky. **1967:** The War Wagon; Welcome to Hard Times. **1968:** The Scalphunters; Head. **1969:** Paint Your Wagon; The Wild Bunch; The Good Guys & the Bad Guys. **1970:** Beneath the Planet of the Apes; The Ballad of Cable Hogue. **1971:** The Omega Man. **1974:** Mrs. Sundance (tv). **1980:** The Mountain Men. **1985:** Remo Williams. **1987:** Innerspace. **1988:** Border Heat; Bail Out. **1991:** Diplomatic Immunity. *Television*—Maverick; The Monroes; Rawhide; Bonanza; Laredo; Lancer.

SPICE WILLIAMS

A former rock singer, female bodybuilder, and professional wrestler, Williams landed a showy supporting role in the fifth *Star Trek* film. She's a member of the Stuntwoman's Association.

Films—**1986:** Band of the Hand. **1987:** The Wild Pair; The Lost Boys; Stranded; Cyclone. **1989:** Star Trek 5: The Final Frontier; Second Sight; Sexbomb; Hollywood Hot Tubs 2. **1990:** Arachnophobia. **1991:** The Guyver; Murder in High Places (tv). **1992:** Sleepwalkers; Out on a Limb. **1994:** A Low Down Dirty Shame; CIA 2: Target Alexa; T-Force; Sensation. **1995:** Bodycount. **1996:** Set It Off. *Television*—The Fall Guy; Sonny Spoon; High Voltage; Women in Prison.

CINDY WILLS (HARTLINE)

The daughter of Henry Wills, this stunt coordinator married stuntman Gene Hartline.

Films—**1980:** Alligator; Cheech & Chong's Next Movie; Roadie. **1983:** Biohazard; Girls of the White Orchid (tv). **1984:** Gimme an F; Nightmare on Elm Street. **1985:** Superstition; Friday the 13th: A New Beginning; Police Academy 2: Their First Assignment. **1986:** Miracles; Eye of the Tiger. **1987:** Innerspace; Raising Arizona; Traxx. **1989:** Collision Course.

HENRY WILLS
(b. 1921; d. 1994)

The Arizona-raised Wills became one of the premiere horsemen in the business, performing over 1400 horse gags in over 40 years of stunts. Along the way he doubled for the likes of Tony Curtis, Robert Taylor, Dean Martin, Jerry Lewis, Cameron Mitchell, Alan Ladd and Audie Murphy, later moving into stunt coordinating and second unit directing. He was a member of the Stuntmen's Association.

Films—**1939:** Zorro's Fighting Legion; The Kansas Terror. **1940:** The Ranger and the Lady; Young Bill Hickcok; Legion of the Lawless. **1941:** In Old Colorado; Saddlemates; Nevada City; Outlaws of the Cherokee Trail; Doomed Caravan; Pirates on Horseback; The Adventures of Capt. Marvel. **1942:** Romance on the Range; Riding High; Sunset on the Desert. **1943:** Beyond the Last Frontier; Silver Spurs; Colt Comrades; Bar 20; Lost Canyon. **1944:** Trail to Gunsight; Song of Nevada; Bordertown Trail; The San Antonio Kid; Code of the Prairie; Stagecoach to Monterey; Riders of the Santa Fe; The Old Texas Trail; The Big Bonanza; Beyond the Pecos. **1945:** Sheriff of Cimarron; Corpus Christi Bandits; Oregon Trail; Trail of Kit Carson; Rough Riders of Cheyenne; West of the Pecos; Flame of the West; Santa Fe Saddlemates; The Purple Monster Strikes. **1946:** Border Feud; The Phantom Rider; The Plainsman & the Lady. **1948:** Sundown Riders. **1949:** The Fighting Kentuckian; Samson & Delilah. **1950:** The Girl from San Lorenzo. **1951:** Across the Wide Missouri; Westward, the Women. **1953:** The Redhead from Wyoming; Shane; Gunsmoke; Houdini; Son of the Renegade. **1954:** The Stand at Apache River; Four Guns to the Border; Saskatchewan; Black Horse Canyon. **1955:** Run for Cover; Destry; Lady Godiva; Rage at Dawn; Chief Crazy Horse. **1956:** The Searchers; Red Sundown; A Day of Fury. **1957:** Night Passage; The Kettles on Old McDonald's Farm; Last Stagecoach West; Gunfight at the OK Corral. **1958:** Saddle the Wind; Ride a Crooked Trail;

The Badlanders; The Law & Jake Wade. **1959:** Black Horse Canyon. **1960:** The Magnificent Seven. **1961:** One-Eyed Jacks; Posse from Hell; The Wild Westerners. **1962:** Six Black Horses. **1963:** Showdown. **1965:** Major Dundee; The Greatest Story Ever Told; The Sons of Katie Elder; Shenandoah. **1966:** Nevada Smith; An Eye for an Eye. **1967:** In Like Flint; Red Tomahawk; Rough Night in Jericho; Return of the Gunfighter (tv). **1972:** The Cowboys; Night of the Lepus. **1973:** The Soul of Nigger Charley; The Don Is Dead; Oklahoma Crude. **1974:** Zandy's Bride; Shootout in a One-Dog Town (tv). **1975:** The Master Gunfighter. **1976:** Drum. **1978:** F.I.S.T. **1979:** Beyond the Poseidon Adventure. **1980:** Melvin and Howard; The Mountain Men; Coast to Coast. **1981:** Going Ape; Under the Rainbow; Legend of the Lone Ranger. **1982:** The Beastmaster. **1983:** Get Crazy; The Gambler 2 (tv). **1984:** Highpoint. **1985:** Quicksilver. **1990:** Pump Up the Volume. *Television*—Roy Rogers; G.E. Theatre; Wagon Train; Rawhide; Zorro; Bonanza; Cain's Hundred; Laramie; Laredo; The Rat Patrol; The High Chaparral; The Mod Squad; The Delphi Bureau; Kung Fu; The Chisholms.

JERRY WILLS

The stunt coordinator son of Henry Wills, Jerry is a member of the Stuntmen's Association.

Films—**1968:** Chubasco. **1972:** Conquest of the Planet of the Apes. **1973:** The Don Is Dead; Battle for the Planet of the Apes. **1974:** The Towering Inferno; Blazing Saddles. **1975:** The Master Gunfighter; Rollerball. **1976:** The Invisible Strangler (aka The Astral Factor). **1978:** Every Which Way But Loose; F.I.S.T. **1980:** Tom Horn; The Mountain Men; Bronco Billy; The Island; Heaven's Gate; The Gambler (tv). **1981:** Going Ape. **1982:** The Beastmaster; The Thing; Frances. **1983:** Fire & Ice. **1984:** Body Double; The Vindicator;

City Limits. **1985:** Space Rage; Commando; Fright Night. **1986:** Crossroads; Blue City; Raw Deal; Meatballs 3. **1987:** Near Dark; Million Dollar Mystery; Extreme Prejudice; Verne Miller; Ferris Bueller's Day Off; Walk Like a Man; Three O'Clock High. **1988:** Illegally Yours. **1989:** Backtrack. **1990:** The Rookie. **1991:** Suburban Commando. **1992:** Hoffa. **1993:** The Last Outlaw; Man's Best Friend; Tombstone. **1996:** Riders of the Purple Sage. *Television*—The High Chaparral; Mission: Impossible.

JIM WINBURN

A lifetime member of the Stuntmen's Association, Winburn moved from coordinating stunts to directing his own low-budget features.

Films—**1977:** Bare Knuckles; Brothers; The Choirboys. **1978:** Movie, Movie; Halloween. **1979:** Charge of the Model T's. **1980:** The Stunt Man; The Fog; Seems Like Old Times; The Gong Show Movie. **1981:** Charlie Chan & the Curse of the Dragon Queen; Graduation Day; Escape form New York; Modern Problems. **1982:** My Favorite Year; The Sword & the Sorcerer; Tron. **1983:** Heart Like a Wheel; The Big Chill; Mortuary; Flicks (aka Loose Joints); Get Crazy. **1984:** Prime Risk. **1985:** Once Bitten; Pale Rider; Gotcha. **1986:** Jumpin' Jack Flash. **1987:** The Night Stalker; Best Seller. **1989:** Colors; Evil Altar (d); The Wicked Stepmother; Glory. **1990:** The Death Merchant (d). **1991:** Popcorn; The Naked Gun 2 1/2. **1992:** Miami Beach Cops (d/s/p). *Television*—Hunter.

DANNY WONG

Films—**1975:** Rollerball. **1982:** Some Kind of a Hero. **1983:** Going Berserk. **1985:** Rambo 2; Stand Alone; Sunset Strip. **1986:** Big Trouble in Little China.

1987: The Night Stalker; Steele Justice; Wanted: Dead or Alive; Cherry 2000. **1988:** Off Limits; The Dead Pool. **1989:** Cage; Casualties of War; Black Rain; Street Asylum. **1990:** Circuitry Man; The Rookie. **1991:** Showdown in Little Tokyo; Double Impact; Flight of the Intruder; Intimate Stranger; Leather Jackets. **1992:** Rapid Fire; Davinci's War; Inside Edge. **1993:** Dragon; Rising Sun; Martial Outlaw. **1994:** Army of One; Double Dragon; Deadly Target. **1995:** Die Hard with a Vengeance; Blood for Blood; Excessive Force **1996:** Escape from L.A.; Mars Attacks!; Back to Back.

B.J. WORTH
(b. 1952)

A Montana-born skydiving specialist and aerial coordinator, Worth has worked primarily on James Bond films since the late seventies.

Films—**1979:** Moonraker. **1983:** Octopussy. **1985:** A View to a Kill; Fandango. **1986:** The Delta Force. **1987:** The Living Daylights. **1988:** The Rescue. **1989:** License to Kill. **1993:** Hot Shots Part Deux. **1994:** Drop Zone. **1995:** Congo; Goldeneye.

HARRY WOWCHUK

An occasional stunt coordinator and location manager, Wowchuk is a member of the Stuntmen's Association.

Films—**1971:** Jud. **1978:** Deathsport; Piranha. **1981:** Smokey Bites the Dust; The Alchemist. **1982:** Parasite; The Entity; Time Walker. **1983:** The Lost Empire; The Dungeonmaster. **1984:** Repo Man; Ghost

Warrior (aka Swordkill). **1986:** Murphy's Law. **1988:** Alien Nation; License to Drive; Sister, Sister. **1989:** Under the Gun; Made in the USA; See No Evil, Hear No Evil. **1990:** Robocop 2; Marked for Death. **1991:** The Hard Way. **1992:** Deep Cover. **1994:** The Cowboy Way. **1995:** Die Hard with a Vengeance; Batman Forever; Assassins; The Usual Suspects. **1996:** Carpool; Set It Off.

TOM WRIGHT

A supporting actor, second unit director, and stunt coordinator most closely associated with the independent films of John Sayles, Wright began with Stunt Specialists.

Films—**1980:** Underground USA; Midnight Madness. **1981:** Subway Riders. **1982:** The Soldier; I Ought to Be in Pictures; Fighting Back. **1984:** Alphabet City; The Exterminator 2; Beat Street; The Brother from Another Planet; Rappin'; Splash; Torchlight; Beverly Hills Cop. **1985:** Streetwalkin'. **1986:** Legal Eagles; Sid & Nancy; Johnny Bull (tv). **1987:** Outrageous Fortune; The Principal; Overboard; Creepshow 2; Deadly Illusion. **1988:** Shakedown; Arthur 2; I'm Gonna Git You Sucka; Troop Beverly Hills; Heart of Dixie. **1989:** See No Evil, Hear No Evil. **1990:** Blue Steel; Marked for Death; Force of Circumstance; Street Hunter. **1991:** City of Hope; Passion Fish; Past Midnight. **1993:** Weekend at Bernie's 2; Acting on Impulse. **1994:** Men of War. **1995:** Tales from the Hood; Forget Paris; White Man's Burden; Excessive Force. **1996:** My Fellow Americans. *Television*— China Beach; Star Trek, Voyager; Maloney.

AL WYATT

(b. 1920; d. 1992)

A veteran Kentucky-born actor, stunt coordinator, second unit director, and fire specialist, Wyatt doubled for the likes of Randolph Scott, Joel McRae, Errol Flynn, Jon Hall, Buddy Ebsen, George Montgomery, and, most often, Rock Hudson. He was responsible for setting up the famous car/train crash in *Dirty Mary, Crazy Harry.*

Films—**1947:** Last of the Redmen. **1948:** Deadline; Silver River. **1949:** All the King's Men. **1951:** Bonanza Town; Whirlwind; Prairie Roundup. **1952:** The Lawless Breed. **1953:** Mississippi Gambler; Gun Fury; Seminole; The Great Sioux Uprising. **1954:** The Outlaw Stallion; Sitting Bull; Shotgun; Creature from the Black Lagoon. **1955:** Robber's Roost; The Far Horizons. **1956:** Seventh Cavalry; The Creature Walks Among Us; A Strange Adventure; 54 Washington Street. **1957:** Gun Duel in Durango; Last of the Badmen; New Day at Sundown; The Guns of Fort Petticoat; The Dalton Girls. **1958:** The Toughest Gun in Tombstone; The Man from God's Country; The Rawhide Trail; Badman's Country; Stallion Trail; Buchanan Rides Alone; Quantrill's Raiders. **1959:** The Jayhawkers; Night of the Quarter Moon. **1961:** Five Guns to Tombstone; The Steel Claw. **1962:** Sergeants Three; Samar. **1963:** The Castillian. **1964:** Robin & the Seven Hoods; The Quick Gun; The New Interns. **1965:** Von Ryan's Express. **1966:** Duel at Diablo. **1967:** The Long Ride Home. **1969:** Heaven with a Gun. **1970:** The Molly Maguires; Flap. **1971:** The Wild Rovers; Valdez Is Coming. **1972:** The Great Northfield Minnesota Raid. **1974:** Dirty Mary, Crazy Larry; Blazing Saddles. **1975:** Sky Heist (tv). **1976:** Fighting Mad. **1977:** The Worlds' Greatest Lover. **1978:** The Manitou; The Fury. **1979:** Meteor. **1982:** Zapped; Fast Times at Ridgemont High; E.T. **1987:** Innerspace. **1988:** Jack's Back; Dangerous Love. **1991:** Stone Cold. *Television*— Playhouse 90; Wyatt Earp; Cimarron City; Batman; The Wild Wild West; Cimarron Strip; I Dream of Jeannie; The Streets of San Francisco; Barnaby Jones; The Quest; Gunsmoke; Gene Audry; Wells Fargo.

ALLAN WYATT, JR.

Films—**1977:** Exo-Man (tv). **1978:** Avalanche. **1979:** Meteor. **1980:** In God We Trust. **1982:** Six Pack. **1983:** Eddie Macon's Run. **1984:** Lovelines. **1985:** D.A.R.Y.L. **1986:** The Texas Chainsaw Massacre 2. **1988:** Maniac Cop. **1989:** One Man Force. **1990:** Payback. **1991:** Nothing But Trouble; The Marrying Man. **1992:** Universal Soldier; Out on a Limb. **1993:** Forced to Kill; Aspen Extreme. **1995:** Separate Lives; Bigfoot; Blackout. **1996:** Fast Money.

WALTER WYATT

A former rodeo rider, Wyatt got his start working on John Wayne Westerns.

Films—**1969:** The Undefeated. **1970:** Little Big Man. **1972:** The Cowboys. **1973:** Cahil, U.S. Marshal; Hijack! (tv). **1974:** Blazing Saddles. **1976:** Banjo Hackett: Roamin' Free (tv). **1978:** Hooper; Convoy; Nat'l Lampoon's Animal House. **1979:** Goldie & the Boxer (tv). **1980:** The Blues Brothers; Tom Horn; The Baltimore Bullet; Smokey & the Bandit 2; Wholly Moses; For the Love of It (tv). **1981:** The Boogens. **1982:** Lookin' To Get Out. **1983:** Christine; Stroker Ace; Cujo; D.C. Cab; Nightmares. **1984:** The River Rat. **1985:** Into the Night; Silverado; Runaway Train; Moving Violations. *Television*—Quest.

DANNY WYNANDS

Films—**1990:** Pacific Heights; Captain America. **1991:** Stone Cold; The Rocketeer. **1992:** Honey, I Blew Up the Kid; Maximum Force. **1993:** Point of No Return; Extreme Justice; Full Eclipse; Man's Best Friend. **1994:** Fist of the North Star; Army of One; Wagons East; Blown Away; Night of the Running Man. **1995:** Demon Knight; Waterworld; Jade; The Criminal Mind; One Man's Justice. **1996:** Broken Arrow; Jingle All the Way. *Television*—Superboy.

BOB YERKES

Brayton "Bob" Yerkes was an acrobat, tightrope walker, and trapeze artist before joining the Stuntmen's Association. As a sideline, he rents out circus equipment to the movie industry. Credited with inventing the modern air bag for stunt use, his son Mark is also in the industry.

Films—**1954:** The Silver Chalice. **1974:** The Towering Inferno; Earthquake. **1976:** Drum; The Amazing Dobermans. **1979:** H.O.T.S. **1980:** In God We Trust. **1981:** Going Ape; Sideshow (tv); When the Circus Comes to Town (tv). **1982:** One from the Heart; The Sword & the Sorcerer; Poltergeist; Forced Vengeance. **1983:** The Man with Two Brains; Psycho 2; Return of the Jedi. **1984:** Tuff Turf. **1985:** Commando; Back to the Future; Remo Williams; Gotcha; Rainy Day Friends (aka L.A. Bad). **1986:** Ratboy; Ferris Bueller's Day Off; Psycho 3; Hollywood Vice Squad. **1987:** Brenda Starr. **1988:** Who Framed Roger Rabbit?; Short Circuit 2. **1989:** CHUD 2; Midnight Warrior; Honey, I Shrunk the Kids. **1990:** Big Man on Campus; Problem Child; Back to the Future 3. **1991:** Hook; The Guyver. **1992:** Mom & Dad Save the World; Class Act; Out on A Limb; Mr. Saturday Night. **1993:** Robin Hood: Men in Tights; A Case for Murder (tv). **1994:** Silence of the Hams; Color of Night; The Stand (tv). **1995:** Virtual Combat. **1996:** Larger Than Life.

MERRIT YOHNKA

A stunt coordinator and supporting player, Yohnka is a member of the International Stunt Association.

Films—**1987:** House 2; Dead Man Walking; Timestalkers (tv). **1988:** The Prince of Pennsylvania; Purple People Eater; Border Heat; Angel 3; They Live. **1989:** Transylvania Twist; Street Asylum; Time Trackers; Masque of the Red Death; Ministry of Vengeance; Brain Dead; The Revenge of Al Capone (tv). **1990:** Slumber Party Massacre 3; Syngenor; Maniac Cop 2; Peacemaker; Real Bullets; Leatherface 3; Streets; Watchers 2; Trancers 2; The Rain Killer; Driven to Kill. **1991:** Shattered; The Perfect Weapon; The Unborn; The Rocketeer; Blood & Concrete; Shakes the Clown; Dance with Death. **1992:** Trespass; Rapid Fire; Innocent Blood; Poison Ivy; The Gun in Betty Lou's Handbag. **1993:** Sommersby; Dragon; Judgment Night; Rescue Me; Cyborg 2; Dangerous Touch; Forced to Kill; The Hit List; Quick. **1994:** Cabin Boy; Body Shot; Blown Away; Trading Mom; Color of Night; Vanishing Son (tv). **1995:** 3 Ninjas Knuckle Up; Temptress; Tank Girl; Sudden Death; One Man's Justice; The Silencers. **1996:** The Trigger Effect; Fast Money. *Television*—Otherworld; Wolf.

JOE YRIGOYEN

A lifetime member of the Stuntmen's Association, the veteran Yrigoyen was a horse specialist best known for doubling Gene Autry and Richard Widmark. The father-in-law of Mickey Gilbert, his brother Bill also performed stunts.

Films—**1935:** Square Shooter. **1936:** Winds of the Wasteland. **1937:** Old Wyoming Trail; Outlaws of the Prairie; Two-Fisted Sheriff. **1938:** The Man from Music Mountain. **1939:** Daredevils of the Red Circle; Dick Tracy's G-Men; Zorro's Fighting Legion. **1940:** The Adventures of Red Ryder; Melody Ranch; Drums of Fu Manchu. **1941:** King of the Texas Rangers. **1943:** Daredevils of the West; The Masked Marvel; Captain America. **1944:** Zorro's Black Whip; Tuscon Raiders. **1945:** The Crimson Ghost; The Daughter of Don Q. **1946:** The Phantom Rider; King of the Forest Rangers. **1947:** Saddle Pals; Trail to San Antone; Robin Hood of Texas. **1948:** The Adventures of Frank & Jesse James. **1949:** Ghost of Zorro; Federal Agents vs. Underworld Inc. **1950:** Dark Command; Colorado Sundown. **1952:** Commander Cody; Montana Belle; Border Saddlemates; Marshal of Cedar Rock; Overland Trail Riders; Jungle Drums of Africa. **1953:** The Woman They Almost Lynched. **1955:** The Road to Denver; Panther Girl of the Kongo. **1957:** Gun Duel in Durango. **1958:** The Legend of Tom Dooley. **1959:** Ben Hur; Pier 5 Havana; Warlock. **1960:** Seven Ways from Sundown. **1961:** Posse from Hell; The Second Time Around. **1962:** How the West Was Won. **1963:** Four for Texas. **1964:** A Distant Trumpet; Taggart. **1965:** The Sons of Katie Elder; Shenandoah. **1966:** Alvarez Kelly. **1967:** Africa, Texas Style. **1969:** Paint Your Wagon; The Wild Bunch. **1972:** The Cowboys. **1974:** Blazing Saddles. **1979:** The Prisoner of Zenda. *Television*—G.E. Theatre; Man & the Challenge; Gunsmoke; Cowboy in Africa; Bonanza; The Deputy.

FRED ZENDOR

A veteran Swiss-born supporting player, Zendor doubled numerous times for Bob Hope. He was also an aquatic specialist who often served as a technical advisor and stunt coordinator for ocean-themed films.

Films—**1946:** O.S.S. **1947:** Unconquered; Road to Rio; Where There's Life. **1948:**

Whispering Smith; Joan of Arc; The Pale-face; State of the Union . **1949:** Sorrow-ful Jones; The Great Lover; Samson & Delilah; Battleground. **1950:** Union Sta-tion; Fancy Pants; Let's Dance. **1951:** Dar-ling, How Could You?; Submarine Com-mand; The Lemon Drop Kid; My Favorite Spy. **1952:** Son of Paleface; Road to Bali. **1953:** War of the Worlds; Off Limits; Here Come the Girls; The Caddy. **1954:** Casa-nova's Big Night; 20,000 Leagues Under the Sea; Living It Up. **1955:** The Seven Little Foys. **1956:** The Ten Command-ments. **1958:** The Old Man & the Sea; Hot Spell. **1960:** Spartacus. **1961:** Voyage to the Bottom of the Sea. **1963:** Come Blow Your Horn. **1964:** Man's Favorite Sport; Where Love Has Gone. **1965:** A High Wind in Jamaica. **1966:** Fantastic Voyage. **1969:** Butch Cassidy & the Sundance Kid. **1970:** The Hawaiians. **1971:** Sometimes a Great Notion (aka Never Give an Inch). **1972:** The Poseidon Adventure. **1975:** Jaws; Lucky Lady. **1979:** Beyond the Po-seidon Adventure. *Television*—Voyage to the Bottom of the Sea.

DICK ZIKER
(b. 1940)

A Wyoming-born stunt coordinator and second unit director, Ziker was recruited for his first film due to his surfing skills. He went on to double Mike Connors, James Brolin, and Robert Urich, making a name for himself as one of the industry's high-est paid and most versatile talents. A member of Stunts Unlimited, he's re-sponsible for a rousing sequence in *The Great Train Robbery* which has Sean Connery atop a train speeding beneath a series of low-lying bridges.

Films—**1964:** Ride the Wild Surf. **1968:** The Young Runaways. **1969:** The Unde-feated. **1970:** The Strawberry Statement. **1972:** The Night Stalker (tv). **1973:** The

Don Is Dead; White Lightning; Trader Horn; Westworld; The Stone Killer. **1974:** Three the Hard Way. **1975:** Mitchell. **1976:** Carrie; Gator; Gable & Lombard. **1977:** Heroes; The Choirboys. **1978:** Hooper; Straight Time; Thank God, It's Friday. **1979:** The Great Train Robbery. **1980:** The Blues Brothers; Smokey & the Bandit 2. **1983:** Independence Day; Cross Country; Nat'l Lampoon's Vacation; Rumble Fish; Scarface; To Be or Not to Be. **1984:** Against All Odds; Bachelor Party; Run-away; The Outlaws (tv). **1985:** To Live & Die in L.A.; Moving Violations; Love on the Run (tv). **1986:** Police Academy 3: Back in Training; The Money Pit; The Wraith; Back to School. **1987:** The Omega Syndrome; Real Men; Burglar. **1988:** Off Limits; Mac & Me; Die Hard; Rambo 3; Alien Nation; The Presidio; Tequila Sun-rise; My Stepmother Is an Alien. **1989:** Who's Harry Crumb?; Gleaming The Cube; Lethal Weapon 2; Blind Fury; Star Trek 5: The Final Frontier; Sea of Love; Tango & Cash; Nat'l Lampoon's Christ-mas Vacation; Riding the Edge. **1990:** Days of Thunder; Robocop 2; Total Re-call; Last of the Finest; The Adventures of Ford Fairlane. **1991:** Mobsters; Shattered; Terminator 2; Thelma & Louise; The Last Boy Scout. **1992:** Memoirs of an Invisible Man; White Sands; Rapid Fire; Lethal Weapon 3; Whispers in the Dark; Cool World; Patriot Games; Forever Young; Under Siege; Beyond the Law. **1993:** Falling Down; Made in America; The Last Action Hero; Rising Sun; The Real McCoy; Carlito's Way. **1994:** Pentathalon; The Shadow; Clear & Present Danger; Puppetmasters. **1995:** Under Siege 2; Jade; Money Train. **1996:** Executive De-cision; Eraser; The Rock; The Glimmer Man. *Television*—The Rat Patrol; Mis-sion: Impossible; Mannix; Charlie's An-gels; Vegas; 240 Robert; Today's FBI.

CHUCK ZITO

Active on both coasts as a stunt performer and supporting player, Zito has doubled regularly for Eric Roberts. He has worked as a professional bodyguard and served as the president of the East Coast Hell's Angels.

Films—**1991:** Hudson Hawk; 29th Street; The Last Boy Scout; Neon City. **1993:** Carlito's Way; Nowhere to Run; Best of the Best 2; Love, Cheat, & Steal. **1994:** Jimmy Hollywood; The Chase; True Lies; North; Love Is a Gun; Sensation; Money to Burn. **1995:** Kiss of Death; Bad Blood; New York Cop; Mallrats. **1996:** The Juror; Heaven's Prisoners; Eraser; The Rock; Maximum Risk; Daylight; The Funeral; Red Line.

Appendix:
Stunt Organizations and Services

Bay Area Stuntman's Association
612 Lancaster Way
Redwood, City, CA 94061
(415) 952-3121; (213) 857-8618 (L.A.);
  (800) 400-3124

Drivers Inc.
5601 Sepulveda Blvd.
Van Nuys, CA 91411
(818) 994-4199; (818) 994-9383 (fax)

East Coast Stuntman's Association
355 W. 39th St.
New York, NY 10018
(212) 581-6470

International Stunt Association
3518 Cahuenga Blvd. West #300
Hollywood, CA 90068
(213) 874-3174; (213) 874-3159 (fax)

Joni's Stunt People (ans. service)
(818) 980-2123

Mid-West Stunts
756 Edge Lake Point
Schaumberg, IL 60194
(312) 885-1179

Professional Driver's Association
5518 Vineland Ave.
N. Hollywood, CA 91601
(213) 462-2301; (800) 999-9732; (805)
  987-4024 (fax)

Rawn Hutchinson's Precision Drivers
P.O. Box 2052
Toluca Lake, CA 91610
(213) 650-2072; (602) 919-8886

Stunt Specialists
211 Muriel Ave.
N. Plainfield, NJ 07060

Stuntmen's Association of Motion Pictures
4810 Whitsett Ave.
N. Hollywood, CA 91607
(818) 766-4334; (818) 766-5943 (fax)

Stunts Unlimited
3518 Cahuenga Blvd. West #207
Hollywood, CA 90068
(213) 874-0050

Stuntwoman's Association
13601 Ventura Blvd. Ste. 94
Sherman Oaks, CA 91423
(818) 886-8755

Teddy's Service (ans. service)
(213) 462-2301

United Stuntwoman's Association
3518 Cahunega Blvd. West
Hollywood, CA 90068
(213) 874-3584; (213) 462-2301

Bibliography

Adams, Les, and Buck Rainey. *Shoot-Em Ups.* Metuchen, N.J.: Scarecrow, 1985.

Barabas, SuzAnne, and Gabor Barabas. *Gunsmoke.* Jefferson, N.C.: McFarland, 1990.

Bartlett, Chuck, and Barbara Bergeron. *Variety Obituaries.* New York: Garland, 1970–1994.

Baur, Tassilo. *Special Effects and Stunts Guide.* Los Angeles: Lone Eagle, 1993.

Cann, John. *The Stunt Guide.* Los Angeles: Action PAC, 1991.

Canutt, Yakima, and Oliver Drake. *Stuntman.* New York: Walker, 1979.

Corcoran, John, Stuart Sobel, and Emil Farkas. *The Original Martial Arts Encyclopedia.* Los Angeles: Pro-Action, 1993.

Davis, Bruce, and James N. Roberts. *Annual Index to Motion Picture Credits.* Beverly Hills, Calif.: Academy of Motion Picture Arts and Sciences, 1978–1995.

Emmons, Carol A. *Stuntwork and Stuntpeople.* New York: Triumph, 1982.

Gianakos, Larry James. *Television Drama Series Programming.* Metuchen, N.J.: McFarland, 1990.

Ireland, Karin. *Hollywood Stuntpeople.* New York: Messner, 1980.

Johnson, John "J.J." *Cheap Tricks and Class Acts: Special Effects, Makeup, and Stunts from the Fantastic Fifties.* Jefferson, N.C.: McFarland, 1996.

Krafsur, Richard P. *American Film Institute Catalog of Feature Films.* New York: Bowker, 1976.

Lentz, Harris M. *Science Fiction, horror & Fantasy Film and Television Credits.* Jefferson, N.C.: McFarland, 1983; *Supplement 1: Through 1987,* 1989; *Supplement 2: Through 1993,* 1994.

Maltin, Leonard. *Leonard Maltin's Movie Encyclopedia.* New York: Plume/Penguin, 1995.

_____. *Movie and Video Guide.* New York: Signet, 1996.

Marill, Alvin H. *Movies Made for Television 1964–1986.* New York: New York Zoetrope/Baseline, 1987.

Miklowitz, Gloria D. *Movie Stunts and the People Who Do Them.* New York: Harcourt Brace Jovanovich, 1980.

Monaco, James. *Who's Who in American Film Now.* New York: New York Zoetrope/Baseline, 1987.

Nash, Jay Robert, and Stanley Ralph Ross. *Motion Picture Guide.* Chicago: Cinebook, 1987–1994.

Oliviero, Jeffrey. *Motion Picture Players' Credits.* Jefferson, N.C.: McFarland, 1991.

Paietta, Ann C., and Jean L. Kauppila. *Animals on Screen and Radio.* Metuchen, N.J.: Scarecrow, 1994.

Phillips, Mark, and Frank Garcia. *Science Fiction Television Series.* Jefferson, N.C.: McFarland. 1996.

Rainey, Buck. *The Shoot-Em Ups Ride Again.* Metuchen, N.J.: Scarecrow, 1990.
_____. *Those Fabulous Serial Heroines.* Metuchen, N.J.: Scarecrow, 1990.
Roberson, Chuck, and Bodie Thoene. *The Fall Guy.* New York: Hancock House, 1980.
Terrace, Vincent. *The Encyclopedia of Television Series, Pilots, and Specials.* New York: New York Zoetrope/Baseline, 1986.
TV Guide. Triangle Publishing, Pennsylvania. 1957–1996.
Variety Film Reviews. New York: Bowker, 1986–1990.
Weldon, Michael J. *The Psychotronic Video Guide.* New York: St. Martin's/Griffin, 1996.
White, Patrick J. *The Complete Mission Impossible Dossier.* New York: Avon, 1991.

Index